Holocaust Averted

Bulgarian Jews in World War II

Second Edition

MIROSLAV MARINOV

MPM Publishing Co.

Toronto 2018

Holocaust Averted – Bulgarian Jews in World War II

Second Edition

© 2018 Miroslav Marinov

MPM Publishing Co., Toronto
Http://www.mpmpublishing.com
Info@mpmpublishing.com

All rights reserved. No part of this publication may be reproduced or transmitted in any form or by any means, electronic or mechanical, including photocopy, recording, or any information storage or retrieval system, without permission in writing from the publisher, except in the case of brief quotations embodied in critical reviews and other non-commercial uses permitted by copyright law.

Any copyrights not held by publisher are owned by their respective authors. All trademarks and brands referred to in this book are for illustrative purposes only, are the property of their respective owners and not affiliated with this publication in any way. Any trademarks are being used without permission, and the publication of the trademark is not authorized by, associated with or sponsored by the trademark owner.

Cover design © 2018 MPM Publishing Co.

ISBN: 978-0-9950065-6-0

CONTENTS

1 BULGARIA AND THE HOLOCAUST AN INTRODUCTION....1
2 JEWS AND BULGARIANS IN MEDIEVAL BULGARIA.........12
3 THE OTTOMAN YOKE..18
4 BULGARIANS AND JEWS IN THE STRUGGLE FOR
LIBERATION..30
5 A NEW LIFE IN LIBERATED BULGARIA.........................45
6 A COUNTRY IN TURMOIL – THE TWENTIETH
CENTURY..54
7 KING BORIS III, HITLER AND THE JEWS.......................68
8 PERCEPTIONS OF THE JEWS IN BULGARIA
(THE SURVEY OF B. PITI)..93
9 GERMANY AND THE ANTI-JEWISH LAWS IN
BULGARIA..112
10 DANNECKER, BELEV AND THE JEWS IN THRACE AND
MACEDONIA...140
11 FIRST DEPORTATION ATTEMPT – MARCH 1943..........181
12 SECOND DEPORTATION ATTEMPT – MAY 1943............220
13 EXILED – BULGARIAN JEWS IN CAMPS AND LABOR
GROUPS...249
14 THE FIRE IN CAMP KAILUKA – ARSON OR
ACCIDENT?..287
15 BULGARIAN JEWS ON THE EVE OF THE SOVIET
INVASION...301
16 COMMUNIST TERROR AND JEWISH EXODUS..............327
17 EPILOGUE – SAINTLY DANES AND LOWLY
BULGARIANS..357
APPENDIX...377
BIBLIOGRAPHY OF BOOKS AND OTHER
SOURCES..384
ILLUSTRATIONS..403

ACKNOWLEDGMENTS

For reasons that will become clear in the book, the fate of the Bulgarian Jews in World War II is still a "fringe" issue in Holocaust history, subject to conflicting interpretations and real or manufactured controversies. Because of that, this project, which took years to complete, did not receive the external support that those dramatic events in the European history deserved.

Nevertheless, there are a few people and organizations that I would like to thank for their invaluable help in the various stages of my work on the book.

I would like to thank the former Bulgarian King Simeon II who kindly responded to my questions and clarified a few historical facts, which contributed to my understanding of those times of the Bulgarian history.

Gratitude is due to Mr. Samuel Arditti, a relentless seeker of the historical truth, whose passion inspired my quest to investigate deeper that time of the Holocaust history.

I would like to express my indebtness to all the people, dead or alive, who left memoirs and records about those times. Regardless of their personal or political views, the written and verbal heritage, which they left behind, made it possible to restore the picture of that difficult era of heroism and martyrdom.

I am also grateful to Holocaust Education Week (Toronto) and the Canadian Institute for Jewish Research (CIJR), which gave me opportunities and venues to share my findings with wider audiences.

And last, but not least, I want to thank my wife Toshie. Without her constant support, faith in the project and unwavering optimism, this book would have never been completed.

1 BULGARIA AND THE HOLOCAUST
AN INTRODUCTION

> *Rescue those being led away to death; hold back those staggering toward slaughter. If you say, "But we knew nothing about this," does not He who weighs the heart perceive it? Does not He who guards your life know it? Will He not repay everyone according to what they have done?*
>
> Proverbs 24: 11-12 (NIV)

The "controversial" nature of the topic of this book prevented me from getting monetary and other support, which is readily available for safer "mainstream" projects. It took longer to complete it, since the speed of my work depended on my ability to cover the costly research at every given moment. Sometimes, when that ability waned, I had to interrupt my work. On the bright side, the lack of monetary support liberated me from ideological or censorship constraints that are often attached to such research assistance. I saw this project as an opportunity to clarify the facts and restore as much as I can the honor of the Bulgarian people blackmailed by all those organizations and individuals who did nothing or very little at the time, but now present themselves as beacons of moral superiority.

World War II was a catastrophic time for the European Jewry. The people that, despite centuries of persecution, managed to become one of the pillars of the Western civilization, suddenly was declared a mortal enemy of the West. The idea of getting rid of the Jews for the sake of racial purity crystallized in the mind of Adolf Hitler and found willing followers. It then evolved from a plan to expel them to faraway places to the reality of systematic physical annihilation.

Helped by their powerful war machine, Hitler's Nazis managed to put into practice their "final solution of the Jewish Question" by either occupying or bullying many countries. In one of the European countries the plan didn't work as expected. Bulgaria, despite being a member of the Nazi Axis, succeeded in averting the Holocaust of its Jewish citizens.

There were over 48,000 Jews in Bulgaria before the war and by its end their number grew to over 50,000.

In every other European country, a significant number of the Jews were exterminated. Hungary and Italy resisted the deportations until Germany took control and finished its disgraceful deed. Romania also refused to deport its Jews but operated its own killing fields in Transnistria and extermination camps on its own territory. Albania's 200 Jews avoided the catastrophe because Germany did not find it feasible to chase them in the mountains. Danish people saved a few hundred Jews by transporting them to Sweden.

Yet the saving of the Bulgarian Jews is little known to the world. One of the most authoritative book on the topic, Frederick B. Chary's "The Bulgarian Jews and the Final Solution, 1940-1944" was published in 1972 and is out of print. There are other books in Bulgarian, like the ones written by Benjamin Arditti and later by his son Samuel Arditti but they are not known enough in the West. The only recent one was Michael Bar-Zohar's "Beyond Hitler's Grasp: The Heroic Rescue of the Bulgaria's Jews" published in 1998.

The final push to write the book you are reading now came after I visited the Toronto offices of an organization, whose task is to keep the memory of the Holocaust alive. The young lady who gave me a tour of the premises looked bewildered when I told her that the Bulgarian Jews survived World War II. She had never heard of it.

Of course, this is not a result of ill will. There are reasons for that historical blackout. In fact, the only indisputable statement in this fascinating rescue story is that there were more Jews in Bulgaria in the end of the war than at the beginning.

Everything else, like how this happened, who was responsible, and what exactly was done, is a subject of fierce and often vicious arguments and debates.

While growing up in communist Bulgaria, I remember that Jews were hardly ever discussed. Officially, there were less than 5,000 of them left in the country. 90% of the survivors moved to Israel shortly after the victory of the "socialist revolution" in 1944. The remaining kept low profile - it took me a few years to figure out that my teacher of Russian in Grade 5, Comrade Levitskaya, was actually Jewish and not just Russian. Seen from the distance of time, that wasn't surprising. Bulgaria severed its diplomatic relations with Israel after its victory in the Six Day War in 1967. The press was spewing fire and brimstone against "imperialist Israel" and its Zionist ideology, the new "form of racism and racist discrimination" as the infamous UN resolution of 1975 stated - a resolution adopted with the help of Bulgaria and the other communist countries. In the 1980s even an embassy of the non-existent state of Palestine popped up in Sofia, the capital.

Since most of the Bulgarian Jews had relatives in "imperialist Zionist Israel", it was wise to keep quiet and condemn Zionism whenever possible. As of the events of World War II, we knew about the concentration camps in Poland run by Germany and the mass killings of Soviet citizens. The fact that a very large number of them were Jews, was rarely emphasized.

Although there was some modest exhibition about the Bulgarian Jews in World War II in the capital Sofia, those events were little known. In the mid-1980s the issue was suddenly raised, probably due to the desire of the Bulgarian communist dictator Todor Zhivkov to improve the economic relations with Israel. The promoted version was that the Bulgarian Communist Party and personally Comrade Zhivkov saved the Jews. He was fond of mentioning it in his speeches. The authorities even released a pseudo-historical movie, "The Echelons of Death", showing the young leader leading monumental efforts to defeat the government. Of course, nobody at the time dared to say that the BCP was too small to have any political influence and that Zhivkov was a minor functionary. There were even rumors that he was nominated for Nobel Peace Prize for his "efforts".

The fall of communism and its most valuable consequence - freedom of speech - opened the floodgates of discussions of topics that were previously suppressed. The fate of the Bulgarian Jews was one of them. Suddenly, Israel became again a respectable country, especially after the anti-Zionist UN resolution was rescinded. The flow of books and articles was significant and within it, a new trend became visible, the attempt to question what happened and to diminish its significance.

Such an attitude is not surprising to those who are familiar with the historical dynamics in Europe. There has always been a clear distinction between Western and Eastern Europe. The dominance of communism in the East that ruled for a few decades made the differences more visible, but they existed long before that time. The situation was partially influenced by religion - Eastern Christian Orthodoxy vs. Western Catholicism (although some of those countries were not Orthodox). Both areas had different development patterns and different economic success. The West was an example that the East had to try to emulate to be successful. The European Union, a monumental attempt to unify and transform the continent, did little to erase the differences. The different mentality created different outcomes, in which the sophisticated West was not always the wise partner. It's true that the economies of Greece and other countries took turn for the worse, but on the other hand, some irrational decisions of the West left the East wonder if its leaders were capable of clear thinking. The flood of millions of unqualified Third World immigrants that Germany and other countries facilitated, thus increasing crime and straining the welfare state, caused an acute reaction from the East, where both leaders and ordinary people were painfully familiar what such "newcomers" could do to their countries.

As of Bulgaria and the other Balkan countries, their status is even lower. They have always been treated as pawns in the games of the great powers, with all negative consequences. Bulgaria had been a strong country for the most of its early history, but the occupation by the Turks in the late 14th century put an end to its power. Although it was liberated 500 years later, it could never reach the same level of independence. The same happened to the rest of the Balkan countries. Due to the strategic importance of the area, those countries were forced to choose between various powers that competed for influence.

That has resulted in long conflicts and a tangle of painful past events that provoke new fights. In North America (at least until recently), history was something distant and hardly known, unless you studied it at school. In the Balkans, history is very much alive and remembered and an event that is a few hundred years old can trigger a new event that is based on the old feelings. And that hasn't always been beneficial to the local Jews who found themselves in the middle of those conflicts.

All that makes the events in Bulgaria during the Holocaust so confusing to the West. It is a paradox that is difficult to explain. On one hand, we have Germany, the undisputed European leader in creativity and industrialization, with rich cultural traditions, which, contrary to its image, came up with the idea to exterminate a whole nation. Not only was the idea implemented but it met little resistance from its ordinary citizens. Other highly developed countries, like France and the Netherlands did little to oppose the genocide and even helped it.

In her introduction to a book about the Holocaust (Morcan, 2016), the Dutch survivor Hetty E. Verolme-Werkendam describes the attitude in the Netherlands:

> "How unspeakably evil the Nazis were. They told the Dutch people that those detained would simply be put to work in Germany to support the war industry. The Nazis also told the Dutch public that detainees would be given a home and that the father in each detained family would work in a factory and the mother would stay home to care for her children. That's how the Nazis managed to orchestrate a quiet and orderly transportation of 105,000 people from the Netherlands.
>
> On the 1st of February 1944 we were on the train to Bergen Belsen where for 10 months we were together with my parents. After eventually being separated from my parents it was my task to take care of my little brothers and also 40 other younger children. With the help of two Polish nurses we managed to stay alive as a group and were liberated by the English army on the 15th of April 1945."

It is hard to believe the Dutch were so naive, maybe they were willfully blind or unwilling to face reality. About a year earlier, the same initiative for "quiet and orderly transportation" of the Bulgarian Jews to the "Eastern regions of Germany" was met with fierce resistance from Bulgarians and Jews alike. There were more than enough rumors and facts that confirmed the grim reality. Even before 1943, the truth about what was going on in Poland had reached the West through the regular news provided by the Polish government in exile, located in London.

That historical reality creates an embarrassing situation, where the morally superior Western Europe has a hard time explaining why it took part in a genocide involving its own citizens, while a "backward" agricultural country in the backyard of Europe did its best to save thousands of its own citizens. There are two ways out of such a situation. First, one can pretend that it never happened.

That is why for so many decades nobody noticed (or pretended not to notice) that almost all Bulgarian Jews survived the Holocaust. It was a quite successful approach, since so many people in the West are totally unaware of what happened in Bulgaria.

The second option is to denigrate Bulgaria, to show that it had some sinister intentions that somehow failed to materialize. Everything negative that happened during the war is pointed out as the country's fault, totally ignoring its role in the European pecking order. Bulgaria didn't have the luxury of all the choices that other countries had, yet that doesn't stop critics from judging the past according to questionable standards.

Such an attitude is not new. For example, in 1979, Vicki Tamir, an American of Bulgarian Jewish background, published the book "Bulgaria and Her Jews: The History of a Dubious Symbiosis" (Tamir, 1979). The author grew up in Bulgaria but emigrated with the large exodus in the late 1940s. Probably due to personal grudges over the World War II experiences, her work transitions from criticism to open hostility toward the Bulgarian people over their supposed rampant anti-Semitism.

Based on her own experiences that she extrapolates vigorously over the long Bulgarian history, she blows out of proportion isolated cases or simply makes statements that lack factual proof (like when she contradicts herself saying that the Bulgarian Army was closed to Jews, yet soon after that she says that three Jews achieved colonel's rank). Due to her anti-Christian hostility, she sees the Orthodox Christianity as the source of the Bulgarian anti-Semitism, forgetting that the Bulgarian Orthodox Church was one of the major factors in saving the Jews. Then she tries to contrast the uncultured Bulgarians to the sophisticated Sephardic Jews. According to her, the Bulgarians under Ottoman rule forgot their history, while the Jews never did that. And she laments that Bulgarians, as related to the Khazars, did not convert to Judaism to become more civilized.

As we will see soon, this is a grossly distorted picture of the Bulgarian history and the relations between Bulgarians and Jews. However, in the last few years, more and more people are peddling such biased opinions.

These opinions mushroomed after the country joined the European Union. Achieving uniformity by wiping out any national pride from the past seems to be the general strategy of the bureaucrats in Brussels.

Recently, I read an interesting interview that displayed the trend: "We Need to Study the Complete Technology of the

Bulgarian Holocaust, Expulsions, Stigma, Camps" (Методиева, 2016). Conducted by a former editor who worked for the Bulgarian Helsinki Committee (one of the projects of George Soros in Bulgaria), it included two gentlemen, members of the Bulgarian chapter of B'nai Brith. They didn't forget to mention the trains with Greek Jews that went to Poland through Bulgaria (though guarded by Germans). One of them quoted a speech of the Bulgarian President at the time, Rossen Plevneliev, who said that the Bulgarian Jews in the end of World War II were more than in its beginning. Then the interviewee continued with sarcasm, "The life here had been so good that they multiplied! This is the large picture of evil, Jews are likened to sheep, their rights were taken away, they were stopped from working in their trades, in the end they were sent to the camps... Some of them were youth communist activists, others, members of the Communist Party, a third group - right-wing anti-fascists. This is not discussed, no one wants to consider communists heroes."

He continued, "They want to deprive us of our individuality. Every family has its history. Our grandparents were part of the resistance against the pro-Nazi government of Bogdan Filov. They don't let us speak and tell us that we are ungrateful, we are communists... They treat us like in the times of the Law for Defense of the Nation [a 1941 law that discriminated against Jews, abolished in 1944 - M.M.] ..."

The other gentleman added: "That's why the Holocaust education is deeply wrong. Holocaust is not just killing Jews. It includes the whole technology - expulsions, depriving of civil rights, labor camps, stigma... Bulgaria had all of that. Have you heard of the fire in the concentration camp near Kailuka? How many Jews had been burned alive there! ... When I was working with Stephen Spielberg's Shoah project in the 1990s, I recorded the tales of many Jewish families. There wasn't a single family that didn't lose one or two children!"

My impressions of B'nai Brith in North America are that it is an organization that does a great job in fighting anti-Semitism. However, there is something odd in the views of the two Bulgarian members. The lamentations about the "forgotten" communists are not hard to figure out. After the war ended, over 90% of the Jews left for Israel and the majority of those who remained were devout communists. As we will see later, the communists played a substantial role in driving most Jews out of Bulgaria. Though a minority in the communist movement in World War II, Jews fought in it. But let's not forget - that movement wasn't just antifascist (a term, hardly applicable to the Bulgarian realities), they fought for the victory of Stalinism, which eventually brought one of the worst catastrophes in the Bulgarian history. Any noble intentions that the Bulgarian and Jewish communists may have had were wiped out by the red terror of the late 1940s. Strangely, the two gentlemen fail to mention the crucial positive role played by the Zionists in Bulgaria in those times.

Mocking the fact that the Jews survived and even multiplied is odd, to say the least. Yes, conditions have often been bad, and just as often Bulgarian people had no control over them. However, life is the supreme value. Without life, without survival, nothing else matters. I wonder how many of the Jews waiting for their turn at the Auschwitz gas chamber would have traded that for a crowded room in a Bulgarian village where many spent months and avoided deportation.

Those views reveal a strange interpretation of the Holocaust. The truth is that the deliberate mass annihilation of the Jews is the central concept of the Holocaust. Encyclopaedia Judaica's definition: ""Holocaust" is the term used for the systematic state-sponsored murder of millions of Jews by the Nazis and their collaborators during World War II" (Encyclopaedia Judaica, 2007, 9, p. 325-326). The Historical Dictionary of the Holocaust defines it in the following way: "HOLOCAUST. The word derives from Greek and Latin and is translated as "something wholly burnt up" and, in its broader meaning, "a total destruction." The Holocaust refers to the Nazi objective of annihilating every Jewish man, woman, and child who fell under their control. By the end of World War II, approximately six million Jews had been murdered by the Nazis and their collaborators." (Fischel, 2010, p. 115).

Most of the Jews that I had interviewed over the years had similar understanding. Turning every suffering into a Holocaust is unfair to the real victims. The Bulgarians under Turkish occupation (from 1393 to 1878) were mistreated, often killed, forcefully converted to Islam, sold as slaves, etc., so by that wide definition that was a Holocaust. Let's also compare that "extended" definition with the events in Rovno, Ukraine, in November 1941, where the German Einsatzgruppen, aided by local Ukrainian police, exterminated the whole Jewish population. Over 23,500 people were forced to strip, dig ditches near the forest and shot in the course of three days; many children were buried alive (Burds, 2013). A month earlier, at Babi Yar, also in Ukraine, the same groups killed over 34,000 Jews in two days (Trubakov, 2013).

Comparing the events in Bulgaria during World War II with those horrific tragedies and calling both Holocaust is an insult to the memory of the victims.

As of the Kailuka and other camps in Bulgaria, they were a far cry from the German concentration camps. It was created for politically active Jews, mostly communists but later it also included Zionists. The fire started after a party in one of the one-storey sheds. At the People's Tribunal in 1944-1945, organized by the communist to sue those who worked for the previous governments, they tried to determine how it started. The testimonies were contradictory - it was either an arson or a candle accident. The accused guard wasn't convicted. The place had only one exit and a narrow space between the two rows of bunk beds, which made the evacuation difficult. Many people ran out through the windows, see (People's Court Session No.16, 1945). In the interview, the literally used expression was "how many tens of Jews burned", which in Bulgarian implies a very large number, near a hundred, but in fact 10 people perished that day. Yes, every death is a tragedy but again, there is no comparison with the millions exterminated in the Nazi death camps. As of the claim that every Jewish family had lost one or two children during the war, it means that we are talking a number as high as 10,000 children and that is far from the truth.

We need to be careful when making such sweeping generalizations. Under Stalin, even the mildest expression of opposition to the regime could have severe consequences - jail, camp in Kolyma, even death. In Bulgaria, under Todor Zhivkov, also a communist dictator, for similar transgressions you could get some beating from the People's Militia (the police), harassment, loss of job but rarely jail. It was still a nasty communist order but not Stalinism. Like the two B'nai Brith gentlemen, who looked at the "whole technology of the Holocaust" thus watering down the concept, I could claim some "whole technology of communist persecution" but I would be embarrassed to put myself at the same level as the great Soviet dissidents. Although I still dislike Zhivkov, in a way, I appreciate the fact that he didn't act like Stalin.

I hope this is a good illustration of the complexity of the issue with the Bulgarian Jews. There are many interpretations of the events and many get confused. The problem is that many people and organizations have a simplistic approach to the Holocaust. It is seen as an American Western, where they expect to see a clear distinction between good and evil. On one side, we have the evil Nazis and fascists of different stripes, on the other side are the helpless Jews and their noble saviors. The reality is quite different.

The prominent Bulgarian politician Prof. Alexander Tsankov, was almost unanimously considered fascist. As a Prime Minister in 1920s, he fiercely persecuted communists (for a good reason) and earned himself the reputation of a "blood-drinking" monster. Yet he was always opposed to the persecution of the Jews and in March 1943 signed the famous letter of several parliamentarians against the planned deportation of the Jews. The Jews themselves (and I am not talking about communists) fought since the moment the anti-Jewish law was put into motion. They petitioned the government, used their connections with politicians and eventually succeeded. The same applies to many other people and groups at the time. And people, who don't behave according to the prescribed stereotypes, create confusion.

Probably that is the reason that Bulgaria, where all Jews were saved, has been honored by Yad Vashem with only 20 Righteous Among the Nations titles, which are awarded to those who went through great difficulties to save Jews during the Holocaust. Common sense tells us that it takes more than 20 people to save 50,000. On the other hand, in Ukraine, where, after everything was done, there were very few Jews left, the Righteous are 2,544. Or let's take Lithuania – this tiny country, much smaller than Bulgaria, started the war with over 200,000 Jews, but by its end over 95% of them had perished, killed not only by Germans, but also by Lithuanians, Ukrainians and even Jewish police (we will get back to this later), yet the Righteous there are 889 (Righteous Among the Nations, 2016).

What I want to say is that an objective discussion of the war events in Bulgaria will inevitably offend somebody. Further in the book, I hope to present and untangle the complexities of the Bulgarian history and explain how it affected Bulgarians and Jews and their relationship. Series of historical events created certain mentality and a way of thinking that resulted in rescuing the Jews in World War II.

I have also tried, whenever possible, to present the events through the voices of those who lived through them. There are numerous unpublished testimonies and memoirs that gather dust in various archives and, so far, have escaped the attention of researchers. I include them in this book, fully aware that many of them cover the events from a very personal point of view and their perception of what happened is often colored by that. However, I still think that those manuscripts, with all of their possible prejudices help us understand better that complicated period of history. All translations from books, documents, articles and other materials are my own.

Miroslav Marinov

2 JEWS AND BULGARIANS IN MEDIEVAL BULGARIA

Bulgaria has a long and turbulent history that, to a great degree, predetermined the events in the 20th century. A short sketch of that history will help us understand better the conflicts in the area. Located in the periphery of Europe and blessed and cursed at the same time as the crossroad between Europe and Asia, the Bulgarian lands have seen countless invaders. The long list of nationalities attracted to those rich lands included Romans, Slavs, Proto-Bulgarians, Byzantine Greeks, Tatars, Circassians, Turks and many others.

Year 681 A.D. is considered the first year of the Bulgarian state. However, the Jewish presence precedes the Bulgarians by several centuries. After the Jewish War, the Second Temple in Jerusalem was destroyed in year 68 A.D. Some of the Jews who lived there were taken as slaves by soldiers from the Roman legions that participated in the destruction of the Temple. Those legions were stationed south of the Danube river in the lands owned by the Roman Empire. The enslaved Jews were considered the first Jews to live in Bulgaria. Two ancient tombstones found near the village of Guigen and the city of Vidin prove that fact (Keshales, p.9).

The void caused by the destruction of the second Jewish Kingdom and the expulsion of most Jews was filled by a new religion, Christianity, whose preachers started to spread the ideas revealed in the New Testament. One of the most famous among them was Apostle Paul. We have his letter to the people from Salonika, included in the New Testament, which is a proof that there were many Jews in the city at the time, which probably means that in the rest of Bulgaria there were also other Jewish communities.

The animosities between Jews and Romans continued in that part of the empire. According to records from year 379 A.D., due to persecution of Jews in what is now northern Bulgaria, the Roman Emperor Theodosius ordered his representatives to stop the mistreatment (Keshales, p.11).

In year 476 A.D., the Western Roman Empire fell under the blows of northern tribes, while the Eastern part survived for about another thousand years under the name Byzantium. In the year 679, the Proto-Bulgarian tribe of Khan Asparukh crossed the Danube. They found in the new land considerable number of Slavs and Thracians. "When the Proto-Bulgars arrived in the Balkans the area was already far from ethnically homogeneous. To the south of the Balkan Mountains the Thracians mixed with Roman settlers whilst there were Greek settlements throughout the region, but particularly on the coast where they remained until the twentieth century. Cultural mixing continued in succeeding centuries as a result of incursions by a series of tribes, including Avars, Huns, Tatars, Pechenegs, and Magyars..." (Crampton, p.7).

Mixing of different ethnicities and races was the way the Bulgarian nation was formed. That history made it impossible to apply Hitler's concepts about "racial purity" in Bulgaria during the war. The American writer Will Monroe noted that complexity in his book "Bulgaria and Her People with an Account of the Balkan Wars, Macedonia, and the Macedonian Bulgars":

> "Although the Bulgars are usually classed as Slavs, the original ethnic stock came from the Finnic group of the Sibiric branch of the Turanian race in Asia. The forebears of the Bulgarians were kin to the Tatars, Finns, and Huns. We first hear of them in the fifth and sixth centuries, when they occupied tracts of land between the Ural Mountains and the Volga river. In the seventh century they crossed the Danube, subjugated the Slavic tribes in the Balkan peninsula, and took over the language, customs, and institutions of the conquered Slavs." (Monroe, 1914, p.182).

The mixing of different ethnic elements affected the language as well: "The language of the Bulgars belongs to the eastern branch of the Slavic family of tongues, but it has undergone more modifications than any other Slavic speech. The highly synthetic character of the Slavic languages is only slightly apparent in the

Bulgar. It is the only Slavic language that has articles which are attached to the terminations of nouns and adjectives, and it is the only Slavic language that makes use of the infinitive. Cases have disappeared, and instead of declining the nouns, prepositions are used, as in English. Some of the dialects of remote sections, as well as a few of the old ballads, show traces of the inflection of nouns, thus proving the antiquity of the language." (Monroe, 1914, p.187).

There is a strong evidence about continuous Jewish presence in the new country. In year 811, Khan Krum, one of the early Bulgarian rulers, brought large numbers of Jewish prisoners from Thessaly, after one of his wars with Byzantium. Those Byzantine Jews, along with other immigrants who arrived later, established communities at Nicopolis (near the Danube river), Sofia, Vidin and Silistra.

In the 9th century, the traditional Bulgarian religion became a hindrance to the goals of the rulers. The country was expanding and in order to be considered equal among the other European nations, it became more and more evident that the Bulgarians had to convert to Christianity. Although the Christian Church appeared to be unified, there were already cracks in that unity, displaying distinctions between the Western Papal Rome and the Byzantine Constantinople, which later, in 1054, split into Catholic and East Orthodox churches.

Bulgarian Khan (later Prince) Boris had to decide which form of Christianity to adopt. The competition over the conversion of the Bulgarians was the first major conflict between Rome and Constantinople. Khan Boris sent to the Pope a long questionnaire about the principles of Christianity. Some of those questions prove that the Jewish customs were well known. The Khan wanted to know about the day of rest, noting that some take Saturday as such day. He also inquired, if in Christianity it is necessary to slaughter animals in certain rituals.

Finally, Khan Boris decided to accept the Byzantine version of Christianity. He and most of the aristocrats converted in year 865 and were followed by the rest of the country. Still, there was resistance led by one of the sons of then Prince Boris, but it was brutally suppressed. A contributing factor to the conversion was the Slavic alphabet created at the request of the Byzantine Emperor in the 850s to facilitate the missionary work of the Constantinople church. The Greek alphabet was used until then, which created problems, since Greek lacked many of the sounds in the Slavic languages.

Two Byzantine scholars of Slavic background, the brothers Cyril and Methodius (Kiril and Metody in Bulgarian) created the new alphabet. The first, more complicated version called Glagolitsa, was later replaced by a simpler version based on the Greek script. Many are convinced that the letters for the sounds "sh" and "ch" (that don't exist in Greek) were borrowed from the Hebrew letters "shin" and "tsadi". It is also believed that during their missionary work among the Khazars, the brothers studied the Hebrew grammar. They also went to Rome, where they successfully debated the Pope and his clergy to obtain permission to spread the Christian scriptures in Slavic languages, instead of Latin and Greek. A few years later, the disciples of Cyril and Methodius found refuge from Western persecution in the Bulgarian Kingdom, where they established schools for high learning and flourishing cultural centers.

Gradually, the Bulgarian state grew under King Simeon I, the son of Prince Boris, who expanded its territory through wars. The 40-year peaceful period during the reign of his son King Peter was followed by slow decline, which was used by Byzantium for its own expansion. The empire eventually took over Bulgaria in 1018 and occupied it for over 100 years.

After several unsuccessful attempts to liberate the country, the successful uprising led by the brothers Assen and Peter managed to expel the Byzantine rulers from Bulgaria in 1185. That was the beginning of the Second Bulgarian State, which again expanded its territory, starting with King Kaloyan's reign from 1197 to 1207. Kaloyan entered a temporary union with the Catholic Church.

During that period, the Jewish population in Bulgaria increased. In 1189, the country established relations with some Western countries - Venice, Ragusa and Genoa. Since the majority of the merchants in those states were Jews, they established offices in Bulgaria and became actively involved in the trade between those countries.

Under the rule of King Ivan Assen II (1218-1241), Bulgaria gained even more territories than under Simeon I, reaching the shores of three seas - Adriatic, Aegean and Black (see the map in the end of the book). In 1235, the King severed the ties with the Catholics and renewed the links with the Orthodox Constantinople, leading to the restoration of the Bulgarian Patriarchate.

In 1352, possibly under Western influence, the church issued an edict to expel the Jews from Bulgaria as heretics. It is not clear if it had any lasting effect, because the Jewish communities continued to flourish in Bulgaria. At that time, the Jews gained some influence in the Bulgarian royal court. King Ivan Alexander, who assumed power in 1331, was a widower; he later married Sarah, a woman from the Jewish community of the capital Tirnovo. She converted to Christianity under the name Theodora, but still maintained ties with her community. It is said that she was intelligent and was active in governing the country.

In 1355, King Ivan Alexander divided the kingdom in two, which is said to have been Theodora's initiative. She wanted to ensure the future of her son Ivan Shishman. The latter became ruler of the Tirnovo Kingdom. Ivan Alexander's son from his first marriage, Ivan Sratsimir, took over the Vidin Kingdom. Dobrudja, the north-east part of Bulgaria, remained under the rule of a local lord, Despot Dobrotitsa.

The divisions of the Balkan countries had tragic consequences in the long term. Bulgaria was weakened in a time marked by the aggressive expansion of the Ottoman Turks. Their army was taking Byzantium piece by piece and regularly plundered the other Balkan countries. By the end of the 14th century, the Turks managed to conquer most of the Balkan Peninsula.

The Tirnovo Kingdom fell in 1393, which was followed by the conquest of the Vidin Kingdom in 1396. During the siege of Tirnovo in 1393, the Bulgarians fought heroically against the Turks and so did the Tirnovo Jews. There is a legend that after the city fell, one Jew came out to greet the sultan and declare his loyalty to him. The sultan despised his behavior and had him killed. The spot where that event supposedly happened became known as Jewish Grave.

The area around Constantinople, a small debris of the once great empire, managed to resist the Turks for over 50 years, but everybody knew that they were doomed. After a long siege, the magnificent city finally fell in 1453 and its citizens were subjected to plunder, murders and rapes. Finally, the Ottoman Empire had a complete control over that part of the world.

The fall of the Second Bulgarian Kingdom was a catastrophe, from which Bulgaria never fully recovered. The Turks occupied the land for nearly 500 years. Most aristocrats were either exterminated or chased away; most libraries were burned down, churches destroyed (followed by a ban on building new churches). It was as if the Bulgarians were sent back in time.

The Ottoman Empire was a backward feudal state, whose economy was based on plunder and severe exploitation of "infidels". It never developed anything worth mentioning. While the countries in Western Europe moved slowly through the

Renaissance toward industrial power, the Turks were in constant stagnation. The feudal model, frozen in time, dragged down each and every one of the conquered nations.

The brutal Ottoman rule had profound consequences for the existence of Bulgarians and Jews. There were some differences in the way both nations were treated, although both were considered second-class subjects of the sultan.

The next chapter will deal with the economic and cultural impact of the Ottoman Empire on the conquered people. Even though they were deprived of rights, the desire to be independent was never extinguished and most of them stubbornly resisted the Turks, which eventually led to the collapse of the empire.

3 THE OTTOMAN YOKE

The order, imposed by the Ottoman invaders, was unlike anything that the inhabitants of the Balkans and especially the Bulgarians have ever seen. Collectively, as nations, they found themselves placed in an inferior position. As Will Monroe had observed:

> "The five centuries that separate the fall of Tirnovo and the fall of Plevna have been aptly characterized as the dark ages of Bulgarian history. For five hundred years the Bulgars bore the double yoke of Turkish political oppression and Greek ecclesiastical tyranny. The Turks carried fire and sword throughout the kingdom. They laid waste towns and villages. Churches and monasteries were sacked and burned. Fertile plains were converted into desolate wastes. Peasants fled to the mountains or crossed the Danube and found refuge in Russia. Some of the nobles embraced the Moslem religion and were rewarded with place and power for their apostasy. Highways were neglected. Khans and caravansaries fell into ruin. The flower of Bulgarian youth was carried to Constantinople to he trained for the janissaries. The fairest of the maidens of the land were seized to grace the harems of their Turkish masters. Every Christian above the age of fourteen years had to pay a poll tax; there was a tax on every head of cattle, and a tenth of all the products of the soil was claimed by the Ottoman government. Regular payment of taxes was greatly augmented by the irregular extortions of Turkish governors, who were allowed to recoup themselves for the bribes they had paid for their jobs. And worst of all, the peasants were fixed to the soil and required to work a certain number of days each week on

the estates of their feudal lords. But the political and economic bondage of the Turks was scarcely less irksome than the religious and intellectual bondage of the Greeks. The entire spiritual government of the Bulgars was turned over to the Greek Phanariotes of Constantinople, for handsome financial considerations, of course! Less than a year after the fall of Tirnovo the venerable Patriarch Eutemius was expelled and the Bulgarian see was subordinated to the patriarch of Constantinople" (Monroe, 1914, p. 25-26).

Some scholars say that the new empire, by liquidating the old state borders, "allowed talented Balkan figures, irrespective of their religious origins, to walk on a world stage, something which the totalitarian constraints of communism or the visa restrictions of the 1990s have effectively prevented in our own day" (Gallagher, 2001, p. 25-26). Although that is partially true, we should remember that this came at a price. It wasn't actually a "world stage" but rather an Ottoman stage, which was viewed with hostility by the rest of the world. Those who wanted to flourish on that stage had to follow closely the Muslim way of life. Those who tried to keep their own traditions, were condemned to a difficult existence.

Henry Barkley, an English engineer who spent years working for the Turkish railways in 1870s, notes in his book "Between the Danube and the Black Sea" that even in the late stages of the empire, the rule of law wasn't a priority:

> "The Bulgarians (and also the Turkish villagers) are loud and incessant in their complaints of the injustice and tyranny of the Turkish officials. All - from the governor-general to the hangman - think it right and just, when on a journey, to quarter themselves on the peasants without ever thinking of paying; and at the same time, they demand the services of their host and his family, and the best of everything there is to be had. The largest and most prosperous of the villages are built as far as possible from the main roads leading to and from the fortified towns such as Widdin, Balchuk, Shumla, etc. If they are on the line of march the troops live on them at free quarters, their carts and beasts are seized for transport purposes, and the owners themselves forced to accompany them as drivers and are obliged to find food for themselves and fodder for the cattle, for all of which they receive no recompense. In consequence of this all the villages that, from force of circumstances, have to be near some main road, are a miserable collection of hovels offering but

small temptation to the traveller" (Barkley, 1876, p. VI).

To the Turkish authorities, that was a natural way of governing. The Ottoman Empire was an absolutist monarchy, where the sultan had unlimited power. His capricious decisions were never questioned because he was simultaneously a political leader and a supreme military commander. "The sultan was apparently all-powerful, and it has been customary, since the time of Machiavelli, to compare Ottoman absolutism with the position of monarchs in Europe, where the prerogatives of the nobility restricted the power of kings. This traditional picture is, however, an oversimplification" (Imber, 2002, p. 318).

The spiritual justification for that unlimited absolutism was Islam. Since its very beginning in the Arab desert, Islam has been an expansionist religion, closely linked with politics. It spread much faster than Christianity because it was forced on the conquered nations - they had to either submit to the Muslim supremacy or die. Another British writer of 19th century, Edward Freeman, observed in his book "The Ottoman Power in Europe, Its Nature, Its Growth and Its Decline":

> "The truth is that the Mahometan religion is, above all others, an aggressive religion. Every religion which does not confine itself to one nation, but which proclaims itself as the one truth for all nations, must be aggressive in one sense. That is to say, it must be anxious to bring men within its pale; in other words, it must be a missionary religion. Now Mahometanism is eminently a missionary religion; but it is something more. It is aggressive in another sense than that of merely persuading men to embrace its doctrines. It lays down the principle that the faith is to be propagated by the sword. Other religions, Christianity among them, have been propagated by the sword; but it is Mahometanism only which lays it down as a matter of religious duty that it should be so propagated. No ruler who forced Christianity by the sword on unwilling nations could say that any precept of the Gospel bade him do so" (Freeman, 1877, p. 60).

Therefore, it is impossible to expect from such a government to provide any equality or even respect to the subjects that adhere to other religions. An anonymous Greek author reflected in 1868 on the same issues, reaching similar conclusion: "In every country which the Turks invaded, they made use of brutal force and of the most treacherous means for proselytising the Christians to the

Mussulman creed. Provinces inhabited exclusively by Christians, unable to resist the oppression of the Turks, were compelled to prefer conversion to the faith of their conquerors, all the ordinances of which they outwardly observed, while in their consciences they remained Christian... Having divided the land into feudal estates, and having settled upon them as conquerors, they left to the Christians the cultivation of the soil, the trade and commerce of the Empire, and intellectual pursuits, to exercise them for the benefit of their lords. All that the Turks reserved to themselves was, the so-called administration of the country by force of arms" (East and West, 1868, p. 5).

According to the Islamic theology, Christians and Jews were at least one level above the despised pagans. Since the Bible revealed some of the teachings covered in the Koran (or rather some of its principles were plagiarized in the Koran), they were considered "people of the scriptures" and were supposed to receive some protection. It was mentioned in the beginning of this chapter that another yoke was the Greek dominance over the Bulgarian church affairs.

The sultan and his administration didn't make distinction between the different ethnicities within his Christian subjects. Even though the Christian and the Jews were supposed to have some religious autonomy, it was the Turkish authorities that decided who was going to lead their communities. "Senior churchmen or rabbis held office by virtue of a royal warrant. This would probably involve a cash payment but, once appointed, the office holder gained tax exemptions and extensive legal and fiscal autonomy within his community". In support of this point, Colin Imber quotes a document issued by a sultan in the 15th century:

> "Because the bearer of this Noble Decree, the priest named X, has brought European florins as a gift to my Noble Treasury, I have granted him the Metropolitanship of Y. I have commanded that, in whatever way previous Metropolitans exercised their Metropolitanship over the priests, monks and other Christians of that area, [he should do the same]; and whatever churches, vineyards and orchards they had the disposal of, he too should have the disposal of them. He should be exempt from... taxes. The priests, monks and other Christians should recognise him as their Metropolitan, and have recourse to him in cases which pertain to the Metropolitanship" (Imber, 2002, p. 216).

For nearly two centuries after the fall of Bulgaria, the construction of new churches was prohibited, and the old ones were either looted and destroyed or turned into mosques. Eventually, the ban was lifted with humiliating conditions - the height of the new churches was not to exceed a rider on a horse (meaning a Turk, horse riding was prohibited for Bulgarians). One of those churches still stands in downtown Sofia (see the pictures in the end).

Not only was the system unfair, but it was also corrupt. However, that was just a part of the problem. Judicially, Christian and Jews, had to submit to the Islamic law, the sharia. Unlike other law systems, which were in the process of constant development, sharia could not be questioned because its principles had a "divine" origin, derived directly form the Koran.

Although a limited number of issues, related to religion, could be handled within the two communities, most of the other legal problems had to go through the system of sharia courts that the Turks established all over the empire. "From as early, presumably, as the fourteenth century, the Ottoman sultans established a network of Islamic courts, so that every town throughout the Empire had one to serve both the town itself and the surrounding area. All the sultan's subjects therefore came within the jurisdiction of an Islamic court. Muslims used these courts exclusively, whether in cases which involved Muslims alone or in those involving both Muslims and non-Muslims. However, the courts were also open to non-Muslims who, as records testify, often brought their affairs to be settled there, even in defiance of their own religious authorities. Occasionally, for example, Jewish women would take advantage of the more generous provisions of Islamic law to claim their inheritance through the Islamic rather than through the Jewish courts. A Muslim, on the other hand, had no access to a non-Muslim court, nor did a non-Muslim in any case which also involved a Muslim. The Islamic courts were therefore, the primary courts of the Empire" (Imber, 2002, p. 217).

The law system reflected the Islamic worldview, which divided the world into two parts: the darülislam, the realm of Islam, subject to Islamic law and governed by Islamic rulers, and the darülharb, 'abode of war', controlled by infidels, that should be eventually conquered (Graf, 2017, p. 73).

The "dhimmis", as they called Christians and Jews who had the misfortune to live in the realm of Islam, were also subjected to economic exploitation. Numerous taxes were levied on them and the situation was complicated by the way taxes were collected.

Often, a feudal lord had to pay to be granted control over an abode, and since he had the right to collect taxes, he imposed higher taxes to compensate for the money paid to the sultan. Farmers were obligated to work several days in the month on the feudal lord's fields.

There was also a special tax, which was kind of a protection racket, called cizie (jizie). Christians and Jews were charged in exchange for the safety of their lives and properties. In a corrupt absolute monarchy like the Ottoman Empire safety, especially of low-class subjects, was problematic, but the tax was another source of income. The only way out of the tax was the conversion to Islam.

Kemal Karpat, in his book "Ottoman Population, 1830-1914" explains how that tax was handled in the late Ottoman Empire:

> "The Christians were divided into categories according to their wealth: good (ala), medium or average (evsat), low (edna), and, occasionally, "incapable of work". Children were not counted. The three main ciziye categories had been maintained almost from the inception of the Ottoman state. In 1831 the tax rates were 48, 24, and 12 kurus, respectively, for the three categories of low, but soon afterwards they were raised by 20% to provide the additional revenue for the sultan's modern army... The rates began to climb sharply after the turn-of-the-century and that the increases became progressively greater throughout the first third of the 19th century" (Karpat, 1985, p. 22).

So, the tax was rising until the end because the empire was never able to develop modern industrial economy. Another, even more horrific tax that existed for a few centuries, but was eventually abolished, was the so-called "blood tax". It was directly linked to maintaining the Janissary Corps, the elite military units that had to guard the sultan and his court and fight in the Ottoman wars.

The cruelty of the Turks was reflected in the way the Janissaries were recruited. Every few years, army units descended on Christian villages and towns, looking for healthy, strong and good looking young boys. They were taken by force and sent to the Janissary barracks in Istanbul. After converting to Islam, they were trained as warriors to join the Janissary Corps. It was a horrific experience for their families. Some sent their children to hide in the woods, others even mutilated them to avoid the recruitment. The famous Bosnian writer Ivo Andric described that in his novel "The Bridge on the Drina": "It was already the sixth year since the last collection of this tribute of blood, and so this time the choice had been easy and rich; the necessary number of healthy, bright and good-looking lads between ten and fifteen years old had been found without difficulty, even though many parents had hidden their children in the forests, taught them how to appear half-witted, clothed them in rags and let them get filthy, to avoid the aga's choice. Some went so far as to maim their own children, cutting off one of their fingers with an axe. The chosen children were laden onto little Bosnian horses in a long convoy. On each horse were two plaited panniers, like those for fruit, one on each side, and in every pannier was put a child, each with a small bundle and a round cake, the last thing they were to take from their parents' homes. From these panniers, which balanced and creaked in unison, peered out the fresh and frightened faces of the kidnapped children. Some of them gazed calmly across the horses' cruppers, looking as long as they could at their native land, others ate and wept at the same time, while others slept with heads resting on the pack-saddles" (Andric, 1977, p. 21-22).

The same grim reality existed in Bulgaria, described by Anton Donchev in his book "Time of Parting" (Donchev, 1968), where he goes even deeper into the attempts to forcibly convert the Bulgarians in the Rodopa Mountain. Some scholars are willing to ignore those cases, basing their views on Islamic theology: "The Qur'an itself is very clear on the matter, enjoining the faithful that 'there shall be no compulsion in religion'. And another section adds, 'Had your lord pleased, all the people of the earth would have believed in Him, one and all. Would you then force people to have faith?' On the other hand, as the discussion of inadvertent conversions in the next chapter suggests, there is some evidence which does point to the existence of less than voluntary converts to Islam. The consensus among the majority of Ottomanists, however, is that, throughout the Empire's history, forced conversion, if it occurred at all, was an exception" (Graf, 2017, p. 77). A deeper look into the history of Bulgaria and the other Balkan countries confirms that the Koranic theology regarding tolerance was not taken seriously by the Turks.

Eventually, the Janissaries became too powerful and demanding. During the decline of the empire, when there were not many wars and not enough plunder, they demanded higher salaries and became a threat to sultan's power. The corps was disbanded, not without a bloody resistance.

Another humiliating ordeal that Christians could suffer was slavery. Under Islam, slavery was perfectly legal. The enslavement of Bulgarians for various reasons started soon after the fall of the medieval Bulgarian Kingdom. The last batch of Bulgarian slaves were a few thousand women and children from Eastern Bulgaria, captured by the Turks during the liberation war of 1877-1878 and ready to be sold. They were rescued by the Russian troops. The process of locating and saving slaves continued after the Bulgarian state was restored. Article 61 of the first Constitution of Bulgaria says: "Nobody in the Bulgarian Principality can buy or sell human beings. Every slave, regardless of gender, faith and ethnicity, becomes free after stepping on Bulgarian territory" (Конституция).

This issue wasn't covered in history lessons under communism and I always thought that the statement was just a feel-good figure of speech, but it addressed a very serious real problem. It is worth noting that in early 19th century, Great Britain pressured the Ottoman Empire to abolish the enslavement of Africans in order to avoid the embarrassment of slavery in its colonies. However, the British never had a problem with the white Christian slaves taken by the Turks from the conquered nations.

According to Tobias Graf, slavery was a large business for the Turks, it was "estimated that between 1580 and 1680, the heyday of the Barbary pirates, on average a total of 35,000 slaves lived in North Africa alone at any given moment. Assuming an 'overall attrition rate' of Barbary slaves of up to 25 per cent, caused by death, manumission, and absconding, he surmises that about 8,500 slaves had to be taken every year merely to maintain the slave population of the Maghrebi littoral alone. Enslavement thus was a real possibility for anybody who travelled the Mediterranean or moved close to the borders with the Ottoman Empire. Anecdotal evidence suggests that Christian-European captives and slaves were ubiquitous at least in such imperial centres as Istanbul, Cairo, and Alexandria" (Graf, 2017, p. 74).

Slaves were used in various works and most often as domestic help. Blond Slavic women with blue eyes were sought because sexual relations with slave women and children (meaning rape) were legal. Even a slave's conversion to Islam wasn't enough to ensure freedom. It was up to the owner to decide when he was going to free a person.

Curiously, rich Jews were also allowed to own slaves, though the right was sometimes revoked. The inferior status of the Jews as dhimmis meant, they could lose privileges at any time at the whim of the authorities. Prof. Yaron Ben-Naeh from the Hebrew University (Jerusalem) has done an extensive research of documents, presented in his paper "Blond, Tall, with Honey-Colored Eyes: Jewish Ownership of Slaves in the Ottoman Empire", which also covers the slavery in general.

He discovered that the documents were related exclusively to female slaves:

> "Slavery thus seems to have been limited to those who would provide household services of the kind exclusively performed by women, including sexual ones. This helps explain why nearly all the slaves were white females, principally of Slavic origin captured during Ottoman campaigns, or by their Tatar collaborators in Eastern Europe, with only a few of other provenance - Circassian, Caucasian, Hungarian, and Austrian. Black slaves are not mentioned. Physical descriptions of female slaves remark about fair hair and light-colored eyes, although, possibly, this simply reflects the general characteristics of the captured and enslaved women; male preference, however, should not be ruled out..." (Ben-Naeh, 2006, p. 317).

The slave owner had the power to limit the period of the slavery and although, according to the custom, the slave was expected to pay for freedom, it was not always necessary, as it was stated in the following document: "...who was the vekil and the eldest son of Avraham veledi Elya the Jew, who lives in the Kiremitci Ahmed Celebi neighborhood in Haskoy and whose vekale was testified by Yasef son of Mihayil and Ilya son of Nahem the Jew's, came to the court and reported on the presence of the cariye of the said Avraham, Eponiye daughter of Romane, who was tall, had blue eyes, detached eyebrows, and was of Russian origin: 'The said Abraham made an agreement with the said Eponiye, that if she will serve him four years with loyalty, at the end of the period she will be free like the other free people.'" (Ben-Naeh, 2006, p. 318).

That arrangement was another result of the Turkish greed, which made the empire ignore its own laws: "The absolute prohibition of slaveholding by non-Muslims gave way to ownership of slaves who were not Muslims, however, in return for the payment of a special tax. In the 1570s Jewish communities, at least in the larger cities, apparently agreed to pay such a tax in return for the right to own slaves, which was likely paid in addition to the jizye (the poll tax paid by [all] dhimmis)', we may assume that slaves owned by non-Muslims rarely converted to Islam, but more often adopted the religion of their non-Muslim owners" (Ben-Naeh, 2006, p. 322).

The situation of the Jews under the Ottoman Empire is often described as peaceful and beneficial to their culture. Although they had some privileges, they were still dhimmis, with all the negative consequences. It was mentioned earlier that many Jews were already in the Bulgarian lands before the Turkish conquest. However, their number increased substantially due to the anti-Semitic hysteria in Western Europe in the 15th century.

Year 1492 was the turning point when Spain expelled the Jews from its territory and they found refuge in the Ottoman Empire. Many of them settled in the large cities, like Istanbul and Salonika, but some joined or established Jewish communities on former Bulgarian territories. "The following centuries saw the migration to Bulgaria of Eshkenazi [Ashkenazi] Jews, mainly from the German lands, whose descendants now form only about 10% of local Jews. Jews were mainly traders, tax collectors, money lenders, manufacturers, doctors and bore the brunt of Ottoman oppression although they were freed from the head tax (haraq) and blood tax (devsirme) levied on the Christians. In some cases, they were even allowed to mint their own gold and silver coins as those dated to the 14th-16th century and discovered near the mining town of Etropole indicate" (Stefanov, 2002).

In 1670s, the British physician Edward Brown traveled in the Ottoman Empire and noted in his book that the Jews in Bulgaria spoke mostly Spanish: "The Jews [in Greece] speak commonly Spanish, as they do in Macedonia, Servia and Bulgaria; and High-Dutch in Hungaria" (Brown, 1673).

The protection provided by the Turks was not a life in paradise. It was a choice between second-class existence in the Ottoman Empire and a likely death in Western Europe. According to the research of Julia Phillips Cohen, presented in her book "Becoming Ottoman: Sephardi Jews and the Imperial Citizenship in the Modern Era", there are many myths about the Jewish life: "Contrary to the statements modern Ottoman Jews pronounced time and again- and to the impression that has remained largely undisturbed until this day—there were moments when the bonds Jews had with the Ottoman government were by no means guaranteed. This was certainly the case during the reign of Bayezid II from 1481 to 1512 - the very same sultan who welcomed Iberian Jewish refugees "with open arms," as so many versions would have it. Bayezid II not only encouraged Jewish refugees to settle in his domains, but also spearheaded campaigns directed against newly opened synagogues and applied significant pressures on Jews to convert to Islam" (Cohen, 2014, p. 3). In other words, the Jewish newcomers were treated similarly to Christians, with the same bans. She continues further:

> "Put simply, the story of the special Ottoman-Jewish relationship is a myth. By labeling it thus, I do not mean to suggest that those who penned the myriad documents or gave the countless speeches testifying to the special nature of Ottoman-Jewish relations were insincere. Rare glimpses into the private lives of late Ottoman Jews indicate the extent to which they internalized their identification with the empire" (Cohen, 2014, p. 4).

Gradually, the Jews began to lose their status, linked to their role in textile production, international commerce and other fields. Part of the problem was the general economic decline of the Ottoman Empire, but demographics also played a role.

> "The demographic situation of Ottoman Jews no doubt contributed to their relative invisibility to imperial state administrators. Compared to the Greek Orthodox and Armenian communities, composed of some 2,000,000 and 2,400,000 souls, respectively, in the mid-nineteenth century, the number of Jews in the empire never reached above 500,000. Smaller than other non-Muslim communities, impoverished, and lacking foreign protectors, Ottoman Jews do not seem to have garnered either the particular favor or the special concern of the Sublime Porte during this period" (Cohen, 2014, p. 6).

Sometimes, Jews became victims of the inner struggles within the empire, prominent businessmen were especially vulnerable, some were even killed.

> "The first of these was Yehezkel Gabbay, Mahmud II's chief moneychanger, who was an ally of the increasingly unwieldy Janissary Corps. His connections with the Janissaries, together with his ongoing rivalry with the lessee of the royal mint, an Armenian Ottoman subject named Kazaz Artin led to his demise. In 1823 Gabbay was exiled to the Ottoman city of Antalya, where he was killed. Then, in 1826, as Sultan Mahmud II took steps to streamline the Ottoman military, he purged the infamous Janissary Corps and had two other Jewish communal

leaders who were financially attached to the institution executed. For a community already struggling economically, this spelled disaster. Thousands of Jews who had in one way or another been tied to a Janissary-based economy were left without a livelihood, while the Jewish community lost its most prominent leaders almost overnight" (Cohen, 2014, p. 6).

By the mid-19th century, it was clear not only inside but also abroad that the Ottoman Empire was in an irreversible decay. It became known as the "Sick Man" of Europe. International powers, like Great Britain, tried to keep it afloat but still many territories were lost - Greece, Serbia, Romania, Egypt and others. The attempt to introduce administrative reforms providing equal rights in the 1830s failed. Turks still held captive several restless nations that were suffocating under their yoke.

In 1876, a Bulgarian uprising started a chain of events that had profound consequences for Bulgarians, Turks and Jews alike.

4 BULGARIANS AND JEWS IN THE STRUGGLE FOR LIBERATION

The mid-1870s were a turbulent time in the Balkan part of the Ottoman Empire. There were several attempts of the enslaved nations to liberate themselves. Uprisings were nothing new in the oppressive Turkish state, they started as soon as it conquered some nations. However, the weakened empire found it more and more difficult to contain them. The frustration with the infidels who rejected the fake benevolence of the sultan led to atrocities that doomed the empire.

In 1875, there was a powerful uprising in Bosnia and Herzegovina, which tried to end the Turkish occupation. The same year, an unsuccessful attempt for an uprising was made in the area of the Bulgarian town of Stara Zagora. The next year, a much larger revolt was planned that was supposed to involve all Bulgarian territories. Weary of the previous revolts, the Turks were ready to suppress it brutally.

These times caused a clash between Bulgarians and Jews - they became victims of a vortex beyond their control. I will write about it further in this chapter.

The events of the spring of 1876 seemed unexpected. It looked like the Bulgarians by that point reached a stage where they could live with the Turkish authoritarianism and find ways to survive. Henry Barkley that I already quoted, confirmed the situation in 1876:

"Beyond complaining of the injustice of the Turkish officials, and the way they are plundered by the troops and police, the

Bulgars have always appeared to me patient under the Turkish yoke, and I never became cognisant of anything like an organised conspiracy against the Government... The Bulgarians are not by any means a warlike race. They are very industrious, penurious, and rather apathetic. As workmen and employees, I preferred them to all others. They are both persevering and intelligent; and very shortly, under English instruction, attained to a higher class of work than, as far as I can recollect, was reached by any other native of those regions" (Barkley, 1879, p. VIII).

The author sees the same attitude in their everyday family life:

"As the children grow up they continue to live in their father's house, and one may often see two or three generations under the same roof. They are the most good-tempered people possible; and though I have spent months in Bulgar houses, I never heard of a family quarrel. I never lived among any race where female virtue is more highly prized than it is among the Bulgarians, and I can safely assert that though our English workmen, men of all sorts and all characters, lived for months at a time in Bulgar villages on the most intimate terms with the women, yet there was never the faintest whisper of scandal. The village girls, though always ready for a laugh or a talk, never drift into levity of conduct, but seem innately to possess virtue and self-respect. As a race, both men and women are well grown and good-looking, and one can see, from their lissome erect carriage and healthy appearance, that from infancy they have been well fed and well clothed. If only absolute security for person and property could be obtained, I believe Bulgaria would be one of the most prosperous countries in Europe..." (Barkley, 1879, p. IX).

Januarius Macgahan, the prominent American journalist, who was the first one to make public the horrific Turkish atrocities after the April Uprising, had a similar opinion:

"I think people in England and Europe generally have a very imperfect idea of what these Bulgarians are. I have always heard them spoken of as mere savages, who were in reality not much more civilized than the American Indians; and I confess that I myself was not far from entertaining the same opinion not very long ago. I was astonished, as I believe most of my readers will be, to learn that there is scarcely a Bulgarian village without its school; that these schools are, where they have not been burnt by the Turks, in a very flourishing condition; that they are supported by a voluntary tax levied by the Bulgarians on themselves, not only without being forced to do it by the Government, but in spite of all sorts of obstacles thrown in their way by the perversity of the Turkish authorities; that the instruction given in these schools is gratuitous, and that all profit alike by it, poor as well as rich; that there is scarcely a Bulgarian child that cannot read and write; and, finally, that the percentage of people who can read and write is as great in Bulgaria as in England and France" (Macgahan, 1876, p. 24-25).

So, the question remains: why did those peaceful people, who cared more about families and education, decided to rise against a powerful enemy? It is obvious that the Ottoman Empire was strangling their initiative, but was that enough to start a revolt?

A possible answer is provided by the Bulgarian sociologist Ivan Hadjiyski who in the 1930s studied extensively the uprising, interviewing many survivors. In his book "Psychology of the April Uprising", he concluded that the heavy taxes and the Turkish corruption were not a sufficient reason for what happened. In his opinion, it was the political and military decay of the Ottoman Empire, which by the 19th century was incapable of maintaining the inner order and peace. In the 18th century, the government successfully handled the large robber armies of the Kurdjaliy (about 25,000 people) with the help of the Bulgarians whom it armed.

In 1863-1864, the sultan decided to move to Bulgaria about 200,000 of over a million Circassians who were displaced after the Russo-Circassian War of that time. The plan was to strengthen the Muslim element in those lands. Hoping to make them work in the agriculture, the government forced Bulgarians to clear of trees vast lands to prepare fields for the Circassians. The latter had no intention to become peasants and started robbing their new neighbors, a "trade" that was one of the main reasons for their war with Russia. The Circassian robberies and other atrocities were outrageous, but the Turkish government was unable to restore order. The chaos encouraged thugs from other ethnicities - Turks, Bulgarians and gypsies - to "earn" living the same way.

Hadjiysky's interviewees told him that women didn't dare to go work on the fields alone. If they were not raped, the robbers at least took their bags with bread. To prevent theft of the animals, the farmers had to lock them up at night in their basements and barricade the doors. "If a Circassian saw in the field a lone peasant with a cow, he took the cow, galloping away on his horse. If the peasant was alone, he took his bag or shoes, but never left the peasant the way he found him. That forced people to travel in groups" (Хаджийски, 2002, p. 220).

The rich merchants had to hire large armed groups to deliver their goods and stay alive. Many of them also had to support the widows of men killed while working for them. The situation made everybody a target, nobody, poor or rich, was safe and their lives changed drastically. There was a rumor that the Circassians were just the first step in a plan of the Turkish government to kill all Bulgarians in 1876. The tragic reality pushed thousands of people to become a part of the hastily organized uprising. Before the Circassian problem nobody thought about an uprising (Хаджийски, 2002, p. 254).

A committee of Bulgarian revolutionaries met in Bucharest. The strategy was to divide the country into four "Revolutionary Districts" led by "Apostles" with the task to organize the uprising. The preparation was more successful only in the 4th district, around the city of Philippopolis (Plovdiv). The Turkish authorities suspected that something was being planned and after receiving tips, sent an army unit to arrest the instigators in the town of Koprivshtitsa. There was a clash, in which the mudur (local military commander) was killed. The incident forced the organizers to rise 10 days before the planned date.

The Turks managed to arrest most of the commanders in three Revolutionary Districts and serious battles took place only in the 4th. Although some towns declared independence, they could not resist for long, being only about 8,000 poorly armed rebels. The central government sent against them a regular army with artillery, about 10,000 soldiers, and over 80,000 Turkish civilians, the so-called bashibozuk. The latter consisted of volunteers who were allowed to keep everything they could loot. Most of the towns, Klisura, Panagyurishte, Batak, Perushtitsa and others fell within days. The majority of people, and especially women and children, were raped and killed. It is difficult to estimate the total number of the victims, but the numbers vary from 30,000 to 75,000 according to different historians.

Since most Jews lived in larger cities, which were not affected, there were no records of Jewish participation in the uprising. Macgahan describes the curious case of a Jewish peddler he met who got stranded in one of the towns:

"He came to us and gave us an account of what had befallen him. The insurgents, suspecting he might go away from the village and relate what was going on, arrested him in order to prevent any such movement, and they finally decided to ensure his silence and secrecy by forcing him to renounce Judaism. He says they put a Bulgarian cap on his head, and gave him the Christian name of "Ghiorghy," or George. It does not appear that they went so far as to baptise him, however; nor does it seem that they placed much confidence in his conversion, for they kept him in prison in a private house, and would not let him leave the village. This fear was not altogether unfounded, as it turned out; for when the Turks arrived and set him at liberty, he went about the town with the Bashi-Bazouks, and pointed out to them the rich people, and the fine houses where they would find the most booty. Apart from the violence they did his feelings in converting him, and giving him the name of "Ghiorghy," he acknowledges that the people were very kind, and gave him plenty to eat and drink during the week he was in their power. He was quite impartial in his relation of what he saw and heard, not seeming to care a fig which side won, and recounting what occurred in the most indifferent and cynical manner" (Macgahan, 1876, p. 76-77).

Despite the rumors that something horrible had happened in the towns near Philippopolis, it took until June for the news to reach the world. Two forces tried to suppress the truth, naturally, one of them was Turkey, the other one was Great Britain, its staunch supporter. The British Consul in Istanbul initially denied the atrocities and later blamed both sides.

An active role in unveiling the truth was played by the American Consul-General Eugene Schuyler who went to inspect the affected area in July and August 1876. He was accompanied by Januarius Macgahan, who at the time worked for the British Daily News. They spent there several weeks and thanks to their reports, we have a detailed information about the atrocities. After the publication, the Turkish government denied everything as lies and exaggerations. The English government of Lord Beaconsfield (a.k.a. Benjamin Disraeli) continued to maintain that the information was unconfirmed, despite that fact that it had the original diplomatic reports.

Upon their arrival in Philippopolis, they received from the diplomats of several countries their estimates of the number of victims:

> "In the districts about Philippopolis and Tatar Bazardjik alone there have been about fifty villages burnt, without counting those that have been only pillaged, and that nearly 15,000 people have been slaughtered. This is the lowest estimate, and it does not include the districts about Sofia and those north of the Balkan. The French and Russian Consuls and the railway officials give much higher figures and would put the number of villages burned at over a hundred, and the killed at 25,000 to 40,000. There are people who put the number of killed at 100,000… The Greek Consul, who is not friendly to the Bulgarians, tells me of 12,000 wretched women and children marched into Tatar Bazardjik, nearly all of whom suffered the vilest outrages. He tells me of Bulgarian fathers who killed their wives and children in order to put them out of reach of the ferocity of the Bashi-Bazouks. The German officials tell me of the bodies of men cut up and flung to the dogs in villages near their own railway stations; of little children of both sexes maltreated and brutalised until they died; of a priest, whose wife and children were outraged and slaughtered before his eyes, and who was then put to death, after the most fearful torture, the details of which are too abominable to be retold." (Macgahan, 1876, p. 11).

The perpetrators of all that had no reason to fear punishment:

> "Chefket Pacha, for instance, who burned the village of Bazardjik, and slaughtered nearly all of its inhabitants under more than usually revolting circumstances, should have been one of the first to feel the strong arm of the law. But having done all this, he has been promoted to a high position in the Palace of the Sultan at Constantinople. Again, there is the ease of Achmet Aga, a captain of a company of Bashi-Bazouks, who likewise distinguished himself by his ferocity. He wished to burn Philippopolis and was only withheld from doing so by the energetic action of the governor, who has since been removed, and who threatened to attack him with the regular troops. It was he who slaughtered 8,000 people at Batak and burned 200 women and children alive in the school." (Macgahan, 1876, p. 12).

Despite the claims of Lord Beaconsfield and Lord Derby in London that the Turks were merely responding to Bulgarian atrocities, no such events were discovered by Schuyler and Macgahan:

> "They could not have obtained it from the Turkish Government, for the reason that even the Turkish authorities here do not claim more than 500 Turks killed altogether, of whom the greater part, they admit, were killed in battle, with arms in their hands; and further, because while they claim some thirty women killed, they have not so far given Mr. Schuyler proof that a single woman or child was killed or outraged. Kiani Pacha told him that the Mudir of the village of Avratalan had been killed with his wife and daughter. Mr. Schuyler found, upon inquiry, that the wife of the Mudir was absent in a different part of the country when the fight occurred, and that the report of her death was therefore untrue; while as to the daughter, he learned that the Mudir never had a daughter" (Macgahan, 1876, p. 13).

On their way to Batak, they met thousands of destitute refugees, mostly wounded and raped women. On a hill overseeing the village, they found a heap of headless skeletons and decomposing corpses, belonging to nearly 200 girls and women, who were held there by the Turks to be raped and beheaded. No Turks were killed in Batak, so they could not claim a revenge. After entering the village, Macgahan went to the school and the church:

> "The schoolhouse, to judge by the walls that are in part standing, was a fine large building, capable of accommodating two or three hundred children. Beneath the stones and rubbish that cover the floor to the height of several feet, are the bones and ashes of 200 women and children burnt alive between those four walls. Just beside the schoolhouse is a broad shallow pit. Here were buried a hundred bodies two weeks after the massacre. But the dogs uncovered them in part. The water flowed in, and now it lies there a horrid cesspool, with human remains floating about or lying half exposed in the mud... The church was not a very large one, and it was surrounded by a low stone wall, enclosing a small churchyard about fifty yards wide by seventy-five long. At first, we perceive nothing in particular, and the stench is so great that we scarcely care to look about us, but we see that the place is heaped up with stones and rubbish to the height of five or six feet above the level of the street, and upon inspection we discover that what appeared to be a mass of stones and rubbish is in reality an immense heap of human bodies covered over with a thin layer of stones... We were told there were three thousand people lying here in this little church-yard alone, and we could well believe it. It was a fearful

sight - a sight to haunt one through life. There were little curly heads there in that festering mass, crushed down by heavy stones; little feet not as long as your finger on which the flesh was dried hard, by the ardent heat before it had time to decompose; little baby hands stretched out as if for help; babes that had died wondering at the bright gleam of sabres and the red bands of the fierce-eyed men who wielded them; children who had died shrinking with fright and terror; young girls who had died weeping and sobbing and begging for mercy; mothers who died trying to shield their little ones with their own weak bodies, all lying there together, festering in one horrid mass. They are silent enough now" (Macgahan, 1876, p. 27-28).

Similar gruesome sights met Schuyler and Macgahan in other villages. Survivors shared their ordeals:

"One woman told us, wringing her hands and crying, that she and her daughter, a girl of fifteen, had been violated in the same room, another that she was violated in the presence of her children. A girl of eighteen avowed, shuddering and bowing her face in her hands, that she had been outraged by ten soldiers. A woman, who came to us on crutches with a bullet still in her ankle, said she had been violated by three soldiers while lying wounded on the ground groaning in agony. Young, delicate, fragile little creatures, ten and twelve years old, were treated in the same brutal manner. A woman told us that her daughter, a tender, delicate little thing of twelve, had been seized and outraged by a Bashi-Bazouk, although she had offered all the money she had in the world - although she offered herself - if he would spare the child. Another told us of a poor little thing of ten violated in her presence, with a number of other girls. Still another told us how a dozen young girls, twelve or fifteen years old, had taken refuge in her house, hoping to escape detection; how they had been discovered; how two of them had been outraged, and killed, because they had resisted, and how the others then submitted to their fate, white, shivering, their teeth chattering with fright" (Macgahan, 1876, p. 44).

The outrage over the atrocities spread all over the world. In Russia, the writers Ivan Turgenev and Fyodor Dostoyevsky wrote about that. The latter even placed some related images in the sick mind of Ivan Karamazov in "Brothers Karamazov". In England, Queen Victoria and many of her politicians were horrified.

Lord Beaconsfield still stood firm, denying everything. His

justification was that the Ottoman Empire had to be kept alive by all means, because if its territory was taken by Russia, it could close the Bosporus and the Suez Canal, hindering the access to India. In his pamphlet "Bulgarian Horrors and the Question of the East" (that sold nearly 200,000 copies) the opposition leader William Gladstone condemned the Prime Minister: "In answer, then, to Mr. Forster, Mr. Disraeli said, "We have no information in our possession which justifies the statements, to which the Right Hon. gentleman refers." The disturbances appeared to have been begun "by strangers, burning the villages without reference to religion or race." A war was carried on between "Bashi-Bazouks and Circassians," on one side, and "the invaders" on the other, and no doubt, "with great atrocity," much to be deplored. Since that time, measures had been adopted to stop these "Bashi-Bazouks and Circassians." "I will merely repeat," he concluded, "that the information which we have at various times received does not justify the statements made in the journal which he has named." (Gladstone, 1876). In another pamphlet, a year later, he called for an action against Turkey (Gladstone, 1877).

In late 1876, an international conference was called in Istanbul to decide how to resolve the crisis. The European powers decided that Turkey should provide autonomy to its European possessions. Encouraged by Lord Beaconsfield's support, the sultan disregarded the recommendations.

In the British Parliament, Lord Beaconsfield continued to defend Turkey:

> "After taunting Sir William Harcourt with his Rhodian eloquence, the Premier went on: [That Sir William Harcourt] should counsel as the solution of all these difficulties that Her Majesty's Government should enter into an immediate combination to expel the Turkish nation from Eastern Europe does indeed surprise me. (Cheers.) And because we are not prepared to enter into a scheme so Quixotic as that would be, we are held up by the hon. and learned gentleman and the right hon. gentleman the member for Bradford as having given our moral, not to say our material assistance to the Turkish people and the Turkish Government. We are always treated as if we had some peculiar alliance with the Turkish Government, as if we were their peculiar friends, and even as if we were expected to uphold them in any enormity they might commit. I want to know what evidence there is of this. We are the allies of the Sultan of Turkey; so is Russia, so is Austria, so is France, and so

are others... I am sure that as long as England is ruled by English Parties who understand the principles on which our Empire is founded, and who are resolved to maintain that Empire, our influence in that part of the world can never be looked upon with indifference... There is nothing to justify us in talking in such a vein of Turkey at this moment. It is a state of affairs which requires the most vigilant examination and the most careful management. But those who suppose that England ever would uphold, or at this moment particularly is upholding, Turkey from blind superstition and from a want of sympathy with the highest aspirations of humanity, are deceived. (Cheers.) What our duty at this critical moment is, is to maintain the Empire of England..." (Thompson, 1886, p. 373-374).

Still, the author concluded that this position ruined Disraeli's career:

"Moreover, Mr. Disraeli had come to be regarded as the apologist of Turkey, and the advocate of an ultra "red" policy, in a more special manner than other members of the Cabinet, and it began to be noted that a great change was coming over the general appreciation in which he was held. Mr. Disraeli has done himself more harm in the House of Commons by his jaunty replies in reference to the questions put to him as to the atrocities in Bulgaria, than by any escapade of his Premiership" (Thompson, 1886, p. 375).

Many in England shared that opinion. Edward Freeman grudgingly admitted in the already quoted book of 1877:

"It is with a blush that an Englishman writes such words as these. It is with shame and sorrow that an Englishman has to confess that, when another nation undertakes the work which should above all things have been the work of England, the utmost that he can dare to hope for is that England may not be a hinderer in that work. We have no wish for Russian aggrandizement, for Russian ascendency, for Russian influence in any form. We believe that the exclusive ascendency of Russia in the South-eastern lands would be an evil; only we do not hold it to be the greatest of evils. We would fain see England, Russia, any other civilized power, have its fair share of influence in those lands. But, if we are reduced to a choice between Russia and the Turk, then we must choose Russia"

(Freeman, 1877).

Disraeli's refusal to acknowledge the suffering caused a negative reaction in Bulgaria, which even had some anti-Semitic connotations in some opinions. It didn't help that strictly speaking, he was not a Jew, he converted to Christianity as a child.

The displeasure of the other countries with sultan's refusal to provide autonomy, pushed Russia to take action on its own. In 1877, the Russian Emperor Alexander II invaded the Ottoman Empire. To the Bulgarians, it was a war of liberation. The Russian troops were joined by over 7,000 Bulgarian armed volunteers.

The war made the situation of the Jews in the empire very complicated. Although Turkey wasn't the best, it still provided some protection. On the other hand, Russia was notorious for its rampant anti-Semitism. While in Western Europe things were slowly improving for the Jews, their brethren in Russia faced living and work restrictions, murders and mass pogroms.

The fear that in the case of a victory, Russia could establish a dependent pro-Russian state in Bulgaria was terrifying. So, the ways of Bulgarians and Jews temporarily parted.

Prominent rabbis in Istanbul declared Turkey "the salvation of the House of Israel". Jews wanted to present themselves as loyal citizens, ready to confront Russia. When it became clear that the war was imminent, many Jewish volunteers expressed their desire to join the Ottoman army. Julia Phillips Cohen notes:

> "...By April Russia declared war on the Ottoman state. Ottoman Jews responded to the news with public demonstrations of patriotism and a new sense of urgency. Within a matter of weeks, Jews in the Ottoman capital filed into the Ahrida Synagogue, located in Balat on the southern shore of the Golden Horn. They gathered to pray for the victory of the Ottoman army. According to various reports, all of Istanbul's Jewish notables were in attendance. An impressive number of civil and military representatives also figured among the guests. In addition to official personalities, synagogue-goers - reportedly numbering in the thousands - arrived to participate in the important event. Their numbers were so great that crowds of expectant onlookers spilled over into the surrounding courtyard and streets" (Cohen, 2014, p. 34).

In his sermon, Chief Rabbi Halevi presented Russia as the image of evil, resembling Egypt, where Jews were persecuted constantly. He declared the Ottoman realms a sacred terrain for the Jews. Praying for the Ottoman victory was not enough, the Jews had to fight for it (Cohen, 2014, p. 36). Strictly speaking, he was correct about the sacred meaning of at least a part of the empire - the territory of ancient Israel was part of it.

The Jews persisted in their support:

> "Even after Muslims began to speak of the war with Russia as a jihad, or holy war for Islam, Ottoman Jews did not desist from claiming the cause as their own. Instead, Jewish journalists introduced their audiences to the terms and concepts involved. Reminding their readers that Abdulhamid II was not only the sultan of the Ottomans but also the caliph of Muslims the world over, they told of the donations that poured in for the Ottoman war effort from Muslims in India and of the rebellion of Muslims under the Tsar... Russia was not only the "enemy of Islam," after all, as a Muslim author suggested in the pages of the Ottoman-language journal Basiret of Istanbul in the midst of the war, but also the enemy of the Jews" (Cohen, 2014, p. 38-39).

It is not clear how much the Bulgarians and Russians knew about all that, but there was tension between them and the Jews. Turkey tried to use the mistreatment of Jews to counter the criticism of its atrocities in 1876. Some Jews were expelled or even killed by Russians in the towns of Vidin, Kazanluk, and Stara Zagora. In other places, Jews joined forces with Bulgarians to save their towns.

The Turks were planning to burn down Sofia and even started the fire, but the town was saved by a Jewish fire brigade. After the liberation, as a sign of gratitude, the first Bulgarian ruler, Prince Alexander Battenberg, granted exclusive rights to the Jewish firefighters. They also appeared in uniforms at all military parades.

The city of Rouschouk (Russe) was saved from fire and slaughter by two prominent citizens - the Jewish doctor Beniamino Raphael Nahmiyas and the teacher Ivan Veder. Just before the Russian invasion in 1877, the local Turkish pasha planned to withdraw after killing most people and taking their possessions. The two delegates convinced him not to do it (Rescue of Russe in 1877).

Many years after the liberation of Bulgaria, in 1940, the Central Consistory of the Jews in Sofia collected facts about the contributions of Jews in the Bulgarian struggle for freedom. The document, "Facts and Activities of the Bulgarian Jewry in Defense of Bulgaria", was part of the protest letters that opposed the proposed Law for Defense of the Nation. It briefly traced the history of the Jewish presence in Bulgaria and revealed some little-known facts.

Elieser Kalev was in 1874-1875 a member of the Turkish administration in Plovdiv. He was influential in the local government, which gave him the chance to save from prison or death many Bulgarians, among whom were Tsoko Chorbadji Yeshioolu, Stefanaki, Stoyan Chorbadji, Todor Kableshkov (prominent revolutionary), Kocho hadji Kalchov.

After the separation of Bulgaria in 1878, Moshe Solomon from Yambol was delegate in the East Rumelian Assembly, he was also a chairman of the local Jewish community. He maintained ties with the most active Bulgarians in the city, shielded them from persecution in creative ways, and provided other service, for which he was harassed by the Turks. Later, he became the first teacher of Bulgarian language in the Jewish School in Yambol.

Davichon Saranga from Stara Zagora spent most of his life in Istanbul and helped many Bulgarian rebels to get out of jail by becoming their surety. During his travels to Vidin to organize local liberation committees, the great revolutionary Vasil Levski had often found refuge in Jewish houses, one of them belonged to the Pinkas family.

Many cases of Jews protecting Bulgarians from the Turkish authorities were described by the traveler Felix Kanitz. Moshe Solomon Tadjer from Kyustendil risked his life in 1876 to save Vasil Levski's adherents, the brothers Manol and Dimitur Dromarski, Hristo Grebenarov, and others.

Haim H. Davidov from Dupnitsa, known to the locals as "Old Haime", saved in 1876 the town from massacre and arson through his courageous confrontation with the dreadful leader of the bashibozuk, Kel Asan. Also, as a juror in the anti-rebel Turkish court, he saved many Bulgarians from death.

After the start of the Liberation War of 1877, many Bulgarians found refuge from the Turks in Jewish homes. In his house in Sofia, Chelibon Farhi hid the Father Superior of the Dragalevtsi Monastery Avxenty, a prominent revolutionary. Due to the uncertainty among the population after the withdrawal of the Turkish Army and the delayed entry of the Russians in Sofia, the citizen Shemuel Asher Levy insisted that Father Avxenty send people to notify the Russians that Sofia is free, and they can enter.

That's what happened. On January 6, 1878, General Gourko entered the town, greeted by a delegation with a few Jewish participants: Harebi Almozlino, the Rabbi of Sofia, Shemuel Asher Levy, Shemuel Ruben, and Haim Isaac Eshkenazi.

During their withdrawal from Sofia, the Turkish Army and Turkish population started many fires and wanted to burn down the town. The bashibozuk looted stores. The Jewish youth armed itself hastily with weapons from an abandoned armory and formed a militia, which saved Sofia from looting, devastation and fire. The improvised Jewish fire brigade extinguished the fires. This voluntary Jewish fire brigade continued its work even after the liberation (and was recognized by Prince Alexander Battenberg) (Факти, евреи защитили България, 1940, p. 1-5).

The war continued for two years with many casualties. The fate of Stara Zagora resembled that of the towns destroyed after the April Uprising in 1876. In 1877, it was taken by the Russians, who although not very friendly toward Muslims and Jews, still maintained order. After an unexpected counterattack by the army of Suleiman Pasha, the Russians withdrew toward the Balkan Mountain.

The Turks turned into their usual genocidal mode. Out of a population of 25,000, over 14,500 were slaughtered and about 10,000, mostly young boys, girls and women were abducted and sold as slaves. Some of them were saved later. The book of Dimitur Ilkov "Contribution to the History of Stara Zagora", based on testimonies and field research lists some of the horrors (Илков, 1908).

There were again gruesome cases of cruelty. In the large house of a rich Bulgarian about 500 people found refuge. The Turks set the house on fire. When people inside tried to run out, the waiting Turks started killing them with swords. Then they broke the door to another part of the house, with 200 people inside, meeting no resistance. They caught the owner and cut off his arms at the shoulders. The rest were begging for mercy, bringing money and gold. All were killed anyway. A young priest among them had his beard set on fire, then the Turks poured gas all over him and burned him alive.

They acted the same way in any house where the Bulgarians tried to hide. People were skinned alive, others were nailed to trees by the arms and the feet. When the Russians returned, the city was empty. The Jews, who were not affected by the massacre, left with the retreating Turks.

Stara Zagora was the last Bulgarian experience with Muslim

barbarism. The Turkish army was completely defeated. Russia was ready to take Istanbul, but Lord Beaconsfield sent the British fleet there as a threat. On March 3, 1878, a treaty was signed in the suburb of San Stefano. Bulgaria was free.

However, as we will see later, England and the other powers did everything in their power to spoil the victory.

5 A NEW LIFE IN LIBERATED BULGARIA

The San Stefano agreement, signed after the end of the Russo-Turkish War, restored the Bulgarian state. In the borders of the new country, the treaty included all territories populated by ethnic Bulgarians, as you can see in the map of Bulgaria in 1878, in the end of the book. Thus, Macedonia, Southern Thrace, and Dobrudja, along with the main territory, became parts of Bulgaria.

However, since the agreement was signed after a military defeat only by Russia and Turkey, the European powers didn't recognize it. The same year they organized the so-called Berlin Congress, where the major European countries redesigned Bulgaria. "From 13 June to 13 July 1878, representatives of the signatories of the Paris peace treaty of 1856, which had ended the Crimean War, assembled in Berlin under the chairmanship of Bismarck. There was no participation of the Balkan states, although their governments were allowed to send representatives to present their views at the sessions that concerned their interests. What ensued, under the cynical guidance of Bismarck, was a diplomatic carve-up of the region that ruled out the creation of a viable pattern of states. Decisions were made about Macedonia, Bulgaria and Bosnia which would return to haunt the peace of Europe in subsequent decades" (Gallagher, 2001, p. 46). In the same map, you can see that Macedonia and Thrace were given back to Turkey. The Bulgarian state was reduced to a vassal principality of Turkey, which included only Northern Bulgaria and the Sofia Sanjak. Southern Bulgaria was given autonomy under Turkish rule.

These decisions were an enormous blow against Bulgarians. The division became the main reason for many wars that the

Balkan countries fought later.

In 1879, in the city of Tirnovo, the first National Assembly was called. A rabbi represented the Bulgarian Jews in it. Under the observation of the Russian authorities, it was supposed to create a constitution, which was modeled under the Belgian Constitution. Most of the national revolutionaries in the past were supporters of a republican order, but the idea of monarchy was eventually imposed. It required an aristocrat to be appointed as a Prince, but the Bulgarian aristocracy had been exterminated long time ago and the Constitution didn't allow the creation of noble titles. Thus, the throne was offered to the young German Prince Alexander Battenberg, who assumed his position as Alexander I.

As we saw earlier, the main concern of the Jews was the connection between Bulgaria and Russia. However, the Constitution was democratic and guaranteed equal right to all ethnicities in Bulgaria, something that lacked in Russia. The two countries were slowly parting ways. In March 1881, the reformist Emperor Alexander II was killed by leftist Russian terrorists. His son, Alexander III, was less inclined to engage in further reforms. Bulgaria started to drift away and look for new ties with Western Europe.

The Berlin Congress demanded equal rights for minorities and that was not followed by some countries. Romania didn't implement any of it - Jews were mistreated, starting from the 1860s.

> "As early as 1866 efforts of Old Kingdom Jews to gain emancipation ran aground Article 7 of the 1866 Romanian Constitution by specifying that only foreigners of Christian faith could become naturalized Romanian citizens, issued in an era of civil limitations for Romanian Jews. Under pressure from the Great Powers the Romanian parliament modified Article 7 of the country's constitution in October 1879... However, the revision of Article 7 was still used to block the Romanian Jews from obtaining full civil and political rights... The new law required Jews who requested Romanian citizenship to petition the prince. The petitioner would then have to wait 10 years and if he or she could demonstrate continual residence in the country and "usefulness to the country" the request might be granted by a special act of the legislature. From a Jewish population of nearly 200,000 in 1911 only 2,000 Romanian Jews had successfully acquired citizenship" (Brustein, Ronnkvist, 2002, p. 213).

The Romanian Jews received full citizenship rights only in 1923, but that did not diminish anti-Semitism. Even the Orthodox Church of Romania expressed hostility toward Jews. A full-blown fascist ideology developed in the 1930s (see Ioanid, 1990).

The Bulgarian Jews were treated differently. They didn't suffer the employment restrictions common in Romania and Russia. Their numbers were relatively small. The census of 1880-1881 shows that of a total of 2,823,865, the Bulgarians were 1,919,067 and the Jews - 18,519 or 0.66%. Later, after the unification with Rumelia, according to the 1887 census, the numbers increased to 3,154,375 total, 2,326,250 Bulgarians and 23,571 Jews (0.75%) (Crampton, 2007, p. 432).

Another visitor noticed the equal treatment of the Jews:

> "I found Bulgarians of all classes, if less hospitable, more serious and better read than Servians. The former are also more up-to-date as regards the treatment of the Jews, who in Sofia, at any rate, enjoy the same privileges as in that earthly paradise of the modern Israelite - England" (Windt, 1907, p. 214).

The reign of Prince Alexander I was marred by fierce political struggles. Russia didn't like him; a coup was organized against him. At certain point, he even suspended the Constitution. There was even a government in 1882 with the Russian General Sobolev as Prime Minister. The most critical point in Prince's career came in September 1885 when a group of revolutionaries and politicians organized a bloodless coup in Eastern Rumelia, overthrowing the Turkish Governor. Then they demanded that Prince Alexander sign a proclamation for the unification of Bulgaria. He knew that all European forces would be against such an act, but signed it anyway, aware that it would bring an end to his rule.

Russia condemned the unification and withdrew all the high commanders from the Bulgarian army, leaving it only with the Bulgarian captains. Almost all Bulgarian troops were stationed at the Turkish border, expecting an invasion over the coup. However, Bulgaria was stabbed in the back - with Western support, the Serbian King Milan attacked the country. Turkey gave assurances that it would not attack, so the troops headed toward the capital Sofia, which was in a dire situation.

They arrived just in time to face the Serbs just a few kilometers from Sofia and defeated them at Slivnitsa. The Bulgarians were willing to continue all the way to Belgrade, but the Western countries demanded that they stop the offensive, thus, saving

Serbia.

Hundreds of Jewish volunteers joined the army and fought heroically. Prince Alexander praised them as the new Maccabi warriors. The next year, he was forced to abdicate. After a long selection process among the European aristocrats, the Parliament approved the German Prince Ferdinand Saxe-Coburg-Gotha as a new ruler.

Ferdinand was an intelligent but pompous and vain person who paid excessive attention to the glamorous side of his power. Unlike Prince Alexander, he liked extravagant events and redesigned the royal palace to match his ego. A good side effect of all that was the new look of Sofia, it gradually turned from muddy provincial town into a "miniature Brussels", as some travelers called it:

> "Sofia is a miniature Brussels. One of these days it may rival Buda-Pest, or rather Pest, the most modern, spick-and-span town in Europe. Twenty- five years ago there were eleven thousand people in Sofia. Now there are over seventy thousand. But Sofia is still in an unfinished state. The old town, as the Turks left it, has nigh gone. But the new town has not come in its completeness" (Fraser, 1906, p. 65).

The same writer had a rather unpleasant opinion about the Prince: "Ferdinand is astute. Yet his cleverness is not of the kind to be appreciated by Bulgarians. During the last twenty years he has had an excellent opportunity to get a grip of the hearts of the people. He has done nothing of the kind. Rightly or wrongly, they are convinced that he neither likes them nor their country. If they are wrong, he ministers to the mistake by preferring to live in other countries than in that of his adoption. His official allowance is about a million and a quarter of francs, money drawn from peasants. They think it ought to be spent in Bulgaria, and not in Vienna or Paris. He is not popular. Despite his shortcomings, Prince Ferdinand is a factor for peace—a greater factor than the rest of Europe gives him credit for. Were his influence removed there is little doubt Bulgaria would pick a quarrel with Turkey and plunge the Balkans into war..." (Fraser, 1906, p. 66). Ironically, Fraser's prediction, written in 1906, will turn wrong - Ferdinand will lead Bulgaria into several wars.

The position of prince vassal of Turkey hindered Ferdinand's ambitions, so on October 5, 1908, he proclaimed Bulgaria's independence and became Tsar (King). This time, the act didn't cause significant negative reactions.

At the time, Jews were already integrating into the Bulgarian society, while preserving their culture:

> "Jewish ease in assimilating into Bulgarian society was bolstered by several factors. In contrast to Jews in many parts of Europe and much like the Jews in Italy, Bulgarian Jews were more likely to speak the local dialect of the community than Yiddish or Ladino. By 1910, less than 2 percent of the Bulgarian Jewish population was illiterate in the Bulgarian language. In a 1934 survey, 40 percent of the Bulgarian Jewish population gave Bulgarian as their principal spoken language; the other 60 percent referred to themselves as bilingual. Not only did Jews learn and speak Bulgarian, their mastery of the language favorably impressed their countrymen" (Brustein, 2004, p. 441).

An important factor in the active social life of the Bulgarian Jews become Zionism:

> "Jewish life in Bulgaria, while modestly successful, did not find Jews well-integrated, since consistent government, social, and economic policies discouraged an active Jewish role in Bulgarian society. But by the end of the nineteenth century, stimulated primarily by Zionist influences, Jewish culture began to thrive. Zionists helped develop an educational system for the Bulgarian Jewish community that emphasized Jewish studies, and under the direction of the Jewish Central Consistory, Bulgarian Jews created a three-tiered educational system that began with kindergarten and ended with the progymnasium. The Jewish community provided 80% of the funding for this system, while the rest came from local and national governmental sources" (Georgeoff, 1985, p. 274-308).

The popularity of the Zionist movement was noticed by Theodor Herzl during his visit in Bulgaria in April 1896. His train stopped briefly at the Sofia railway station:

> "In Sofia a touching scene awaited me. Beside the track on which our train pulled in there was a crowd of people-—who had come on my account. I had completely forgotten that I was actually responsible for this myself. There were men, women, and children, Sephardim, Ashkenazim, mere boys and old men with white beards. At their head stood Dr. Ruben Bierer. A boy handed me a wreath of roses and carnations—Bierer made a

speech in German. Then Caleb read off a French speech, and in conclusion he kissed my hand, despite my resistance. In this and subsequent addresses I was hailed in extravagant terms as Leader, as the Heart of Israel, etc. I think I stood there completely dumbfounded, and the passengers on the Orient Express stared at the odd spectacle in astonishment" (Herzl, 1960, Vol.1, p. 368).

The better conditions, under which the Bulgarian Jews lived, attracted Jews from other countries, where conditions were much worse.

"In the early 1900s a number of Russian Jews sought refuge in Bulgaria after the pogroms in their homeland, their numbers in towns such as Plovdiv, Ruse, Sofia, and Varna rising noticeably between 1900 and 1905. They were easily absorbed into the existing Jewish communities. Although these immigrants saw Bulgaria as a safe haven anti-Semitism was not unknown in Bulgaria. There was an anti-Semitic outburst in Lom in 1904 which threatened to spread to Vidin" (Crampton, 2007, p. 434).

In 1909, the construction of the new magnificent synagogue in Sofia was completed. It was large, capable of accommodating over 1,000 people. Many Jews and non-Jews attended the opening. King Ferdinand was a guest of honor.

Ferdinand didn't limit his support for the Jews to attending only official events. He was willing to help Jewish causes directly. In the 1890s, Theodor Herzl was traveling around Europe, seeking support for his proposal to restore the Jewish state. In July 1896, in Carlsbad he met for the first time Prince Ferdinand after arranging a meeting:

"[Ferdinand] was waiting behind some shrubbery. Ten steps away from him I took off my hat, and he advanced two paces toward me. There actually was no introduction. He gave me his hand, and I immediately began to present the Jewish cause...

I expounded my project for him with laconic brevity. He was quickly gripped. "It is a magnificent idea," he said; no one has ever talked to me about the Jewish Question this way. But I have often thought about what you say. Actually, I was raised by Jews. I spent my youth with Baron Hirsch. So, I know the whole background; people often reproach me for being half a Jew. Your idea has my full sympathy—but what can I do for it?"

"I should like to ask Your Royal Highness to prepare the

Czar for my plan and. if possible, to obtain an audience for me.

"That is very difficult," he said doubtfully; "it is a matter which involves religion. As it is, I don't stand in well with the orthodox. There are delicate matters in that area in which I often have to subordinate my convictions to political necessity."

...He stated repeatedly that he was a friend of the Jews and was pleased when I told him that the Sultan and the Grand Duke of Baden were, too.

...He nodded his satisfaction and promised me his full support, on condition that this be kept secret. In Russia, he said, at most. Grand Duke Wladimir might be interested in the matter. All others speak of the Jews as though they were not human. I should send him, the Prince, my book in German, Russian, and English" (Herzl, 1960, Vol.2, p.436-437).

The generally positive attitude toward Jews in Bulgaria didn't mean that there was no anti-Semitism. R. Vulcheva, in an investigation published online, explored the anti-Semitic elements in the Bulgarian press in late 19th - early 20th century. "There was a limited number of openly anti-Jewish publications and elements of such views in mainstream newspapers. Bulgaria also had specialized papers defending Jews, which showed some tension in the society" (Вълчева, 2006).

According to her, one of the reasons for low anti-Semitism was the material condition of the Jews. Just a handful of them were worth more than 1 million leva ($800,000). The rest were small merchants, poor craftsmen and workers.

One of the earliest anti-Semitic books was published in 1839 by a former rabbi who converted and became a monk under the name Neofit. In it, he supported the view that Jews used Christian blood in their rituals. One of the early anti-Semitic articles was published in Plovdiv, in the paper Maritsa in 1882. It claimed that the next goal, after the liberation from the Turks, was the expulsion of the Jews, who are going to flock into Bulgaria after leaving Romania.

The first openly anti-Jewish paper, Bulgaria for Bulgarians, appeared in September 1893. It slandered the Jewish community that they stole children. The accusation wasn't taken lightly - the same year, the editor was sentenced to four months of jail and a fine of 40 francs. However, he was allowed to continue publishing. In 1894, another paper, People's Liberty, attacked the Jews again, declaring them "robbers who send our wealth to the Rothschilds and corrupts our gullible youth with their modernity." The next year, the same publication called for founding an anti-Semitic party to protect the existence of the Bulgarian people. Its membership would be restricted only to Bulgarians, and the goal - to restrict the rights of the Jews and closing Bulgarian borders to them; Jewish businesses should be boycotted, etc.

It is not clear if such a party was ever created and the publications had a short life. A few years later, in the city of Burgas was created an Anti-Semitic Committee, but it seems that its activities were limited to writing letters demanding stopping the immigration of Jews, restrictions on buying real estate, prohibition from trade out of the cities, ban on working on commission, death penalty for those of them who kidnap Christian children, banning Jewish businesses from obtaining credits, etc.

Actual physical attacks against Jews were extremely rare, there was nothing like the pogroms in Russia and Romania. The ugliest story involving accusations against Jews unraveled in the town of Vratsa in 1898. A young child was found dead. A rumor was spread that Yohanan Avraam Benbasat and his mother Sarucha Benbasat killed the child with large needles to drain the blood and use it for their rituals. As Yohanan's son reports in his memoirs, both were respected members of the local community. A rabid crowd attacked their house. Their Bulgarian neighbor yelled to them to jump over the backyard fence and get into his house. One of the kids got badly scratched during the flight over the fence and later died. Yohanan and his mother were arrested, he spent a year and she - six months in jail respectively.

The prosecutor demanded the death penalty for both. The Jewish community hired a good lawyer, Dr. Konstantin Stoilov, future Prime Minister of Bulgaria. They were acquitted. Meanwhile, the mother of the dead child that started it all, admitted that she was paid to accuse the Jews. She was arrested but killed herself in custody before the trial (Memoirs of the son of Yohanan Avraam Benbassat).

In 1904, there was another case in the town of Lom. A young man disappeared for several days and the locals accused the Jews of ritual murder, because this happened just before Easter. Many insisted on starting an investigation among Jews, but the local police commissioner was reluctant to act. Finally, the commissioner agreed to search one of the Jewish houses after receiving a tip. Many people gathered around the house during the search, but the crowd was under control. Nothing was found.

A few days later, the body was found on the bank of the Danube, close to the town. Three doctors examined it and concluded that the man drowned, there were no signs of violence.

The mob wasn't satisfied. When the cart with the body entered the town, the mob already was trying to attack the Jewish quarter. They insisted to carry the body through the quarter and provoke a riot against the Jews. A mounted police unit blocked the street, but a few people walked around it. They were hit with batons, soon a real fight between the police and the crowd erupted. Another police unit arrived. Eventually, the procession was directed to a different street, but the crowd pelted with rocks a few Jewish houses, after which it dispersed with the promise to be back.

The funeral was held a few days later. The mayor declared martial law, and the police blocked the main passages to the Jewish quarter. The crowd insisted on entering it but was stopped. A small group managed to sneak in and break windows of Jewish businesses and houses. About ten houses were robbed before some of the perpetrators were caught.

The local press speculated that the rage wasn't accidental, the attack was planned. Some Jews were successful wheat traders, in competition with Bulgarians. Some people wanted their businesses destroyed.

Despite these disgraceful incidents, anti-Semitic actions never took root in Bulgaria. Some historians blame Russia - the "blood libel" cases there were ubiquitous, often causing horrific pogroms with hundreds of victims.

6 A COUNTRY IN TURMOIL – THE TWENTIETH CENTURY

The territorial divisions after the Berlin Congress in 1878 left large territories with Bulgarians and other nationalities in Turkish possessions. Macedonia became the center of the struggle for liberation. Revolutionaries were constantly plotting how to defeat the Turks and return the land to Bulgaria. The large Ilinden Uprising in 1903 was one of those attempts. It was suppressed with the usual Turkish brutality. In 1908, the power in the dying Ottoman Empire was taken by a group of officers, the Young Turks. They promised profound reforms, but they were just as oppressive as the old government.

Fed up with the situation, several Balkan countries - Bulgaria, Serbia, Greece and Montenegro - joined forces against Turkey. Within several months, Turkey was defeated and most of the territories populated with Bulgarians and Greeks were taken back. That was the First Balkan War, however, about a month after the peace agreement was signed, a quarrel over dividing the lands caused a new conflict. King Ferdinand's stubborn refusal to negotiate led to an attack by the Bulgarian army, which tried to push Greece and Serbia from the disputed territories. The Bulgarians were pushed back, Serbia and Greece made a secret agreement and attacked on June 17, 1913. That was the beginning of the Second Balkan War. On June 28, Romania attacked Bulgaria from the north. Later, Turkey also started a fight with Bulgaria.

Bulgaria tried to enter into an armistice with Serbia and Greece, but they refused. Tens of thousands of civilians were killed in the battles. The Greeks burned down Bulgarian towns and villages, destroying the harvest and killing women and children. Since Bulgaria was practically isolated, its foes provided all the information about the war, often distorting it. The information that reached the press was so disturbing that it prompted an investigation by a special commission in 1914, under the auspices of the Carnegie Endowment for International Peace (USA). It interviewed survivors and local authorities and published its findings in the voluminous "Report of the International Commission to Inquire into the Causes and Conduct of the Balkan Wars", published in Washington, D.C., in 1914.

On the issue of the destroyed villages, the commission stated:

> "The list of burned villages which follows will be found to be accurate, in the sense that it includes no villages which have not been burned. But it is far from complete, save as regards the Kukush and Strumnitsa regions. Many other Bulgarian villages were burned, particularly in the Serres and Drama districts. In many cases we have not been able to discover the exact number of houses in a village. It will be noted that the list includes a few Turkish villages in Bulgarian territory burned by the Greeks, and a few villages burned by the Servians [Serbs. – M.M.]. The immense majority of the villages are, however, Bulgarian villages burned by the Greek army in its northward march. The number of burned villages included in this list is 161, and the number of houses burned is approximately 14,480. We estimate that the number of houses burned by the Greeks in the second war cannot fall short of 16,000" (Report on Balkan Wars, 1914, p. 314-315).

A haunting memorial of the atrocities were the letters of Greek soldiers, found in the mail of the nineteenth regiment of the Greek seventh division, captured by the Bulgarians in the region of Razlog. The Report published the facsimiles with English translations. Here are a few samples:

> "RHODOPE, 11th July, 1913.
> "This war has been very painful. We have burnt all the villages abandoned by the Bulgarians. They burn the Greek villages and we the Bulgarian. They massacre, we massacre, and against all those of that dishonest nation, who fell into our hands, the Mannlicher rifle has done its work. Of the 1,200 prisoners we took at Nigrita, only forty-one remain in the prisons, and everywhere we have been, we have not left a single

root of this race.

"I embrace you tenderly, also your brother and your wife SPILIOTOPOULOS PHILIPPOS" (Ibid., p. 308).

"Mr. Panaghi Leventi, Doctor, Aliverion, Euboea.

"I also enclose herewith, the letter of congratulation from my commandant, Mr. Contoghiri in which he praises my squadron, which on the occasion of the short stay of a few days of our division, received the order at five o'clock, to march to the north of Serres. During the march, we engaged in a fight with the Bulgarian comitadjis [resistance fighters. – M.M.], whom we dispersed, after having killed the greater part. We burnt the two villages of Doutlii and Banitza, the homes of the formidable comitadjis, and passed everything through the fire, sparing only the women, the children, the old people, and the churches. All this was done without pity or mercy, executed with a cruel heart, and with a condemnation still more cruel.

"Merocostenitza, 12th July, 1913. The outposts of the Army.
"Love to you and also the others,
"(signature unreadable), sergeant" (Ibid., p. 308).

"Mr. Sotir Panaioannou, in the village of Vitziano, parish Ithicou Tricala de Thessalie.
"River Nesto, 12th July, 1913.
"Here at Vrondou (Brodi) I took five Bulgarians and a girl from Serres. We shut them up in a prison and kept them there. The girl was killed and the Bulgarians also suffered. We picked out their eyes while they were still alive.
"Yours affectionately:
"COSTI" (Ibid., p. 308).

"Zissis Coutoumas to Nicolas Coutoumas.
"With the present I give you some news about the war that we have made against the Bulgarians. We have beaten them and have reached the Turkish-Bulgarian frontier. They fled into Bulgaria and we massacred those who remained. Further, we have burnt the villages. Not a single Bulgarian has been left. God only knows what will come of it. I have nothing more to write you. I remain, your Son Zissis Coutoumas. Many compliments from Thimios. He is well as also the other young men here.
12th July, 1913" (Ibid., p. 309).

"M. Zaharia Kalivanis, Erfos-Milipotamos, Rethimo, Crete.
"RHODOPE, 13th July, 1913.

"(Seal of the Commandant of Public Safety, Salonica)

"We burn all the Bulgarian villages that we occupy and kill all the Bulgarians that fall into our hands. We have taken Nevrocop and were well received by the Turks, many of whom came to our ranks to fight against the Bulgarians. Our army is in touch with the Servian [Serbian. – M.M.] and Roumanian armies, who are 32 kilometers from Sofia. With regard to ourselves we are near the ancient frontier.

"S. Z. KALIYANIS" (Ibid., p. 309).

"M. Aristidi Thanassia, Kaniniati, Commune of Athanamow, Trikala, Thessaly.

"14 July, 1913.

"DEAR COUSIN:

"I have received your letter of the 1st and I am very glad that you are well, as, after all, so are we up to now. Let me tell you, Aristidi, all we are going through during this Bulgarian War. Night and day, we press on right into Bulgarian territory and at any moment we engage in a fight; but the man who gets through will be a hero for his country. My dear cousin, here we are burning villages and killing Bulgarians, women and children. Let me tell you, too, that cousin G. Kiritzis has a slight wound in his foot and that all the rest of us, friends and relations are very well including our son-in-law Yani.

"Give my greeting to your father and mother and your whole household, as well as my cousin Olga.

"That is all I have to say,

"With a hearty hug. Your brother,

"ANASTASE ATH. PATROS" (Ibid., p. 311).

"M. George P. Soumbli, Megali Anastassova, Alagonia, Calamas.

"Rhodope, 12th July, 1913.

"DEAR PARENTS:

"We got to Nevrokop, where again we were expected, for again we fought the entire day, and we chased them (the enemy) to a place where we set on them with our bayonets and took eighteen cannon and six machine guns. They managed to get away and we were not able to take prisoners. We only took a few, whom we killed, for those are our orders. Wherever there was a Bulgarian village, we set fire to it and burned it, so that this dirty race of Bulgars couldn't spring up again. Now we are at the Bulgarian frontier, and if they don't mend their manners, we shall go to Sofia.

"With an embrace,

"Your son,
"Pericli Soumblis
"7th Division, 19th Regiment, 12th Company, Salonica" (Ibid., p. 311).

"11 July, 1913.
"I have not time to write much; you will probably find these things in the papers. It is impossible to describe how the Bulgarians are being treated. Even the villagers – it is butchery – not a town or village may hope to escape being burned. I am well and so is cousin S. Kolovelonis.
"With a loving embrace,
"Your brother,
"N. BRINIA" (Ibid., p. 314).

Some of the Bulgarians found refuge thanks to help from local people, like this Bulgarian merchant, who was saved by Jews:

"Dimitri Anguelov, wine merchant of Serres, arrested on July 7, was shut up in the school, escaped with a Jewish prisoner on Friday, and was concealed by Jews of the town" (Ibid., p. 321).

Will Monroe also visited the devastated areas after the hostilities ended:

"The author found that in those parts of Macedonia through which the Greek army had marched the country was devastated. Grain-fields, vineyards, and all other sources of livelihood had been destroyed. In his travels in Bulgaria and in excursions in the Bilo and Rhodope mountains he met thousands of refugees who told him they were fleeing from the atrocities of the Greek army. Most of the refugees were women and children; they had walked through the mountains for many days, some of them for twenty-five days; most of them fled with only the clothing on their backs. He met a party of refugees in the mountains near Ichtiman. It numbered one hundred and five persons when they started from Macedonia, but in a march of twelve days, twenty-five of the children and one old man had died...
The author interviewed hundreds of these refugees. Their descriptions of atrocities committed by the Greeks were heartrending, and would have been incredible, but for the overwhelming testimony on all sides. This is the gist of the

stories they told the author: We were urged not to leave our homes, that the Greeks would do us no harm. But when we lingered until the Greek troops arrived, our villages were surrounded, the cavalry in many places being employed for the purpose, and all those who attempted to escape were indiscriminately sabred, men, women, and children. In cases where seeming- friendly emissaries sent by the Greek army persuaded the villagers to linger, no mercy was shown. The men were compelled to give up to the Greek soldiers any arms that they possessed, after which they were shot. The pillagers gave themselves up to orgies of rape, which were terminated by the murder of the Bulgarian women they had ravished. A few escaped to tell the fate of the villagers that trusted to the promised mercy of the Greek emissaries. There was general agreement in their accounts of the fiendish conduct of the Greek soldiers. The narrators came from remote parts of Macedonia. They had left their villages by different routes and had crossed by passes in the Rilo and Rhodope mountains that were miles apart. Unthinkable as were the tales they told, collusion was even more unthinkable. The report of the commission appointed by The Hague tribunal to examine the question of culpability for the atrocities committed in the second Balkan war verifies the tales told the author of this book by the hundreds of refugees that he interviewed" (Monroe, 1914, p.135).

In the end, Bulgaria lost most of the territories it gained the year before, including southern Dobrudja, which went to Romania. The New York Times reported about protests from Bulgarian Jews over the transition:

"Bulgarian Jews protest.
Oppose cession of land to Romania, an anti-Semitic country.
Paris, Thursday, February 27. – A Sofia telegram published here today states that the Central Consistory of the Jews of Bulgaria addressed a petition to the Bulgarian Premier against the cession of any territory to Romania because the latter country, contrary to the Treaty of Berlin, refuses civil rights to Jews, and these disabilities might apply to Bulgarian Jews living in the ceded territory. The premier replied that he was confident that the mediatory Powers would satisfactorily solve the difficulty" (New York Times, 1913).

It is not clear if the Powers solved their problem. Bulgaria suffered a devastating defeat, which remained in history as the First National Catastrophe. After a couple of peaceful years, in 1914, a Serbian terrorist killed the Austria-Hungary's heir Erzherzog Franz Ferdinand in Sarajevo, which started World War I. In 1915, King Ferdinand plunged his country in it on the side of Germany. The war was lost. The poor conditions of the Bulgarian army and communist agitation in 1918 caused the Soldiers' Rebellion of 1918. Several army units turned against the Government and marched to Sofia.

In a town near the capital, they declared Bulgaria a republic. A few days later, they were defeated. Bulgaria had to sign a humiliating peace treaty in Neuilly. Alexander Stamboliysky, the new Prime Minister who signed it, spent most of the war in jail for opposing it. After signing, he broke the pen in protest.

This was the Second National Catastrophe and Ferdinand didn't survive it. He was forced to abdicate. He left the country, never to come back. His son ascended to the throne under the name Boris III. The new King inherited a country in disarray, burdened by huge reparations owed to the countries of the Entante, the alliance of Great Britain, France and Russia, which defeated Germany and its allies. The economy was at a low point, affected by the war. Some of the politicians involved in the war were put on trial and jailed.

King Boris III was very different from his father. He detested the flamboyance and vanity of Ferdinand. He had the ability to communicate with common people and understood their problems. His simple way of life and empathy made him popular with his subjects. I will say more about his style of governing in the next chapter.

The new Prime Minister Stamboliyski perceived the King as weak, with insignificant political abilities; he even contemplated declaring Bulgaria a republic in the future and joked that the King, as a nice person, could become its first president. As one of the leaders of the Soldier's Uprising in 1918, he was part of the attempt to declare a republic at the time.

Stamboliyski's Agrarian Union was a peasant party. Its leaders were dissatisfied that the ordinary poor peasants were neglected and underrepresented in the Government. However, they went into the opposite extremity, declaring the city dwellers enemies of the peasantry. The peasants received preferential treatment - people with such background were routinely chosen to fill important government positions. This behavior quickly descended into corruption and election-rigging, common for many previous governments in Bulgaria. Stamboliyski's attempts to appease Yugoslavia were seen by patriots as a blow against the unification of Macedonia with Bulgaria. The monarchists detested his plans to turn the country into a republic. The right-wing parties were routinely harassed by peasant gangs (called "Orange Guard"), which were dispatched to disrupt their activities.

The dissatisfaction with the Government ended with a bloody coup. On June 9, 1923, a group, called Democratic Alliance, took power and Alexander Tsankov, professor of economics at Sofia University, became the Prime Minister. Stamboliyski was captured and a few days later killed. There was a spontaneous peasant rebellion, but it wasn't supported by the communists – they saw it as a fight between the city and the village bourgeoisie and remained neutral. Later, in September, the communists changed their position and organized the September Uprising over the whole country. It was sponsored by the Soviet Union as a "socialist revolution" and later branded the "first anti-fascist uprising in the world".

It was led by the prominent Bulgarian communists Georgi Dimitrov and Vasil Kolarov but was poorly organized and active only in north-west Bulgaria. The rebellion was suppressed quickly and resulted in severe laws against communists. They continued their activities poorly disguised as a Bulgarian Workers Party.

Although the communist movement in Bulgaria was strong, it was dominated by ethnic Bulgarians. Many Jews, despite being poor, stayed away from communism and their numbers in those organizations was very small, while in other countries, the Jewish communists were much more prominent. The Zionist movement was much stronger. That was one of the reasons that in Bulgaria communism was never seen as a "Jewish conspiracy".

At the time, Trotsky's theory of the "permanent revolution" was still accepted in Soviet Russia and Communist International (Comintern) was looking for weak spots, where it could provoke a socialist revolution. Bulgaria was seen as an important target for communist expansion. From the documents published after the Soviet archives were opened, found in the collection "The Comintern and the Idea of the World Revolution" (1998, in Russian), it becomes very clear that an uprising was planned in Bulgaria for 1924 or 1925.

Protocol No. 77 of the meeting of the Politburo of the Russian Communist Party (Bolsheviks) on March 13, 1924, reported a discussion of the situation in Bulgaria with the participation of Zinoviev, Chicherin, Litvinov and others, including the Bulgarian

Kolarov. Politburo decided:

> "It considers very likely the revolutionary exacerbation of the crisis in Bulgaria, and supports the evaluation of the possible prospects, provided by the Bulgarian Communist Party and the Comintern. Politburo thinks that the Bulgarian revolutionary movement should rely only on internal revolutionary forces: the Bulgarian workers and peasants. Specifically, the party must remember that the USSR, due to the current situation, cannot help in the near future the Bulgarian revolution with military force (or even military demonstration) ... The proposal of Comrade Unshlicht for providing larger sums of money through the Comintern is accepted" (Коминтерн, 1998, p.463).

In August 1924, the Executive Committee of the Comintern prepared a detailed instruction for the Central Committee of the Bulgarian Communist Party and its Underground Military Organization regarding the preparation of an armed uprising. It recommended sudden decisive attacks on barracks and whole regions with the purpose of full annihilation of the resistance (Коминтерн, 1998, p.498). Paragraphs 20 and 21 gave instructions on forming terrorist groups:

> "20. To execute mass terror during the uprising against government leaders in control of hostile forces (army, police, fascists, etc.), must be created deep underground terrorist groups under the direct control of high military leaders, not lower than regional level. The selection of members for the terrorist groups should be conducted very carefully.
> "21. It is necessary to plan in advance mass terror against the leaders of the hostile forces, to be executed along with the general plan for taking power. The terrorist acts at present time, in the beginning of August, should be considered premature." (Коминтерн, 1998, p.501).

In 1925, the communists, inspired by the Comintern, made another attempt for revolution with weapons and explosives financed by Moscow. It was considered the right moment to unleash the terror recommended by the Comintern. The plan was to kill a high-ranking official, possibly the King, bomb the funeral and start an insurrection to overthrow the weakened government.

In the week before Easter, King Boris III left for a hunting trip to the Balkan Mountain, north of Sofia. There were four other people in his car - driver, a military officer, an ornithology professor from the university, and a farmer who assisted the King in hunting. While going through a mountain pass, the car was stopped by an armed group. They opened fire, the professor and the hunter were killed, and the driver seriously wounded. The King and the officer fought the gang off. Then the King stopped a passing bus, took the wounded and the dead bodies and drove it to the nearby town. Then, he returned with a military unit, and chased the gang (all attackers were later killed). Upon his return to Sofia, the King was cheered by the people for his miraculous salvation.

Meanwhile, in Sofia, after the failed attack against the King, the communists were looking for another high-ranked target. The same day they shot General Konstantin Georgiev who was about to enter a church with his granddaughter for the evening service during the Holy Week. Some historians say that the attack against the King and the murder of Gen. Georgiev were not related, but it is difficult to explain such a perfect coincidence.

The funeral of the general was to be held on April 16 in the St. Kral Church (a.k.a. St. Nedelya). Nobody knew that a few days ago, members of the military wing of the communist party bribed the groundskeeper of the church who let them stuff the main dome with about 150 kg of explosives and bottles of acid to increase the damage. There were nearly 2,000 people in the church. At certain point, Metropolitan Stefan, who presided over the funeral service, decided to move the coffin closer to the altar to accommodate the large crowd, so the officials were not under the dome. Moments later, the dome exploded and collapsed on the church floor.

It was an apocalyptic picture. It seemed that everybody was dead, until the survivors started to crawl out of the rubble. Several cabinet ministers were wounded but none was killed. The number of victims was huge, there are no exact records, but it varies from under 200 to 260 (according to the memoirs of Queen Ioanna, the wife of King Boris). Among the dead was the wife of Colonel Avram Tadjer, a prominent army commander, and many other Jews. Over 500 people were wounded and maimed. The King was on his way to the church, but since he had to attend the funerals of his friends killed in the mountain, he was late and that saved him. This communist disgrace still remains one of the worst terrorist acts in the European history.

Prof. Tsankov unleashed counter-terror against the communists and their party was practically destroyed. Soon, disagreements within the Democratic Alliance led to the fall of the government. That was followed by a period of political instability, with many political parties bickering and fighting over power. It made Bulgarians even more cynical about their politicians.

On May 19, 1934, the instability ended with another coup. A group of masonic officers, members of the political group Zveno (Link), led by the Colonels Kimon Georgiev and Damyan Velchev, took power. They dissolved the parliament and abolished the political parties. They improved the relations with Yugoslavia and established diplomatic relations with the Soviet Union (though they still persecuted local communists). They attempted many reforms to improve the economy, but their republican leaning didn't find support. The group remained isolated, with little political influence and within a few months their government resigned.

The King used the situation to consolidate the power in his hands. He didn't restore the political parties. When he called elections a few years later, the candidates were supposed to present only their constituents, without declared party affiliations. In the communist historiography, years later, the colonels' rule became known as "military-fascist" dictatorship, while the King's consolidation was "monarcho-fascist" dictatorship, although it is a big stretch to talk about fascism in Bulgaria.

The event that probably forced the King to act was the ascend of Adolf Hitler. After becoming a Chancellor in 1933, the latter made his desire to revise the unfair post-World War I borders and his hatred for Jews known to the world. The King was aware that Europe was marching toward a new war and stability was essential for Bulgaria to survive. His intention was to keep the country neutral, but that was extremely difficult.

Bulgaria was approached by other Balkan countries to join a pro-British alliance. The Soviet Union tried to pull the country into its orbit through propaganda from the underground communist party. Those efforts took a strange form when the USSR signed a pact with Germany in 1939:

> "The Nazi-Soviet Pact may have bewildered many Party members, but ironically it put the BKP itself in a strong position. After years of persecution, the Party discovered that its new stance toward Germany coincided with official government policy. And in one important respect the Party line was even more favorable to Germany than the government position: the government refrained from caustic attacks on the Western Powers in an attempt to maintain correct if not

friendly relations, but the BKP was under no such restraints. It did advocate the signing of a mutual assistance pact with the USSR, but as the government's reluctance to do so was supposedly based only on technicalities, there was no open conflict on this issue.

The Communists were therefore allowed a measure of relative freedom at a time when right-wing activity was being officially restricted because of events in Romania. On September 22, 1939, the Romanian Prime Minister, Armand Calinescu, was assassinated by members of the Iron Guard (a mystical and violent Romanian nationalist organization), and it was feared that fascist groups in Bulgaria might attempt some similar action. As a result, the activities of the local right-wing groups, especially the Ratnitsi [Ratniks] and Legionnaires, were curtailed and their members warned that they risked dismissal from government positions, universities, and the armed forces. Emboldened by its new prominence, the Communist Party launched a vocal attack on the Western Allies and their Bulgarian supporters. Members of the democratic opposition were accused of advocating Bulgaria's entry into the war on the Allied side instead of supporting the official policy of neutrality" (Miller, 1975, p. 17).

Another factor impeding the neutrality was the important role of Germany in the Bulgarian economy. Bulgaria was heavily dependent on it for its exports.

"Like every other Balkan country, Bulgaria traded extensively with Germany; but Bulgaria depended on German trade more than any other country in southeastern Europe. Almost 70 percent of Bulgaria's exports in 1939 went to Germany, compared with 6 percent to Italy, 3 percent to England, and 1 percent to France. By comparison, Hungary and Yugoslavia sent only about 50 percent of their exports to Germany, and Greece and Rumania sent considerably less. At that time Germany may have been more interested in the trade than in its political consequences, but the two became increasingly intertwined" (Miller, 1975, p. 7).

In 1940, Italy attacked Greece and invited Bulgaria to join the war, but the King refused. Other countries tried also to get Bulgaria's attention. In the same year, the Soviet Union demanded through Germany the return of Bessarabia, occupied by Romania since 1918. That was used by Bulgarian diplomats to demand the return of Dobrudja, which was an undisputed Bulgarian territory, taken by Romania after the Balkan Wars. Both Germany and the Soviet Union supported the demand for their own reasons. "On August 21, 1940, agreement between Rumania and Bulgaria was reached at Craiova. According to the treaty signed on September 7, Bulgaria received all of the Southern Dobruja, including the towns of Silistra and Balchik; the 110,000 Rumanians in this area were exchanged for 65,000 Bulgarians from the Northern Dobruja. Bulgarians greeted the treaty with jubilation" (Miller, 1975, p. 29-30). All residents, including Jews, received Bulgarian citizenship. I will provide more details about the return of Dobrudja in another chapter.

Meanwhile, the German pressure was getting stronger. Hitler wanted access to the southern Balkans and Bulgaria and Yugoslavia stood on his way with their attempts to maintain neutrality. Bulgaria was slowly caving in by appointing a pro-German Prime Minister, Prof. Bogdan Filov, and accepting anti-Jewish laws but didn't want to become a full member of the Axis. In her memoirs, Queen Ioanna writes about those times:

> "On January 1, 1941, Prime-Minister Filov traveled to Germany with the German ambassador in Sofia. However, on January 3, the King confirmed to the ex-Prime Minister Toshev his decision to keep the neutrality. On January 5, the American radio stations reported that Hitler demanded from Bulgaria "free passage" of an army of about 500,000, already at the border, but kept there by Prime Minister Filov. Then Hitler called Boris personally: "My divisions, he said, are stranded at the Danube but must pass through Bulgaria. They are headed toward Greece. You are aware of the urgency and importance of that military move that must resolve quickly the strategic difficulties in the southern Balkans. I want my troops to enter Bulgaria as our ally and not as a country to be conquered. I expect your response in two hours." The King replied: "The decision that the Fuehrer expects cannot be made in Bulgaria by the King alone, it must be presented by the government and voted in the parliament" (Царица Йоанна, Спомени, p. 112).

Hitler didn't follow through with his 2-hour ultimatum, but he didn't change his intentions. Eventually, Bulgaria capitulated, and Prof. Filov traveled to Vienna to sign the Axis pact. The Germans didn't even wait for the official ceremony - they entered Bulgaria a few hours before the signing. Yugoslavia held the resistance a few extra weeks but on March 25, 1941, the Prince Regent signed the pact. Upon his return, he was deposed in a coup and the new government reversed the decision. It took Hitler only a week to invade and dismember Yugoslavia. The Bulgarian government was asked to occupy Macedonia and southern Thrace. Although the move wasn't planned, and the occupation was considered temporary by the Germans, the status of the lands had to be decided after the war, the government propaganda presented that as unification of Bulgaria. More details about these events will be provided further in this book.

7 KING BORIS III, HITLER AND THE JEWS

I dedicate a separate chapter to King Boris III because his behavior before and during World War II continues to be highly contested. He is often praised as a savior of the Bulgarian Jews and at the same time condemned as a fascist anti-Semite. A definite answer can't be provided without consideration for the complex situation of Bulgaria at the time. Also, I covered the events in the first forty years of the 20th century, as you will see, they had a profound impact on the King's way of thinking.

It is important to note that the task of understanding the King as a person and ruler is made difficult by the lack of personal records. He seemed to be an extremely cautious person who avoided leaving written traces of his actions, maybe because in the brutal political reality in Bulgaria anything personal could be used against him. The King did not leave memoirs. After his death no will was found in the palace or anywhere else. The few letters he left behind were signed with pseudonyms and in most of them he referred to himself in third person. All the information we have about King Boris comes from the records of people who worked or lived with him. And again, because of their personalities, which saw things differently, his image and behavior also seem elusive and vary according the views of those people. This unique situation is the reason why it is so hard to define the King.

As a soldier in the Bulgarian army in the Balkan Wars and World War I, he saw clearly all the mistakes his father made. Ferdinand's grand ambitions obscured his ability to think rationally. He was ready to plunge the country in wars that were difficult, if not impossible, to win. After the initial success in the

First Balkan War, Ferdinand contemplated taking over Istanbul. He underestimated the human suffering that his ambitions caused, the dead, the loss of money to reparations and destroyed factories. And all that eventually cost him his throne and even threatened the dynasty.

King Boris detested the shiny uniforms and other royal regalia. When he was crowned, he wore a simple military coat. After King Ferdinand abdicated, he left Bulgaria with his children Prince Kiril and Princess Evdokia (Princess Nadezhda was already married in Germany). The new King remained alone in the palace and those lonely days and nights probably helped him to reflect on what happened in the wars and how he was going to act in the future.

He lacked Ferdinand's condescending attitude when communicating with people he considered below him, which made his father such a hated person. Boris was willing to listen and mingle with ordinary people. Even after the attempt on his life in 1925, he didn't surround himself with bodyguards. I never heard about any further attacks, except, possibly, from the politicians and the military who sometimes plotted his demise.

King Ferdinand preferred to keep the heir to the throne at his side, so Prince Boris was educated in the Royal Palace by visiting teachers and professors. That education created in him a lifelong interest in natural science. In a letter to the author of this book of February 28, 2018, the son of King Boris, King Simeon II, recalled, "I unfortunately have little knowledge of what King Boris liked to read and which were his prime interests. For sure, he was a keen naturalist and entomologist and an accomplished botanist."

In his book about the King, Pashanko Dimitroff covers in detail his work in natural sciences and activities for preserving the wild life in Bulgaria:

> "Nature, its beauty and secrets, its vastness and mystery had a dominant and healing effect on Boris's own nature. It was not just love, curiosity and admiration, it was veneration which imposed its guides upon his attitude and behaviour. His friends were scientists, his companions were botanists, ornithologists and their assistants. Every trip to the country became a kind of pilgrimage and a safari, and he never returned to his palace without specimens of plants, butterflies or insects. His favourite reading was books and magazines on geography and the natural sciences. His interest in nature, encouraged, and sometimes forced on him, from early childhood by his father, became a passion that left many memorials on the country. Ferdinand

was the driving force behind the Zoological Gardens in Sofia and a superb Museum of Natural History. Boris followed him by founding the Botanic Gardens with its enormous variety of alpine flora, an Entomological Institute, the Marine Institute in Varna on the Black Sea and numerous Nature Reserves, where he introduced grouse, pheasant, deer, fallow deer, mouflon and many other varieties. As a conservationist Boris became very unpopular by introducing licences and seasons for hunting, chase and fowling. Killing bear, even carnivorous bear, required a special permit. Poaching was punished with severe penalties" (Dimitroff, 1985, p. 127).

King Boris's habit to keep a low profile and consider carefully all circumstances before making a decision, was often mistaken for weakness in the brutal Bulgarian politics. His desire was to avoid all pitfalls that Bulgaria ran into during his father's reign. That's why he refused to give up on the country's neutrality for such a long time.

Boris was content to forfeit the pomp and the glory of the royal power and let politicians handle the government affairs. People who knew him attest that sometimes he was prone to pessimism and depression and even considered abdication, but it seems the sense of duty took over every time.

Those who accuse him of anti-Semitism, can't point out at a single proof for it. The King had always had good relations with the Jews. He supported their causes, attended events and was grateful for their support. One of the earliest documents of his reign, from 1919, his second year, is a telegram to the Bulgarian Zionists:

"September 9, 1919 - to the Chairman of the Bulgarian Zionists

"It was a real pleasure to receive the greetings you sent on the occasion of the Ninth Conference of the Bulgarian Zionists. Accept my heartfelt gratitude and best feelings for the Bulgarian Zionists who have always been good citizens of our fatherland.

The King" (Telegram Boris III)

He had good relations with the Central Consistory of the Bulgarian Jews. Some rich Jews in the otherwise modest community did important charity work that benefited the country. In 1937, the Jewish banker Angelo Kuyumdjiski established a foundation to support the education of poor students, starting with 7 million leva of his money (Нотариален акт, 1937). His initiative was highly appreciated by the government and the Education Minister send him a letter of gratitude (Благодарствено писмо, 1937).

The Jews supported educational organizations, like the "Jewish People's University", as the documents of its registration show (Досие за пререгистриране, 1930). Thanks to their respect for knowledge, the literacy rate among the Bulgarian Jews was much higher as a percentage than in the other ethnic groups. There were also numerous charities ran by Jews, like the Ashkenazi Charity Society "Support", which was also supported by the Government (Досие за пререгистриране, 1938).

Considering the ethnogenesis of the Bulgarian nation, it was absurd to speak about racial superiority in Bulgaria and most people were aware of that fact. Even King Boris, who didn't have a single drop of Bulgarian blood in him, was seen as more Bulgarian than many others because of his deeds. Despite various attempts to start it, there was never a successful fascist movement in Bulgaria. Bulgarians, even today, treat politicians with suspicion and skepticism (and for the most part they are right). Emerging of somebody charismatic like Hitler or Mussolini that people would follow blindly, is practically impossible in Bulgaria. Even the attempts to introduce a communist "cult of personality" in the times of Stalin, of the Bulgarian communist leader Vulko Chervenkov looked comical.

Though it hindered the unity of the nation, this situation prevented people from falling into an abyss, following the steps of a crazed fanatic. In that regard, there are similarities between Bulgarians and Jews, since the latter seem to be equally skeptical when dealing with politicians.

One of the earliest books on the Holocaust, published in 1943 by the New York Institute of Jewish Affairs, "Hitler's Ten-Year War on the Jews", clearly stated the low level of anti-Semitism in Bulgaria:

> "Anti-Semitism was very weak until collaboration with Hitler. Of the small and unsuccessful anti-Semitic groups, the fascist army league, Rodna Zaschita [Zashtita. – M.M.], was the most conspicuous. This organization, active between 1925 and 1930, was finally suppressed by the government, only to be reinstated five years later under foreign pressure, together with other fascist and anti-Semitic groups. In 1934, when a synagogue and the home of a Jewish resident were bombed, the government ordered the arrest of 140 anti-Jewish agitators.
>
> "In July 1939, members of the outlawed anti-Semitic

organization Ratnitsi perpetrated anti-Jewish excesses in the town of Pazardjik. In September adherents of the same organization were arrested in Sofia for plundering and destroying Jewish shops. The Bulgarian government issued an official statement reaffirming its determination to suppress anti-Jewish disorders and to put an end to the subversive activities of the Ratnitsi and the National Legionnaires. Persons supporting these outlawed organizations were to be interned in concentration camps. On February 4, 1940, the government declared that it recognized no distinction between Jews and other law-abiding Bulgarian citizens and strongly condemned the anti-Jewish excesses.

"But the Bulgarian government, subjected to strong German pressure, was forced to take back with its left hand what its right hand had given. Refugees from Germany, Austria and Czechoslovakia were again placed on the rack, and Jews from Italy and Greece, many of whom had lived in Bulgaria for decades, were given a foretaste of Nazi method. After 1937, when through manipulated trade pacts the Reich achieved economic domination over Bulgaria, Nazi political influence grew rapidly. Throughout most of 1939 the Kiosseivanoff Cabinet was cautiously but consistently pro-German. Influenced by Nazi promises of assistance in the pressing of Bulgarian territorial claims against Rumania and Greece, as well as German threats of military and economic reprisals if Bulgaria failed to "cooperate", Bulgaria was between the devil and the deep blue sea" (Hitler's Ten-Year War, 1943, p. 113-114).

The comparison of Bulgaria being "between the devil and the deep blue sea" is spot on.

The ability of King Boris to use his charm and diplomatic abilities to get the best deals for his country, were severely tried by the towering figure of Adolf Hitler. Hitler was unlike anything that befell on Europe before (or at least in modern times). Confident, paranoid and fanatical, he knew how to get things his own way. He was not afraid to bulldoze countries and people to achieve what he wanted.

In her memoirs, Queen Ioanna shares the King's impression of Hitler:

"My husband gained a rich experience in his interactions with Hitler. In those times, I mean shortly before World War II, Boris had seen him and thought he was a real mystery. He told me once: "Hitler's way of speaking is abundant, powerful, and very convincing, though it looks like he is reading a lecture. No objection or remark can stop that overwhelming flow of eloquence. Any discussion becomes impossible, he doesn't allow anyone to add even a word and he wouldn't hear it anyway." I asked him, if he thought that Hitler had original ideas, his own philosophy. Boris said: "He definitely has projects, ambitions, that he talks about, as he described them in "Mein Kampf" - it's a brutal bluntness that he will realize by all means possible. There is some strange amalgam in that man, defined by realism and mysticism, clear reason and dark instincts, will and religious fanaticism. These tendencies could drive him far ahead. All in all, he is a man possessed by the devil, in the etymological sense of the word"'" (Царица Йоанна, Спомени, p. 103).

Boris knew that direct confrontation with such a difficult and contradictory person like Hitler could have fatal consequences for him and his country. Heroic confrontation looks good in movies and fiction books, but when it brings disastrous consequences, it doesn't seem like an attractive option. Boris was painfully aware of all the opportunities in front of him and none of them was heroic or even winning. Italy, due to its size and importance, could openly disagree with Germany on some issues without fatal consequences.

If he confronted Hitler openly, the tanks would have run over his small country and all Jews and other "undesirable" elements would have been deported. By avoiding that, the King could save many communists, who after the war expressed their "gratitude" by executing his brother and expelling the Queen and her children from Bulgaria.

He could have submitted to Hitler and followed his directives with exactly the same result.

Instead, he chose to pretend to agree with everything, while sabotaging the German efforts behind the scene. He joined the war but didn't send troops against the allies. He allowed the expulsion of Bulgarian Jews to provincial towns but didn't deport them to the German camps. It definitely isn't heroic behavior, and some may call it cowardly, but it is easy to judge from the safe distance of several decades. At the time, avoiding conflicts and delaying decisions saved hundreds of thousands of lives, though Boris was confident that Hitler would lose after attacking the Soviet Union, he didn't know how much time he had.

Somehow, that tactic worked with Hitler – he suspected that

Boris was hiding something and called him "fox" but at the same time, found his many excuses reasonable. Maybe it was because Hitler despised the Slavs probably as much as the Jews but tried to find something positive in the Bulgarians. In the collection of recorded dinner conversations, "Hitler's Table Talk, 1941-1944", Hitler pontificates:

> "The Russians never invent anything. All they have, they've got from others. Everything comes to them from abroad—the engineers, the machine-tools. Give them the most highly perfected bombing-sights. They're capable of copying them, but not of inventing them. With them, working-technique is simplified to the uttermost. Their rudimentary labour-force compels them to split up the work into a series of gestures that are easy to perform and, of course, require no effort of thought" (Hitler's Table Talk, 2000, p. 182).

Bulgarians get off easier:

> "It is not possible to generalise on the extent to which the Slav races are susceptible to the Germanic imprint. In point of fact, Tsarist Russia, within the framework of her pan-Slav policy, propagated the qualification Slav and imposed it on a large diversity of people, who had no connection with the Slavonic race. For example, to label the Bulgarians as Slavs is pure nonsense; originally, they were Turkomans. The same applies to the Czechs. It is enough for a Czech to grow a moustache for anyone to see, from the way the thing droops, that his origin is Mongolian" (Hitler's Table Talk, 2000, p. 473).

Of course, the most vitriolic of Hitler's points were reserved for the Jews: "One must act radically. When one pulls out a tooth, one does it with a single tug, and the pain quickly goes away. The Jew must clear out of Europe. Otherwise no understanding will be possible between Europeans. It's the Jew who prevents everything. When I think about it, I realise that I'm extraordinarily humane. At the time of the rule of the Popes, the Jews were mistreated in Rome. Until 1830, eight Jews mounted on donkeys were led once a year through the streets of Rome. For my part, I restrict myself to telling them they must go away. If they break their pipes on the journey, I can't do anything about it. But if they refuse to go voluntarily, I see no other solution but extermination. Why should I look at a Jew through other eyes than if he were a Russian prisoner-of-war?" (Hitler's Table Talk, 2000, p. 235). King Boris was right about Hitler's nature in his talk with the Queen, it boiled down to "brutal bluntness that he will realize by all means possible". It was difficult, if not impossible, to promote such views in Bulgaria.

Of the Bulgarian royal family, Hitler liked the exiled King Ferdinand who, at the time, lived in Germany: "If one can reproach the Tsar Ferdinand with having been more rapacious than a Jew in money-matters, one must nevertheless acknowledge that he was admirable as regards his audacity and decisive spirit. If we'd had him on the Imperial throne of Germany instead of William II, we'd certainly not have waited until 1914 before unleashing the first World War. We'd have acted as long ago as 1905. Just as the cunning fox succeeded, after the collapse in 1918, in preserving the throne for his son, in the same way I think he'd have found some way for Germany to save herself from the disaster" (Hitler's Table Talk, 2000, p. 390).

Hitler was aware that the Bulgarians were not trustworthy and did not support his "new world order". He noted it in his talk:

> "In Bulgaria, on the other hand, everything is uncertain. Thus, I was struck to learn that after the conclusion of the Tripartite Pact the President of the Bulgarian Council was scarcely acclaimed by the population of Sofia, despite the major importance of this pact to Bulgaria. And I was not less struck to know that at the same time the population of Sofia was enthusiastically welcoming a Russian football team. The fact is that Bulgaria is strongly affected by Panslavism, both on the political and on the sentimental level. She's attracted by Russia, even if Sovietised. I recognise that the King of Bulgaria is a very intelligent, even cunning, man, but he doesn't seem to be capable of guaranteeing the stability of his régime. He himself confessed that he couldn't change a single Minister or relieve a general of his command without endangering his crown. He has to act very cautiously, he says, beginning with granting sick-leaves and then retaining these men's attachment with the help of numerous favours" (Hitler's Table Talk, 2000, p. 379).

The words that I highlighted show that Boris's tactics worked - we know that he was in control of the affairs in his kingdom most of the time but managed to create in Hitler the idea of uncertainty, which allowed him to maneuver and postpone important decisions and avoid Hitler's rage.

He managed to do the same with Joseph Goebbels who initially didn't like the King. In his Diary's entry for January 25, 1942, Dr. Goebbels states:

> "Several reports indicate that anti-German sentiment in certain Bulgarian Government circles is slightly on the increase. Especially Czar Boris is said to be playing a somewhat double-faced game. He is a sly, crafty fellow, who, obviously impressed by the severity of the defensive battles on the Eastern Front, is looking for some back door by which he might eventually escape. This is a very shortsighted policy which will, of course, immediately be reversed, once our offensive has started again..." (Goebbels, 1948, p. 47).

Not a very flattering description, to say the least. But only two months later, Dr. Goebbels met the King again during his visit in Germany and wrote the following on March 28, 1942:

> "King Boris expressed the wish of talking with me at leisure. I visited him at Bellevue Castle where he is residing for a few days. Our talk, which was really to take up only twenty minutes, stretched out for more than two hours. The King is extraordinarily charming and has returned from the Fuehrer full of new ideas, suggestions and initiatives. The Fuehrer has this time given him a complete briefing on all matters that concern him. Boris is an impassioned devotee of Hitler's genius as a leader; he really looks upon him as a sort of emissary of God. He shows the greatest understanding for my work. He follows what I do with such alert interest that I am simply surprised at what he knows and what he asks about. My articles in the Reich are part of his required reading. Yes, he told me he even uses the arguments advanced in these articles in all his diplomatic negotiations. He is full of admiration for the sensitiveness of our psychological approach in leading the German people which, he claims, differs most strikingly from that of World War I. He is a real people's King. He describes to me how he travels incognito through Bulgarian villages to learn about the sentiment of the people. Undoubtedly sentiment was pro-Russian even a short time ago, but under the impact of the presence of German troops it has veered over noticeably to our side. The King has observed marked friendliness to Germany even in such sections of the country as were hitherto known for their pro-Russian sympathies. He is very happy that the Fuehrer does not expect more of him than that he be a

stabilizing factor in the Balkans" (Goebbels, 1948, p. 151).

It is hard to believe that the propaganda doctor described the same person. The "sly, crafty fellow" who looked for ways to escape from the war, suddenly turned into "an impassioned devotee of Hitler's genius as a leader". All it took, was a praise of the chief propagandist's articles. Boris was an educated and cultured man, fluent in German and other languages and well-read. It was very unlikely that his bedtime reading and source of tips for his diplomatic negotiations were the mediocre articles of Josef Goebbels, which, in their tactics, differed little from Stalin's propaganda.

It is impossible to tell what the King really thought during the two-hour conversation, but he either entertained himself or hated the fact that he had to impress somebody like Goebbels. But that was the price he had to pay to keep his country intact and he succeeded. Again, there is no glamor and heroism here, but nothing else would have worked.

The ability of the Bulgarian King to communicate with other leaders and officials was noticed by another high-level employee in the German Ministry of Foreign Affairs. The Deputy Director of its commerce policy department, Dr. Carl Clodius, had contacts with the King during World War II over the status of the lands occupied by Bulgaria. In 1944, Clodius was arrested by the Russians and spent years in the USSR. During an interrogation about his role in Bulgaria, he characterized the King in the following way:

> "However, foreign policy was his true calling. His father was German, his mother – French, his wife – Italian. Besides, he was closely related to the British royal court, for which he, as all members of the house of Coburg, had high hopes. All that made him a real cosmopolitan. He spoke five or six languages, felt at home in almost all countries of Europe, and in his numerous travels, he could use his extensive connections for the interests of his country. This ensured his strong influence on the Bulgarian foreign policy even when his position in the country has not yet been firm enough. From 1936, he conducted in person many political negotiations with representatives of foreign countries. Following his cautious nature, he tried to derive all benefits for the future of Bulgaria, and while he did not give up any Bulgarian revisionists demands, he did not manifest them in the international arena and strived, as long as possible, not to associate Bulgaria with anything" (Тайны

дипломатии Третьего рейха, p. 239).

One of the best summaries of the achievements of King Boris III belongs to Christo Boyadjieff, Bulgarian diplomat who worked for the King and spent years in exile after the communist invasion. In his book on saving the Bulgarian Jews, he wrote:

> "As a ruler, Boris was inclined to sacrifice a little in order to save as much as possible. He consented to send occupation troops to Thrace and Macedonia to insure order and provide administration but refused to send his soldiers to the Eastern Front. He imposed on the country his personal rule because, in those troubles times, he feared that a pro-German Government might escape his control and open the door unconditionally to the Nazis. He never hesitated to compromise when necessary. When in September of 1940 the destiny of Dobrudja was under discussion between Bulgaria and Rumania at Craiova, the majority of his Government and National Assembly were against the Rumanian request to keep Northern Dobrudja. This unreconciliatory stand menaced the signing of the Treaty. King Boris intervened personally and convinced the Bulgarian politicians to accept the Rumanian demand. In doing so he consolidated the return of South Dobrudja, with the consent of Great Britain and the Soviet Union...
> Any pro-German coup d'état would have led, as F. Chary maintains, to the deportation of the entire Jewish community. To avoid these disastrous alternatives, the King kept the reins of Government in his hands. To be successful in such a policy he needed an obedient Prime Minister, a compliant Council of Ministers, and a rubber-stamp National Assembly. Supplied with such tools he could pursue his policies, probably the best for the country at that historical moment. The principal characteristics of his policy were; temporization as long as possible, and, when all resources were exhausted, give as little as possible... By using his closest collaborators' attachment to Germany for his far-sighted policy. King Boris proved that, under the mask of a hesitant and weak character, he hid a fine mind that knew how to take full advantage of the extremely limited arms and means at his disposal. Only under the umbrella of the alliance between Bulgaria and Germany could the King had acted as he did" (Boyadjieff, 1989, p. 145-147).

A prime example of the diplomatic skills of King Boris III was the campaign to get back southern Dobrudja from Romania.

Unlike Macedonia, this fertile land has always been Bulgarian but was lost as a consequence of the unfair treaty that ended the Second Balkan War in 1913. Its area was 7,565 km², with a population of about 300,000. Various ethnicities inhabited it, about 134,000 (47%) were Bulgarians, 106,000 (37%) Bulgarian Turks, the Gypsies and the Tatars were about 12,000 each, and the Romanian population was only about 6,000. There were also a few hundred Jews living there.

Its re-unification with Bulgaria was a national dream but it became possible only in 1940 in the context of the struggle for influence over the Balkans of several powers, which the King skillfully utilized. That process was documented in the German diplomatic correspondence at that time (Нойков, 1995, p. 12-17).

In May 1940, the deputy chief of the Commerce Policy Department of the German Foreign Ministry Carl Clodius was sent on a mission to Bulgaria. He met the King and a few Bulgarian politicians. In his report to the Minister Joachim von Ribbentrop, Clodius observed that all important political decisions were made by the King and eventually everything depended on his opinion. The King told him that the Bulgarian national interests could be served best, if the country was on the side of Germany, and the return of Dobrudja was important in fulfilling Bulgaria's aspirations.

On June 27, 1940, Stalin's Government issued an ultimatum to Romania and 24 hours later annexed with force Bessarabia and Northern Bukovina. King Boris III saw this as a suitable occasion to attempt to solve the Dobrudja question and raised the issue at a meeting with the German Ambassador, asking for Germany's help. He said that resolving that issue would not only correct the injustice of the 1913 treaty, but it also would improve the relations between Bulgaria and Romania. The King emphasized that, if nothing was done on the issue, it could be expected that in the coming days the public in Bulgaria, aided by the communists, may start a vicious campaign against him and the Government. He needed that solution to avoid a possible coup d'état that would put the country under Soviet control.

In a telegram to his ministry, the ambassador agreed with the position of the King, which was also shared by the Ambassador of Italy, and noted that providing that help to Bulgaria would strengthen the German positions in the region. Ribbentrop gave a vague response, promising a favorable solution to the Bulgarian territorial demands after the end of the war.

In the end of June 1940, the Bulgarian Ambassador in Berlin, advised by the King, warned the German Foreign Ministry that if Germany continues to distance itself from the Dobrudja question, and does not at least recognize the Bulgarian demands as legitimate, there is a serious danger that under the pressure of the public opinion Bulgaria may receive the territory as a "gift from the hands of the Soviet Union and not from Germany".

The lack of response did not discourage the King. In July, he sent to Berlin Prof. Alexander Stanishev, Chairman of the Bulgarian-German Association in Bulgaria, who graduated in Germany and had good connections. However, the officials he met did not give a straight answer. Another emissary, Marko Riaskov, former Finance Minister, went to Germany later the same month, but again, he was not successful.

Meanwhile, the Soviet Government declared officially that it recognized the Bulgarian territorial demands to Romania as legitimate. It also stated that it would provide the necessary assistance to fulfill them. The possibility of Bulgaria falling under Soviet influence forced Germany to change drastically its position. On July 27, Hitler met in Germany with a Bulgarian Government delegation, led by Prof. Bogdan Filov, the Prime Minister. He unequivocally confirmed that he supported the return of southern Dobrudja to Bulgaria. On July 30, the Foreign Ministry instructed the German Ambassador to Romania to inform the Romanian Government that "the Fuehrer considered the return of southern Dobrudja in its 1913 borders, including the towns of Silistra and Balchik, a very appropriate and just solution, to which Romanians should agree without further delay".

On August 4, King Boris received in the palace the German Ambassador and had a long conversation with him. He expressed his sincere gratitude to Adolf Hitler for his position on the Dobrudja question, that was the first ray of light after the prolonged difficult times. Further in the talk, the King expressed his concerns that the Romanians may not be willing to resolve the issue and give back the town of Silistra. He used again the rivalry between Germany and the Soviet Union, saying that he could not tell the Bulgarian people to give up Silistra when the growing communist propaganda in the country suggested that Bulgaria could get back the whole Dobrudja with the help of Russia.

He used the same points in his meeting with the German Ambassador to Turkey, von Pappen, who stopped briefly in Sofia on his way to Ankara. The King added that even the British Ambassador informed him that his Government agreed that Dobrudja should be returned. That position was confirmed later by Sir Winston Churchill as well.

This situation put additional pressure on Germany and forced it to act, if it did not want to lose its influence and prestige in Bulgaria. Germany brought Romania to the bargaining table and after long negotiations, a treaty was signed between Bulgaria and Romania on September 7, 1940, according to which the whole territory of southern Dobrudja was returned to Bulgaria. All attempts of the Romanians to keep the two important towns were firmly rejected by the King. Another provision of the treaty was the population exchange. By 1940, many Romanians had been moved to southern Dobrudja, while thousands of Bulgarians and Turks were expelled to the northern part of Romania, often in a brutal way, involving violence, murder and starvation, which had been documented by local activists with testimonies and photographs, see for example "The Roumanian Atrocities over the Bulgarian Population in Dobroudja Abducted into Moldova" (Patchoff, 1919). The treaty ensured that the expelled Bulgarians and Turks would return, and the Romanians move out of Dobrudja.

The return was an enormous diplomatic success for Bulgaria and the King, a crown achievement after decades of frustration and attempts to get back the occupied land. However, according to reports, the Germans were unhappy that the King did not give them credit in his manifesto for their role in resolving the issue, which was in contrast with the reactions of many other people who praised Hitler.

The Bulgarian citizenship of the people from all ethnicities living in Dobrudja was restored. The treaty was never disputed, even after World War II, and Bulgaria kept its sovereignty. It is important to remember that when we cover later the events in the occupied Macedonia and Thrace. Those lands, despite the official propaganda, never became part of Bulgaria, they were always considered under temporary Bulgarian rule and their fate was to be determined after the war.

Shortly after that, a new force tried to get involved in the competition for influence over Bulgaria, the USA. On January 21, 1941, Colonel Donovan, representative of the US Government, arrived in Sofia and met the King. From the records of what the King shared with other people, it became clear that the Colonel had little knowledge of the Balkan history and current situation. He demanded that Bulgaria remain neutral and, if necessary, it had to oppose Germany on the battle field, in return it could count on the generosity of the USA and England. The King sarcastically remarked that England's generosity had been well known for the last 20 years. Donovan then stated that now Bulgaria could be destroyed if it took the wrong position. The demands seemed cynical and brutal, considering the fact that neither England or the USA were capable of helping any country in Europe, especially Poland and Greece, which were devastated despite the protection guarantees. On top of that, another report noted that Donovan lost a bag with important documents in Sofia and couldn't remember where, he was visiting a night club the night before (Нойков, 1995, p. 26-27).

The King's habit of doing things his own way, a way that tries to reduce the possible damage to his country, led to more negative scrutiny from the Germans. This became obvious after the pressure to deport the Bulgarian Jews increased. This will be covered in detail later, but here it is important to not how King Boris's actions were seen by the German informants.

The surprising reluctance of the Bulgarian politicians to embrace the "final solution" of the Jewish Question was aggravated by the King's resistance to the deportations. He argued with the high leadership of the Third Reich over these issues and tried to help Jews.

On July 21, 1942, Joachim von Ribbentrop was surprised by the report of the German Ambassador to Bulgaria Adolf Beckerle that the King was in contact with Jews, despite the Government campaign against them. The incident involved telegrams exchanged between the King and the Chairman of the Central Consistory of the Bulgarian Jews Yosif Gheron regarding the birthday of Crown Prince Simeon. The King wrote: "I sincerely thank you and the Bulgarian Jews for the greetings and the kind wishes that you sent for the birthday of the Crown Prince. The King". Although Beckerle wasn't happy about this, the Foreign Ministry advised him not to deal with the case anymore (Нойков, 1995, p. 45).

Another interesting document scrutinizing King's actions, was a secret report from Standartenfuehrer of SS Walter Schellenberg, a high official in the German state security services, sent on November 9, 1942, to the Foreign Ministry. Schellenberg expressed concern about the unsatisfactory development of the Jewish Question in Bulgaria and especially the role of the King. The measures against the Jews were met with disapproval by people and there were even attempts from the Royal Palace to help Jews. Prof. Filov told him that some of the reasons were that the godfather of Princes Maria Louisa (King's daughter) was Alexander Malinov, married to a Jewish woman, while one of the granddaughters of Prince Simeon's godfather General Danail Nikolaev was married to a Jew.

Further, Schellenberg noted that Peter Gabrovski, the Minister of Interior, told many times Alexander Belev, the Commissar for the Jewish Questions, that the Royal Palace wanted certain softening of the measures against the Jews. What was even worse, in addition to advocacy for Jews from many members of the parliament from the Government majority, the King himself through various people from his circle in some cases asked the Commissariat to help Jews. For example, King's secretary Balan inquired at the Commissariat about a sick Jew who lived near one of the palaces, the words Balan used were: "The King orders..." Schellenberg disliked the Jewish attitudes in Bulgaria – the Jews wore their yellow stars with arrogance and the Bulgarian people supported them. Some of them put next to the stars pins with the images of the royal family. All that caused Jews, who before that accepted their fate, to disobey the laws (Пойков, 1995, p. 46-47).

The next year, in April 1943, during a visit to Germany, the King met Ribbentrop and discussed the Jewish Question. Although he had to agree to the deportation of the Jews from the occupied territories, he could allow the deportation of only a small number of Jewish communist elements from old Bulgaria, the rest of the 25,000 Jews from Sofia were to be sent to provincial towns within Bulgaria, because they were needed to do some public works. Ribbentrop expressed his disapproval and stated that the Jewish Question required a radical solution. The details of these events are covered further in this book.

It is important to note that the King did not deport even those communist Jews that he promised to the Germans.

The German reports clearly showed that people were unhappy with the anti-Jewish policies. It was not just the ordinary people, but also prominent politicians and intellectuals. We will examine their positions as they were reflected in a fascinating document published in 1937, which will be covered in the next chapter.

The activities of King Boris III regarding the topic of this book are part of the events covered further. However, his story will be incomplete without the details of one of the mysteries of the 1940s – the untimely death of the King at the age of 49 in August 1943. The speculations about what exactly happened abound even today due to the secrecy that surrounded his life.

In mid-August, the King was invited by Hitler to visit him in his headquarters. He sent an airplane piloted by his trusted pilot Lt.-Col. Bauer. The scheduled day for the flight was August 13, which was also Friday. The superstitious King did not want to fly on that day and rescheduled the flight for Saturday. After his meeting, he returned to Bulgaria on Sunday on the same plane. As it always has been the case, the King and Hitler met in private, face to face. Boris, who was fluent in German, did not need an interpreter, and since no notes were taken at the meeting, it is hard to determine the content of the conversation. Since this was their last meeting, followed by a chain of events that ended with the King's death, there are plenty of speculations about the issues that Hitler and Boris discussed. We have to rely on isolated phrases and comments made by the King after he came back.

According to Frederick Chary:

> "Hitler apparently did not ask the Bulgarian monarch to send troops into Russia. Boris told Filov that the journey was not satisfactory, but that they had discussed only an expanded role for Bulgaria in the Balkans. The Germans still believed that an Allied invasion there was forthcoming. With Italy in confusion and the Germans in retreat in the East, Hitler asked Bulgaria to supply two divisions to fight in northern Greece and eventually in Albania—essentially backing up German troops. Boris promised only one. He now had little confidence in the German ability to stop the Russians or in that of the Western powers to stop the spread of communism into the Balkans after the war. The journey had made him very weary and downcast" (Chary, 1972, p. 158).

Michael Bar-Zohar described the situation in a similar way:

> "When he returned to Sofia, the King told Filov that the Germans had asked him for two infantry divisions, to be positioned in northern Greece and eventually Albania. The King had cautiously replied that he was ready to place a division in readiness in Macedonia, but for that he needed the arms promised by Germany. He was assured the arms would arrive soon. "They were confident concerning the Russian front," the King told Filov. "However, they did not indicate in what manner they planned to deal with the situation." That was how the King described his meeting with the Führer to his prime minister, Bogdan Filov, whom he knew to be a fervent supporter of Germany. Yet, he blurted a single sentence that expressed a deep concern: "Today, during our flight back, I wished that enemy planes had shot our plane down, so it all would be over"" (Bar-Zohar, 2013, Ch.19).

The request to add another division of the Bulgarian Army to the occupational corps in Macedonia was not something unusual or a game-changing event in the war. If that were the only issue discussed, it is strange that the King was so depressed that he wished his own death on the way back. Maybe Hitler raised other issues as well, which Boris could not discuss openly in Bulgaria. As we will see later, Prof. Filov was part of a large intelligence network that the Germans maintained in Bulgaria, which followed every step of the monarch.

As the person who spent most of her life near him, Queen Ioanna may have some hunches or knowledge about the situation, which preceded the August events. In her memoirs she wrote: "When Hitler sent an invitation to Boris, Bulgaria was already looking for contacts with the Allies. The British did not even want to hear about it. They were saying that Bulgaria had always deceived them... Only two people accompanied the King, General Nikola Mihov, Minister of War, and an aide-de-camp. The talk's topics were prepared and announced in Sofia – "Analysis of the general military and political situation" and "Discussion about the role of Bulgaria in the war". Boris and the two men flew to Germany and after they landed in Sofia, he was greeted by Prime Minister Filov. "Boris told him hastily, "I did not retreat on any issue, did not give them a single soldier." His face was paler than usual, and he looked tired. To ensure the flight security, the plane had to move to different heights and oxygen masks had to be used" (Царица Йоанна, Спомени, p. 119). Then, the Queen notes that the King returned on Tuesday, August 17.

Shortly after that, the Queen left Sofia with her children to spend a few days in the palace of Tsarska Bistritsa. The King stayed in Sofia. She also wrote that he was distraught by the tense situation in Germany. Sevov, the King's adviser and unofficial chief of his personal intelligence, informed him about the current opinions of the political circles in Bulgaria and specifically of Prof. Filov.

> "Filov was determined to ask the King for an intervention against Russia. At 7 p.m. Princes Evdokia called him. After a short talk, the King returned to his desk and his secretary Grouev handed him some papers, but a few minutes later, the King said, "It's enough for today, we will continue tomorrow. I don't know what is wrong with me. I have never felt so bad." After a pause, he added, "Of course, the meeting was very tiring." It was clear he meant his meeting with Hitler.
>
> "Later, he retreated to his private apartment. In the

bedroom, he suffered vomiting cramps. He went to the bathroom and fainted. When his valet did not see him coming out, he alarmed the staff. The King was already unconscious. Dr. Daskalov and other doctors were called, they found symptoms of left coronary artery thrombosis. The same night, they called Berlin to request the help of a known specialist in internal diseases, Dr. Seitz" (Царица Йоанна, Спомени, p. 121).

Additional sources confirm that the request was received by Hermann Goering, who looked for Dr. Seitz. It turned out that the same day, his clinic was bombed. The doctor survived but had to be pulled out of the rubble and rushed to the airport to fly to Bulgaria on a special airplane. Two other German doctors assisted Seitz, but the condition of the King did not improve, he remained unconscious. The staff did not want to bother the Queen and the children, so she did not know anything.

Finally, she was notified:

> "To a degree, I was comforted by the thought that Prince Kiril was with the King. But the next day, they called me from Sofia to say that he was very sick, but it was not necessary to go back. Finally, on Wednesday night, the staff told me, after a full day of worries, that the Palace doctor, Daskalov, and the Palace Inspector Ghenchev, arrived with an urgent message. I had a sad premonition. Both told me that Boris was very sick, and they worried. To avoid an unnecessary disturbance, they did not tell me anything for two days. But now, they had to let me know, because nobody knew what was wrong with the King" (Царица Йоанна, Спомени, p. 122).

The Queen was rushed to Sofia. Addressing the later speculations about who caused the King's death, she expressed doubt about the German fault, because of the help that came from Germany:

> "Here I must say, in connection with the later hypotheses about the death of my husband, that the German authorities were quick to provide to the two doctors a speedy military airplane, whose flight had a priority. All flights in the corridors of the planes, on which Seitz and Eppinger flew from Berlin and Vienna, were cancelled... On Thursday, August 26, and Friday, August 27, the doctors gathered again to write their bulletins. Only later, I found out that one of them refused to sign the

diagnosis" (Царица Йоанна, Спомени, p. 123).

After Boris's death, there were speculations about his health, many tried to blame some undiagnosed diseases for his untimely demise. The Queen firmly rejected such theories. She recalled that for the thirty years she knew him, he had only one episode of sciatica, result from a cold he caught during a hunting trip in Rila Mountain. Despite the emotional distress in mid-August, he still looked physically healthy after the meeting with Hitler.

The Queen was convinced that the King did not die of natural death:

"His death was caused by a criminal action. I should note the utmost secrecy of the medical council, to which, for obvious reasons, I was not allowed. It was said, and I confirm it here, that the doctors promised to keep their conclusions secret. The commission was composed of at least ten doctors, Bulgarian and foreign, among whom was Kirkovich, who knew the King since the Balkan Wars. On Thursday in the afternoon, Boris opened his eyes. I was holding his hand. He said, "Why are you here?" I lied, "I arrived for a Red Cross ceremony." He did not reply. That was all. He passed away on Saturday [August 28], the day of the feast of the Assumption.

"Two days later, my sister Mafalda arrived. Nobody could have guessed, even me, who was overwhelmed by the mechanism of a misfortune that looked unbearable, the fate that awaited her a few days later; her arrest by the Nazis, her detention in camp Buchenwald, and her martyrdom" (Царица Йоанна, Спомени, p. 124).

As it will become clear below, Hitler accused Princess Mafalda that she poisoned the King, but she arrived in Sofia two days after his death.

The day King Boris died, Radio London announced the hypothesis that he was poisoned, most likely by Hitler. The Queen also recalled another testimony about the possibility of poisoning. The family of the former Prime Minister Prof. Alexander Tsankov escaped to Vienna days before Bulgaria was occupied by the Soviet Union. In Vienna, Prof. Tsankov's wife consulted Dr. Eppinger in late 1944. Later, she shared with another Bulgarian émigré, Hristo Statev, that Eppinger told her that the King was poisoned. Statev wanted to get more details about the claim, but Mrs. Tsankova did not know anything else. Statev prepared a questionnaire and asked her to visit again the doctor to answer the questions. Dr. Eppinger refused to answer and told her to forget what he said before. A year later, the doctor committed suicide (Царица Йоанна, Спомени, p. 126).

In the archive of King Ferdinand, who lived in exile in Coburg, Germany, there was a copy of the medical expertise of the death of King Boris III with a handwritten note of Princess Evdokia (published in Bulgarian in the book "From the Secret Archive of King Ferdinand"). King Boris's sister supported the version of murder committed by the German authorities:

> "The most important is left out of this document. It is a proof of the limitless meanness and lies of the doctors. King Boris died of embolism, but they did not say what caused that embolism.
>
> "King Boris died after he was at Hitler's headquarters on August 15-16, 1943, and after two days of stormy quarrels with Hitler and his generals he refused to declare war on Russia or to send "volunteers" to the Russian front. The King himself, upon his return from the meeting with Hitler on August 16, told Strashimir Dobrovich, former chief of his cabinet, "I refused again, this time for good. It was a terrible fight, I won, but I will pay for it!"
>
> "On his way back on the airplane, at 6,000 m height, they gave him an oxygen mask, with which they poisoned him, burning his aorta.
>
> "This is the truth.
>
> "Evdokia" (Бележка от Княгиня Евдокия).

The hypothesis of poisoning was confirmed by the powerful German Ambassador to Bulgaria Adolf Heinz Beckerle. The next day after the King's death, August 29, 1943, Beckerle sent a telegram to his boss, the Foreign Minister Joachim von Ribbentrop. He requested that the three German doctors, who treated the King, visit him at the embassy before their departure. They complained that the whole time they were kept in the palace like "prisoners" to avoid leaks, so they could not contact Beckerle earlier. The palace staff did not let them go even after the King died:

> "Other than that, they received the diagnosis. The Bulgarian doctors were very restrained. Dr. Seitz said that he talked with the King, while he was still conscious, and he knew that his situation was difficult and thought that he would die because it was clear to him that he had angina pectoris. The King thought it was caused by his hike to the Rila peak Musala the week

before.

"I asked them, because of the understandable suspicion, if they thought it possible that an external action (poisoning) was the cause for the disease and the death. The three doctors immediately and unanimously confirmed it on the basis of the King's body losing strength. Eppinger said it was a typical "Balkan death." Could this be confirmed as the cause of death? It could be considered probable. "However, it could not be claimed with certainty without an autopsy. They recommended an autopsy, at least of the brain, and even almost requested it. Initially, it was refused, but after the embalming, the staff decided to allow it. However, at that point, an autopsy did not make sense, so the doctors gave up. My personal impression is that, despite the limited scientific information in this case, the doctors are convinced that it was a violent death. Then, they said that due to the professional secret, I will be the only person to know their opinions, and after they go back, they will provide only limited information about the King's disease to the German circles.

"I supported their intentions and told them that they should keep the secret as a government obligation, which goes even beyond their professional confidentiality. If a need arises, by an order from the highest place, they will be heard once again. Then, they asked that in such a case, they wanted to be heard not one by one, but together. In the end, the gentlemen stated that they did not require any payment.

"I will be following all rumors and will report the most important of them. I think that for now this issue should be kept strictly secret and unless asked again, we should not interview the doctors again. At this point, we should try to direct, which I think possible, the future Bulgarian foreign policy to follow our direction and make sure that the regents are on friendly terms with Germany and are fully engaged with our views about the war.

"Beckerle" (Леверсон, 1993, p. 80-82).

Hitler also thought that the King was poisoned, and it was a conspiracy concocted by the Italian royal court. He suspected them mostly because of the participation of the Italian King in the overthrowing of Mussolini. Joseph Goebbels writes about that, while commenting on the appointment of the regency council of the underage King Simeon II, Boris's son. It is in the entry for September 11, 1943 (the entries from July 30 to September 8 are missing from all editions of the diary). Here is what he writes:

"A new Regency Council has been constituted in Sofia, composed of Prince Kyrill, Premier Filoff [Filov], and War Minister Michoff [Mihov]. This Regency Council is positively on our side; we can go places with it. The Fuehrer intends to transmit to Prince Kyrill the findings of the German doctors on the poisoning of Czar Boris, which he believes was in all likelihood inspired by the Italian Court. For it is very suspicious that Princess Mafalda, the worst wench [groesste Raabenaas] in the entire Italian royal house, was on a visit in Sofia for weeks before King Boris's death. It will be remembered that she is a sister of the Bulgarian Queen" (Goebbels, 1948, p. 442). Goebbels is wrong or deliberately deceptive – Princess Mafalda arrived in Sofia two days after the death of the King.

Goebbels continues with the deeper conspiracy that Hitler saw behind the events: "The King can no longer be spared in our propaganda. The Fuehrer once more expressed his conviction that Princess Mafalda was the trickiest bitch [geriebenste Aas] in the Italian royal house. He thought her capable of having expedited her brother-in-law Boris to the hereafter. It was also possible that the plutocratic clique administered poison to Mussolini, for Mussolini's illness, too, was somewhat mysterious. No words need be wasted about the treacherous Italian generals, he said. They had so besmirched Italy's military honor that it could not be washed clean for a long time to come. The plot hatched against us in Rome was backed by the monarchy, aristocracy, society, higher officers, Free Masons, Jews, industrialists, and clerics. The Duce became the victim of this plot. We have no intention of going his way. We are going to prevail, come what may. The Fuehrer invoked final measures to preclude similar developments with us once and for all. He ordered all German princes discharged from the German Wehrmacht. I proposed to the Fuehrer that all the estates of the former ruling families be seized as quickly as possible. Real estate is the foundation of economic independence, and economic independence always furnishes a basis for political influence. The Fuehrer was quite in accord with this point of view" (Goebbels, 1948, p. 445).

Princess Mafalda, the daughter of King Victor Emmanuel and sister of Queen Ioanna, was married to a German aristocrat, Prince Philip of Hesse. She became the first target of Hitler's crusade against the "treacherous aristocracy". Since she lived in the occupied by the Germans part of Italy, she was arrested and sent to the concentration camp Buchenwald in Germany. She died there on April 19, 1945.

The opinion of Michael Bar-Zohar about the reasons for the possible murder of the King is based on his "unauthorized" contacts with the enemies of the Reich:

> "If King Boris was indeed assassinated, it certainly was not as a punishment for his August 15 refusal to send the Bulgarian army to fight the Russians. The only logical reason might have been the fear in Germany that he intended to pull out of the war and sign a separate peace with the Allies. Persistent rumors about secret peace talks between Bulgaria and the Allies were circulating in RSHA circles in Berlin. At the beginning of August 1943, the king's adviser, Iordan Sevov, went on a mysterious trip to Ankara. The Germans believed that he had established contact there with Allied diplomats" (Bar-Zohar, 2013, Ch.19).

Frederick Chary is willing to consider foul play, but eventually tends to agree with the idea of death from natural causes:

> "Whether the rumors were true or not, they could have motivated an assassination by the RSHA [Reich Main Security Office] without Hitler's knowledge. Nevertheless, without more definite evidence it is difficult to give full credence to the assassination hypotheses. The consensus of historians currently writing in Bulgaria is that Boris died of natural causes. One thing is clear: the Nazis would not have murdered Boris for his refusal either to send troops into the Soviet Union or to deport the Jews to Poland" (Chary, 1972, p. 161).

Another version, though less explored, is the Russian link. The long-term interest of Russia and later of the Soviet Union in the control of the two straits (Bosporus and Dardanelles) had resulted in frequent interference in Bulgaria's affairs. The death of the King could destabilize the country politically, so the Russians could have been involved. Besides, the Soviet security forces routinely used chemical substances to eliminate their enemies. Although the Soviet Embassy in Sofia was never closed, a possible Soviet takeover was unlikely, because the Bulgarian communist movement was weak, and the Germans had a considerable military presence in the area.

The mystery of King Boris's death remains unsolved until today. Things are getting even more complicated. He was buried in the largest Bulgarian monastery in the Rila Mountain, the Rila

Monastery. After the communist coup, his body was removed and re-buried in the park of Palace Vrana. Later, it disappeared from there and it is not clear what happened. Some claim that the King's remain were thrown away in a nearby river, others say that the body was flown to Moscow at the order of Stalin (he did the same with Hitler's remains), there are other versions as well.

It is unlikely that anyone will tear the shroud of secrecy that covers the case. The witnesses, sworn to secrecy, are already dead, the archives have not yielded any relevant information, although a large part of the Bulgarian Government archives is still hidden in Russia, stolen shortly after the occupation of Bulgaria in 1944. Maybe the solution of our case is hidden there as well.

> Over a year after the death of King Boris III, Beckerle, who was arrested and held by the Russians in Moscow, revealed that the Nazi Germany attempted to appoint as Prime Minister someone who will follow the German policies more consistently. According to the interrogation protocol of March 23, 1945, he said: "After the death of King Boris, I was ordered by Hitler and Ribbentrop to try to appoint as Prime Minister the leader of the National-Liberal Party [Alexander] Tsankov and form a government able to follow even more decisively pro-German policies. We knew Tsankov from the events in 1923, when he, as a Prime Minister, dealt decisively with the Agrarian Party of Stamboliyski (who was killed) and cruelly suppressed the democratic movement. Besides, the military situation of Germany was getting worse by the day after the defeats on the Eastern Front, so we had to put in power an energetic person with dictatorial traits, able to keep by force Bulgaria's collaboration with Germany. Tsankov could be that person" (Тайны дипломатии Третьего рейха, p. 50).

Fortunately, that did not work. The moderate career politician Dobri Bozhilov formed the next government, which was the beginning of substantial changes in the Bulgarian politics.

8 PERCEPTIONS OF THE JEWS IN BULGARIA (THE SURVEY OF B. PITI)

It was already mentioned that the anti-Semitism in Bulgaria never had deep roots. It always remained a marginal view, which didn't permeate the culture of the country. When, under German pressure, the Government introduced the discriminatory legislation against the Jews, no prominent intellectuals supported it (if we don't count the Prime Minister Prof. Bogdan Filov who was a well-known historian and archeologist), on the contrary, the flood of objections and protests showed the deep revulsion to the unfair law.

In contrast, other countries in the area had a long tradition of anti-Semitism. In Russia, this view affected leading intellectuals, writers and philosophers and even influenced common people's attitudes, leading to centuries of ugly pogroms that culminated in collaboration with the Germans during the Holocaust. The situation in Romania was similar. The discrimination against Jews, present there since the country became independent, spilled into the intellectual discourse. Prominent philosophers like Emil Cioran and Mircea Eliade were nationalists, but also anti-Semites (Volovici, 1991). The nationalist movements with anti-Semitic undertone were very popular among different groups of society, from the high intellectuals and politicians to the fascist extremists of Codreanu's Iron Guard.

Bulgaria had similar fascist organizations, especially the Ratniks and the National Legions, but they never reached the influence and popularity that the Romanian Iron Guard had.

There is a fascinating document that provides a glimpse into the Bulgarian perceptions of the Jews. In 1937, the Jewish journalist Buko Piti made a survey about anti-Semitism among over 60 prominent Bulgarians – former Prime Ministers (including the notorious Prof. Alexander Tsankov), cabinet ministers, community leaders, writers, scientists, artists, military officers, etc. He published the results in his book "The Bulgarian Public on Racism and Anti-Semitism". All participants opposed anti-Semitism in strong terms, emphasizing that it did not have deep roots in Bulgaria and the ideas of racial superiority were foreign to the Bulgarians (Пити, 1937). 3,000 copies of the books were printed.

As it was customary at the time, the political books had to be reviewed by the political police for incriminating ideas. The dossier of the book has been preserved in the Bulgarian archives. Interestingly, the agent who reviewed it did not find anything objectionable in it, even though most opinions where opposed to the Nazi racial doctrine. Here is the report:

"Ministry of the Interior and the Public Health
"Directory of the Police, Section Political Police
"July 15, 1937
"To the Director of Section "B"

"REPORT
"Mr. Director, I am bringing to your attention the following:
"I reviewed the book that was given to me: THE BULGARIAN PUBLIC ON RACISM AND ANTI-SEMITISM, edited by B. Piti.

"The book was published by an Editorial Committee for Education and Action against Racism and Anti-Semitism. It was printed in June 1937 on printer's press and contains 203 pages. The book was a result of a survey among prominent representatives of the Bulgarian society, science, literature and arts. It contains the opinions of 23 public figures and 39 scientists, writers, journalists, actors, artists, and others about, 1) racism as theory and practice; 2) anti-Semitism, and 3) the Jewry at large and specifically about the Jews in Bulgaria. Some of the opinions, especially of those already deceased, have been taken from newspapers and magazines from the near past.

"The editor B. Piti provides in the introduction to the book a historical review of the emergence and development of anti-Semitism.

"The interviewed representatives of the Bulgarian society, science, etc., without an exception, declare the theory of racism senseless and outdated, condemn anti-Semitism in all of its forms, and provide flattering opinions about the Jews in Bulgaria.

"The book has been reviewed and approved by Section Press Control.

"I did not find in the foreword, the introduction and the text of the book any information or quotes that could be a reason for incrimination.

"Foreign press agent Number К3516" (Досие на книга против антисемитизма, 1937).

The foreword by the editors explains the reasons for the survey, related to the new order in Germany:

"The racial theory emerged immediately after the National Socialism came to power in Germany. More specifically, the racist ideology found its interpreters among the National Socialists in Germany. When it was applied in practice, the racial theory brought a lot of bitterness not only in the lives of the Jews. The consequences of the racist policies are known to every cultured person and it is not our task to discuss them… For reasons of civil and humanist nature, we distributed a survey in our country with three questions, which specify the nature of racism as a theory and practice:

What do you think of racism as a theory and practice?

How do you explain anti-Semitism?

What is your opinion of the Jews and specifically of the Bulgarian Jews?

To form a clear idea about the attitude of the Bulgarian social and cultural thought toward the questions, we approached prominent public figures, writers, actors, artists and others, and their responses are printed in this book in alphabetical order" (Пити, 1937, p. 3-4).

This is followed by an introduction by Buko Piti who provides a detailed history of anti-Semitism from antiquity to modern days. He writes about how the anti-Jewish sentiments in Europe are being manifested in the 1930s and about their absence in countries where there are few Jews, like China and Japan.

The opinions of the surveyed people are included in separate chapters; there are 62 of them. The condemnation of anti-Semitism as a form of racism and bigotry is unanimous, although the authors sometimes use different arguments. Interestingly, criticism comes from artists who blame some Jews, especially the rich ones, for their lack of interest in supporting the Bulgarian Jewish culture. The excerpts from typical opinions included below can give you an idea about the perception of the Jews and criticism of Hitler and the National Socialism, despite of their growing power. The names of the politicians included here are followed by their years in power (added by me) before the publication of the book.

Alexander Malinov, former Prime Minister (in 1908-1911 and 1918), noted that "the Bulgarian Jews are satisfied with us and we are satisfied with them, because they are good and loyal compatriots. This is a real situation and it shows why in our country we have never had and will not have a serious anti-Jewish movement. The efforts of specific persons or small political groups to create it will not succeed. Our nation abhors anti-Semitism. In the places, where it exists, the reasons are not the racial specifics of the Jewry. I think that they are not even economic, but most of all political. However, for our political goals, we will continue to strengthen our best feelings and attitude toward the national minorities and specifically the Jews" (Пити, 1937, p. 21).

Prof. Alexander Tsankov, former Prime Minister (1923-1926), was described by the communist historians as the quintessential Bulgarian fascist, due to his long struggle to contain communist influence in Bulgaria. Yet it was never mentioned that he was a staunch supporter of the Bulgarian Jews in the times of persecution after 1941. In B. Piti's book, he also expressed those views, he thought that any prejudice against Jews contradicts the Christian principles (Пити, 1937, p. 23).

Andrey Liapchev, former Prime Minister (1926-1931), also thought that "the attempts to create an anti-Semitic atmosphere in Bulgaria are based on evil intentions. Without any doubt, they are perpetrated by extortionists and robbers. It is not necessary to give them more attention. Maybe some ignorant people and simpletons will follow them, but they will understand and feel soon enough how evil those attempts are" (Пити, 1937, p. 24).

The banker Atanas Burov, former cabinet Minister (Minister of Commerce 1919-1920, Minister of Foreign Affairs 1926-1931), stated that "from the point of view of our national interests, there is no bigger absurd than the promotion of anti-Semitism in Bulgaria. We have so many compatriots still living under foreign yoke [in Romania and Yugoslavia – M.M.] that we cannot and should not enter the role of haters of other wronged and oppressed peoples and races. On the contrary, with our tolerance and respect of those races, we can win their support for the cause that we defend. From that point of view, the help from the Jews has always benefited Bulgaria" (Пити, 1937, p. 26).

Vergil Dimov, former cabinet Minister (1932-1934), goes into details about the role of the Jews in Bulgaria:

> "Racism explains anti-Semitism. There are two reasons for it: first, because the larger part of the Jewry has always supported progressive ideas and has been on the forefront of democracy, and second, in their fight against the Jews, the ruling classes have always tried to divert public attention from their political failures, pointing at the Jews as their cause. Jews are an old and distinguished people. Mankind and civilization owe a lot to that persistent, hard-working and civilized people that has provided many bright minds and exceptional geniuses, who have contributed substantially to the culture and progress. The Bulgarian Jews have always been and still are good citizens, who, in times of tribulations and national tensions, have fulfilled with dignity the duty to their homeland. As people with strong feeling for social participation, the Jews take part in the life of the country as public figures, culture creators, and businessmen... That is why among our people there are no anti-Semitic trends. Anti-Semitism is absent from the freedom-loving and democratic spirit and life of the Bulgarian people, known for their religious tolerance and humanism" (Пити, 1937, p. 31).

Grigor Vasilev, former cabinet Minister (1930-1931) wrote, "as a Bulgarian, who values most the national culture and the immortal Bulgarian ideals, I state that the all-encompassing collaboration and the close friendship between Bulgarian and Jews is a principle that I urge the younger Jewish and Bulgarian generations to follow. Bulgarians and Jews will follow shoulder to shoulder that path, despite all suffering, they should see themselves as loyal friends in happiness and misery. Only people who lack morals and honor can create and believe the miserable slander against the world Jewry" (Пити, 1937, p. 35).

Dimitrana Ivanova, leader of the Bulgarian Women's Union, praised the Jewish women: "We congratulate the Jewish women for their newest initiative to organize all Jewish women's associations into a united Jewish women's union. We expect that it will help Jewish women to take even bigger part in the social and political life of our country, to show even more interest in the struggle for equal participation of the female Bulgarian citizens in that life and make easier the fulfilling of the goals of the Bulgarian

Women's Union, which should be goals of every woman in hour country" (Пити, 1937, p. 37).

Dimitur Ghichev, former cabinet Minister (Minister of Agriculture 1931-1932, Minister of Commerce 1932-1934) emphasized the contradiction between anti-Semitism and patriotism:

> "It is a sign of intellectual and moral emptiness when a people tries to find its prosperity and greatness in rejection and persecution of others. We do not deny patriotism, it is a sacred feeling, but the rational patriot loves and protects what is his own, while he respects and tolerates the others. Chauvinism and xenophobia don't equal patriotism. Anti-Semitism is a special form of xenophobia. In some places, it is caused by religious fanaticism and ignorance, elsewhere, it is based on economics. When political regimes and ruling groups wanted to divert the minds of the masses from the real reasons for their miserable conditions, they used the helpless Jews, turning them into a lightening rod for the anger accumulated in people's souls. In countries with a democratic spirit and order, anti-Semitism is unknown. Democracy creates tolerance and solidarity" (Пити, 1937, p. 41).

Dimo Kazasov, former Minister (1923-1924) in the cabinet of Prof. Alexander Tsankov, eventually joined the first pro-communist government after the coup in 1944. Later, he was declared one of the Righteous Among the Nations from Bulgaria. An important point that he makes here is that the tolerance of the Bulgarians is a consequence of the horrible ordeals they have often gone through in their history:

> "Looking at our tragic history, we can clearly see that both in the theory and practice of racism and anti-Semitism are reflected the factors and the facts, which created the humiliation and suffering during our national slavery. Treating those factors with respect or even indifference means to respect the chains that we have already broken. We know what slavery, oppression and injustice mean and that knowledge does not allow us to wish to anybody the suffering caused by those shameful social conditions. And if we, the Bulgarians, have had, have and will have a deep respect for the fate of a homeless nation like the Jews, it is because we, as a people, have carried the burden of such a fate. This respect is also respect for the suffering of our national soul" (Пити, 1937, p. 45).

Dr. K. Stanishev, was a former Chairman of the Macedonian National Committee. This was one of the several organizations working on the liberation of Macedonia. As I mentioned in a previous chapter, the borders imposed by the Berlin Congress in 1878 left large territories with Bulgarian population out of the country. That resulted in decades of bloody struggle for liberation, in which some Jews also took part. Well known is the case of Rafael Kamhi, an important activist of the Macedonian Bulgarian organization and participant in the uprisings. He was arrested in early 1943 and together with the other Jews in Salonica, was to be deported to Poland by the Germans. With the enormous efforts of politicians, Macedonian activists and even the King, despite the German hostility and reluctance to let him go, he was released and given asylum in Sofia (Довеждането на Рафаел Камхи).

In his entry, Dr. Stanishev writes about that contribution of the Jews:

> "The poverty among Jews is the same as the poverty of other of our citizens. It is enough to peek into the houses on Tri Ushi and Positano Streets and elsewhere in Sofia where Jews live, to understand that the majority of them struggles with abject poverty. And as we remember that these countrymen of ours just like us defended the national cause in the wars, I can't understand the efforts of some intellectuals, though they are very few, to blackmail the Jews in the Bulgarian mind. Because, if we follow this new way of thinking, how could we, the Bulgarians, justify our desire that other peoples treat us like their own citizens, we can't ask for it, if the origin, faith, and customs of people who have lived here for centuries irritate us. During Sultan Hamid's regime in Turkey, we, the Macedonian Bulgarians, were supported in our struggle for freedom only by the Jews, because the other Christian peoples living there were against us. Later, on the international arena, our cause was again defended fiercely by many honorable Jews, prominent Bulgarian citizens and soldiers. So, we have no reasons to violate the harmony among our citizens and to divide them according to "racial background"" (Пити, 1937, p. 52).

The contribution of Kosta Todorov, former ambassador, analyzes in detail the history and contradictions in the racial theories and how they influenced the worldview of Adolf Hitler. It is the longest chapter in the book. He writes: "The new racial theory, which today is the main ideology of the Third Reich, is based on several pseudo-scientific historical studies of non-German origin. The Frenchman Count Gobino, a person driven more by political passion than by history and science, published in 1852 the book "An Essay on the Inequality of Races", where he claimed that the blue-eyed, blond and tall Aryans are the supreme race that creates culture." Further, he notes that some people in Germany accepted this view, while the best minds of the German science rejected completely those pseudo-scientific fantasies.

Another source of that theory, according to Todorov, is the incorrectly understood Darwinism: "Racism also uses the theory of Darwin of the struggle for survival, without the understanding that Darwin sees this struggle as struggle of the species against the other species, so in his theory "the species" is the whole mankind. Within this "species" exists mutual support, while the struggle for survival confronts biological and other forces that are foreign to the "species". Alfred Rosenberg [the philosopher of the Third Reich – M.M.] tried to prove the moral, intellectual and other superiority of the German race with historical examples. He thought that the fall of the Roman Empire was due to the "bastardized", mixed blood, and didn't understand that this was an argument against him, because the major contributor to the mixing of the Roman blood had been the German tribes, so the fall of the Roman Empire should be attributed to their inferior blood."

There are also newer examples: "It is a fact that Poland starts to disintegrate when it is ruled by a Saxon dynasty. And the Prussian type, which according to Hitler is able to create states, has been created by the mix between Germans and Polabian Slavs. There is no doubt that the racial theory has no justification. It is a political slogan, introduced to justify the future German invasion of other people."

Then the author turns to anti-Semitism, which flourishes in times of social crisis. Even during the crises in ancient Rome, Jews have been accused of ritual slaughter, and the same is valid in Russia, where calls for pogroms masked the incompetence of the government in solving people's problems.

> "I think that anti-Semitism is an evil, not only because it is immoral, but also because it covers up the important questions about state and social order and leads people to animal violence against a helpless minority."
>
> "The Jews are neither "superior" nor "inferior" race. The Jews are like all other people, with the same needs, the same positive and negative traits that are possessed by all civilized people... They play and will play a very positive role in the inevitable future fraternity of all peoples in the world... In

Bulgaria, where anti-Semitism is foreign to the masses and is followed by a prejudiced minority, Jews live peacefully. The vast majority of them are creators. If we see among them speculators, crooks and usurers, they are not worse than Bulgarians involved in the same activities" (Пити, 1937, p. 53-56).

Mihail Madjarov, former cabinet Minister (Minister of the Public Works 1894-1899, Foreign Minister 1919-1920) wrote:

"The Jews are intelligent, industrious, and frugal, all very important qualities. They have provided many talented people in all sectors of the intellectual, social and economic life of mankind. Nobody can question the contributions of the Jews as scientists, philosophers and writers. In our country, the Jewry is a minority loyal to the duties and the laws. In the difficult times that Bulgaria suffered, the Jews showed their patriotism. They took part and fought valiantly in the war, and suffered just like us, the Bulgarians, from the harsh life in the country after the Great War. I don't see conditions for anti-Semitism in Bulgaria. I passionately support the Jews. Since a young age, I have had Jewish friends. Good Christians cannot dislike Jews" (Пити, 1937, p. 59-60).

Nikola Mushanov, former Prime Minister (1931-1934), also raises a voice against anti-Semitism:

"The Jews earn their living mostly in commerce and industry and less in agriculture. They are skillful and nimble in their trades and many are relatively richer than other people. This situation causes jealousy in some. While this is a part of Jewry that is well-off, the masses of the Jews live in abject poverty. On some occasions, I have observed the bad conditions, in which the poor Jews live, and there are many of them in Russe, Sofia, and abroad. The nature of the Bulgarian people is democratic and not xenophobic. There have been cases of attacks against Jews by some anti-Semites. However, those are isolated cases, which could be explained with the fact that similar Bulgarians also hate and persecute other Bulgarians" (Пити, 1937, p. 62-63).

Dr. Nikola Sakarov, former Member of the Parliament, and politician with leftist views, also condemned anti-Semitism:

"It is not serious to think that the 18,000,000 Jews scattered all over the Earth could be the reason for the economic, financial or political misfortune of certain circles or countries. One fifth of the Jewry lives today in Poland and about 6,000,000 of them are in America. Palestine, as the national home of the Jews for the last twenty years, still has accepted less than half a million Jews. And yet, in the last two years, we have witnessed cruel assaults against the Jews there. It was not because, as some say, the Jews lowered the culture level there. On the contrary, the economic and general culture in Palestine rose in only 20 years to a level that was the envy of all peoples of near Asia and that was mostly in the agriculture, a sector, in which, as many thought, the Jews could not achieve anything. The Jews rather became victims of the plans of European forces that fought each other for centuries on the east Mediterranean shores and in other territories of the Near and Far East. Even the formal beneficiaries of the new Palestinian state are not completely free from suspicion of pursuing egotistical political interests" (Пити, 1937, p. 64-65).

The prominent Bulgarian sculptor Prof. Andrey Nikolov is one of the few that are critical of the rich Jews for not supporting the arts. However, he is also critical of anti-Semitism:

"Anti-Semitism, beyond any doubt, is a sign of barbarism, which makes the peoples infected by this psychosis look bad, if we, of course, could accuse whole peoples of following anti-Semitism...

"The young Jewish generation in Bulgaria has already shown its real creativity. However, as a whole, the Jewry in our country seems to lock itself voluntarily in a spiritual ghetto. And that, I think, is the reason why they don't encourage and help the work of their own people. Unfortunately, the myth that many believe, that Jews help only those among them with proven talents, remains just a myth.

"Our Jews, unfortunately, don't worship the manifestations of the creative spirit. I am not aware of cases where the Bulgarian Jewry supported Jewish talent – writers, artists, musicians or others. The rich Jews, like all others who possess material wealth, worship only the Golden Calf that Moses destroyed with lightening. I would like to be proven wrong and now is the good time for that. At the gallery on 9 Preslav Street, now there is an exhibition of the works of a great Jew, creator in the Jewish culture – the sculptor Boris Schatz. At the same gallery they have also exhibited the paintings of a young talented artist – David Peretz, who grew up in poverty, graduated in poverty from our Arts Academy and created in poverty his wonderfully beautiful paintings. Both are some of the most prominent Jewish artists in Bulgaria. Boris Schatz has equally contributed to Bulgaria and the old Jewish homeland, Palestine. It will be a sin and a crime that the Jewry will commit against itself and against the Consistory and the Jewish community, if they don't buy all exhibited works of the great sculptor Boris Schatz, as well as some of the paintings of the young talented artist David Peretz and don't establish a Jewish art museum in Bulgaria. The attention of the Bulgarian Jews to the posthumous exhibition of Boris Schatz would be the only consolation for his son Batzalel, who spent all his money to come to our country and organize, with my help, an exhibition of his father's works" (Пити, 1937, p. 86-88).

The popular author Anton Strashimirov explains the raging anti-Semitism in Germany with the negative results of World War II.

"But what could one say about what happens in Germany? Isn't it clear? The atrocities against Jews in that country are not just a consequence of the horrible tragedy of the Germanism at large but are also a stage in the dangerous expansion of that tragedy. A flourishing people of seventy million was transformed in certain historical moment into a powerless mob of pariahs, condemned to starvation and cannibalism. Could such tragedy be expressed only in persecution of Jews? No, this is just one of the stages. The raging dark storm will strike beyond the deaths of the innocent local Jews and will flood the world! We can confirm it, we, the tiny Bulgarian nation, because we feel it in the tragic fate of our homeland...

"The German Jewry has had many achievements. It is enough to mention the names of the following Jews: Mendelssohn, Heine, Boerne, Marx, Lasalle, Freud, Adler, Ehrlich, Einstein, Hertz, Minkowski, Strauss, Schnitzler, Wassermann, Kellermann, Zweig, E. Ludwig, part of the legion of pioneers in all areas of culture...

"In our country, there is no ground for anti-Jewish hostility. If the Jews want also to be liked, it is necessary that they leave the shell of obscurantism and the prejudices of chauvinism and free themselves completely of the old Turkish spirit. The Bulgarian Jewry should lift itself up and catch up with its brethren in other countries" (Пити, 1937, p. 90).

Prof. Assen Zlatarov, a scientist in the field of biochemistry, also traces the roots of Hitler's anti-Semitism to the popular racists theories, initiated by Gobino. "And these anti-worker teachings attracted the starving philistines and lumpen-proletarians and created the force of Hitlerism! The national socialism cleverly masked those theories and reduced everything to a struggle of Arians against Semites. Hitler supports that view, in a speech delivered on April 12, 1932, he said: "There are no classes and they can't even exist. The class is caste, and the caste is race." A Hitlerite "handbook", distributed in hundreds of thousands of copies, stated: "The total population of the world, excluding apes, half-apes, and bats, is one billion and six hundred million primates, nine hundred million of whom are people and the rest are humanlike creatures (with two arms) in different stages of development. Here are included the Malays, many Egyptian and Mongol tribes, Jews, etc." According to Hitler, the Slavs also belong to those inferior creatures" (Пити, 1937, p. 92-94).

The conservative literary critic Vladimir Vasilev traced the roots of the current persecution of Jews in Germany to the consequences of World War I.

> "What do I think about the German racism? I am not familiar with the theories, but it seems to me that the theory of racial "superiority" is just an excuse. A totally unnecessary excuse. There are other reasons for blackmailing the Jews in Germany that need to be condemned. Seventy million people are suffocating, there is not enough room in their lands, they are in a mortal grip, trying to break their chains and, in these efforts, chains break at the thinnest links. Why weren't the Jews persecuted in Germany before? Why don't we see such persecution in today's France and England? Why even the fascist regime in Italy doesn't see the need to chase the Jews? Because this world is the victors' world. And before cursing Hitlerism, we should curse those who inevitably push a great people toward that doctrine." (Пити, 1937, p. 100-101).

One of the great Bulgarian actors at the time, Vladimir Trandafilov, condemns the racism in Germany:

> "The fashionable racial theory, which was imposed so

suddenly and brutally in Hitler's Germany, is nothing more than an ideological transformation of the old theory of anti-Semitism, that was born with the blessing of the Christian Church and found its reliable support in the organization of the Christian state. The only difference is that anti-Semitism was inspired by the sad fact of the crucifixion of Christ and by the intolerance of the religious dogmas, while racism exploits the idea of a racial, pure German state, whose structure should be deeply cleansed from all evils of the Jewry to ensure the pure German reproduction of the German spirit. This is a nationalist ideology of most anachronistic nature" (Пити, 1937, p. 102-103).

Prof. Dimitur Mihalchev was the best-known Bulgarian philosopher at the time. Educated in Germany, follower of the teachings of the German philosopher Johannes Rehmke, he expressed a true surprise about the way things deteriorated in that country.

"And now we are faced a new social hysteria! A shameful persecution of the Jews has begun in Germany, along with showing a mean disrespect for their fruitful contributions. It is not difficult to explain the emergence of that psychosis, but this doesn't mean that it can be justified. The Jews are nimble, energetic and clever. They have gifted people good in commercial, financial and thought speculation. That's why their enemies have been jealous of them. In our case, they are dangerous competitors of the average German. There are probably just over a million Jews in Germany but their participation in the economic and spiritual life of the country is not proportionate to their number, meaning that it is not seventy times lesser than the German participation, but it is much bigger. That's why, the popular social movement that we see today in Germany, in its demagogic attempt to use the sentiments of the large masses, is looking for the weakest and lowest in the psychology of the masses – their jealousy to a common target. That's what has caused the speculations about the Jewish "danger"" (Пити, 1937, p. 113).

Dobri Nemirov, the Chairman of the Union of the Bulgarian Writers, has harsh words about most of the Bulgarian Jews, due to the perceived lack of support for cultural initiatives:

"My opinion about the Bulgarian Jewry and its

intelligentsia? Well formulated question – the Jewry is one thing; its intelligentsia is something different. The Jewry is the total mass of people, in which we can see the image of the race with its defective and positive features. Something positive is the participation of the Jews in the material culture, where they work successfully, due to their experience, in an effortless way. But the Jewish masses at large must have their spiritual needs, must relate to the Bulgarian spiritual and cultural life. The Jews here have equal rights, so their duty to our spiritual life is as important to them, as it is to the Bulgarians.

"However, when sacrifices are needed for our spiritual and cultural life, the Jews think that their mission doesn't go that far. The Jewry treats our culture harshly. It is not involved in philanthropy, it doesn't feel the duty to support Bulgarian publishing, Bulgarian theater, Bulgarian arts and science. It is not interested in the writer, the artist and the scientist, doesn't value the people of spirit. Considering this, we may ask how many cultural initiatives have been supported, how many orphanages have been helped, how many cultural institutions and how many social ideas have been initiated by the Jewry...

"But the Jewish intelligentsia is something different. It is part of our life, it participates in all successes and failures of our culture and contributes to its treasure. Still, it remains foreign to the common Jewish circles. Its achievements are not appreciated by the Jews. I can mention names that bring honor to the Jewry. And yet, I think that only the Jewish intelligentsia will continue to contribute" (Пити, 1937, p. 115-116).

The composer Prof. Dobri Christov wrote: "Hitler's persecution of the German Jews caused a strong reaction against him from the world Jewry and the whole civilized world. Jews are persecuted because the peoples, among which they live, don't know them enough. If nationalities knew each other well enough, maybe we would have never witnessed the revolting bloodshed that causes pain in our hearts when we realize that people's highest mission is to create spiritual and material goods and live in peace and love for each other" (Пити, 1937, p. 118-119).

The great Bulgarian writer Elin Pelin, a friend of King Boris III, will play a role in saving the Bulgarian Jews in 1943. Here he emphasizes the importance of tolerance: "I have always valued the noble Bulgarian quality to treat with friendship and respect the Jews who live in our homeland. The Bulgarian Jews, as exemplary citizens, deserve to be treated in the best possible way. The Bulgarian Jewish intellectuals live with the Bulgarian spirit, aspirations, joys and sorrows. Fully adapted to our conditions, they carry in their hearts and souls Bulgarian feelings" (Пити, 1937, p. 121).

Prof. Emanuil Popdimitrov, a well-known writer, talks about the loyalty of the Bulgarian Jews:

> "The emancipation of the Bulgarian Jews has developed in them civil loyalty and, as we saw during the wars, a true patriotic spirit. The case of the Bulgarian Jews, who already live in Palestine, is touching. When meeting Bulgarians, they express fraternal feelings. On the market today, you will find excellent Palestinian oranges, grown by them, special export to Bulgaria, and on their packages, you can see the image of Hristo Botev. This is not an advertisement, but real respect for a hero who died for the freedom of his people. Because the modern Jews also need such heroes, they had them and will have them again.
>
> "As a representative of the Bulgarian minorities at the European national congresses, I had the chance to see how the Jewish representatives not only worked with us, but also expressed sincere compassion. The minority issues are also Jewish issues. They were created and pushed forward as a principle, above all, by the Jews. Our enslaved compatriots, who live out of our borders, owe the Jewish minorities, especially the one in Bulgaria, deep gratitude for the support that the Jewry has given and always gives to the unfairly treated Bulgarians, as it was the case in August 1929 in Geneva, at the congress of the European minorities, when some wanted to exclude the Bulgarians in East Serbia from participation." (Пити, 1937, p. 122-123).

The writer Ivan Nikolov provided another view of the delusions of racism:

> "Racism is a theory, which postulates that a race, which is more perfect and talented, is supposed to rule over the other races. This theory is being developed and preached with a special persistence and it is the basis of most of the ideas of National Socialism. The theory of the superiority of the German race over the rest, especially over the so-called non-Aryan races, is the starting point of Hitler's teachings. A consequence of those teachings is the mass expulsion of Jews from Germany. Memorable are the words of the German philosopher Keiserling about the inferior origin of numerous nations, among which is

the Bulgarian nation. His opinions about Bulgarians and Jews are equally condescending. The ideologists of racism do not care what science and biology state about these issues. According to science and common sense, there are no superior and inferior races. The races are so mixed, that it is ridiculous to even talk about pure races...

"In the nations developed in conditions of political freedom, the anti-Semitism is anachronistic and useless. Peoples that are free politically have the ability to think and see. It is known that only in nations that are behind in their political development anti-Semitism has roots and grows, not only among the semi-intellectuals but also among common people. The people in the real sense of the word – peasants, workers, craftsmen, have always possessed common sense and avoided such type of a heresy. I have lived in Russia for many years, this is the classical country of the anti-Jewish pogroms, and I can say openly and honestly and with a clear conscience that the common Russian people have not taken part in those pogroms and even detested them... The pogroms were the work of the same clique, which caused the catastrophe of the Russian Empire.

"The Bulgarian Jews have been not only good and loyal citizens, but also good Bulgarians. People like me, who have visited Palestine, have seen there the Jews from Bulgaria, their houses, villages, with the portraits of Levski, Botev and other heroes, have heard their songs, as well as the Bulgarian folk songs, witnessed how many don't go to bed before the program of Radio Sofia ends – such visitors feel ashamed that the anti-Semitic hydra already hisses in Bulgaria, although its voice is still weak. The small nations should be wiser" (Пити, 1937, p. 128-130).

Iordan Kovachev was a colorful figure in the Bulgarian intellectual life. A writer, philosopher, lawyer, and follower of the teachings of Leo Tolstoy, he was persecuted for his leftist views in old Bulgaria. After the communist takeover, he was persecuted again and spent years in communist concentration camps for supporting the political opposition to the regime. He cannot accept the persecution of Jews: "Anti-Semitism, as a historical fact, collective evil and theory, is much older than racism and even more senseless and barbaric than racism. It could survive for so many centuries and could disgrace even our times only because the true, inner, moral culture advances very slowly and because during an enormous period, the Jews have been the safest target for looting and the easiest scapegoat, attacked by all scoundrels who want to cover up their incompetence. Persons, social movements and nations that don't work on eradicating once and for all the hatred for Jews and other people, are in decay and deserve only pity" (Пити, 1937, p. 134-135).

The journalist Krustyu Stanchev wrote:

> "We don't have in Bulgaria anti-Semitism as a social movement and will not have it. All attempts to create an anti-Semitic movement in our country have failed pathetically. Our compatriots, the Jews, know and feel the real attitude of the Bulgarian people toward them. Random excesses of some people only show how groundless anti-Semitism is in our country...
>
> "We respect Jews as our good citizens and our Jewish compatriots respect the Bulgarians as tolerant people. Our totally negative opinion about racism and anti-Semitism determines our attitude toward all Jewish people. The Jews are a nation like any other. They have a long history. Other nations that have lived along with them have disappeared and their names lost. The Jews have remained, even after endless persecution, and not only survived, but have also kept their vitality" (Пити, 1937, p. 144-145).

The popular theater actress Rosa Popova noted:

> "There is no racial superiority, there are only human beings. If the various castes could be called races, I would divide the whole mankind in two races – oppressors and oppressed. If we place all human beings under equally good conditions for education and spiritual development, we will see that the racial issue will disappear on its own. Inequality ruins both sides.
>
> "Was it by chance that the great Shakespeare, the son of the proud Albion, was the first one in literature to condemn with his noble spirit and humanism the racial differences through the characters of the Moor Othello and the Jew Shylock? Doesn't Desdemona show that love can discover under the dark skin the beauty and nobility of the soul? And didn't Shylock say: "When you kill us, don't we bleed?" That's blood, which has the same elements as the blood of any other person. There are no privileged races and nations, there is just one mankind, and it is a crime to create false superiority and obstacles among nations" (Пити, 1937, p. 171-172).

Another performing artist, the opera singer Stefan Makedonski, condemned the expulsion of the Jews from Germany:

> "They expelled the Jews from Germany but forgot that the same Jews gave Germany some of its brightest minds – some of the greatest performers in theater and opera, achievers in science, medicine, and industry, all of whom were the pride of the German culture. It seems to me that the harm caused by the National Socialists to the German culture was worse than the loss of the colonies after the war. The competition among most European countries and America to offer positions at their universities to emigrant professors is a clear sign of protest against the persecution in Germany. The attention of [the Turkish President] Kemal Ataturk is striking – he is proud that in the universities of the new, rebounding Turkey, one can find professors who came from Germany; he opened the gates of his homeland to many scientists, professors and writers. I believe in the future of mankind and I know that in the end reason and freedom will prevail" (Пити, 1937, p. 178-179).

The great poet Theodor Trayanov finds another reason to criticize the Jewish elites in Bulgaria:

> "You want to know my opinion about the Jewish intelligentsia? I'll be blunt, it is not very flattering. Because the self-imposed crude materialism and the devastating and limiting spirit of the ghetto prevent it from developing its energies and talents of a chosen people, which have been hidden for centuries, and becoming part of the nation and the land where it lives. Wherever those spiritual energies are released, we see cultural achievements. It is enough to mention, as an illustration, two names: Mois Benaroya, a deep and perceptive essayist, and Isaac Daniel, a theater director of European stature" (Пити, 1937, p. 191-192).

This is just a part of the opinions of the 62 prominent people included in the book. As you can see, anti-Semitism is unanimously condemned. Its most powerful manifestation at the time, Nazi Germany, is also criticized harshly, despite its growing influence in Bulgaria.

It is interesting to note the critical opinions, which came predominantly from artists. While traditionally Jews have been criticized for their perceived excessive influence over the public life, their critics in Bulgaria make the opposite point. They are disappointed that the Jews do not contribute according to their vast abilities and talents. Not a single writer found any sign of a Jewish conspiracy for dominance. This observation is important, because it explains the fierce resistance that met the proposed anti-Jewish laws and later, in 1943, the concerted efforts of intellectuals, politicians and common people to prevent the proposed deportations of the Bulgarian Jews. The warnings of the anti-Semites in the government about the deep Jewish influence sounded shallow and ridiculous when so many educated Bulgarians were able to see the truth.

The other important observation is that sometimes a small group can impose its sinister ideology, contrary to everything that the majority believes, with the help of a strong external power (Germany in this case) and cause potentially devastating consequences.

9 GERMANY AND THE ANTI-JEWISH LAWS IN BULGARIA

I hope it became clear that Bulgaria did not have a tradition of anti-Semitism, commonly seen in many European countries. The sporadic cases of hostility against Jews never gained wider acceptance. Despite the attempts to develop anti-Semitic political movements, such initiatives did not find fertile ground in Bulgaria and it was hard to imagine them gaining popularity on their own.

Some of the intellectuals surveyed in "The Bulgarian Public on Racism and Anti-Semitism" noted that the Jews did not participate enthusiastically in the Bulgarian cultural and social life. However, Jews were active, they maintained many organizations in the field of sports, culture and charity. The nature of most of them was Zionist and they operated in the open and took part in international events, as you can see in the photos at the end of this book. Neither the Bulgarian Government, nor the people objected to those organizations; nobody wanted to restrict them.

The rise of the National Socialism in Germany, with its deeply rooted hostility against Jews, drastically changed the situation. Unlike the Weimar Republic, which was preoccupied with its inner struggles caused by a disastrous economic situation, Hitler's Third Reich embarked on a more aggressive foreign policy to increase the influence of Germany. The German interests in the new places of influence, required compliance with the new German ideology, including its attitude toward Jews.

With rare exceptions, the passing of anti-Jewish laws was demanded by Germany from every country, which found itself in the Reich's orbit, either as an ally or a puppet state. Hitler's personal obsession with Jews as the prime source of all misfortunes of mankind was the driving force behind those laws. Japan was the only ally that did not have an anti-Jewish law, not only because of lack of Jews on its territory, but also because of the way Japanese saw the Jews, which eventually led to saving of tens of thousands of Jews in Japan and on the occupied by the country territories, see (Marinov, 2017) for details.

It is wrong to see Hitler as an eloquent madman who managed to seduce the gullible persons around him and rise to power. Hitler's worldview, to a great degree, was a reflection of the ideological environment of his times. The animosity toward Jews in Germany, with all of its excesses over the centuries, is well known. Even Karl Marx, Hitler's nemesis, who came from a Jewish family, was against the Jews because of the usual stereotypes. The resolution of the "Jewish Question", in the young Marx's views, would come when the Jews are fully assimilated and cease to be Jews (Marx, 1959, p. 45). Lesser thinkers had similar views, published books and pamphlets, and Hitler devoured many of them when he lived in Vienna in the early 1900s.

The myth of the cheated majority that knew nothing about Hitler's intentions is shattered when we look at the way Germans accepted Hitler's war on the Jews. The British historian Ian Kershaw notes that in his book "Hitler, the Germans, and the Final Solution": "Remarkable as it may sound, the Jewish Question was of no more than minimal interest to the vast majority of Germans during the war years in which the mass slaughter of Jews was taking place in the occupied territories. The evidence, though surviving much more thinly for the war years than for the prewar period, allows no other conclusion" (Kershaw, 2008, p.198).

The point of view that the Jews were something different and foreign to Germany, regardless of the long common history, made their isolation and removal from society much easier for the Nazis. "Moreover, the Jews, a generally unloved minority, had become, as we have just seen, almost totally isolated from the rest of German society. For most people, 'the Jew' was now a completely depersonalized image. The abstraction of the Jew had taken over more and more from the 'real' Jew who, whatever animosity he had caused, had been a flesh-and-blood person. The depersonalization of the Jew had been the real area of success of Nazi policy and propaganda on the Jewish Question" (Kershaw, 2008, p.199). Thus, the deportations that started in 1941, received little attention from the German public. Even the German churches, Catholic and Protestant, didn't articulate any significant opposition to the regime, with rare exceptions like Dietrich Bonhoeffer.

Hitler's charisma and the Reich's excruciating power would not have been able to win without the cooperation of millions of people. It is important to remember that when we talk about the anti-Semitic laws in Bulgaria.

Unlike Romania, Russia, and later Germany, Bulgaria never had or contemplated such laws until the late 1930s. Contrary to what the history textbooks said during communism, there was no fascism in Bulgaria. Fascism requires a charismatic leader with messianic aspirations, blindly followed by millions. It also presupposes strong government control over the economy and the political life. The parliamentary system in both Germany and Italy was practically suspended. In Germany's case, some of the methods and institutions of fascism were "borrowed" from Lenin and Stalin's Soviet Russia, despite Hitler's opposition to Marxism; he adopted the camp system for undesirables, developed by Lenin in the 1920s.

King Boris III preferred to work behind the scenes and, unlike Hitler and Mussolini, never relied on fiery speeches to increase his popularity. His main objective was to lead his small country through the coming war with minimal losses. Despite the dissolution of the political parties after 1934, the Parliament continued to function, representing many political forces with different ideologies, even communists were MPs in the late 1930s and early 1940s. There were no charismatic promoters of the Nazi ideas in Bulgaria. Most of them, like Minister Peter Gabrovski, were mediocrities who could not inspire a large following. Without the strong pressure from Germany, none of their ideas could have been implemented in Bulgaria. And whenever implemented, they were accepted as an inevitable compromise to calm down the potential German rage.

Prof. Alexander Tsankov, the personality closest to a fascist leader, was too academic, too intelligent to fill a Fuehrer's role. Besides, he was a staunch defender of the Jewish rights. Two Nazi-like youth organizations had some following, the Union of Bulgarian National Legions (Legionnaires) and the Warriors for the Advancement of the Bulgarian National Spirit (Ratniks). The King was suspicious of them because the Germans could use both groups against him, in the way the Romanian Iron Guard movement was used against the Romanian Government in 1930s. Before the pro-German government faction became stronger, the

Bulgarian fascist youth organizations were not allowed to operate openly.

The leaders of those organizations were obscure figures, virtually unknown to most people. Only the leader of the Legions, General Hristo Lukov, a war hero, had some prominence but since he had already retired, he didn't participate actively in the political life.

Prof. Bogdan Filov, appointed by the King as Prime Minister in 1940 to appease Germany, was a strong supporter of Nazi Germany but was not well known as a politician. Before that, he had a scientific career as an archeologist and historian of Medieval Bulgaria. Two figures that were to play pivotal role in the Jewish issues, came from the Ratniks organization. The Interior Minister Peter Gabrovski was one of their leaders. The future Commissar for the Jewish Questions, Aleksander Belev, was also an activist in the movement.

In the late 1940, the government proposed a law that would restrict the rights of the Jews, accusing them of being a danger to the state. That was the notorious Law for Defense of the Nation (Zakon za zashtita na natsiyata, ZZN). It is not to be confused with the Law for Defense of the State, adopted by the government of Prof. Alexander Tsankov in the 1920s.

The proposed law consisted of two sections - Section One "About the Secret and International Organizations", dissolved organizations like the Free Masons and any other international entities that had representation in Bulgaria (even the Pen Club, whose chairman was Prof. Filov, was shut down). They had to stop their activities immediately, their members had to declare their international ties and the groups' properties were to be seized.

More important was Section Two "About the Persons of Jewish Origin". Article 15 defined a Jew as a person with at least one Jewish parent with the exception of people born in mixed marriages of a Jew and Christian and baptized Jews (Закон за защита на нацията, 1941, p. 6). The definition emphasized the religious background as a defining factor, while Hitler's Nuremberg laws focused on race.

All Jews were expected to be registered with the government. They were prohibited from using the Bulgarian endings -ov, -ev, ich, and others in their names. The Jews were not allowed to occupy elected positions. The law prohibited Jews from serving in the regular army, leaving as the only option the Labor Army. They could not use servants and housekeepers of Bulgarian background. The ownership of agricultural land was prohibited. As Marshall

Miller notes:

> "Raul Hilberg has pointed out, "In its effect, it was not exactly a mild law, for the Bulgarians did not start out with mildness. Restraint was applied only afterwards, when the prospects of a German victory began to fade." Jews were forbidden to engage in a large number of occupations, and a numerus clausus was introduced to limit the percentage of Jews allowed to practice medicine, law, engineering, and a number of other professions, as well as to enter universities. Jews were not allowed to have gentile servants and were required to register their property and possessions; their dwelling places could not be changed, and money could not be sent out of the country.
>
> "It should be pointed out, however, that the Bulgarian law was milder than might have been expected from the German models. First, the definition of a Jew was somewhat narrower than in the German edicts. Second, Article 33 exempted the families of Jews who had been awarded medals for bravery, which meant that about one-tenth of the Jewish families in Bulgaria were freed from restrictions. This also affected the quota system, for it was decided not to include them in the numerus clausus, whose calculations were further modified by basing the percentages on the population of the cities rather than of the country as a whole. As a result, in Sofia the number of Jewish lawyers had to be reduced only from 20 to 18, engineers from 6 to 4, musicians from 14 to 8, and doctors from 21 to 13." (Miller, 1975, p. 95).

Prof. Filov's government had a hard time convincing people that the 50,000 Bulgarian Jews were such a grave danger to the state. The speeches of Peter Gabrovski and other anti-Semitic members of the parliament during the debates couldn't provide anything but tired clichés. On the other hand, representatives of the opposition, like Nikola Mushanov and Petko Stainov pointed out the Jewish contributions to Bulgaria and accused the government of cruelty.

The idea behind the law was to insulate Bulgaria from destructive foreign influence. However, even within the government parliamentary majority, there were politicians reluctant to accept such unjust law. The politics of secrecy over those issues made it difficult to see the truth, although some hints about the real situation were presented in the Ratniks' circular in Appendix A. An interesting explanation of the polarization within the government can be found in the testimony of the lawyer Dr.

Georgi Lipovanski, an active Member of the Parliament from the government majority, during his trial before the People's Tribunal in 1944:

> "Chairman: What was your position about the Law for Defense of the Nation. Did you vote for it? If you reacted to it, when and where did you do it?
>
> "Lipovanski: Dear People's Justices! As the Chairman of the Bulgarian-Hungarian Business Chamber, I traveled to Hungary at least once a year and had the opportunity to see how the Hungarians treated the Jews. Here is what I was told by Mr. Revitsky and the former Prime Minister Kallay: "It is not known how the war will end, but regardless of how it ends, England and America will never disappear, the financial power in those countries is held by the Jews, and since Hungary will need financial help irrespective of the war outcome, we will treat the Jews in ways that will allow us to maintain our ties with England and America." This was a reasonable policy and after every trip, I told our cabinet ministers that they should follow it. The Jews must not be mistreated, we should tolerate them because they can help us.
>
> "C.: In what other ways, besides talks with ministers, have you expressed this ideology?
>
> "L.: I discussed it with [Prime Minister] Filov, but my impression was that for him the question was already resolved, and nothing could change his position. In the commission that debated the law, I tried to suggest some softening, I proposed to exclude from the law the children from mixed marriages. But Mr. Filov didn't want to accept even that change and was upset.
>
> "C.: You should have censured him.
>
> "L.: But King Boris wouldn't allow to censure him.
>
> "C.: So, King Boris was the ruler.
>
> "L.: Of course, he ruled the country. If we, the opponents, had left, who knows how much worse the law could have become.
>
> "C.: When the parliamentary debates of the law started, why didn't you express your position in a speech?
>
> "L.: I expressed it in the commission... The only thing I could do was to abstain from voting. However, any MP who tried to raise his voice was slandered as being corrupt. Mr. Gabrovski set everything in such a way that we were cautious and afraid to disagree...
>
> "C.: Did you vote?
>
> "L.: No.

"C.: Did you attend the session?

"L.: Yes, I attended" (Народен съд, разпит на Георги Липовански, 1944, p. 272-273).

Politicians, who were outside of the parliament at the time, were also against the law, like Dimo Kazasov, a socialist who had an entry in the book against anti-Semitism covered in the previous chapter. In a letter to Prime Minister Bogdan Filov, dated November 18, 1940, he expressed his strong opposition to the law and its absurd restrictions:

"The sons of the Jewish nation play a prominent role in the political, economic, spiritual and scientific elites of large and small countries. The war on Jews in our country will be noticed in those circles and will place us in the position of a moral conflict with the public in those countries, although we must maintain cultural and economic ties with them for the sake of our interests. Large nations with a rich material and spiritual life, like Italy and Germany, can afford the luxury of such a conflict, but a small nation like ours must avoid it. We need as many friends as we can attract and more support and help from others. The foreign enemies' interests are served not by those who want to keep the ties with everybody, but by those who want to break them. What a strange and monstrous nationalism – to condemn our nation to such an isolation!

"You justify the proposed law against the Jews with the need to eliminate the foreign influence and protect the Bulgarian nationality, if so, why don't you want to see:

1) 650,000 Turks, who as a group, have much more properties than the Jews and who, with their conservatism, slow down our economic progress and are the target of foreign propaganda.

2) 70,000 Romanians, target of foreign propaganda.

3) Countless foreign schools in Bulgaria, where thousands of young Bulgarians are subjected to foreign influence and propaganda.

I don't recommend the persecution of Turks and Romanians, but I ask you, why do you see the straw, but remain blind for the log?

In a country like ours, which badly needs economic initiative and expansion to extract the hidden natural resources and opportunities, you march against an entrepreneurial minority like the Jews that was born, lives and contributes to our country and place it at a level below Gypsies who are twice as many as the Jews and lead purely parasitic way of life in our economy. Does the prosperity of the country require punishment for economic initiative and privileges for parasites?" (Казасов, писмо до Филов, 1940, p. 1-5).

Very strong opposition came from the Jewish community, the main target of the new law. It was channeled through the Central Jewish Consistory, which represented the community. In the literature about these events, its role is often underestimated. However, its quiet work behind the scenes, though unsuccessful in stopping the law, contributed greatly to the saving of the Jews from deportation two years later. The Central Jewish Consistory sent out numerous letters proving wrong the baseless accusations of Jewish control over the affairs of Bulgaria. The role of the Jews in the Bulgarian history was explained in detail. It added to the letters statistical data to debunk the idea that Jews were criminals or plutocrats who controlled the Bulgarian economy.

In Sofia, where most of the Jews lived, the distribution by trades and professions showed that they hardly controlled anything. The majority were not prosperous, with 7,247 housewives, 1,422 merchants, 247 barbers, 828 unemployed, over 7,000 students and small children, etc. About 2% of the Jews sacrificed their lives for Bulgaria - 952 Jews in the army perished in wars from 1885 to 1918 (Професии на евреите в София, 1940).

Even the crime rate among Jews was lower than in the rest of the country. In the period 1920-1935, in Bulgaria were committed 12,923 murders, 14 of them by Jews. Since Jews were 0.85% of the population, to match the official rate, Jews had to commit 110 murders, but there were only 14. For prostitution, the Consistory listed a total of 2,792 prostitutes, 41 of them Jewish and noted again that to match the national rate, there should have been 258 Jewish prostitutes (Престъпност сред евреите, 1940).

In a statement of the Central Consistory dated October 22, 1940, the phony arguments of the promoters of the law were refuted one by one. The refutation started with the fact that the Bulgarian Jews had established long time ago unbreakable ties with the Bulgarian people; they have supported their homeland in happiness and sorrow. The Bulgarian culture, in all of its forms, had been inseparable from the lives of the Jews. Since Roman times, Jews have resided in the Balkans. During the Turkish yoke they coexisted peacefully with Bulgarians and supported their struggle for independence. Many Bulgarian revolutionaries found refuge in Jewish houses. After the liberation, the Jews took part in the struggles, fighting for Bulgaria. It was emphasized again that 952 Jews perished fighting in the liberation wars, out of a population of about 45,000, which makes 21 per thousand. Considering the fact that the Jews live in cities, the percentage of their sacrifice is higher than that of the Bulgarian urban population.

Bulgarian Jews helped their country to defend the rights of the Bulgarian minorities in other countries. Colonel Avram Tadjer arranged the participation of Prof. Emanuil Popdimitrov and others in the congress of minorities, the only international tribune at the time, where the problems of the Bulgarian minority could be discussed in 1932.

The letter continued: "Bulgarian Jews in Palestine are known for their patriotism, as many travellers have noted. They speak Bulgarian, sing Bulgarian songs, decorate their homes with the images of the Royal Family and proudly call themselves Bulgarians. They spread the glory of Bulgaria in Palestine."

The accusations that the Jews controlled the economic life in Bulgaria were not true. On the contrary, the situation of many Jews was difficult. Their number was miniscule – 46,558 according to the 1926 census or 0.7% of the population. It dropped, compared to 0.93% in 1905. Most Jews lived in cities, 45,261 as of 1926, with only 1,307 in the villages, at the time of the letter, they were even fewer. Only 75 Jews worked in agriculture and only 14 owned farms. So, the most important treasure of the Bulgarian people, their land, wad entirely in Bulgarian hands. There were no Jews involved in mines, forestry or quarries.

"The Jews are not represented in the government bureaucracy, which has about 200,000 employees at different levels and only about 10 of them are Jews. If the quota of the law is accepted, the Jews should have 2,500 of them in the government apparatus. Since they don't occupy such positions, they have no influence on the education of youth or state affairs.

Their participation in theater, press, music, literature and arts is also very limited (as they were criticized by artists in the survey book – M. M.). So, they don't control those fields. It is regrettable, and the Consistory would be happy to see more Jews involved in the cultural life."

Jewish bankers and industrialists were also mentioned. According to the latest statistics, there were 84 Jewish industrialists and not a single banker. Even the clerical staff of the largest banks was entirely Bulgarian. The only Jewish bank, a cooperative institution, was Gheula Bank of Sofia, with capital of about 25 million leva, collected by the Sofia Jews. There were 2 or 3 smaller cooperative banks with capital of 250,000 to 3 million leva.

"The vast majority of the Jews make a living by manual labor. Out of 25,000 Jews in Sofia, 1,422 are merchants with their own shops; 723 are peddlers, whose capital is a box with small merchandise, while the total number of merchants in Sofia is 9,000. The claim that Jews control the commerce is groundless. The same could be said about the professionals. There are 84 Jewish doctors, 58 lawyers, 25 engineers, 70 dentists or a total of 237. The number doesn't show Jewish dominance.

"The conclusion is that the Jews in Sofia and the rest of Bulgaria are mostly poor or with limited earnings, craftsmen, sales clerks, workers, small merchants with very limited income and in rare cases with small capital. The Jewish misery is on display in the quarters where they live. The proposed law will only worsen their situation and will condemn them to starvation.

"There is no reason to restrict the Jewish activities. Some of them hurt the honor of the Jews, especially the ban of future participation in the Bulgarian Army. The Jews have always served proudly in it and want to continue. This injustice is offensive to the Jews.

"The closure of Jewish enterprises and stores, which employ predominantly Jews, will deprive them from the opportunity to feed their families." (Изложение на Централната консистория по ЗЗН, 1940, р. 1-10)

Other organizations were also vocal with their criticism of the proposed law. Letters of protest to various officials were sent by the unions of doctors, lawyers, artists and other organizations. The Bulgarian Orthodox Church took immediately a position of disagreement with the new anti-Jewish policies and maintained it until the end of the war. At the same time, the Church approved the section of the law dealing with international organizations and wanted the law to prohibit foreign religious organization and to state specifically that only Catholicism, Anglicanism, Armenian Christianity, Lutheranism, Methodism, Judaism and Islam are allowed on the condition that they are led by Bulgarian citizens (Писмо от митрополит Неофит, декември 1940).

The high clerics of the Church were not fond of Germany. Metropolitan Stefan, later an Exarch, was even suspected of working for the British intelligence. In "Protocol of the interrogation of Obergruppenfuehrer of SA A. Beckerle, January 30, 1950", the former German Ambassador in Bulgaria Beckerle said that Stefan was a British agent (Beckerle spent years in the Soviet Union, after his arrest by the Russians in 1944):

> "It was difficult to deal with Patriarch [the term was used incorrectly, he was an Exarch. – M.M.] Stefan, because his high position in the Bulgarian Orthodox Church made him untouchable. The German intelligence revealed the close ties of Patriarch Stefan with the British intelligence, with which he communicated through the popular in Bulgaria Masonic lodges and the church organizations under his control. Patriarch Stefan took every opportunity to travel abroad, where he was seen meeting many times representatives of the Church of England and British spies disguised as clerics… Stefan was hostile to the USSR and his main fear was the rapprochement between Bulgaria and the Soviet Union. Because of that, he thought necessary to support the Germans in their fight against the USSR" (Тайны дипломатии Третьего рейха, p. 64).

On November 14, 1943, the Holy Synod of the Bulgarian Orthodox Church (its governing body) met to discuss the situation and a response to the proposed Law for Defense of the Nation was discussed.

The main speaker at the meeting was Metropolitan Kiril from Plovdiv. In the very beginning, he stated that the starting point for building an opinion was clear – since the Church adhered to the principles of the Gospel and the Christ's teachings about the equality of all people, regardless of background, race and culture, it must defend the Jews as well, first those who were baptized, and also the non-Christian Jews.

Then he went into details about the nature of Judaism, which differed from the Old Testament religiosity, which traditionally was ascribed to the believes of the Jews. Judaism was the result of a long religious and political history of the Jews that had become dominant in the Jewish mindset. Kiril saw three major characteristics of Judaism: 1) following of earthly values, 2) religious and national self-isolation and exclusivity, 3) hostility toward Christ and Christianity. The earthly spirit of the Jews could be seen even when they were not connected to the Jewish synagogue community. An example of that was Karl Marx who reduced the whole social development to the work of economic forces and elevated an anti-Christian and anti-spiritual ideal for social development. Karl Marx was a typical case of Judaist hostility toward Christ and the Christian faith. This hostility was maintained in the Jewish soul by the synagogues and was as old as Christianity. In the Talmudic literature you could find insults against Christ and the Christians and expectations that the God of Israel would liberate the Jews from their domination. A Jewish prayer, found several decades earlier, called "Shmone Esre", was supposed to be uttered three times a day by every Jew; it asked God to destroy Christians and their dominance.

Such religious beliefs had their impact on the national psychology of the Jews and their deep attitude toward Christianity. The Jews displayed hatred for Christ, which was manifested and encouraged in different ways. Anti-Judaism is an old phenomenon, which existed even before Christ for various reasons, which are the same for today's anti-Jewish sentiments. One of the main reasons was the religious and national isolation and exclusivity of the Jews. Judaism was anti-Christian, but Christianity was also anti-Judaist from the beginning. The anti-Jewish sentiments among Christian nations were old. They also existed in a naïve form among the Bulgarian people – the Jews crucified God, chased the Apostles, persecuted the Church. Other than, Bulgarians have been tolerant, and the Jews could complain of mistreatment. But there was still some wariness toward Jews.

Further, he noted that he shared those facts to emphasize that the evaluation of the law by the Church was based on a principled Gospel point of view and not on ignoring the reality. It was important to analyze the situation of the Jews in Bulgaria. Many of them were poor, but often this was hard to see, because they had a well-established mutual help network. There were also rich Jews who controlled many factories in Bulgaria. The Jewish capital's share in the commerce was substantial. Until recently, the Jews did not participate in the cultural life, but this was changing, and their influence was felt. Jewish capital was influential in enterprises that determined the direction of the cultural life in Bulgaria. Also, some Jews already treated purely Bulgarian cultural questions and interpreted the Bulgarian past, unfortunately, from a negative position.

He suggested further that the Church should be careful with its response to avoid misunderstanding. It must insist on humane and just treatment of the Jews, while at the same time providing fair treatment for the Bulgarian people. Preserving the Bulgarian character of the culture was important and no influence on its trends by Jewish capital should be allowed. In the economy, without introducing restrictions on the Jewish labor as a labor to earn a living, the Bulgarian people must also be treated fairly, in case if the Jewish financial, commercial and industrial capital violated that fairness. It was not fair if the people in these lands were pushed away from their proper position in the economic life.

The Church should be careful when writing its letter not to create the impression that it is indifferent to these issues and defends the Jewish capitalist enterprises, this was not its position. The Church defends individuals and their labor (Свети синод, Протокол №12, 1940, p. 71-75).

It is obvious that the Church was trying to strike a balance between defending its doctrines and helping the Jews in a difficult situation. It also had to avoid potential clash with the government, as every one of the fifteen independent Orthodox Churches, the Bulgarian Church was confined within the national borders and it depended on the government and the opinions of the common people.

At the same meeting, Metropolitan Stefan of Sofia reminded the Holy Synod that the most beautiful traits in the history of the Bulgarian people were their tolerance and hospitality. Tolerance was shown when the Bulgarians accepted the suffering Armenian people, who, after the massacres in Istanbul, found a quiet and humane refuge in Bulgaria. At international conferences, Bulgarians had been praised for their tolerance of all minorities, especially when compared with the Romanians. He thought that it was necessary to have restrictions on the Jews only in one area – the domestic help, they should not have Christian housekeepers, but the restriction could be expanded in the sense to not allow Christian girls to work as servants for people from other faiths (Свети синод, Протокол №12, 1940, p. 75).

Metropolitan Paissi of Vratsa added that the law had to include provisions for defending the Orthodox faith, especially from foreign religious propaganda and Protestant sects. The Orthodox faith had preserved the Bulgarian people through the ages, especially during the Turkish slavery. The strengthening of that faith must include its growth by accepting newly baptized Jews into the Church, so there should not be a deadline for the conversions, as it was stated in the proposed law. The other Jews, had to be treated according to the principles of truth and humanism (Свети синод, Протокол №12, 1940, p. 76).

The Holy Synod held another meeting the next day, November 15, 1940, to approve a letter to the Speaker of the People's

Assembly with a position about the proposed Law for Defense of the Nation; all Metropolitans were present except Boris of Nevrokop and Evlogi of Sliven. The only Metropolitan who voted against the letter was Iosif of Varna and Preslav.

The letter started with the admission that the government was expected to defend the nation from various dangers. However, the proposed law had serious shortcomings that could bring more dangers to Bulgaria. The first thing the Holy Synod questioned was the lack of distinction between the Israelite Jews and the Jews baptized by the Orthodox Church before September 1, 1940. The baptized Jews had joined the Bulgarian nation and had the same culture, believes and customs as the Bulgarian Christians. Both groups could not be treated the same way.

Another problem were certain provisions against the Israelite Jews, which were unfair and not useful for the defense of the nation. If there were any such dangers, the measures against them had to address actions and not ethnicities and religious groups, however, in its present form, the law created the impression that it aimed at a special treatment of an ethnic minority in Bulgaria. The defense of one nation should not include injustice and violence against other nations.

Also, the law did not protect in any way the spiritual unity of the Bulgarian people, especially their Christian beliefs. The Holy Synod proposed four amendments to the proposed law:

"1. All Jews, who have been baptized or are going to be baptized, should be treated in the same way as the Orthodox Christian Bulgarians.

"2. The provisions against the Jews as an ethnic minority should be dropped and replaced by measures against all real dangers to the spiritual, cultural, economic, and social life of the Bulgarian nation.

"3. The law should include measures against all anti-religious and anti-church propaganda, which strives to erode the religious-national spirit and destroy the faith of the Bulgarian people.

"4. It should outline specific measures to limit foreign religious propaganda, which breaks the spiritual unity of the Bulgarian people and makes them an easy prey of foreign aspirations and goals (Свети синод, Протокол №13, 1940, p. 82-87). The letter, prepared by the Holy Synod, was sent the next day to Prime Minister Bogdan Filov, signed by Metropolitan Neofit (Писмо от митрополит Неофит, ноември 1940).

In agreement with the opinion of the Holy Synod that baptisms of Jews must continue, regardless of the time limits imposed by the Law for Defense of the Nation, the Sofia Diocese issued a confidential circular signed by Metropolitan Stefan, which encouraged the priests to baptize Jews who wanted to convert to Christianity. It also determined the order of the procedure and warned that the ceremonies had to be performed without charging any money (Окръжно на Софийската Митрополия, 1940).

Other than the Church, many professional organizations that had Jewish members expressed their strong criticism of the new law. The influential Doctors' Union sent a critical letter to the government against the law on November 5, 1940, stating:

> "We are afraid that if the law is adopted, it will damage the good name and reputation of our tolerant and magnanimous nation, which have been preserved for centuries. Guided by those views and considering the known fact that the Bulgarian Jews have always been loyal citizens, the Bulgarian Doctors' Union, as a professional organization, cannot remain indifferent to the fate of its Jewish members, though we admit that the judicial contradictions between the proposed law and the Constitution are beyond its competence. First of all, the number of Jewish doctors in the country is extremely small compared to that of all doctors. There are 3,200 Bulgarian doctors in the whole Kingdom, as opposed to 146 Jewish doctors. 74 of them are in Sofia and the rest are scattered all over the country. Only 18 of them occupy government or municipal positions, so we can't even think of any negative influence on our public life caused by that miniscule number. Let's not forget that most of the few Jewish doctors in government positions are in village areas and their dismissal will harm people's health at a time when hundreds of such village positions are vacant and for various reasons are not taken by Bulgarians" (Изложение от БЛС против ЗЗН, 1940).

The Bulgarian Lawyers' Union also sent a letter on October 30, 1940. In it, its leadership emphasized the legal violations, especially the contradiction between the new law and the Constitution of Kingdom Bulgaria:

> "The proposed law introduces many significant and humiliating restrictions on the Jewish minority in Bulgaria. In his speech, the Minister [Gabrovski] doesn't explain the need of such a law in our country. On the contrary, we learn that he is

convinced that: "The Bulgarian state and the Bulgarian people have always strived and succeeded in preserving their national character. The Bulgarian state is fully national, and our nation has preserved its purity to a degree, which few countries in Europe could boast". So, if the Minister himself states that the Bulgarian state is fully national, and our nation has preserved its purity, there is no need to create a law that would restrict and degrade morally a category of Bulgarian citizens. The Jews in Bulgaria have not threatened our economy, culture or the purity of the Bulgarian nation. It would be an extreme mistake to claim that the Jews have some special influence on our spiritual, political and economic life. On the other hand, it will be unfair to say that the Jews don't fulfill their obligations as citizens. That is why we cannot find any justification, with regard to the interests of the state and the nation, in taking such limiting and humiliating measures against the Jewish minority in Bulgaria. Not only are they unjustified, but they also contradict to the democratic and free spirit of the Bulgarian people, who in the long and difficult period of the [Turkish] yoke and in times of bitterness and suffering have not seen the Jews in the camp of their enemies and oppressors...

"We must note that there are no professional reasons to restrict our Jewish colleagues. The Jewish lawyers have been, in general, good members of the organization, fulfilling their professional and moral obligations as lawyers...

"However, beyond anything said so far, the legal side of the question is the most important to us. The proposed legislation will be another blow against our Constitution, which specifically prohibits the division of the Bulgarian citizens into inferior and superior categories. All Bulgarian citizens are equal before the law (article 57). All Bulgarian citizens have political rights (to vote and be elected, to occupy civil and military positions, etc.), and all those who live in the Kingdom have civil rights, i.e. all rights covered by the civil law (article 60). How can you match these and other texts from our Constitution with the proposed restrictions on the Jewish minority in Bulgaria? It is obvious that the Constitution has been violated, and the ministers and members of the parliament must prevent that, because they have given an oath to preserve and defend the Constitution. Considering all that, we ask you to abandon the proposed law, which is unnecessary, harmful to society and against our judicial rules and justice" (Изложение от СБА против ЗЗН, 1940).

The plans to introduce the new discriminatory law reached

quickly the ordinary people who were also outraged. Many telegrams have been preserved in the archives, sent by craftsmen, carpenters, tailors, cobblers, bakers and others to the Royal Palace and the government. The dominant argument in their criticism was that Bulgaria was known as a tolerant country and the restriction of the rights of the Jews was disgraceful and contradictory to the traditions of the country (Телеграми от занаятчии против ЗЗН, 1940).

The Bulgarian pharmacists were a curious exception from the almost unanimous condemnation of the anti-Jewish laws. In 1941, the government introduced a special law that liquidated the Jewish pharmacies. They were not closed but rather placed under government control. That caused a storm of protests from Bulgarian pharmacists, but they were not protesting the confiscation. They were upset by the fact that the government now owned pharmacies that competed directly with the private Bulgarian pharmacies and the latter could be driven out of business. The protesters demanded that the government concessions be given only to Bulgarian pharmacists (Телеграми от аптекари, 1941-1942).

Despite the protests, the law passed in the early 1940. However, as it often happens in Bulgaria, the implementation of its provisions was inconsistent. For example, the restrictions affecting Jewish professionals didn't work as expected. "Occupations were distributed only among the major cities with Jewish population; Sofia, Plovdiv, Ruse, Varna, and some others. Yet many Jewish professionals, businessmen, and merchants were able to keep on with their work despite the quotas, even in restricted areas. Because the need for doctors was so great, the government impressed displaced Jewish doctors into service under the Law for Civilian Mobilization, requiring them to practice in the cities or in small villages. They also mobilized key industrialists, veterinarians, dentists, and others" (Chary, 1972, p. 42).

One of the provisions of the ZZN in Article 25 was that the Jews had to register their wealth. It wasn't explained why, but a few months later, a new legislation took advantage of the registration. It was a law for charging the Jews with a one-time tax, based on the amount of their wealth. "Minister of Finance Dobri Bozhilov stated that the chief reason for proposing this tax was the debt the Jews owed Bulgaria for "over sixty years of exploitation." The Subranie [People's Assembly] enacted a law which required the Jews to submit to the Ministry of Finance a statement of their total wealth within seven days after the law's publication. (They had already registered their property under the ZZN.) All Jews with property valued over 200,000 leva ($2,430) were subject to the tax: 20 percent on property valued above 200,000 leva but under 3 million leva ($36,500), and 25 percent on property valued above 3 million leva. The law applied to all Jewish property in Bulgaria regardless of the citizenship of the owners, and Bulgarian Jews abroad were also liable to the tax" (Chary, 1972, p. 43). The acquired money from this tax and other expropriations was later placed under the control of the Commissariat for the Jewish Questions in the fund "Jewish Communities", which was supposed to cover the needs of the displaced Bulgarian Jews.

In his memoirs, the Zionist activist Yako Baruh recalled the effects of those harsh laws. All Jews practicing some free professions, like pharmacists, small merchants, artists, actors, an so on, had to stop working and the pharmacies and small stores had to be liquidated. Within a short time, those enterprises were given, under different arrangements, to Bulgarians and in some cases the Jewish owners continued to work for them, controlling the business secretly. Other categories of free professions, like lawyers, were allowed to operate but only among Jews.

Further, Baruh notes that the commerce ventures were also restricted to operating only among Jews. "Others had to find their own way to operate, either by liquidation or as joint ventures with Bulgarian merchants. Many Jews found Bulgarians without capital and created joint ventures by giving them part of their capitals and under various arrangements established nominally Bulgarian businesses with people who, in rare cases, had commercial experience, but most often had little knowledge of business. In these business combinations as well, the Jewish merchants gave some of the capitals to their Bulgarian partners, thus buying their names.

"Very few Bulgarian Jewish merchants liquidated their enterprises and most often formed different combinations, for which it was always easy to find willing Bulgarians. These joint ventures were popular in the industrial businesses and factories owned by Jews, when the latter sometimes provided, with or without payment, portion of the shares they owned" (Барух, Спомени 1941-1943, p. 10).

Germany wasn't satisfied with the half-hearted anti-Jewish policies of the Bulgarian government. The reason were Hitler's evolving ideas for solution of the "Jewish Question". In the early years, the Nazis were inclined to expel the Jews from Germany and the occupied territories. England's White Paper of 1939 severely restricted Jewish immigration to Palestine, so that venue was closed. The idea of Goering and others to send all Jews to Madagascar could not be implemented, see (Memorandum on Expulsion of Jews to Madagascar, 1940, p.154-155). After the invasion of the Soviet Union, with its millions of Jews, the goal switched from expulsion to extermination. The Wannsee Conference of January 20, 1942, outlined the mechanism of that new policy. That increased the pressure on Bulgaria.

In December 1941, the Nazis decided to increase the pressure on the European countries for resolving the Jewish Question, as this memorandum, issued in preparation for the Wannsee Conference states:

> "DESIRES AND IDEAS OF THE FOREIGN OFFICE IN CONNECTION WITH THE INTENDED TOTAL SOLUTION OF THE JEWISH QUESTION IN EUROPE
> 1. Deportation to the East of all Jews residing in the German Reich, inclusive of those who live in Croatia, Slovakia, and Rumania.
> 2. Deportation of all Jews living in the territories occupied by us who were formerly German citizens but lost their citizenship and are now stateless in accordance with the latest supplementary decree to the Reich Citizenship Law.
> 3. Deportation of all Serbian Jews.
> 4. Deportation of the Jews handed over to us by the Hungarian Government.
> 5. To declare our readiness to the Rumanian, Slovakian, Croatian, Bulgarian, and Hungarian Governments, to deport to the East the Jews living in these countries.
> 6. To influence the Bulgarian and Hungarian Governments to issue laws concerning Jews similar to the Nuernberg Laws" (Desires for Solution of the Jewish Question, 1941, p. 198).

In June 1942, the Bulgarian Government introduced a new law giving extraordinary powers for resolving the Jewish Question. A new agency - Commissariat for the Jewish Questions (Komisarstvo za evreiskite vaprosi, KEV) was created. It had very broad powers. It was expected to organize the deportation of the Jews to Germany. As its first Commissar was appointed Alexander Belev, an employee of the Ministry of the Interior and a staunch anti-Semite, trusted by the Germans. His presence in Germany during the Wannsee Conference was a sign that the Nazi Government wanted to prepare him to implement the "final solution" in

Bulgaria. Many people in Bulgaria were convinced that Belev was a German agent. Although he was born in Bulgaria and had a Bulgarian father, his mother was Italian, and according to some rumors, she had Jewish background.

Thank to a testimony at the People's Tribunal in 1945, we can get a glimpse at the inner workings of the new Commissariat. The witness was Svetoslav Petrov Nikolov, former inspector in the Commissariat for Jewish Questions.

He was appointed about a month after the institution was established on October 1, 1942. At the time, most of the people working there had no clear idea about its purpose. They were doing no real work and were just studying the laws about the Jewish Question. Nikolov did the same for about 15 days. The first thing they did, was to create the so-called "ghetto" – asking Jews to leave their homes and move. Belev's Deputy Pencho Lukov was in charge of sending the invitations asking the Jews to move:

> "People's Prosecutor Rahamimov: Tell us about the employees that worked diligently for the anti-Semitic actions and their motives.
>
> "Svetoslav Petrov Nikolov: Everybody's work was very slow because it was not clear what the new institution was supposed to do. They didn't understand the tasks, which Belev, as a person who inspired the Commissariat, had in mind. Belev expected them to show initiative but they didn't know what to do. He was often irritated by the situation and treated them in a very rude way. Eventually, he adopted a different tactic – he started writing leaflets with tasks that were distributed every day. We called them "butterflies". They were typed by Miss Panitsa, everybody got them.
>
> "R.: Which employees with anti-Semitic views took the initiative?
>
> "N.: Everything was slow, if anything started to move, it was because of the inner drive that Belev had for his work. He was extremely nervous, dynamic, even demonic.
>
> "R.: Then, why did you endure that harassment for so many years? You refused to go to Thrace and Macedonia [for the deportation].
>
> "N.: I didn't like the action and used my mobilization in the anti-aircraft defense force to get away.
>
> "R.: Did you understand that action?
>
> "N.: Yes, I did. I assumed that most of my colleagues did as well and they didn't go there enthusiastically, but they were civil servants and the whole personnel of the Commissariat was

civilly mobilized.

"R.: Then how would you explain the cruelty of the Commissariat? Where their representatives were absent, the Jews could keep their money, but when they were there, they took everything.

"N.: It was a result of the strict orders that everybody received.

"R.: Were those orders legal? Did ZZN say that the Jews must be deported within half an hour?

"N.: The orders were illegal.

"R.: Then why did they follow them?

"N.: In defense of the workers there, I can say that there were cases of objections to Belev's orders that they saw as illegitimate. For example, Lukov refused to sign many letters that he thought were illegal.

"R.: Then why did Lukov take such an active role in the deportations of 12,000 Jews? If he thought it was illegal, he would have refused.

"N.: He came from the judicial system, former prosecutor. He thought that every civil servant had to follow his obligations. But he also arranged the use of the Bulgarian Railways because of personal connections with the ministry. He managed to provide enough trains, had he not done it, the Jews would have been exposed to more hardships...

"R.: Did they have many Ratniks in the Commissariat?

"N.: Yes.

"R.: Why did that happen?

"N.: Belev wanted to surround himself with trusted people. He was disappointed by most of the personnel. He felt that they blackmailed him and didn't collaborate with him. Being a Ratnik, he attracted to the institution other members and thought that he could rely on them in the future measures against Jews."

Then Rahamimov asked for the names of Ratniks that worked in the Commissariat, Nikolov mentioned a few people, but added that the organization was secret, and it wasn't clear who belonged to it.

"R.: What was the role of [Miss] Panitsa?

"N.: Before, she worked at the Ministry of the Interior, but Belev needed a trusted person and hired her.

"R.: Why?

"N.: I don't know, but he thought she could keep secrets. Pavlova, he didn't trust, she was often hostile toward him. She didn't trust the Ratniks and thought they took bribes. She was rude, but to everybody.

"R.: To the Jews?

"N.: To Jews and lawyers as well, but that was a character flaw resulting from her upbringing. A friend of her told me she behaved the same way since her student years. Sometimes, she was rude even to me. There was corruption in the Commissariat, but it was done in secret.

"R: Who of the workers took bribes?

"N.: It was thought all of them. I had reports about some cases, but after one of them, he [Belev] yelled at me and wanted me to resign. For example, one of his appointees was registered at the police for 5-6 robberies, I wanted to charge him, but Belev refused, he didn't want the public to know of those employees.

"R.: Was the institution corrupt?

"N.: I had that impression – you probably know that the Jews were in a situation that forced them to look for favors by all means. So, some delivered those favors.

"R.: What do you know about Serdica Bank?

"N.: During my investigations of the corruption, after Belev didn't take measures to fight it, I continued my work and found out about Serdica Bank. When Belev was still working at the Ministry of the Interior, together with [Minister] Gabrovski, they removed the whole board of the bank, as required by the ZZN, because its members supposedly had progressive views. Then, Belev was appointed as an interim director of the bank. During that short period, a few hundred Ratniks were recruited; they showed up for the first annual meeting and took control over the bank, which at that time had 90 million leva in shares and 15 million leva in deposits. The Ratniks were planning to take over other banks in the same way, since they needed them. After Belev became the chairman of the bank, without any legal justification, he transferred 18 million leva from fund "Jewish Communities" to Serdica Bank, even though those funds were supposed to be held in state banks. I had information that, as a chairman, Belev provided unlimited credit to his Ratniks friends, who, as members of various trade organizations, appeared at auctions for liquidation of Jewish businesses to buy the firms or their shares. Following these investigations, I prepared a secret report to the then Prime Minster [Dobri] Bozhilov. It reached the government and they initiated an audit of Serdica Bank. I don't know the result, but when there was a financial audit of the Commissariat, we found out that the 18 million leva were returned from Serdica to the Jewish fund. Moreover, Belev and Gabrovski, at certain point, ordered that the proceeds from the liquidation of Jewish firms be deposited in Serdica Bank.

"R.: That was obviously illegal. How did the bank use the 18 million leva?

"N.: As I said, I suspected that the Ratniks pursued their political goals through the bank. Maybe the people at the top, like Belev and Gabrovski, wanted to profit from the liquidation of the Jewish properties. That was my guess. I wasn't allowed to investigate the accounts of Serdica Bank and I don't know the result of the audit, but I know that a businessman, a close friend of Belev, received 2 million leva, then another 4 million. They probably had a certain goal. All my findings were reported to the Filov government. Then Bozhilov dealt with them. The Commissariat and Serdica were audited, the Directory of the Police got involved, but the process wasn't completed, and no one was charged. And in the end, after they found out that Belev wasn't as selfless as he presented himself, they fired him, but in order to save his reputation and his career, they made him a District Director in the Ministry of the Interior, so not many noticed his dismissal from the Commissariat" (People's Court Session No.14, 1945, p. 937-953).

In his memoirs, Yako Baruh explained that the budget of the Commissariat, with its large apparatus, had to be covered by the Jews themselves by creating a fund that received revenue from the one-time percentage tax of the blocked money of Jews, "specifically, 5% on sums up to 100,000 leva, 8% on up to 300,000, 10% on up to 1,000,000, and 12% on over 1,000,000. Since the blocked money of a person were often not in the same bank, the percentages were not applied properly because there was no time to investigate and centralize the sums, so they decided to charge everybody 12% with the intention to refund in the future the overcharged amounts. Naturally, that never happened" (Барух, Спомени 1941-1943, p. 14).

However, the inconsistent behavior of the Bulgarians regarding implementing that law, puzzled the Germans who were used to having unity behind the leadership of the Fuehrer. The lack of a charismatic dictatorial figure in Bulgaria made things difficult for the promotion of anti-Semitism. "Opposition to the more extreme laws developed also among the leaders of the government, whose actions sometimes differed from their words. Perhaps the most striking example was that of Gabrovski, the Minister of the Interior, who had been a sponsor of the anti-Jewish legislation. In September 1942, a group of 350 Jews gathered in front of the Ministry to protest its recent decisions. Gabrovski saw them from his office and invited them into the courtyard where, to everyone's surprise, he talked to them for half an hour. The worst was over, he said, and they had no need to worry, for the government had foreseen everything. Then he stood at the gate and personally reassured each of the delegates that there was no danger. This incident caused consternation among the Germans and in the anti-Semitic Commissariat for Jewish Affairs. That same day, Gabrovski ordered the Bulgarian newspapers to make no mention of the Jewish question or the activities of the Commissariat; the situation was already determined, he said, and there was no point in alarming the people. He and Justice Minister Partov also informed Alexander Belev, the head of the Commissariat, that the Court and the Council of Ministers wanted some moderation in the action taken against the Jews; hence the Tsar had still not signed the law restricting the Jews to certain theaters and taverns. Moreover, the Secretary of the Royal Court, Stanislav Balan, acting on orders of the Tsar himself, interceded directly with the Commissariat on behalf of a sick Jew who lived near the Tsar's summer palace" (Miller, 1975, p. 97-98).

The extremists from Ratnik were aware of that and did not like it, a circular that criticized the government for its insufficient work for resolving the Jewish Question, is included in the end of this book.

In September 1942, the Deputy State Secretary of the German Ministry of Foreign Affairs Martin Luther, sent a secret report to Minister Joachim von Ribbentrop about the situation of the Jewish Question in Bulgaria. It expressed concern that the King still maintained ties with the Jews and quoted as an example the greeting from the Central Consistory of the Jews in Bulgaria regarding the birthday of Crown Prince Simeon in 1942, to which the King replied (the exchange was mentioned in Chapter 7).

The telegram caused concerns among the nationalists. On the other hand, the report continued, a new law was introduced that gave more powers to the Bulgarian Government. It provided the definition of Jew, forced the Jews to wear a star, limited their economic influence by liquidation of the Jewish enterprises for good. "A special Commissariat that has not been established yet will arrange all these questions in detail. The blocked Jewish capital will maintain a fund designed for covering expenses of moving the Jews to special places and camps. The formed Jewish communities are the starting stage of the emigration or to dispersing the Jews.

These evacuation plans encouraged the Central Security Service of the Reich to ask the question whether the Reich should intervene and offer its services to the Bulgarian Government, which has shown its interest in the evacuation... The new measures make it possible to assume that the Bulgarian Government will accept voluntarily the German offer to finance the expulsion of the Jews" (Секретна записка от Мартин Лутер до Рибентроп, 1942). It was clear that the Germans were increasing the pressure again and that is how they eventually managed to establish successfully Belev's Commissariat that was going to play an important role in the fate of the Bulgarian Jews.

The crucial role of the German pressure on introducing the anti-Jewish policies in Bulgaria was recognized by activists and politicians who were opposed to the government before the communist coup of September 9, 1944. Several witnesses made such statements during the proceedings of the section of the People's Tribunal in 1945, which dealt with the anti-Semitic crimes.

Grigor Cheshmedjiev was a socialist, member of the Bulgarian Worker's Social-Democratic Party and a parliamentarian from 1919 to 1944. In 1945, he was the Minister of Social Policies in the first government after the Soviet occupation in 1944. He said in his testimony:

> "I think that the Law for Defense of the Nation, the anti-Jewish law, would not have been created without the Hitlerite agents in Bulgaria. Without any doubt, the law was introduced either by suggestion or direct influence from abroad, and I guess, what was happening in Germany also influenced that matter, especially their sermons about the so-called racial differences, pure races, etc. Before the law, the highest echelons of the government were contemplating that we needed to introduce a law against Jews, for the purity of the Bulgarian nation, in order to impress the Germans. I think, in that sense, we, the Bulgarians, went too far with the desire to be liked by the Germans, because, according to the information from Italy, the nest of fascism, which started there in 1921, they did not introduce such laws for persecuting Jews" (People's Court Session No.9, 1945, p. 756).

The Jewish communist activist Isac Fransez, after September 1944, became the Commissar for the Jewish Questions. He made a statement at the hearing:

"CHAIRMAN: If we were not occupied by the Germans, don't you think that the Bulgarian public opinion would have been more assertive, raising voice in the streets of Sofia?

FRANSEZ: Definitely; the Bulgarian people have totally different feelings from those, who are standing trial here, and their supporters. I have no doubt about that, because otherwise we would not have had faith in our struggle, it would have been lost before we started it. But the realization that the progressive Bulgarian people supported us, gave us courage and faith in the future. We, all Jews, regardless of class status, knew that the Bulgarian people were not anti-Semitic, and we felt it in our daily lives. If it were not for that state anti-Semitism, imposed from above, we would have had equal rights. Those at the top had no base among the common people, so they introduced it through government measures. In other countries, the anti-Semitism came from the masses, but that was not the case in our country" (People's Court Session No.9, 1945, p. 783).

The war hero Colonel Avram Tadjer was asked the same question:

"CHAIRMAN: What is your impression, if we were not occupied by the Germans, would such laws be created in Bulgaria? Could they be introduced without German occupation?

TADJER: There were here organizations like Ratniks, Legionnaires... These laws would not have been introduced, because the Bulgarian public opinion was so strong that it would not have yielded" (People's Court Session No.9, 1945, p. 824).

Meanwhile, Jews continued to leave countries that were threatened by the Nazi plans. Many of them had to go through the territory of Bulgaria, which was on the itinerary toward British Palestine, which despite the limitations of the White Paper of 1939, still provided some hope for survival. Often, the desperate Jewish refugees used ships and boats in Black Sea.

One of those boats was involved in the worst disaster involving Jews near Bulgarian territory (the boat was sailing under Panamanian flag but most of its crew were Bulgarians). The boat was 74 years old, its engine was old and faulty, there was no kitchen, the food was insufficient, it had only one toilet and primitive berths. The boat left the Romanian port of Constanta on December 12, 1941, on the way to Bosporus. It had onboard 781

Jewish passengers, about 100 of them children, and a crew of 10.

> "The Bulgarian crew did not appear to have any of the professional skills of seamen. Within a few hours the engine failed and for an entire day it drifted slowly until a Romanian vessel responded to its distress signal. The captain, for a fee of three million lei, which the passengers paid in jewelry and cash, made temporary repairs to the engine which lasted until the Struma reached the Bosporus on 14 December where it broke down again.
> "On the following day, it drifted towards a minefield and was taken in tow by a Turkish ship to Istanbul and placed in quarantine. At dawn on 23 February, ten weeks after it had been nursed into Istanbul, the captain of the Struma, a Bulgarian national, was ordered by the Turkish coastguard to set sail for the Black Sea. The captain refused, and the refugees joined his protest by hanging out bed-sheets with the letters "S.O.S" painted on them. Over the sides of the boat they draped signs in French with the words "Jewish immigrants" and "Save us!" The Turkish patrol boat withdrew but came back with 150 armed police who boarded the Struma and forced the passengers below decks. The Struma was then taken under tow and released into open waters. Just before dawn, some seven miles from land, it was torpedoed and sank. Almost twenty-four hours passed before Turkish boats arrived on the scene but by then they found only one survivor, David Stoliar. Stoliar was allowed to enter Palestine two months later, after recuperating in a Turkish military hospital. It was only after 1990 that access to Soviet archives confirmed that a Soviet submarine had mistakenly identified the Struma as an enemy vessel and fired the fateful torpedo" (Deletant, 2012, p. 89-90).

Ironically, the actions of the Russian Allies were the cause of the deaths of 791 people, 781 of them were Jews. If we add the victims of bombings of Sofia and other towns and villages in 1943-1944, it was the Allies that killed on Bulgarian territory so many people, whom they were expected to protect.

Great Britain also played role in this tragedy. The ship Struma was stopped by the Turks under British pressure, because the refugees onboard did not have visas for Mandate Palestine. The country that was authorized by the League of Nations to prepare the territory as a "Jewish home", did not change its policies after the tragedy. On the contrary, "on March 5, 1942 the British War Cabinet responded to the Struma sinking by reaffirming its decision not to allow "illegal" Jewish refugees admission to Palestine" (Groth, 2011, p. 151).

The new laws were just the beginning of the grave problems for the Jews in Bulgaria and other countries in the area. The Wannsee Conference, held in Berlin in January 1942, marked a fundamental change in the Jewish policies of the Nazis. While before they were willing to expel the Jews from Europe, the new approach was to exterminate them. The conference collected the statistics of the Jewish population in Europe (48,000 in Bulgaria) and planned its gradual destruction. It was supposed to start from the countries or territories under Nazi Germany's influence or occupation.

10 DANNECKER, BELEV AND THE JEWS IN THRACE AND MACEDONIA

The tragic fate of nearly 12,000 Jews in the occupied Macedonia and Aegean Thrace, who were detained and transported to the German concentration camps in Poland, is one of the highly contested events in the recent Balkan history. As I mentioned elsewhere, an objective and impartial treatment of that history is practically impossible, because every event involves the diametrically opposing views of the sides involved, often based on older events that predetermine the behavior of the participants.

In this case, during the last two decades, there is a trend to blame Bulgaria for the events, supported by certain circles in Greece, Serbia and the newly-established state of Macedonia. Digging deeper, we will find that the animosities are rooted in older events, like the pro-Bulgarian liberation movement in Macedonia in the early 20th century, while the territory was occupied first by Turkey and then by Greece. The hostilities erupted again during the Second Balkan War of 1913, when Bulgaria was the target of Greek military atrocities, which were investigated in the "Report of the International Commission to Inquire into the Causes and Conduct of the Balkan Wars", quoted in Chapter 6 (Report on Balkan Wars, 1914). That was followed by an ethnic cleansing of the Bulgarian-speaking population in the area by both Yugoslavia and Greece between the two world wars. The tensions did not subside, and World War II only worsened the situation.

From that point of view, it is important to figure out the big picture. Was Bulgaria a country that had a significant control over the "new territories"? What was its involvement in the events of March-April 1943?

Due to its strategic position, Bulgaria was a key country for the world powers that wanted to control the Balkans. We saw how in 1877-1878, the attempt by Russia to take control of the straits of the Sea of Marmara caused a clash with England, from which Bulgaria suffered. Many decades later, the situation was similar, with the Soviet Union trying to take control of the straits and prevent England from invading. Nazi Germany, the newer player, needed Bulgaria for the passage of its troops to Greece and as a buffer to a possible invasion of England. So, depending on the situation, Bulgaria was both courted and threatened by the powers that wanted to control it.

Although King Boris III wanted to keep neutrality, the pressure from both Germany and the Soviet Union was too strong. The so-called Sobolev Action in 1940, named after the envoy of Stalin's Government, was organized by communists to pressure the rulers of Bulgaria to sign a pact similar to the one signed between the USSR and Germany. The statement of the Soviet Government was that it didn't object to Bulgaria joining the Axis after signing the pact, it even suggested that the Soviet Union may also join it (Chary, 1972, p. 20). The "peace" between the two European powers made the communist movement passive. They avoided criticism of Germany, even though it persecuted Jews and communists.

The secret documents about the relations between Germany and the Soviet Union, uncovered after the war and published in 1948 in the book "Nazi-Soviet Relations 1939-1941: Documents from the Archives of the German Foreign Office", confirm the King's pessimistic view of the situation. There was not much that Bulgaria could do, because it was just a pawn in the supremacy games of the two world powers.

It was difficult to take the "friendship" offer of Sobolev in late 1940 when watching how the events unravelled in another small country that had a friendship agreement with the Soviet Union – Lithuania. The secret unpublished protocol to the infamous Treaty of Nonaggression Between Germany and the USSR of August 23, 1939, predetermined the fate of the Baltic states: "In the event of a territorial and political rearrangement in the areas belonging to the Baltic States (Finland, Estonia, Latvia, Lithuania), the northern boundary of Lithuania shall represent the boundary of the spheres of influence of Germany and the U.S.S.R. In this connection the interest of Lithuania in the Vilna area is recognized by each party" (Nazi-Soviet Relations, 1948, p. 78).

The Soviet Union stationed its army garrisons in Lithuania and shortly after that, started accusing the local government of mistreating the Soviet military, as a German Memorandum of June 11, 1940, about talks with Lithuania, shows: "The Lithuanian Minister called on me today to inform me of the further progress of the discussions with the Soviet Union. After the Soviet Union had raised the question of the safety of the Soviet garrisons in Lithuania and had rejected the suggestion for a mixed commission to investigate the incidents, the Lithuanian Government had of its own accord taken a series of measures which it thought would satisfy the Soviet Union, it might perhaps be admitted that relations between the Soviet garrisons and the Lithuanian population had earlier been treated too casually. Restrictive and control measures had now been taken, and many arrests and house searches made, etc. It was known that no reply was received to the Lithuanian suggestion of sending the Foreign Minister to Moscow. It was, therefore, all the more surprising that not the Foreign Minister but Minister President Merkys was summoned to Moscow.

> "On June 7 Merkys had had his first conversation with Molotov. The latter had reproached him severely regarding the safety of the Soviet garrisons and, in this connection presented a great many detailed incidents. Molotov had in particular maintained persistently that Butayeff, a member of the Red Army, who according to Lithuanian reports had committed suicide, had been shot by Lithuanians. He had expressed his dissatisfaction very plainly and stressed that the Lithuanian Ministry of the Interior was not equal to its task" (Nazi-Soviet Relations, 1948, p.146).

It was just a prelude to a more serious action against the tiny country. In a telegram of June 16, 1940, the Foreign Minister Joachim von Ribbentrop alerted the border authorities that the Lithuanian President Smetona, with his family and other functionaries, has crossed the "green frontier" and upon entering Germany, the group was interned by the Gestapo. There were also requests from Lithuanian troop contingents to cross the German border, which were considered and were about to be granted, after the troops were disarmed. To avoid a conflict with the Soviet Union, the State Police had to take "measures necessary so that the border posts concerned may be immediately informed. It is again pointed out that border crossings are to be permitted only upon request of the Lithuanians and that we, for our part, must not do anything to encourage such requests... Ribbentrop" (Nazi-Soviet Relations, 1948, p. 150).

In the later Soviet historical literature, the events that put an end to the three Baltic states, were presented as a socialist revolution that miraculously happened at the same time in all three of them. After the "revolution", the working people spontaneously demanded a unification with the Soviet Union. Probably the same was planned for Bulgaria, which shortly thereafter became the subject of bickering between Germany and the Soviet Union.

In the further communications between the two, it becomes clear that they want to prevent jointly England from taking over the straits of the Sea of Marmara. In a Memorandum of the talks between Ribbentrop and the Soviet Prime Minister V. Molotov on November 13, 1940, it was stated that Germany, Italy, and Japan, on one side, and the Soviet Union, on the other, agreed to prevent further war and "respect each other's natural spheres of influence. In so far as these spheres of influence come into contact with each other, they will constantly consult each other in an amicable way with regard to the problems arising therefrom" (Nazi-Soviet Relations, 1948, p.248-249).

In a conversation between the German Ambassador in Moscow Schulenburg and Molotov on November 26, 1940, the latter demanded additional conditions to the agreement discussed on November 13, which included German withdrawal from Finland, which the Soviet Union considered part of its sphere of influence. The second condition involved Bulgaria: "Provided that within the next few months the security of the Soviet Union in the Straits is assured by the conclusion of a mutual assistance pact between the Soviet Union and Bulgaria, which geographically is situated inside the security zone of the Black Sea boundaries of the Soviet Union, and by the establishment of a base for land and naval forces of the U.S.S.R. within range of the Bosporus and the Dardanelles by means of a long-term lease." Molotov also proposed a new secret protocol to the agreement: "c) a fifth secret protocol between Germany, the Soviet Union, and Italy, recognizing that Bulgaria is geographically located inside the security zone of the Black Sea boundaries of the Soviet Union and that it is therefore a political necessity that a mutual assistance pact be concluded between the Soviet Union and Bulgaria, which in no way shall affect the internal regime of Bulgaria, her sovereignty or independence."

(Nazi-Soviet Relations, 1948, p.258). Similar clause in the agreement with Lithuania did not prevent the Russians from annexing it.

At the peak of the German pressure on Bulgaria to let the Nazi army through the country on its way to Greece, the Soviet Ambassador in Berlin handed a memorandum from the Soviet Government on January 17, 1941, to the German Foreign Ministry:

> "According to all reports, German troops in great numbers are in Rumania and are now prepared to march into Bulgaria, having as their goal the occupation of Bulgaria, Greece, and the Straits. There can be no doubt that England will try to forestall the operations of German troops, to occupy the Straits, to start military operations against Bulgaria in alliance with Turkey and turn Bulgaria into a theater of operations. The Soviet Government has stated repeatedly to the German Government that it considers the territory of Bulgaria and of the Straits as the security zone of the U.S.S.R. and that it cannot be indifferent to events which threaten the security interests of the U.S.S.R. In view of all this the Soviet Government regards it as its duty to give warning that it will consider the appearance of any foreign armed forces on the territory of Bulgaria and of the Straits as a violation of the security interests of the U.S.S.R." (Nazi-Soviet Relations, 1948, p.268).

The German Foreign Ministry responded on January 21, 1941 through State Secretary von Weizsacker:

> "Germany does not intend to occupy the Straits. She will respect the territory under Turkish sovereignty unless Turkey on her part commits a hostile act against German troops. On the other hand, however, the German Army will march through Bulgarian territory should any military operations be carried out against Greece. The Reich Government has, of course, no intention of violating any Soviet Russian security interests nor would this by any means be the case if German troops march through Bulgaria" (Nazi-Soviet Relations, 1948, p.271).

On March 1, 1941, the day Bulgaria signed the Three-Partite Pact and the German troops entered the country, the German Ambassador Schulenburg was summoned by Molotov who expressed a strong displeasure of the situation. Schulenburg wrote to the Foreign Ministry:

"Molotov, who received my communication with great gravity, stated first of all that he was informed regarding the German decision, since the Bulgarian Minister had today already apprised Herr Vishinsky. Molotov thereupon expressed his deep concern that the German Government had, in a matter of such importance to the Soviet Government, made decisions contrary to the Soviet Government's conception of the security interests of the Soviet Union. The Soviet Government had repeatedly stressed its special interest in Bulgaria to the German Government, both during the Berlin conferences and later. Consequently, it could not remain indifferent in the face of Germany's last measures in Bulgaria and would have to define its attitude with regard thereto.

"It hoped that the German Reich Government would attach the proper significance to this attitude. Molotov in my presence drafted in his own hand a rough memorandum setting forth the position of the Soviet Government, had it copied, and handed it to me. The text of the note is as follows:

"1. It is to be regretted that despite the caution contained in the demarche of November 25, 1940, on the part of the Soviet Government, the German Reich Government has deemed it possible to take a course that involves injury to the security interests of the U.S.S.R. and has decided to effect the military occupation of Bulgaria. (emphasis mine – M.M.)

"2. In view of the fact that the Soviet Government maintains the same basic position as in its demarche of November 25, the German Government must understand that it cannot count on support from the U.S.S.R. for its acts in Bulgaria" SCHULENBURG (Nazi-Soviet Relations, 1948, p.278-279).

Later that month, on March 28, in a memorandum about the talks between Ribbentrop and the Japanese Foreign Minister Matsuoka, it was stated about the Soviet zone of influence demands: "But when the Finns defended themselves so valiantly against the Russians, strong feeling for them sprang up in Germany, so that it was now impossible to give up Finland, since an occupation by Russia would lead to complete destruction of the country, as was shown by the example of the Baltic States. The second Russian condition dealt with the guarantee to Bulgaria, together with occupation of the country by Russian troops, concerning which he had already been informed in detail in the earlier conversations" (Nazi-Soviet Relations, 1948, p. 304).

It is clear that both Germany and the Soviet Union saw Bulgaria as a territory to be occupied. However, most of the Bulgarian politicians were unaware of all that. On the surface, it looked like both powers agreed about common goals.

Germany had an urgent need to take control of the territory of Bulgaria and was ready to enter a confrontation with the Russians due to the tense situation in Greece. In the late 1940, Mussolini's forces invaded Greece, hoping for an easy victory, but things became difficult. Because of the British guarantees for support of Greece, Hitler was worried of them getting involved, so he needed a passage through Bulgaria to help his ally. The German pressure on Bulgaria increased tremendously, despite the reluctance of King Boris. (As it was stated in the Memoirs of Queen Ioanna, quoted in a previous chapter, they were determined to get in either as friends or invaders.) That difficult situation was documented in the diary of Prof. Filov, who noted that after his meeting with Hitler on January 4, 1941, the King said that he preferred to abdicate or to go with Russia, despite the Bolshevization. It was clear that the Germans didn't treat Bulgaria with respect – the German Army entered Bulgaria on March 1, 1941, at 12:01 p.m., while the Axis treaty was signed the same day at 4:30 p.m. Even worse – the People's Assembly was called to debate and ratify the treaty on March 2, after the German troops had already crossed the country (Ташев, p. 7).

Still, the situation created the impression that Germany and the USSR were close friends. The Bulgarian MP Georgi Lipovanski, from the government majority, was in his riding in the first days of March 1941, shortly after Bulgaria signed the Three-Partite Axis agreement and the German troops entered the country. He testified at the People's Tribunal in 1944 that the Bulgarian population greeted the Germans. Local peasants, coming from the nearby railway stations, told him that they saw in the German trucks sacks with Russian oats marked in Russian; they also saw barrels inscribed in Russian. The locals were happy that there was mutual understanding between Russia and Bulgaria and that Germany was getting Russian help. The reason for the joy was that Russia and Germany were allies. Many people with leftist views in his riding were also glad to see the Germans, they thought that because of the alliance, Bulgaria would not fight, and it could get back some of the lost lands, the way Dobrudja was returned. When Lipovanski went back to Sofia and shared his impressions with Prime Minister Filov, the latter ensured him that the country will keep complete neutrality and stay out of the war. At the time, it seemed that even Yugoslavia would join the Axis, which it did, but left it after the coup in March 1941.

Lipovanski added further that during the discussions in the People's Assembly on March 2, 1941, it was made clear that the Germans demanded both actions at the same time – joining the Axis and allowing the German troops into the country. He had a talk with another MP, the communist Poliakov, and asked him what the communists were going to do. Poliakov replied: "We did not receive an order and can't support or reject the agreement, but for you, the situation is clear. The most important is that Germany and Russia have mutual understanding." So, Lipovanski concluded that being part of the Axis was not something unusual (Народен съд, разпит на Георги Липовански, 1944, p. 249-250).

Another hasty decision, made under German pressure, was that Bulgaria declared a "symbolic war" against Great Britain and the USA, which had catastrophic consequences a few years later. At a session of the People's Assembly in early March 1941, Prof. Filov announced that since Bulgaria was already part of the Axis, it declared war on Great Britain and the USA. Lipovanski testified that the statement caused confusion and fear among the MPs, the effect was like a bomb, many asked how this could happen, even though the government ensured them that the war was symbolic. They were upset that such potentially fatal decisions could be made without the approval of the Parliament. He would have never voted for it; that was the most fatal mistake of the Government. Another MP told him that the German Ambassador Beckerle called Prof. Filov and strongly demanded such a decision, saying that all members of the Axis have declared war on those two countries. Then Lipovanski contacted a high-ranking employee at the Royal Palace and asked him: "The King is a reasonable person; how could he make such a mistake?" He replied: "There was a strong pressure from Beckerle and his circle. The King resisted for three days and finally surrendered. Then he didn't talk to us for another three days, upset that he made a mistake. That's why he later died, he could never overcome the guilt of that mistake." (Народен съд, разпит на Георги Липовански, 1944, p. 252-253).

Beckerle confirmed that fact years later during his capture in the Soviet Union. In an interrogation protocol of March 23, 1945, he stated: "I demanded from the Bulgarian Government through the Foreign Minister Popov to declare war on England and the USA, according to the obligations they had assumed by joining the Three-Partite Pact. The Bulgarian Government announced that it was in the state of war with England and America" (Тайны дипломатии Третьего рейха, p. 49).

It is important to note here that at this point, every decision about the political and military affiliation of Bulgaria was made under external pressure. Germany forced its invasion without offering any territorial incentives. Other than the invasion of Greece, the status quo in the Balkans remained the same. There were no talks about redistribution of any territories. It looked like Yugoslavia had also joined the alliance by signing the Three-Partite Treaty in March. However, the military coup in Belgrade against the supporters of Germany drastically changed the situation. Unable to resist Hitler's rage, Yugoslavia quickly collapsed after the Germans invaded it on April 6, 1941.

After the collapse of the Kingdom of Yugoslavia and the stationing of the Nazi Army there, the so-called "Einsatzgruppen" began their activities. "The need to free German troops from the area to send them to the Eastern Front, leads to sending Bulgarian troops and administration to the occupied lands. However, they are not independent. In a message, dated April 23, 1941, the Commander of the German Army defines them as "Bulgarian forces under German command." There was no official document allowing the annexation of Vardar Macedonia and the Aegean region by Bulgaria. The Bulgarian troops and administration entered the region according to the agreement between Clodius and Popov of April 24, 1941. Its text shows that the Bulgarian Government has taken only obligations that guarantee the rights of the Germans in the occupied Macedonia, Thrace and Morava region, which were called "areas conceded to Bulgaria". There were no details about the conditions of the transfer; nothing was said about the rights of Bulgaria in the area, other than the note that they will be discussed after the war. The agreement guaranteed the presence of the German Army in the region at the expense of Bulgaria. In article 5, a possibility was mentioned – to allow workers from the former Yugoslav territories to continue to work in Germany in the future. The researcher of the problem of the Bulgarian presence in the Aegean region during World War II, Hans-Joachim Hoppe, thinks that this meant "recruitment of workers for Germany" ... While the returning of Dobrudja in 1940 happened through an international treaty, the territorial gains in 1941 were of military nature and not a single country in the world, including Germany, recognized them" (Ташев, p. 8).

Recruiting people for paid work in Germany was one of the tasks of the German diplomats. In the interrogation protocol of March 23, 1945, Beckerle confirmed it: "In 1941, at a request from Berlin, I managed to mobilize in Bulgaria labor force for work at factories in Germany. In accordance with my demand, they mobilized about 40,000 Bulgarians that I sent to Germany" (Тайны дипломатии Третьего рейха, p. 51). The German Embassy's adviser Anton Mohrmann was doing the same, according to his interrogation on February 26, 1945:

> "As of the negotiations to send Bulgarian workers to Germany, I participated in them directly with the Bulgarian Minister of Trade Zagorov (replaced later by Zahariev) who was authorized to resolve such questions and negotiated with him the necessary number of workers to be sent to Germany. Following my agreement with the Bulgarian Ministers, several thousand Bulgarian citizens were sent to Germany" (Тайны дипломатии Третьего рейха, p. 382).

As a result of the invasion, Germany acquired complete control over the territory of former Yugoslavia. Only after the fact was Bulgaria invited to take part in the occupation. Despite the propaganda conducted by the government of Prof. Filov about "unification", the new territories that have never been part of Bulgaria, were not recognized as Bulgarian lands. This is obvious from the German documents. The German diplomatic correspondence at the time confirms that the Germans were in charge of the distribution and status of the lands they occupied after the fall of Yugoslavia.

When Beckerle was being sent to Bulgaria as an ambassador, he was reminded by Hitler impose the German demands, while at the same keeping alive the dream of Bulgaria's national unification (protocol of the interrogation on March 23, 1945):

> "In June 1941, before my departure to Sofia, I had a meeting with Hitler in the presence of Ribbentrop and Goering. Hitler asked me if I had enough information about the situation in Sofia. When I replied that I did, Hitler said that my tasks as an ambassador to Sofia would not be difficult, because everything was good in Bulgaria... Hitler told me that he had a friendly relationship with King Boris and they discussed all political questions. He advised me to do favors to the King and treat him with tact. The meaning of Hitler's instructions was that I had to pursue aggressively the unconditional fulfillment of all German demands, but without affecting the ambitions of King Boris who was dreaming to become "King – Unifier of the Bulgarian Lands" (Тайны дипломатии Третьего рейха, p. 46).

On April 21, 1941, Joachim von Ribbentrop and the Italian Foreign Minister Count Ciano, held talks in Vienna, where the Bulgarian territorial demands were discussed. The German Minister explained that the Bulgarian King, during a meeting with Hitler, requested the whole territory of Macedonia up to the Albanian-Yugoslav border and especially Ochrid, which he considered a holy Bulgarian city. Hitler agreed in principle with the demands but noted that due to economic and especially military reasons, Italy wanted the border moved further to the east, because of the presence of Albanian people in the area. Ribbentrop also found the Bulgarian demands reasonable, especially after Hitler was sympathetic to them.

Count Ciano reiterated the Italian arguments for moving the border to the east for economic and military reasons that forced Italy to take such a position. He suggested a consultation with Italian military experts that he brought with him. They made their presentation but were unable to answer the detailed questions of Ribbentrop concerning the border proposal in Macedonia. Count Ciano stated that he was willing to compromise – the border around Ochrid could be drawn in a way that would leave the Bulgarian holy places in Bulgarian territory.

Then Ribbentrop said that the German Government was inclined to give the whole Macedonia to Bulgaria, because that will place the territory in the hands of a good and loyal friend of the Axis. Hitler also shared that opinion. Ribbentrop admitted that the German position created disagreements between Germany and Italy regarding the new Bulgarian-Albanian border (Нойков, 1995, p. 125).

On April 24, 1941, King Boris III met in Sofia the Deputy Chief of the Commercial Policies Section in the German Ministry of Foreign Affairs, Carl Clodius, and told him that for ethnic and geographic reasons, Ochrid, Struga, Gostivar, and especially Tetovo, should be given to Bulgaria. The next day, Ribbentrop notified Clodius to tell the King that the Italians had demands for those towns, so they will receive them, however the Minister managed to keep for Bulgaria Ochrid and the surrounding area.

The same day in the afternoon, the King met again with Clodius in the presence of Prof. Filov and other members of the cabinet. The long conversation focused on the proposed by the Germans future Bulgarian border in the Pirot area (part of the Bulgarian territory annexed by Serbia after World War I). In this conversation, the King demanded parts of Greek Macedonia because the area south of Bitola, and especially around the town of

Lerin, had only Bulgarian population. He said the same about the town of Kukush – it was purely Bulgarian town – and it also had to be included in the Bulgarian territory, but only if that didn't disrupt the future German plans (Нойков, 1995, p.29-30).

On April 25, Ribbentrop sent from Vienna a telegram to Clodius with guidance on dealing with the Bulgarian territorial and economic demands. He acknowledged receiving his employee's report, in which Clodius wrote that hopefully Ochrid, Struga, Gostivar and first of all Tetovo would be given to the Bulgarians. Then Ribbentrop made a few points, which he wanted shared confidentially with the King.

He mentioned his negotiations with Count Ciano a few days earlier that covered the future borders. Italy initially wanted a vast area east of the old Albanian border for strategic and ethnic reasons. Ribbentrop had to consider the Italian desires about Tetovo, Struga, Gostivar and Kichevo, but he managed to convince Count Ciano not to include Ochrid and the area in Albania. The Minister was happy that he could get this concession from Italy on behalf of Bulgaria. Further, he wrote that Bulgaria should be satisfied with this solution, moreover, Germany was ready to offer as some compensation part of the northern territory of Serbia (annexed in World War I from Bulgaria).

Besides, Bulgaria was already given a large area in the northern Aegean shores, which currently was populated with Greeks and Turks, but Bulgaria could use it to move there people from the Bulgarian minority that lived out of the country (Нойков, 1995, p.130-132).

On May 4, 1941, Ribbentrop sent a telegram to the German representatives in Sofia about the territorial demands of King Boris III, discussed with Clodius. The Minister gave the following instruction regarding the western Bulgarian borders: "Please notify King Boris that in principle the Government of the Reich agrees with the proposed border line, however, we reserve the right to determine later the specific border." As of Lerin, Ribbentrop stated that the issue was problematic due to the Italian demands. The same was the situation with Kukush – being only 40 km north of Salonika, it was part of the Salonika region, whose future status had not been determined yet, so it was not possible to discuss the Bulgarian demand at this point (Нойков, 1995, p.29-30).

In the telegram, Ribbentrop addressed the Bulgarian territorial demands north of Macedonia, in the Nish area, including the mountain pass St. Nikola. Bulgaria was ready to give up the towns of Bela Palanka and Leskovats, Bulgarian in the past, but now populated only with Serbs. Then he made the statement mentioned above, to advise King Boris that the final borders would be determined later.

Then Ribbentrop raised the issue of the town Lerin, where only Bulgarians lived; it was requested by the King, however, the Italians also wanted that town for inclusion in the future Greater Albania, so because of that, the Bulgarian demand was problematic. The Bulgarian town of Kukush, in the Salonika area, was also problematic, the Germans were not sure whether it should be given to Bulgaria. In the same way, Germany couldn't take a position about another request of the King – to return to Turkey half of the area around Odrin, which was annexed by Greece in 1915, and to give the other half to Bulgaria, which needed it to build a railway link to the old territories. In the end, Ribbentrop emphasized that none of these issues was urgent (Нойков, 1995, p.137).

Another issue that Germany wanted to keep under its control was the exploitation of the natural resources in the newly-occupied territories. On April 24, 1941, Clodius had a talk with King Boris and his Foreign Minister Ivan Popov in Sofia regarding the control of the chrome ore deposits in the Skopje area. In a telegram to Ribbentrop, he reported that Bulgaria was ready to confirm the German ownership of all chrome ore deposits, according to the previous agreement between Bulgaria and Germany regarding natural resources. Clodius noted that the agreement was reached in a friendly way and he didn't think that the King remained with the impression that he was under German pressure. After that, Clodius met Minister Popov, and made other economic and financial requests on behalf of Germany. He was satisfied that the Bulgarian side did not object to their resolution. In the end, Clodius wrote that at this point an official agreement should be avoided and both sides planned to exchange only certified notes about the talks (Нойков, 1995, p. 129).

The only conclusion that we can make from those documents is that Germany was in full control of the area. Regardless of the bickering between Italy and Bulgaria over the redistribution of Macedonia, the Germans had the final word and they were not in a hurry to decide what was going to happen. Only one thing was sure – they wanted complete control over the natural resources in the area. So, regardless of the propaganda spread by Prof. Filov and Gabrovski about the "King Unifier" and the expansion of Bulgaria, the Germans were calling the shots and that would turn fatal for many people who lived in the occupied territories.

Ambassador Beckerle made it clear that the Bulgarian troops in those regions played an auxiliary role, supporting the German rule, as stated in his interrogation protocol of March 23, 1945: "In 1942, the Bulgarian Government sent three divisions of its troops to Serbia and one to two divisions to Greece, which were called Occupation Corps, for suppression of the partisan movement and to support the German occupational regime in those countries" (Тайны дипломатии Третьего рейха, p. 47)

Like Beckerle, Dr. Carl Clodius was also arrested in 1944 and taken to Moscow. In a testimony recorded on June 5, 1946, he admitted that all those territories were given to Bulgaria to manage, because the Nazi Government needed its troops freed for other tasks:

> "The Bulgarian troops were used more and more as an occupational army in Yugoslavia and Greece. In Yugoslavia, the Bulgarians occupied a territory that they advertised as Bulgarian – North-West Macedonia to the Ochrid Lake, to include in it an old holy place, the Ochrid Monastery. Gradually, the Bulgarians occupied almost the entire territory of old Serbia. Though this was done to free the German troops for other tasks, it created more difficulties for Germany regarding the Serbian people. The situation in Greece was similar. Serious troubles there caused the fact that by the spring of 1941, not only West Thrace, but also East Macedonia were given to the Bulgarians to manage. The Greeks did not forget that the Germans, after the Second Balkan War [1913], were interested in the unification of East Macedonia with Greece, but now Hitler gave that Greek territory to the Bulgarians. The anxiety rose higher when later the Bulgarians also took East Macedonia (except the city of Salonika), although here, like in Yugoslavia, the Bulgarian troops were simply replacing the German troops to free them for other tasks. The Bulgarian occupation of North Macedonia also caused tensions between Bulgaria and Italy" (Тайны дипломатии Третьего рейха, p. 241).

Even the police force established in those territories was under strict German supervision. The Bulgarian police was directed by German officers, led by Oberfuehrer Friedrich Panzinger. He was the Attaché of the Security Police at the German Embassy in Sofia. During an interrogation in Moscow on February 12, 1947, he said: "In May-June 1941, under my direct control was introduced a strict police regime in the occupied by Bulgaria regions, Thrace and Macedonia. In these territories, we established police stations and conducted mass punitive operations against anti-Fascists. I personally inspected Thrace and Macedonia with [Police Director] Pavlov, and I controlled the activities of the police forces and provided instructions to strengthen the fight against persons who acted against Germany. Also, in 1941, after an order from Berlin, I conducted a number of activities in Bulgaria to prepare its territory to be used as a springboard in the attack of Germany on the Soviet Union" (Тайны дипломатии Третьего рейха, p. 641-642). Panzinger had strong influence within Bulgaria as well. He maintained a wide network of agents, among whom were Prof. Kantardjiev, favored to become a Prime Minister; Prof. Alexander Stanishev, a prominent surgeon, later Cabinet Minister; Burov, a large merchant; Prof. Alexander Tsankov, former Prime Minister. The total number of his Bulgarian agents was over 40 (Ibid., p. 642).

The problem with the deportation of the Macedonian and Thracian Jews is a thorny issue in the Holocaust history. Some historians think that Bulgaria was solely responsible for it, since it had jurisdiction over the area. However, as we saw, neither Germany nor other countries recognized the sovereignty of Bulgaria in those lands. In contrast, Dobrudja was returned to Bulgaria in 1940 through a treaty recognized internationally, while Macedonia was never part of Bulgaria. The idea of "unification" was nothing more than government propaganda. Chary acknowledges that fact: "The government applied the ZZN and these subsequent laws not only to Bulgaria proper, but after April 1941 to the occupied territories in Greece and Yugoslavia as well. Although Sofia now regarded these provinces as part of the kingdom, Berlin actually recognized only Bulgarian military administration of the occupied territories. The Germans postponed a final settlement, which, to be sure, would have probably awarded the areas permanently to Bulgaria until the cessation of hostilities throughout Europe. Sofia was unhappy with this but could only acquiesce" (Chary, 1972, p. 44).

In his diary, Goebbels specifically says that the occupation of Serbia, specifically the Macedonian lands, was part of the auxiliary role of Bulgaria: "The Fuehrer is showing himself extremely liberal toward Bulgaria. Bulgaria, after all, cannot easily take an active part in the war, since it has almost never lived in peace throughout its young national history. **It can, however, supply auxiliary troops here and there, as indeed it has done, for**

example, in Serbia. For this we can only be thankful to the King" (Goebbels, 1948, p. 151-152, emphasis mine – M.M.).

Hitler's war directives were also clear about the auxiliary role of the Bulgarian troops. His Directive No. 55273/42 of December 28, 1942, states that due to possible allied attacks in Greece, those areas are under German command:

> "2. The following will be under the Commanding General, Armed Forces, Southeast:
> a. In the Croatian area, the "German General in Croatia" (aside from his capacity as Military Attaché) and the commander of German Troops in Croatia".
> b. For the area of former Serbia, the "Commanding General, Serbia" (Trevor-Roper, 1966, p. 205-206).

That was confirmed in Directive 48 of July 26, 1943: "V. A. 1. The Greek territory occupied by German forces and by the Bulgarian 7th Division, including the islands and the neutral zone in Thrace, will be an operational area. Commander-in-Chief South-east will exercise full powers in this area and is authorized to delegate his powers to Military Commander Greece" (Trevor-Roper, 1966, p. 213).

The situation was reflected in German maps (see the illustrations in the end). One such map defined the territories as being under Bulgarian administration. The other one, found in a German school atlas of 1942, clearly shows the old borders of Bulgaria, even though the new territories are marked with the same color.

Also, in the protocol of the Wannsee Conference, which listed the number of the Jews to be targeted in the "final solution", Bulgaria was listed as having 48,000 Jews, i.e. those who lived in the old territories. Those in the occupied territories obviously belonged to Germany.

The attempts of Bulgaria to provide citizenship to people from the area, were met with disapproval by the Germans. Though the Bulgarian ethnicity dominated the area decades before the occupation, that population had been ethnically cleansed by the Greeks:

> "A state that viewed them as a serious menace to its own security could encourage minorities to move. In the mid-1920s, Greece expelled about 53,000 Bulgarians from Greek Thrace and Macedonia in order to make room for 638,000 Greek

refugees from the littoral of Asia Minor. Henceforth 89% of the population of Greek Macedonia consisted of Greeks while Greek Thrace was virtually cleared of Bulgarians. In the 1930s ambitious plans were drawn up by Serb officials to change the national character of the population in Kosovo. The colonization programme occurring since 1918 both here and in Macedonia was to be stepped up and forceful measures were employed to promote the mass departure of Kosovo Albanians. But refugees and displaced peoples could keep national disputes at boiling point, as the uprooted Macedonians in Bulgaria were to prove in the first quarter of the last century" (Gallagher, 2001, p. 89).

In the previous chapter, I already mentioned that 1942 was a crucial year in the German policies toward Jews. The various forms of expulsion were drastically changed to a methodical extermination, as it was decided at the infamous Wannsee Conference in January 1942. However, even the Wannsee Conference protocols used a vague language that didn't state unequivocally that the Jews would be exterminated. Very few people knew about the camps and even the Jewish press initially treated with skepticism the reports about the concentration camp horrors. It took some time for the truth to start emerging, which made the allies of Germany feel uneasy, because most of them never anticipated that they would be forced to take part in mass murder.

Due to the German pressure in the judicial field, Bulgaria already had discriminatory laws against the Jews and, most importantly, a whole institution controlled by the anti-Semite Alexander Belev, which could implement the German decisions in Bulgaria. The Commissariat for the Jewish Questions had the task to organize the deportation of the Jews from Bulgaria. The purpose of that expulsion wasn't clear at the time. It was seen by many as a German action to mobilize large numbers of Jews for public works in Poland, as was the case with recruiting Bulgarians and other nationalities for factory work in Germany. There was no explicit written order from Adolf Hitler about annihilation of the Jews, other than his outburst in speeches and conversations that the Jewish Questions had to be resolved once and forever.

In the same way, the Commissariat was operating in secrecy, having been given full power by the law for resolving the Jewish Question. After selling a large number of Jewish properties, it kept the money in special accounts that it could use for its activities. As it was explained in the testimony of Svetoslav Nikolov in the previous chapter, Belev made some attempts to transfer part of the money to banks controlled by the Ratniks, but that was stopped after the audit. Still, Belev was frustrated with the slow pace of the government anti-Jewish policies. His feelings were shared by Germany and especially its representative in Bulgaria, the ambassador Beckerle. The King despised the latter and found his appointment offensive - Beckerle wasn't a professional diplomat, but a Nazi party activist and former police chief of Frankfurt.

"In September 1942, Ribbentrop ordered that all diplomatic efforts should be made to speed up the deportation of the Jews from the various countries of Europe, and he specifically mentioned Bulgaria. Beckerle reported that the Bulgarian government was delighted with the proposal but that there were certain difficulties; after all, if the government had been unable to deprive Jews of their Bulgarian citizenship, it was unlikely that more radical measures would be possible. Furthermore, he reported, because of the labor shortage in Bulgaria, Filov did not think that the adult male Jews could be spared from their present work of road construction; and the fee of 250 Reichsmarks that the Germans wanted to charge for every Jew "re-settled" was considered much too high.

"It was now clear to the German government that the Tsar was reluctant to take drastic action against the Jews in Bulgaria, but the Nazis believed that he might be persuaded to allow the "resettlement" of the Jews from the newly annexed territories. In January 1943, SS-Hauptsturmfuehrer (Captain) Theodor Dannecker came to Bulgaria as a special representative of Adolf Eichmann to negotiate with Belev for the deportation of the Macedonian and Thracian Jews. If some concession had to be made on the Jewish question, the Tsar preferred to sacrifice non-Bulgarian rather than Bulgarian Jews. Consequently, he gave his approval for the deportation but specified that he had "agreed only to the expulsion to the East of the Jews from the new lands. From the Bulgarian Jews themselves he wanted only a small number of Bolshevik Communist elements." The remaining Bulgarian Jews should be allowed to stay in the country because they were still urgently needed for road construction.

"This was the limit to which Belev was authorized to go, but during the treaty negotiations with Dannecker he made new computations and found that there were not 20,000 but only around 12,000 Jews in the new territories. To reach the desired quota, he needed to include 8,000 Bulgarian Jews in the deportation; he therefore marked out the limiting phrase "from the new Bulgarian lands, Thrace and Macedonia" from the draft copy of the treaty. Moreover, Belev decided that the Jews selected for the first deportation should be not the political activists, as the Tsar had directed, but rather the elite of each community.

"The Dannecker-Belev agreement was signed on February 22, 1943, and secret preparations were begun immediately to assemble the Jews in a few large camps. Border guards were increased to prevent escapes, for the authorities were aware that a few individual Jews had already learned of the plan" (Miller, 1975, p. 99).

In the of the interrogation protocol of March 23, 1945, during his detention in Moscow, Beckerle outline the dominant German role in the deportation: "Following Himmler's instructions received in a telegram, I, in cooperation with Dannecker, the person authorized by the German Government to deal with the Jewish affairs, managed to arrange through Minister Gabrovski the deportation from Macedonia and Thrace of 14-15 thousand Jews, who were sent to Poland, according to my demand. I don't know what happened to them after that" (Тайны дипломатии Третьего рейха, p. 50).

The inner struggles in the government were expressed in the testimony of MP Dr. Georgi Lipovanski at the People's Tribunal in 1945. The hardcore enemies of the Jews, who wanted them expelled and destroyed, were not that many, but they were enough in numbers and had sufficient support from Germany to push forward:

"Prosecutor Angelov: Why was Mr. Filov's position on the Jewish Question so extreme?

"Lipovanski: Now I know why. Every time I came back from Hungary, I would tell him: this is a mistake, you shouldn't do it; Hungarians are smarter and more cultured than us, we must follow them and avoid persecuting the Jews. He was adamant. And from the talks with the other ministers, it became clear to me that the decision was final, and they must have made some special commitment. And now I understand why. Accidentally, I spent some time in a jail cell with [the King's adviser] Sevov. I asked him: "Why did the King surrender?" He replied: "Listen, the situation was even scarier. One day the King called me to the palace and said that Filov visited him and reported that he gave his consent to the Germans, to Beckerle, to surrender all Bulgarian Jews to the Germans." Then Sevov asked the King: "Your Majesty, how did you reply to Filov?" The King answered that he didn't say anything to him. Sevov countered: "But how can Filov want to give away the Jewish Bulgarian citizens? They are your subjects. Tomorrow they may demand other subjects as well, they may demand me. Would you let Filov send me away?" The King realized his mistake and asked Sevov to visit Filov and tell him that the King does not want to hand over the Bulgarian Jews to the Germans. But Filov replied: "I have already agreed and have an obligation to Beckerle, how can I change my mind?" Sevov said: "I don't know, but what I know is that the King is firmly against the deportation of Jews." Filov looked confused: "I'll see what I can do." Then he changed the arrangement and let the Germans deport only the Jews from Aegean Thrace and Macedonia, who were not Bulgarian subjects, while the Bulgarian subjects remained.

"Chairman: The question is not who was pushing the Jewish Question when the agreement between Belev and Gestapo was being implemented, but who started the process, who pushed it initially to the attention of the Royal Palace and the Government?

"Lipovanski: The Germans.

"C.: Wasn't Gabrovski involved?

"L.: Possibly yes.

"C.: Didn't Filov and Gabrovski compete to show more servility to the Germans?

"L.: Sevov told me that Filov had completely sold himself to the Germans.

"C.: Weren't Belev, Gabrovski, and others, members of the Ratnik organization?

"L.: I don't know, I have never been a part of it.

"C.: Was it by accident that Belev became the king of the Jews? Where did he come from? Didn't he come from that organization?

"L.: I don't know... But that was their motivation – serving the Germans and showing them that they were more German than the Germans themselves.

"C.: Why did Gabrovski want to resolve the Jewish Question in such a brutal way?

"L.: Probably because he was preparing to replace Filov as a Prime Minister" (Народен съд, разпит на Георги Липовански, 1944, p. 273-275).

Even though the Bulgarian government approved the

discriminatory laws, many of its members thought the deportation problematic. Benjamin Arditti emphasized in his book the different ideas that King Boris III and Prime Minister Bogdan Filov had about the Jewish "problem". On March 11, 1943, Filov met the King and discussed the deportation of the Jews from Thrace and Macedonia. The King proposed to arrange through the telegraph to send them to Palestine, meaning that he wanted to handle the initiative himself. Filov replied that it was too late, they were leaving in a few days. The King asked where they were being sent. After Filov replied, "To Poland," the King said that they were going to their deaths. Filov tried to make the excuse that the Jews were going to work there, like other Bulgarians. The King replied that it was not the same, the Jews were treated in an inhumane way. Mr. Arditti noted that the Bulgarian Jews were not mentioned in the conversation, which meant that they were not threatened by deportation on March 11. Still, the King and Filov had opposite opinions; Filov tried to convince the King of his opinion, that the Jews should go. He knew about the German plans for extermination and supported them.

The King was against that treatment, on March 9, he cancelled the deportation order for the Bulgarian Jews and on March 11, he was ready to take steps to help the Jews from the new territories. Knowing that Filov and other members of the government will oppose his plan, he was willing to arrange the issue himself, but the Prime Minister was against such action (Ардити, 1952, p. 30-31).

It is likely that despite Filov's refusal, contacts had been made with the Allies about sending the Jews to Palestine. There are documents showing that, when faced with the demand to deport the Jews, Bulgaria inquired about the possibility of moving 60 to 70 thousand Jews to Palestine, this obviously included the occupied territories. Although England received a mandate from the League of Nations to prepare Palestine for the future Jewish state, it practically sabotaged that task.

In a conference with the American President Roosevelt on March 27, 1943, the British Foreign Minister Anthony Eden refused to accommodate the request:

> "Hull raised the question of the 60 or 70 thousand Jews that are in Bulgaria and are threatened with extermination unless we could get them out and, very urgently, pressed Eden for an answer to the problem. Eden replied that the whole problem of the Jews in Europe is very difficult and that we should move

very cautiously about offering to take all Jews out of a country like Bulgaria. If we do that, then the Jews of the world will be wanting us to make similar offers in Poland and Germany. Hitler might well take us up on any such offer and there, simply are not enough ships and means of transportation in the world to handle them.

Eden said that the British were ready to take about 60 thousand more Jews to Palestine but the problem of transportation, even from Bulgaria to Palestine is extremely difficult. Furthermore, any such mass movement as that would be very dangerous to security because the Germans would be sure to attempt to put a number of their agents in the group. They have been pretty successful with this technique, both in getting their agents into North and South America." (Memorandum Eden-Roosevelt, 1943).

The incident adds another layer of disgrace to the behavior of the country that was entrusted to prepare Mandate Palestine to become the "national home" of the Jewish people. The White Paper of 1939, which limited severely the Jewish immigration to Palestine was another disgraceful act.

While abdicating its obligation in Mandate Palestine, which was supposed to be the home of the Jews, especially in the times of the Holocaust, Great Britain got involved in the questionable effort to move 30,000 Bulgarian Jews to Turkey, even though Turkey could not afford to support so many people. This was outlined in the memo "The British Embassy to the Department of State", dated April 19, 1943:

"On the 29th of March, Mr. William Strang handed to Mr. Dunn the draft text of the instructions sent to His Majesty's Ambassador at Ankara and to His Majesty's Minister at Berne with the purpose of arranging with the Turkish and Bulgarian Governments (the latter by way of the Swiss Government) for the evacuation to Turkey from Bulgaria of 30,000 Jews who were, it was understood, to be deported to Poland. The State Department will no doubt have received from the United States Ambassador at Ankara a telegram to the effect that it is the agreed view of the United States and British Ambassadors that there is no prospect whatever of persuading the Turks to agree to receive the 30,000 Bulgarian Jews, and that the only possible solution of the problem would be to arrange for their transport to some other destination" (Foreign Relations US, Vol. 1, p. 292).

In "Memorandum by the Assistant Chief of the Division of Near Eastern Affairs (Merriam)" to the US Government, dated October 15, 1943, it was admitted that Britain mishandled the Mandate. Great Britain went even further with the emigration restrictions. The number of Jewish emigrants to Palestine had to be limited "to the extent of its economic absorptive capacity", and it had to be kept lower than the number of Muslims there at any given time:

> "This would open up Palestine to about 500,000 Jews, which is the upper figure cited by such careful students of the problem as Dr. Nelson Glueck, of European Jews who will have to be taken care of outside Europe. If that number cannot be absorbed quickly, temporary provision for them could be made in Libya, for example. Of course, if it is not necessary to put 500,000 more Jews in Palestine, it would make things that much easier all around. As the Zionists wish for political reasons to place as many Jews in Palestine as possible, it will be necessary to see to it that European Jews are not dragooned into emigrating to Palestine in excess of the emigration that is absolutely required by their situation" (Foreign Relations US, Vol. 4, p. 817).

With millions of Jews facing extermination, that was a death sentence. It created severe problems for a small country like Bulgaria, where many were reluctant to follow the German anti-Jewish policies, but it was difficult to find ways to save the Jews.

In the circular in Appendix A, the Ratnik organization recognized the crucial role of the Germans when it accused the government of failing to deport all Jews: "They agreed to deport only the Jews from Thrace and Macedonia, who belonged to Germany anyway, because that country conquered those lands with blood and handed them to us."

Belev and Eichmann's emissary Dannecker acted in secrecy, with full Germans support in the region. Even though Bulgarian police were used in part to collect the Jews in Macedonia and Thrace, members of the local authorities, appointed by Bulgaria, were unaware of the plan. At the People's Tribunal in 1945, a high Bulgarian government employee appointed in those lands, testified that he was awoken at night by the action to arrest Greek Jews, unaware of what was going on. His name was Petko Lalovski, prosecutor in Gyumyurdjina during the war. He did not approve the occupation, even though he served three years in the new territories, because that was not the way to liberate those lands. He was ashamed of what happened to the Jews there – when the arrests started, he was outraged, went to his office, and confronted the police commandant about the lack of notification. The latter replied that no one other than him and the military commander were supposed to know about that. The prosecutor was powerless while he was watching the harsh treatment of the Jews. Because of his demand for humane treatment of the arrested Jews, later, he was viewed with suspicion (People's Court Session No.15, 1945, p.1378-1381).

The Bulgarian politician Dimo Kazasov, a strong supporter of the Jews, was already quoted in previous chapters of this book. After the war, he became the Minister of Propaganda in the government that organized the People's Tribunal in 1944-1945. As such, he testified at the trial and admitted that Bulgaria was occupied by Germany and the anti-Semitic laws were imposed under German influence, but the Bulgarian government was cruel in applying them. Near the end of the testimony, he expressed his opinion about the deportations from Macedonia and Thrace:

> "COUNSEL M. STOENCHEV: One more thing about the Jews in the old borders of Bulgaria. Mr. Minister, you clearly said that the Bulgarian people felt compassion and supported them. In the atmosphere during the German occupation of Bulgaria, under the influence that the Germans had in the new territories, which were neither officially nor practically acquired by Bulgaria, could the Bulgarian people in the country do something more?
>
> "MINISTER D. KAZASOV: It could not be done in the new territories, because the measures there were applied by surprise. When the Bulgarian people found out that the Jews from Thrace and Macedonia were being sent to Poland, it was already too late. They found out only when the carriages with the Jews passed through Dupnitsa on their way to Lom.
>
> "CHAIRMAN: Besides, the percentage of the Bulgarian population in the new territories was very small.
>
> "COUNSEL M. STOENCHEV: Who initiated the deportations?
>
> "MINISTER D. KAZASOV: **There was no initiative, the German authorities organized the deportations**" (People's Court Session No.9, 1945, p. 739, emphasis mine – M.M.).

Grigor Cheshmedjiev, the Minister of Social Policies, was

quoted in the previous chapter; in his testimony at the People's Tribunal, he was also asked about the deportations:

> "CHAIRMAN: Who should be credited with the cancellation of the deportation from the old territories – the government or the Bulgarian public opinion?
> "CHESHMEDJIEV: I think, the public opinion should be credited.
> "CHAIRMAN: Why did the deportation of the Aegean Jews happen? Was it because of the surprise or because of the low percentage of Bulgarian people in the area?
> "CHESHMEDJIEV: I think, that was simply an order from the Germans" (People's Court Session No.9, 1945, p. 760).

The leading role of the German Embassy in Sofia in the deportation was confirmed by the Embassy Adviser Anton Mohrmann, during an interrogation in Moscow on February 26, 1945:

> "Question: You did not tell us about the violence against the Bulgarian population committed by the Germans to realize their aggressive military plans.
> "Mohrmann: Regarding this issue, I am aware only of the actions of our authorities concerning the Bulgarian Jews. The embassy received an order from Berlin to demand from the Bulgarian Government consent to deport all Jews from Macedonia and Thrace. Beckerle reached an agreement with the Minister of the Interior, managed to obtain the consent of the Bulgarian Government, and all Jews, about 10,000, were deported.
> "Question: Was that done violently?
> "Mohrmann: Yes, the deportation was done in a violent way.
> "Question: Where were all those people sent?
> "Mohrmann: To Poland.
> "Question: What was the purpose?
> "Mohrmann: The deportation was presented as sending the Jews to work in Poland, however, I am not aware of their fate.
> "Question: Who managed the deportation?
> "Mohrmann: For execution of the deportation, from the central office of the SS in Berlin to Sofia was sent a special SS envoy – Dannecker, who managed the whole operation" (Тайны дипломатии Третьего рейха, p. 384).

The German control over the deportations from the new

territories was also confirmed by the testimony of Benjamin Arditti, a Bulgarian Zionist activist, recorded after he moved to Israel: "In March 1943, an echelon with Greek Jews reached the Sofia railway station. The rescue committee of Jewish leaders started a campaign to stop the deportations from the Aegean region through intercession to the Bulgarian authorities and foreign representatives, including the Papal Nuncio. Nothing positive came from the Bulgarian administration, they responded that Thrace and Macedonia were territories occupied by Germany, so the Germans could do whatever they wanted. Besides, those lands were considered "military zones" and the actions there were conducted for military reasons. The Jewish leaders proposed that the captured Jews be detained in Bulgaria, if they could not be sent back to their homes. The Bulgarian authorities replied that they did not control the situation. The fate of the Jews was in German hands" (Ташев, p. 13).

In his book about King Boris III and the fate of the Jews in Bulgaria, Benjamin Arditti confirms that point. He sees as a reason for the failure to save the Jews in Thrace and Macedonia the status of those lands. They were occupied by the Germans, who transferred the administration to Bulgaria. The latter annexed them on its own and the unilateral act was not recognized by Germany. Thrace and Macedonia were always considered German occupation zones. Within Bulgaria, the King and the government could at least argue with the Germans that the country was sovereign, and they could not do whatever they wanted, while in the occupied lands, the Bulgarians were not able to state the same (Ардити, 1952, p. 36-37).

The Jewish Zionist activist Albert Varsano left impressive memoirs about camp Somovit in 1943, the largest Jewish detention camp in Bulgaria, in 250 typewritten pages that unfortunately are still not published. I will write about his experiences in one of the next chapters, but it is important to note here that some Macedonian Jews who managed to escape the echelons were captured and brought to the camp but were not deported to Poland. For example, a group of young people from Aegean Thrace were brought to the camp, though they were not Bulgarian citizens, they were mobilized in Jewish labor groups in Bulgaria and despite of threats from anti-Semites to be sent to Poland, they never were (Varsano, p. 66). At a later day, a young man from Greece, who was on one of the trains but managed to escape, was brought to the camp. He told his story about the horrible conditions on the trains, with people packed like sardines in locked carriages, with little food or air and cruel treatment. Near the Danube, before boarding the boats on March 19, 1943, he and another one managed to escape and hide at a Jewish family in Vratsa. They were captured and sent to the camp but never deported (Varsano, p.100).

Helping the Jews in the occupied territories was a difficult task even for people with authority, as it was shown in the rescuing of the Macedonian liberation activist Rafael Kamhi who lived in Salonika, an area under complete German control. He was 74 years old at the time. The archives have preserved the correspondence that led to his rescue. On March 23, 1943, the Chairman of the Council of the Macedonian Cultural-Educational and Benevolent Fraternities in Bulgaria, General Kosta Nikolov, requested from Prime Minister Bogdan Filov an intervention to allow Rafael Kamhi from Salonika to move to Sofia. The general explained that Kamhi was a prominent activist in the Bulgarian Macedonian movement, with exceptional contributions, and urged Prof. Filov to read the recommendations from three other activists, attached to the letter. It was an urgent request, because the Jews of Salonika were soon to be deported. The three letters covered Kamhi's work in helping Bulgarian activists to avoid capture or murder by the Turkish authorities (Довеждането на Рафаел Камхи).

After the government intervention, the German Commandant of the Military Administration of Salonika issued a certificate on April 2, 1943, stating that Kamhi, now considered a Bulgarian subject of Jewish background, was excluded from the deportation of the Salonika Jews, following the explanation provided by the Bulgarian Government through the King's liaison officer at the German Supreme Commander for the South-East Region. Kamhi was allowed to remove his Jewish Star No.41367, leave the ghetto and move to Bulgaria. The certificate was good for two weeks, during which Kamhi was expected to get his Bulgarian ID papers; it was also signed and stamped by the King's liaison officer. Due to slow processing of the papers, it was extended twice (Удостоверение на Рафаел Камхи, 1943). Kamhi was transferred successfully to Sofia, where he remained even after the expulsion of most Jews in the end of May 1943. After the communist takeover, he left Bulgaria with the other Jews and lived in Israel until his death at the age of 100.

The Bulgarian historian Spas Tashev mentions two other cases. Marco Aaron Perets, Bulgarian subject of Jewish background, was arrested in Thrace during the deportation action in 1943. Later, he was released because he had a Bulgarian ID. Something similar happened to the brother of Harry Nissimov from Sofia who was detained with the local Jews in Xanthi but was released as a Bulgarian subject. In 1934, Bulgaria was the home of 4,989 Jews born in Dobrudja, Thrace or Macedonia, the lands under Bulgarian administration since the end of April 1941. Being Bulgarian subjects, none of them was deported. Foreign citizenship was another factor for the Jewish survival in the region. After the arrests in March 1943, 165 of the Jews detained in Skopje were released as foreign nationals, mostly from Catholic countries like Italy and Spain. In 1941, the Bulgarian administration in Skopje found 160 Jewish families with foreign citizenship or total of 263 people. 28 of those families were Spanish (approximately 46 people). By 1943, their number increased to 74 and since influx from the outside was not allowed, that meant that they must have received passports from the Spanish embassy in Sofia, most likely from the Ambassador Julio Palencia. It is assumed that he saved over 600 Jews by issuing entry visas to Spain (Ташев, p. 19-20).

In a Circular on the Jewish Question, issued by the Ratniks (see Appendix A), the Bulgarian authorities were blamed for warning the Macedonian Jews: "High administrative agencies in Skopje warned the Jews in the city and when the Jews were collected, it turned out that hundreds of the most influential have fled to Albania. And from Sofia and elsewhere, every day Jews are leaving for Istanbul." It was clear that mostly Bulgarians acted to save Jews in the Aegean and Macedonian areas.

Another controversial problem is the passivity of the Yugoslavian resistance movement of Josip Broz Tito, which claimed over 1,000,000 armed fighters. The three large groups of arrested Jews were held in camp Monopol 11, 14 and 18 days respectively. During that period, no attempts were made by the armed communist formations to liberate the captured Jews. Each of the trains was guarded by 30-35 Germans and the photographs showed that they were armed with rifles, not with automatic weapons. It would not have been a problem to attack the trains, which followed the same itinerary to Poland – Skopje-Nish-Lapovo-Zemun (Ташев, p. 18).

Spas Tashev, whose writings I have already quoted in this chapter, published in 2012 a comprehensive study of the events in the occupied territories in 1943, under the title "The Holocaust in Vardar Macedonia and the Aegean Region in 1943 and Its Modern Dimensions", which addresses many of the controversies surrounding that page of the Balkan history.

He provides some very thoughtful arguments that should be covered in addition to the documents quoted earlier. In his opinion, the mixed German-Bulgarian jurisdiction influenced the status of the Jews in the region. The Bulgarian Government gave an option to the Yugoslavian and Greek population to obtain Bulgarian citizenship, but excluded the local Jews, a decision that reflected the Law for Defense of the Nation. However, Circular No.5347, regarding the decree dealing with the citizenship in the new lands, never mentioned the Jews and left a loophole, which was used later by some Jews with foreign citizenship. A note to the Circular clarified that the Bulgarian citizenship option did not affect people with foreign citizenship (Italian, German, American, etc.), who were able to keep the citizenship they had under the Yugoslavian or Greek governments (Ташев, p. 10).

Mr. Tashev clearly states the dominant role of the Germans in the occupied regions. The Germans began persecutions in Vardar Macedonia and the Aegean region long before the mass deportations. Most often, they arrested and deported Jews who traveled from the German occupation area in Serbia to Macedonia in search of refuge. Although those Jews came with an entry visa to Macedonia from the Bulgarian Embassy in Serbia, they had been warned that they couldn't remain in Skopje. The reason was that from April 1941 to October 1944, without any interruption, there was a German military commandmentship at the Skopje railway station, which allowed the Nazis to arrest and deport such Jews (Ташев, p. 11).

Mr. Tashev also provides convincing arguments about the heavy German involvement in the deportations. The detained Jews, after their arrests, were placed in temporary transit camps and then loaded on trains. Upon their arrival in Bulgaria, they were left for a few days in camps in Dupnitsa and Gorna Jumaya. Then they continued on trains and arrived in the Danube port of Lom, from where they were moved to boats on March 20 and 21, 1943, and sent to Vienna and then to Treblinka. Some witnesses have left testimonies about the guards involved in the deportations. The Sofia Metropolitan Stefan, on his way to the Rila Monastery, saw one of the trains and was appalled by the horrible conditions of the Jews. He noted that the train was guarded by Germans and when he reached the monastery, he sent a telegram to the King demanding humane treatment for the prisoners. The German researcher Hans-Joachim Hoppe stated that during the deportation, the Aegean Jews were guarded by Bulgarian police, but they were together with Germans. He thought that the Bulgarian participation continued to Poland, but that was unlikely – the German documentary footage showed that the deportees' document checks were conducted by people in German uniforms who took complete control at Lom. The underground Macedonian communist press of the time also confirmed the German control: "bloody German fascists and their Bulgarian servants collected all Jews" (Ташев, p. 15-16).

Also, the process of deportation, according to materials at Yad Vashem, was guided by the German Ambassador Beckerle, Eichmann's envoy Theodor Dannecker, and Alexander Belev, who arrived in Skopje on March 21, 1943. A photograph shows Belev being guarded by two German soldiers. Yad Vashem confirms the presence of 120 Bulgarian policemen at this first deportation (but not during the other two). On the other hand, the Macedonian historian Alexander Matkovski claimed that only 20 Bulgarian soldiers took part in that deportation. He also quoted the memoirs of Albert Sarfati, who managed to escape, that the first train was guarded by 20 Germans with one officer; Sarfati didn't mention Bulgarian presence. A German propaganda movie, shot by a special crew sent to Macedonia, covered many moments of the deportation, like the guards, the loading of the trains and locking the doors. Everywhere in it could be seen German soldiers, including some wearing SS uniforms. (Ташев, p. 17).

The tragic fate of the remaining Jews was the result of their status of stateless persons, and because of that, Germany saw them as its hostages. For example, during the People's Tribunal in 1945, Belev's secretary Lilyana Panitsa cited a conversation between Belev and Dannecker, the latter said that the Macedonian and Thracian Jews were considered German subjects, who could be deported regardless of the position of the Bulgarian side. That confirmed once again that citizenship was the crucial factor in the Jewish survival. At the People's Tribunal, the Chief People's Prosecutor Georgi Petrov stated that under Hitler's diktat, the government of Bogdan Filov started an inhumane persecution of the Jews. In the final verdict, it was noted that the action for deporting the Jews was more German than Bulgarian. The People's Prosecutor Eli Baruch wrote in his memoirs in 1960 in Israel: "At the People's Tribunal we proved beyond any doubt that the Law for Defense of the Nation, as well as all other laws and decrees against Jews, were issued following a clear order from the German Government" (Ташев, p. 19-23).

Spas Tashev concludes that his research and data analysis

suggest that the deportation of the Macedonian and Aegean Jews in 1943 was initiated by Germany in territories that were controlled by it, with an overwhelmingly German participation.

> "Bulgaria's part in the events was determined by the subordinate role of the country in that period and was performed chiefly by the trained in Germany Hitlerite agent Alexander Belev. Until the beginning of the 1990s, nobody ever denied the leading role of Germany in the events. Samuel Arditti, who lives in Israel, noted the following: "In Israel, since the beginning of the 1950s, people freely argued about the question of the rescue of the Bulgarian Jews. Even the worst opponents of the King never accused him at the time of causing the deaths of the Jews in Thrace and Macedonia. Why? Because even they knew that those lands were not truly Bulgarian. The Germans were the masters of the area and they could do whatever they wanted. To blame the King for the German actions is an enormous injustice"." (Ташев, p. 24).

With all that said, it is still important to note that the collection of the Jews was performed at night, by surprise and with formidable brutality. The Germans and the Bulgarian police under Belev's control had to bring thousands of Jews quickly to the already prepared camp, a warehouse not designed to hold people. Although none of them was killed, they were searched thoroughly, and their valuables confiscated (although they were supposed to be deposited in the special Jewish Fund). The conditions in the camp were deplorable, with insufficient food and water. Some people with valuable skills, like doctors and pharmacists, were released together with their families. The same happened with the citizens of other countries, like Italy, Spain and Bulgaria.

In the archival account of the events, which is in Yad Vashem's archives "Monastir During the Holocaust: Liquidation of the Jewish Community in Monastir" we can find details about the tragedy. After all the Jews were already collected in camp Monopol, on March 21, a group of high-level officers arrived in Skopje, among them were the German Ambassador in Sofia, Adolf Beckerle, and also Alexander Belev and Eichmann's envoy Theodor Dannecker.

The first transport left the next day. It was supposed to take 1,600 Jews but at the last minute about 800 more were added. Since the available food was rationed for 1,600 people, there was shortage of food. "The train had 40 wagons, each with a small pitcher of water and some buckets for toilet purposes. The number of people in each wagon reached 80. One captain and 120 soldiers – all Bulgarian – appointed by the Bulgarian Interior Ministry, supervised the first transport. They accompanied the train until Lapovo, where they were met by German policemen. German security police head Rot took charge of accompanying the transport to Treblinka. Six days later, in the morning hours of 28 March, the transport arrived. Four people had died during the journey."

Three days later, on March 25, a second transport left, carrying 2,402 people. "A German police unit headed by Sgt. Buchner had come to Skopje some two days earlier to organize and accompany the transport. One of the wagons had no windows at all. When the Germans were approached to exchange the wagon for another, the coarse response was that there was no time to find another wagon; the transport had to leave immediately. It arrived at the Malkinia train station on the afternoon of 31 March. Within one hour, 20 wagons had been brought to Treblinka."

The last train took off on March 29, following the same itinerary, the total number of the prisoners was 2,404. "The journey ended on 5 April at 7 am. Between 9 and 11 am, the passengers were taken off the wagons at Treblinka. This transport was also organized and accompanied by groups of German policemen. Five people died along the way."

The records of Yad Vashem confirm that a number of inmates were released from camp Monopol "in line with orders from the Bulgarian authorities: 32 doctors and their families, 35 pharmacists and their families, 74 Spanish citizens and first-degree relatives, 19 Albanian citizens and first-degree relatives, and 5 Italian citizens and first-degree relatives. Among those released were just three members of the Monastir community: the doctor Helena Leon Ishach, her husband and her mother. In addition, five members of the Monastir community managed to escape from the camp: Niko Pardo, Allegra Aroesti-Pardo, Albert Moshon, Albert Sarfati and Joseph Kamhi" (Monastir During the Holocaust).

The account of the witness Dr. Ishah Levi confirms the information above: "The first transport of the Skopje Jews took off on March 22, 1943, the day before only 1,600 persons were scheduled for transport and the food for the trip was distributed among them. In morning of March 22, suddenly they announced that another 800 people will be added, they threw them into the wagons, and most of those 800 people did not receive any of the food because the transport had to leave quickly. The second transport took off on March 25, and this was a group of Skopje, all Jews from Shtip and a group of Bitolja Jews. This transport from Skopje was taken over by a German Gestapo platoon, and the first transport left under the guard of Bulgarian police officers" (Testimony of Dr. Ishah Levi of May 3, 1945; Crimes in Yugoslavia, p.193)

A book published in 1957 in Belgrade by surviving Jews covers in detail the Holocaust in Yugoslavia. In the chapters dedicated to Macedonia, it provides three reports about each of the transports that took the Jews to Treblinka. From Niska Banja (in the Nish region) more German police officers joined the guards of the trains.

All three reports were from the German guards in response to verbal orders from Dannecker to provide information. The first report from April 3, 1943, stated that the train left on March 22 and until it reached the Lapovo railway station, it was guarded by the Third Platoon of the protection police (Schutzpolizei) with commander officer Rott. The report failed to mention any Bulgarian police guarding the train. At Lapovo, the German police of Niska Banja took over. In the police papers, the final destination was marked as camp Treblinka, station Malkinia. The train reached the station on March 28, and since 4 Jews died on the way, 2,334 in total were transferred to the camp. The report was signed by Schutzpolizei Lieutenant Karl (who also signed the other two reports).

The second train was guarded by Second Platoon of Schutzpolizei with commander Handrik, it reached Treblinka on April 1 and 2,399 Jews were moved into the camp. The third report, dated April 12, 1943, states that the third train was guarded by the First Platoon of Schutzpolizei, under the command of officer Buchner, it delivered 2,399 Jews to Treblinka on April 5 (Crimes in Yugoslavia, p.193-194).

The trains that travelled from Aegean Thrace through Bulgaria, to the Danube port in the town of Lom, stopped at a temporary camp in the town of Dupnitsa. The commandant of the camp became known for his brutal behavior and after the communist takeover in 1944, he was tried by the People's Tribunal and sentenced to death. No Jews were killed there or at any other place in Bulgaria, but they were subjected to humiliating searches. "At the first search the authorities collected about 50,000 leva ($607) from the little remaining to the Jews, but he [the witness] had no knowledge of the results of the second. A Dupnitsa doctor who was called into the camp, gave up 20,000 leva ($243) which he never regained. (Paitashev told him that he had spent the money for provisions for the camp.)" (Chary, 1972, p. 111).

The Jews from Pirot (town in Serbia) were also treated harshly. "A group of three policemen and two officials of the district government acting under a search committee led by Bakurdzhiev himself thoroughly searched men, women, and children, forcing them to strip completely. Even those few decencies observed in the operation in Thrace were absent in Pirot. Not only did the searchers take valuables, but they systematically looted the luggage of the Jews." (Chary, 1972, p. 114)

Two trains with Jews arrived in the town of Lom on March 19 and 20, 1943. The only detailed description of the events, other than the official report of Yaroslav Kalitsin from the Commissariat, came from Nadezhda Vasileva, a nurse who helped the Jews on the trains; years later she was recognized as Righteous among the Nations. At the request of the Jewish Scientific Institute of Sofia, in 1947, she provided 21 pages of typewritten memoirs. About half of the manuscript has been translated into English in Volume 3 of "Yad Vashem Studies of the European Jewish Catastrophe and Resistance" (1959). The original Bulgarian document is preserved in the Bulgarian state archive.

There are some discrepancies between her dates of the events and the timetable from other sources. The latter lists as arrival dates March 19 and 20, with the deportation happening on March 20 and 21. Vasileva stated that the events transpired between March 15-20 and she became aware of the trains when she visited a friend, whose house overlooked the railway station. The friend told her that she was distraught by the cries for the last three days. After that, Vasileva provided help to the detained Jews for two days, meaning that the ordeal lasted five days. In a letter, sent on August 30, 1947, to the Institute, she clarified a few dates, stating that her information covered "the time of the evacuation between March 20-23, 1943, of the unfortunate Aegean and Thracian Jews" (Надежда Василева, писмо, 1947).

Shocked by what she saw from her friend's window, Vasileva quickly left the house, driven by her urge to help. She always had good ties with the Jews – growing up an orphan, she was helped by local Jewish families. The first thing she did, was to find a bucket with water to distribute among the thirsty people on the trains. Almost immediately, she was stopped by policemen and Customs guards – one of them hit her with his rifle and threatened to kill her. She refused to back off. Meanwhile, a crowd of Jews and Turks gathered around and brought more water.

In the Yad Vashem translation, otherwise faithful to the original, two sentences describing that moment were omitted: "The crowd was getting bigger, the people were crying and piling up whatever they could bring, they were handing me things that I distributed, those inside the trains wanted matches and candles, and lemons, if we had them, because many were sick of dysentery and were in the dark. I heard blessings in three languages, saw beautiful delicate hands with rings, bracelets and watches; it was clear, they did not do manual labor" (Спомени на Надежда Василева, p. 4).

Another group of people in German and Bulgarian uniforms showed up, some of them aimed rifles at the crowd. Slavi Puntov "came ahead and asked me: "Who asked you to do these crazy things? Go back! I am going to have you arrested!" (Ironically, Puntov was the local representative of the Commissariat and the president of the Red Cross.) During the argument she fainted and when she regained consciousness, Vasileva found herself in a shop, with a few Bulgarian and Turkish men standing around her.

On her way out, she saw a few Jews, the President of the Jewish community Miko Moshe among them. She discussed with them what to do and they managed to get a permission to deliver more food. Helped by several Gypsies, Vasileva continued to distribute lemons, apples, matches, candles, sugar, cheese, yoghurt and other things. Eventually, two Customs guards threatened her with arrest and she stopped. She asked for help the chief doctor of the local hospital, but he said that would be difficult, as new transports were arriving within the next few days. He advised her to continue to help discretely, he knew that the local Jews were preparing some warm food, but they had to present that as supplies coming from the Red Cross, otherwise no distribution would be allowed. Vasileva was aware that without a permission from Puntov, she would not be able to do it. Her Jewish friends managed to get a written permit from Puntov, stating that she could start the next day at 5 a.m.

When she arrived at the station the next day, she saw a pile of food, with a crowd around it. They were told that no Bulgarians or Jews could approach the trains, so she had to use only Gypsies. The food had to be inspected by Commissar Puntov before distribution. He showed up at 6:30 a.m. and started the inspection: "He took out a home-baked loaf of bread, showed it to me and said: "Nothing can stop these Jews! You see that they made signs on that loaf!" He broke it into pieces which he threw away." (The next year, when charged by the People's Tribunal, it was revealed that he had Jewish background, that is why he could read the signs.)

She started the distribution, but saw that some of the Gypsies, along with a Bulgarian railway worker, were filling their pockets and trying to sell the water and food to the Jews on the trains. The stench coming from inside was unbearable and the authorities did not allow to open and clean them. At 10 a.m., Puntov stopped the distribution and told her to come back at 5 a.m. next morning. As soon as she arrived, Vasileva heard that a woman gave birth and an old man had died. The food left from the previous day, disappeared. People were yelling from inside that they had to use the toilet. Since nobody of the authorities was responding, she broke the seal of one of the carriages to let them out. She was threatened with murder again, but the Jews managed to get out. A policeman tried to charge them money for that: "But I was greatly surprised when I saw a policeman shouting to all the people from that wagon: "All who have rings, bracelets, and watches on their hands, hand them over." This was an order. And I was thinking how dear was the price these people had to pay in order to gratify a physiological need!" (Vasileva, 1959, p. 295-301).

These disturbing events, witnessed by Nadezhda Vasileva, were presented differently in the Report from Yaroslav Kalitsin to the Commissar for the Jewish Questions Alexander Belev of March 24, 1943:

> "Report
> "From Yaroslav Kalitsin, Head of the Administrative Section at the Commissariat
> "Dear Commissar,
> "The Jews, collected from the Aegean region, along with those from the town of Pirot, arrived at the Lom railway station in two trains: the first one, on March 19 at 12:01, the second – on March 20 at 10:30. The departure of those Jews from the borders of the Kingdom was done on 4 passenger boats: 1) On March 20, at 14:00, 1,100 people left on boat "Kara Georgi"; 2) On March 20, at 20:30, 877 people left on boat "Voyvoda Mishich"; 3) On March 21, at 14:00, 1,256 people left on boat "Saturnus" and 4) On March 21, at 20:00, 986 people left on boat "Tsar Dushan". A total of 4,219 persons of Jewish background left the borders of the Kingdom from the Lom port.
> "The departing Jews were accompanied by Bulgarian police guards and 4 Bulgarian doctors to provide medical assistance

when needed. The Commissariat mobilized these doctors from the Main Directorate of People's Health and provided all medications, which the doctors thought they may need.

"During their short stay at the Lom railway station, with the help of the Red Cross Society, among the Jews was distributed warm food (lunch and dinner) for 1,200 people. The preparation of the food required 300 kg meat, 100 kg potatoes, 100 kg rice, 40 kg canned vegetables, and the necessary spices. Every 3 hours, the persons from the carriages parked at Lom station South, were allowed to go to the toilets.

"Upon leaving Sofia for Lom, the trains received from the Sofia Rabbinate 5 trunks and 18 packs with various clothes and shoes, to be distributed among the needy Jews. All that was distributed at the port of Lom, with the help of two ladies and four nurses from Red Cross. One trunk with man's vests and some small items remained, because nobody wanted them, so they were left to Red Cross in Lom.

"Two persons died at the Lom railway station and were buried by the local Jews. Both were over 70 years old. The doctors determined old age as the reason of death. There was also a successful birth at the station. The mother was transferred immediately to the boat, she received enough diapers and the necessary medical attention.

"The dispatch of the persons finished without any accidents.
"On March 23 at night, I returned to Sofia.
"March 23, 1943, Sofia
"Head of Department
"(Yaroslav Kalitsin)" (Шарланов, 2009, p. 466-467).

In the portion not included in the Yad Vashem translation, Vasileva provided more information about the events after the deportation. A few days after the boats left, while walking by Slavi Puntov's store, Vasileva was called in. Puntov and his wife waited for the customers to leave, closed the door and started to talk against the Jews, they were not people, they killed Jesus, etc. Then Puntov said that "his safe was full of jewelry and gold, taken from them before boarding the boats, which were sewn in their clothes and other places; he showed me a small wooden box, which later disappeared; when I saw his wife a second time, I reminded her about the safe, she immediately denied, saying they never had a safe" (Спомени на Надежда Василева, p. 12).

The behavior of Slavi Puntov alarmed the authorities. In the spring of 1944, during the Bozhilov government, an inspector came from Sofia to investigate his deeds as the local Commissar for the Jewish Questions. Vasileva heard from a police officer who knew her and wondered why she was not called as a witness. She went to the station and asked for the inspector, Svetoslav Nikolov. This was the same person who investigated Alexander Belev, his testimony at the People's Tribunal was quoted in Chapter 9. She entered a big room, with many Jews, and when one of the local Jewish leaders, Dr. Alfandari, saw her he said: "This is the Bulgarian I was talking about, Mr. Inspector, she was the only one running and helping at that time when nobody dared to help our Thracian and Aegean compatriots." She started to talk, but she remembered only that she and everybody else was crying. Nikolov shook her hand and told her that as a woman and Bulgarian, it was the honorable thing to do and she was the only one to clear the stain caused by other people. Then he asked her to write down everything to be added to his files (Спомени на Надежда Василева, p. 19).

Frederick Chary clarified the inspection in his book. Nikolov audited Puntov because the latter misused money, he "received from the passport bureau over 100,000 leva ($1,210) confiscated from the Jews and another 40,000 leva ($486) confiscated by customs, along with some miscellaneous valuables." Puntov claimed that he deposited the money in the bank, but the auditor could not find such deposit. Then, he tried to make a deposit during the audit, but the bank was already closed for the day. Puntov also asked a Customs official to issue a note for 40,000, instead of 100,000 leva of confiscated valuables. (Chary, 1972, p. 120).

We have a description of the boat trip from Lom, thanks to the testimony of Dr. Mindizov at the People's Tribunal in March 1943. He was called as a witness against the employees of the Commissariat for the Jews Questions. The Commissariat requested five doctors from the Doctors' Union to accompany the Jews on the boats. Nobody wanted to go, because they found the deportation unacceptable. Then Belev told them that if he sent Jewish doctors, the Germans would not let them return.

Dr. Mindizov and others had no other choice but to go. From Lom, he left on the first boat with Dr. Tsenov. The staff included two Germans, an officer and a sergeant, and 15 Bulgarian policemen. The Jews look tired and weary. The food was not good – dried goat meat and hard bread. Too many people were onboard, and it was too hot underneath the surface. A 78 year old man died on the way and two women gave birth. Eventually, they reached Vienna; the order from their management in Bulgaria was to continue to Katowicz. However, the German authorities in Vienna treated everybody badly: "Why does that rabble need doctors? If somebody dies, throw him in the Danube. They should not get any help."

Then the Germans complained that the brought human material was too bad: "Where are the Sofia Jews?" Dr. Mindizov replied that they were needed in Bulgaria, but he sounded rude. He was detained by a German commander who checked his passport and asked him, if he was a baptized Jew. The doctor had to prove physically that he was not a Jew. They let him go. The Germans started to load the Jews on a train and the Bulgarian doctors gave them all medications they had. A German Major, commandant of the port, was counting the Jews and whipping every one of them. He refused to let the doctors go any further with the Jews and sent them back to Bulgaria. The doctor was appalled that the Jews were searched naked at the Lom port and was upset with the bad conditions on the boat. When Dr. Mindizov returned, he complained to the health authorities. It seems they chastised Belev, because when the two met, he was very rude and demanded a report from the doctor. The latter refused and said that he wrote reports only for his bosses.

Going back to the trip topic, Dr. Mindizov said that the Bulgarian police treated well the Jews on the boat. However, every time the boat approached a port, the Jews had to hide under the surface. During the trip, three people ran away. Then, he was asked by the prosecutor:

> "PEOPLE'S PROSECUTOR MANCHO RAHAMIMOV: What did the German mean when he said that they were bad human material?
>
> "DR. MINDIZOV: I thought that he wanted better-fed people.
>
> "MR: So that they can work in factories?
>
> "M: Frankly, I could not understand his idea. I think he was comparing them with the Sofia Jews. He even asked about them.
>
> "MR: I meant were those people sent to work in factories or elsewhere?
>
> "M: My personal impression was that sick women, old people, mothers with babies, cannot work in factories. They sent them to get rid of them.
>
> "MR: Did you know about the crematorium in Katowicz?
>
> "M: I did not know at the time.

"MR: And do you know now?"

"M: My impression was that it was a whole process, transporting them to a sure death. An old woman can't be a worker" (People's Court Session No.9, 1945, p. 817-820).

The communists took power in Bulgaria in September 1944. Shortly thereafter, they organized a show trial to punish politicians, parliamentarians, military officers and intellectuals with ties to the previous governments. It was called People's Tribunal; its Seventh Section was supposed to deal with the anti-Semitic crimes. The only people charged with participation in the deportations in Thrace and Macedonia, were Belev and a few employees of his Commissariat. Not a single police or military officer of those who brutalized the Jews in the occupied territories was charged. On the other hand, prominent politicians and parliamentarians who risked their lives to help Jews, were sentenced to death or life in prison. As usual, the purpose of the communist courts was not to deliver justice, but to eliminate the political competition.

In the introduction to Mr. Tashev's study, the tireless defender of Bulgaria in Israel Samuel Arditti, who has witnessed many events of that time, pointed out that the fate of the Macedonian and Aegean Jews is routinely used in campaigns promoted by foreign interests and leftist citizens of Bulgaria (Jewish and Bulgarian) to discredit the country. The purpose of that denigration is to belittle Bulgaria's role in the rescue of its 48,000 Jews. Mr. Arditti listed numerous factual arguments that must be considered when assessing the events and the political forces at that time.

He is convinced that it is impossible to make moral judgments without considering the situation in southern Europe at that time. Applying modern standards to that complicated period distorts history. The critics of Bulgaria are mum on some basic facts:

"They don't say that Bulgaria was a small and weak state. The Bulgarian Army was brave, but poorly armed. Such a country could not determine who was going to rule the world – democrats, Nazis or Bolsheviks. Bulgaria had already experienced two national catastrophes and King Boris III desperately tried to prevent a new catastrophe. Practically, Bulgaria was a German vassal with seemingly independent Government. The German military headquarters were in the [park] Boris Garden, a five-minute walk from the Royal Palace.

Gestapo even contemplated a coup against the Government with the help from Ratniks and Legionnaires. Thrace and Macedonia were occupied initially by the German Army, without Bulgarian military participation. The Germans were in control and considered the Jews in those lands "their own", as Lilyana Panitsa, the secretary of Belev, testified... The people, who want to degrade Bulgaria, don't consider the strategic and actual participation of the Nazis in the Holocaust in the Aegean region and Macedonia. They exonerate the true criminals, Hitler, Eichmann, and Beckerle. Unwittingly, they become collaborators in the vindication of the beast from Berlin" (Ташев, p. 2-5).

The Germans were not satisfied with those deportations, they wanted to expand their "business" into the old territories of Bulgaria. And Alexander Belev and his Commissariat were willing to help them...

11 FIRST DEPORTATION ATTEMPT – MARCH 1943

The attempt to deport about 8,000 Jews from the old borders of Bulgaria in March 1943, is a direct consequence of the agreement between Dannecker and Belev. Historians and political agitators who want to pin the deportations of the Jews in Macedonia and Aegean Thrace to the sinister Bulgarian politicians and the indifference of the Bulgarian people in general, fail to notice or deliberately ignore the complexity of the situation. In the previous chapter, I covered the issue about the enormous power that Germany had over Bulgaria and the actions of its government. That applies on the changing German attitudes toward "resolving" the Jewish Question, which the part of the Bulgarian political class that sided with Germany was expected to follow.

The secrecy that surrounded all German actions against Jews eventually blurred the picture of the events in March 1943 in Bulgaria. The only undisputable facts that we know are that the Commissar for the Jewish Questions was in the advanced stage of secret preparations to deport about 8,000 Jews from old Bulgaria, with the blessing of Prof. Filov's government, but the order was stopped or cancelled on March 9, 1943. From that point on, we enter the realm of hypotheses and guesses. What did the actors in those dramatic events actually do? Who revealed the secret? Who cancelled the order? Did the people involved know what the Germans have planned for the deported Jews?

It is difficult to give definitive answers to those questions, because we don't have written records about the most crucial decisions of the King and the high echelons of the government. Still, we have memoirs and letters of the participants of those events. None of them understood the whole picture, but the bits and pieces, reveled through their actions in the early days of March, can help us build a more or less accurate timetable of the events. So, their records will be used extensively in this chapter.

Before we start digging deeper, it is important to understand why secrecy was so important to Germany in handling the Jewish Question. Adolf Hitler never made a secret of his hatred of Jews – it was on full display since the 1920s on the pages of "Mein Kampf" and in many speeches he delivered over the years. However, what was considered a collection of annoying anti-Semitic ramblings during the Weimar Republic, became the target of intense scrutiny after the Nazis took power in 1933 and Hitler's writings became the blueprint for the National Socialist revolution.

The first measures against the Jews in 1933 and especially the virulent rhetoric of Hitler and Goebbels, triggered a wide boycott against the German economy, organized by the world Jewry. It was something the Nazis did not expect.

> "While some Jewish efforts were dedicated to the use of diplomacy for defensive purposes, others attempted to use economic warfare, with the hope of toppling the Nazi regime or at least forcing the Nazis to moderate their antisemitic cam¬paign. A number of anti-Nazi boycott groups sprang up sponta¬neously among Polish, American, and Palestinian Jews in Febru¬ary and March 1933, in response to the first news of Nazi antisemitic persecution... While a unified boycott movement might have affected the German economy, unity proved difficult to obtain. The various boycott groups differed among themselves, and some of the most important Jewish organizations including the Board of Deputies of British Jews, the Anglo-Jewish Association, the Alliance Israelite Universelle, and the American Jewish Com¬mittee all opposed the idea of boycotting Germany" (Edelheit, 1994, p. 139-140).

Despite the lack of good organization, the boycott affected the German economy, which still was suffering from the economic consequences of the war defeat and the enormous reparations that crippled the German industries. The Nazi policies changed, assuming a more "flexible" approach. For the time being, the emphasis was placed on Jewish emigration and the Nazis were willing to facilitate it by allowing Jews to export capitals and move to Mandate Palestine. The details of the so-called Haavara agreement, which outlined that process, are out of the scope of this book, but they can be found in various publications like Avraham Barkai's article "German Interests in the Haavara-Transfer Agreement 1933-1939" (Barkai, 1990, p. 249-257) and Edwin Black's book "The Transfer Agreement" (Black, 1990). What is important to note is that the Haavara agreement between the Nazi Germany and some Zionist groups helped thousands of Jews to leave and evade persecution. They managed to save some of their wealth, which was transferred to Palestine, mostly through German exports to the Mandate.

The uneasy collaboration between Nazis and Jews in that period was grudgingly accepted by Hitler as a temporary measure, which was abandoned after the Nazi regime became stronger and switched from emigration to extermination. However, to avoid something similar to the clash of 1933, Hitler thought that keeping those policies secret was extremely important. After the invasion of the Soviet Union, the mass extermination of the Jews started in earnest. To keep the information under control, Hitler issued a strict order concerning "the handling and safeguarding of secrets":

> "25 September 1941
> Basic Order
> 1. No one, no office, or no officer may learn of any matter that is to be kept secret, unless they must absolutely have knowl¬edge of same for official reasons.
> 2. No office and no officer may learn more of any matter that is to be held secret than is absolutely necessary for the carrying out of their duties.
> 3. No office and no officer may learn earlier of a matter to be kept secret or of that part necessary for them unless this is absolutely necessary for the carrying out of their duties.
> 4. Thoughtless passing on of orders, the keeping secret of which is of decisive importance, according to any kind of general distribution key, is forbidden.
> Signed: Adolf Hitler" (Hitler's Order about Secrets, 1941, p. 173).

In Germany, as an orderly and disciplined country, the order was followed strictly and the information about the magnitude of the Jewish catastrophe was kept successfully under the lid. Even in the territories under German control, where most of the atrocities were taking place, many people knew little or nothing about what was going on. In his book on the Jewish survival during the Holocaust, Evgeny Finkel analyzes the responses of the Jewish communities in the endangered territories (mostly Poland, Belarus, Ukraine and elsewhere) and concludes that due to deep secrecy and the never-before seen character of the German actions, many Jews never suspected the real nature of the danger. Even in Krakow, a city close to some major extermination camps, the Germans successfully maintained a deceptive picture through disinformation:

> "The importance of knowledge can also be clearly seen when we analyze the behavior of Krakow ghetto inmates during deportations to death camps. Initially, argue the survivors, no one knew what the term "deportation to the East" meant, and German authorities invested considerable effort in spreading rumors, mainly through their Jewish collaborators, that the deportees were being sent to Ukraine, where they would work in labor camps and agriculture. "No one imagined that those who were deported were being killed," recalled Henry T. "We knew that Auschwitz was a concentration [rather than death] camp, but what was going on there we had no idea," claimed Solomon S. Ida L. believed that Auschwitz was "a special camp for older people." Regina L., like most other Jews in the ghetto, believed that she was being sent to a labor camp in Ukraine, and worried more about her family members who stayed behind, hidden with a Polish peasant, than about her own fate. But prior to boarding the train, she was told by a Ukrainian guard that she did not need new shoes and water because she was going "straight to the oven." Regina L. and her sister jumped off the train and survived. In her case, it was new and unexpected information, received from a person who certainly had not planned to help her, that prompted Regina L. to change her survival strategy" (Finkel, 2017, p. 61).

The intention to destroy the Jews was clearly stated by the top Nazi leadership. Gustav Richter was an adviser on the Jewish Question at the German Embassy in Bucharest. He was providing instructions to Marshal Antonescu and other Romanian leaders on how to get rid of the Jews in the country. Arrested by the Russians after the occupation of Romania, he spent years in the Soviet Union. He revealed important information about the treatment of Jews, as his statement in "Protocol of the Interrogation of the Sturmbahnfuerer of SS Gustav Richter, October 5, 1947" shows:

> "Question: What was meant under "final solution of the Jewish Question"?

> "Richter: The final solution of the Jewish Question meant the complete physical extermination of all Jews in all European territories occupied by German troops. The first secret order about the extermination was issued by Goering to the Chief of the Security Police of Germany Heydrich on July 31, 1941. I personally read that order, at a meeting with Eichmann, who was appointed by Heydrich to manage directly the extermination of the Jews. The German policy toward Jews was formulated clearly enough by Hitler in his speech of February 24, 1943, before the members of the "old guard" on the anniversary of the establishment of the National-Socialist Party. Hitler stated that by the end of the war, all Jews must be totally destroyed" (Тайны дипломатии Третьего рейха, p. 669-670).

Technically, that was not a speech, but a proclamation that Hitler sent to the commemoration of the party's foundation in Munich on February 24. Hitler did not attend the event in person, because just a few weeks earlier his armies suffered the humiliating defeat at Stalingrad. On the Jewish Question, the proclamation states the following:

> "After all, thank God, not only the Jews in London and New York but also those in Moscow made clear what fate might be in store for the German Volk. We are determined to be no less clear in our answer. This fight will not end with the planned annihilation of the Aryan but with the extermination of the Jew in Europe. Beyond this, thanks to this fight, our movement's world of thought will become the common heritage of all people, even of our enemies. State after state will be forced, in the course of its fight against us, to apply National Socialist theories in waging this war that was provoked by them. And in so doing, it will become aware of the curse that the criminal work of Jewry has laid over all people, especially through this war" (Hitler, Speeches 1932-1945, Vol. IV, p. 2763).

The German original of the highlighted phrase is: "Dieser Kampf wird deshalb auch nicht, wie man es beabsichtigt, mit der Vernichtung der arischen Menschheit, sondern mit der Ausrottung des Judentums in Europa sein Ende finden" (Hitler, Reden 1932-1945, p. 1992). Some revisionists question the use of "die Ausrottung", that Hitler did not mean "extermination", but the common usage of the word disproves that objection. Others question the term "das Judentum" – it has a broader meaning than "der Jude" (Jew) and encompasses the Jewish religion, culture and way of life, so they are willing to interpret the phrase as "eradicating Jewishness". Despite the semantic questioning, the practice of Nazi Germany left no doubt that physical extermination was its pursued goal.

The German approach differed profoundly from the policies in Bulgaria. So, a blanket condemnation of the Bulgarian politicians and the Bulgarian people at large about insufficient activism is not fair. If even the people in the eye of the storm were deceived, those who were farther away, could hardly get a correct idea about the German intentions. But even with their incomplete knowledge, they sensed that something wrong was going on and many were trying to help.

Some employees of the "Fascist Government" started helping Jews long before the demand for deportation was made. Bulgaria is often accused that it did not protest the arrest and deportation of a small number of Bulgarian Jews who resided in Germany and some other Nazi-occupied lands. Italy is given as an example of the contrary – it managed to protect its Jews living abroad. Bulgaria was much less important to Germany and its protests hardly mattered, but it is unfair to assume that nothing was done. The Bulgarian diplomat N. Balabanov was one of those who tried to help.

In a letter from N. Balabanov to Benjamin Arditti, dated October 21, 1960, the former Bulgarian Ambassador to Turkey, described his work to help the Jews. Among other things, he explained that when he was assigned to Vichy France in 1942, he witnessed the beginning of persecution of the Jews demanded by Germany. He intervened several times on behalf of Jews who were Bulgarian citizens. He even met the Prime Minister of the Vichy Regime Pierre Laval and managed to improve the situation of many Jews. Balabanov also arranged the release of H. Menahemov from a camp, just before his deportation to Germany (Balabanov to Arditti Letter, 1960, p. 3). It is not clear, if his intervention was successful because Bulgarian Jews in France were still deported, but Bulgaria did not have the military and diplomatic weight that Italy had.

The Bulgarian archives keep information about the fascinating story of four Bulgarian diplomats who started to issue transit visas to Jews crossing Bulgaria on their ways to Palestine. The little-known activities of N. Vachev, Harry Levenson, Lyuben Zlatarov and N. Petsev are at the level of the widely-publicised work of the Japanese Consul in Lithuania Chiune Sugihara who saved about

6,000 Jews by providing transit visas to Japan.

The four diplomats had been aware of the fate faced by the Jews in the European countries, so they started issuing transit visas to Jews leaving for the Mandate Palestine, despite the ban by the Foreign Ministry, risking their careers and possibly their lives.

Among the preserved documents are the memoirs of Lyuben Zlatarov, one of the four diplomats involved. He recalled that, starting in 1941, due to rumors that the European Jews were being sent to camps, the Bulgarian Embassies in Bucharest and Budapest saw a surge in applications for transit visas through Bulgaria for Turkey and Palestine. The new anti-Jewish legislation in Bulgaria prohibited such visas for Jews, except in special cases with the permission of section State Security of the Police Directorate, but they rejected almost all applications forwarded to them by the embassies.

However, the four Bulgarian diplomats, working at the Foreign Ministry in Sofia, felt that such policies went against their convictions and conscience and took the risk of issuing transit visas for Jews. Nikola Petsev was Minister Plenipotentiary at the Consul Directorate and Nikola Vanchev, Harry Levenson and Lyuben Zlatarov were advisers at the same Directorate. On August 12, 1941, Petsev notified the State Security section that temporarily only the Foreign Ministry will be issuing transit visas to Jews, which contradicted the older (but still valid) order. He took an enormous risk, because if someone reported his letter to the higher authorities, he and his collaborators could have been charged with sabotage of government orders. Fortunately, nobody reported the letter. The diplomats continued to help Jews go through Bulgaria under the radar.

The officially granted visas by the government were scrutinized. For example, on January 9, 1943, the Bulgarian Foreign Ministry approved the request of the International Red Cross to grant transit visas for 200 Jewish children from Romania and Hungary for Palestine. The first group of 70 entered Bulgaria without problems. On April 4, the embassy in Bucharest issued another 73 visas to the second group, however, the next day the ministry asked the group not to leave Romania, because it would not be allowed in Bulgaria. The German Embassy in Sofia demanded the cancellation. Ambassador Beckerle explained in a report that the Bulgarian government did not realize that the Jewish Question has not been solved in Hungary and Romania, so the embassy did not want Jews to leave those countries.

At the same time, Beckerle and Filov did not suspect that four employees of the Foreign Ministry kept issuing transit visas secretly. It is difficult to determine the number of the visas because a large part of the archives of the embassies and the Foreign Ministry is missing (shortly after the occupation in September 1944, the Russians took to Moscow many documents that still haven't been returned). There are documents for 430 visas but Zlatarov's estimate was that they let well over 1,000 Jews save their lives by going through Bulgaria (Транзитни визи, архив).

Despite the work of some diplomats and other government employees, the fate of the Bulgarian Jews seemed sealed. Belev and Dannecker needed another 8,000 Jews to fulfill the quota of 20,000 they agreed upon. That became the first attempt to deport Jews from Bulgaria. The operation was supposed to be executed in complete secrecy. However, unlike the orderly and disciplined Germany, where Hitler's call for secrecy was dutifully obeyed, Bulgaria was a rather disorderly country with a chaotic political life, so keeping secrets was not among the traits of most people.

As the Ratniks complained in the document in Appendix A about the poorly executed action in Thrace and Macedonia, government employees provided information to Jews to escape. Something similar happened in March 1943. Belev prepared lists of Jews to be picked up and urgently deported to Poland. They had to include undesirable elements but his idea about an "undesirable" was the class of the most prominent Jewish leaders, mostly Zionists. He wanted to decapitate the Jewish community.

As it was already noted in Chapter 9, the Bulgarian Government did not come up with the idea of the deportation of the Jews. The German proposal to the Bulgarian Government to deport the Jews followed the decisions of the Wannsee Conference of January 1942. Belev was in Germany when the conference took place and when he returned to Bulgaria, he became the tool through which the Nazi Government exercised its pressure on Bulgaria.

On June 1942, the People's Assembly debated a law proposed by the government to give powers to the government to take all measures to resolve the Jewish Question. Some MPs from the opposition were against it, but eventually it was accepted on June 25, 1942. It allowed the government to deal with the Jewish issues without consulting the parliament. That was an unusual decision, which changed the normal order of introducing policies in Bulgaria. Nir Baruh notes that fact: "It is important to emphasize that the transfer of the rights of the King and the People's

Assembly to the Government had no precedent and contradicted the spirit and the letter of the Constitution. Besides, the law applied to the Bulgarian Jews, not to the Jews in Thrace and Macedonia." (Барух, 1991, p. 73)

The decision was followed by Decree No. 70 of August 1942, which confirmed the restrictions imposed on the Jews and became the basis for establishing of the Commissariat for the Jewish Questions. The law was publicized and gave grave concerns to the Bulgarian Jews, but the rest of the society did not react.

In the early 1943, the government of Prof. Filov introduced a few other decrees, which remained secret and were not published in the State Gazette.

Among them was Decree No. 126, which stated that the real estate properties and houses of Jews deported from Bulgaria will be sold to the state in exchange for personal bonds with 3% annual interest, payable in full within 20 years, at prices determined by the government. All the other properties were to be sold and the proceeds deposited to blocked accounts at the Commissariat in the name of the original owner. All properties of the liquidated Jewish communities were to be transferred to the local communities (Постановление на МС №126, 1943). According to Decree No. 116, all deported Jews had to be stripped from their Bulgarian citizenship, if they were citizens at the time (Постановление на МС №116, 1943).

The harsh measures against the Jews affected even the school children. Expulsions of Jewish students from Bulgarian schools became more frequent, despite the protests of teachers and education officials against this injustice. The archives have preserved heartbreaking correspondence between the parents of several Jewish high school students, who were forced to leave school after the anti-Semitic laws were introduced. Very few of these cases were resolved favorably for the children. In one case, a girl that had been adopted by Jews at the age of 1, but was of Bulgarian background, was allowed to continue her studies (Кореспонденция по прилагане на ЗЗН в училищата, а.е. 1836, 1941-1943).

As it was mentioned in Chapter 10, the concrete measures against the Jews to prepare the expulsion from Bulgaria started only after SS Hauptsturmfuehrer Theodor Dannecker, "Eichmann's Apprentice", arrived in Bulgaria on January 21, 1943. He was the main liaison between Gestapo and the Commissariat. Over a month later, on February 4, 1943, Commissar Belev presented a report to Minister Gabrovski, in which he summarized his talks with Dannecker. The German officer introduced himself to Belev as an agent of the German Government authorized to arrange the deportation of the Jews from Thrace and Macedonia. He also told him that the Reich was willing to take all Jews from those regions, as well as the undesirable elements in the old borders, according to numbers determined by the Commissariat. Dannecker demanded that no less than 20,000 Jews should be deported. In January 1943, the German Ambassador Beckerle discussed the Jewish Question with Minister Gabrovski. According to his report, both were satisfied that the measures against Jews did not cause strong reactions. Gabrovski thought that the future deportations should start with the Jews from the new territories. In another report to Ribbentrop, dated February 8, 1943, Beckerle confirmed that the Jews in the "liberated territories" will be deported first (Барух, 1991, p. 74).

On February 16, 1943, Dannecker notified Berlin that the Cabinet, after long debates, approved Belev's deportation proposal. He also noted that Belev was going to arrest some undesirable Jews to ensure that a total of 20,000 are collected. In order to avoid riots, Belev planned to transfer the arrested Bulgarian Jews to the new territories, so that they could join there the transports leaving for Germany. On the same date, Beckerle sent a telegram to Berlin about a message he received from Prof. Filov. The Prime Minister confirmed that the Bulgarian Government agreed to deport 20,000 Jews from the new territories and also stated that Jewish men from old Bulgaria would be mobilized in labor groups for public works. On February 22, 1943, Dannecker and Belev signed an agreement for the deportation of 20,000 Jews from the new territories. In the official Bulgarian copy, somebody crossed out the words Macedonia and Thrace, to make it sound as if it applied to Bulgaria as well. There were no changes in the German copy... The agreement was drawn after a phone conversation with Eichmann and was signed after he received the draft (Барух, 1991, p. 75). Ink with the same color was used for the correction and Belev's signature, which made many people think that Belev made the change.

The agreement demanded payments from Bulgaria to cover the expenses for the deportation, which totalled 2,840,750 Deutsche Mark.

A special Circular No. 5712 was released by the Commissariat on the day the agreement was signed. It asked all of its representatives in all towns to prepare within 24 hours detailed lists of all rich and influential Jewish families. Special emphasis was given to locating leaders with anti-government opinions. The lists were not supposed to include baptized Jews, women and men married to Bulgarians, war heroes, decorated veterans and so on. A second circular, sent by Belev the next day, asked the local commissars in Sofia and Vratsa to provide the lists within five days. The employees scoured the archives of the Jewish communities to prepare the lists. Within days, the names of about 9,000 Jews were sent to the Commissariat and Belev selected for deportation 8,400 of them (Барух, 1991, p. 77-78).

The Cabinet confirmed the Dannecker-Belev agreement on March 2 and made several decisions: ordered the Bulgarian State Railways to transport the Jews without payment; created district commissions for organizing Jewish camps; all deported Jews were to lose their citizenship; the property of the deported Jews was to be confiscated, as it was mentioned above.

The main purpose of the Commissariat for the Jewish Questions was to exclude the Jews from the economic life of the Kingdom. Since the money of the Jews was the major source of the budget of that institution, the liquidation of businesses was the only action that was consistently pursued, although many Jews found ways to keep control of their enterprises under nominal Bulgarian ownership. By late 1942, the Commissariat had liquidated about 2,000 Jewish factories, of which 1870 with capital under 600,000 leva and 150 with capital over that sum. The blocked bank accounts of Jews were transferred to fund "Jewish Communities", which soon grew to 4,715,025 leva. The money was used for the needs of Jewish families and distributed by the Commissariat. The homes of the Jews expelled to other towns were controlled by the Commissariat. They were rented to mobilized employees, newlyweds, families with many children and also used for other government purposes. The stores were rented out (Шарланов, 2009, p. 129).

The Commissariat continued its secret work to prepare trains and locations for deportations. In early March 1943, the Jews in Kyustendil received orders to provide utensils for preparing food at an empty tobacco warehouse. At the same time, curfew was imposed. Meanwhile, in other places, like Plovdiv, the Jews in the local lists were also ready to be picked up and moved to the railway stations.

This will be covered in detail below, but I should mention that the secrecy of Belev's preparations was compromised and several people, including from his own office, put in motion events that spoiled his and Dannecker's carefully built plans.

It is not clear what exactly happened. In his report about the events, the German Ambassador Beckerle mentioned that the deportation was stopped by an order from "the highest place". The highest place in Bulgaria at the time was the King. As I noted before, the King was already convinced that Germany was losing the war but couldn't oppose it openly. He couldn't allow such mistreatment either. R. Crampton is right about the complicated situation:

> "The king followed rather than led opinion on the Jewish question, but once he had been persuaded to forbid the deportations from Bulgaria proper he stuck to his decision. The critical issue was citizenship. Boris argued, as did others opposed to the deportations, that any decision affecting Bulgarian citizens could only be made by the Bulgarian authorities; it was a matter of national sovereignty as well as human decency. No doubt another consideration was that after Stalingrad it appeared ever more likely that the Germans would lose the war, and the United States had already made it known that after the war anyone guilty of persecuting the Jews would be punished. Beckerle eventually recognized that the Jewish question in Bulgaria and the Balkans was different from in other areas; the Bulgarians, he said, had grown up with Greeks, Armenians, and Turks, and therefore did not have the antipathy to Jews found in northern Europe, and he concluded eventually that Berlin should not endanger its political standing in Sofia by pursuing the matter any further" (Crampton, 2007, p. 266).

One of the important figures that revealed the sinister plans of the Commissariat was Belev's secretary, Lilyana Panitsa. A young and intelligent woman, she was sympathetic to the plight of the Jews. When she saw the lists that she had to type, she alerted her friend Buko Levi, a Zionist activist, about the coming deportations. He was among the "undesirables". She told him that she could not delete his name because he was too well known and Belev targeted people like him.

Despite her contributions, about a year later, after the communist coup, she was accused of anti-Semitism and put on trial at the People's Tribunal, along with other employees of the Commissariat. The People's Prosecutor Mancho Rahamimov made a condescending presentation of the charges against Lilyana Panitsa:

> "Lilyana Panitsa, private secretary of Belev. His most trusted person, as such, she was aware of all secret correspondence. She followed and fulfilled all his orders, and when he had been absent, she herself had issued orders... She, along with Belev and Dobrevski, went to the Aegean territories, but didn't have any assigned duties. Even as a private secretary, she had been implementing the policies of the Commissariat. She was satisfied with the deportations and felt unhappy when they stopped. Here, at the People's Tribunal, she confessed everything and stated that her work at the Commissariat had contributed to the persecution of the Jews and thus disgraced the Bulgarian people. The witnesses confirmed that she had done favors of nature that can't be ignored and should be considered in determining her sentence. Despite those favors, she is guilty under the Law for the People's Tribunal and should be punished, though with a lighter sentence" (People's Court Session No.18, 1945, p. 1946-1947).

The accusation is another proof of the farcical nature of the tribunal – it was proven that Panitsa shared with prominent Jews confidential information about the imminent deportation. In his ridiculous statement, the prosecutor accused her of not showing support for Jews at her office; it probably didn't matter to him that such a behavior would blow her cover and bring a severe punishment. She was treated horribly after her arrest, tortured and beaten with sticks by the "People's Militia", see (Ардити, 2014), and she died only a year later at the age of 29. Despite the attempts of Samuel Arditti, Yad Vashem refused to recognize her as Righteous Among the Nations, despite the risks she took to help Jews.

Additional information about Miss Panitsa's family is provided in the testimony of the former German Ambassador Beckerle, during an interrogation in Moscow on January 30, 1950. Due to the age of the "rich woman" he describes, it is doubtful that she was Lilyana Panitsa. However, the activities of the family left little doubt that they were not on the side of Germany:

> "Shortly after I arrived in Bulgaria in 1941 Bollmann [the representative of the Reich Security] shared with me his suspicions about a rich woman in Bulgaria – Panitsa, I don't know her first name; she had wealth of several million leva. She, according to Bollmann's information, was a staunch Anglophile. Her home in Sofia and her cottage at the resort of Pancharevo, were hospitable places to meet employees of the

British Embassy. Through her son-in-law, a well-known merchant, she had conspirative contacts with the English spy Smith-Ross. Bollmann told me that after the British Embassy moved from Bulgaria to Turkey, the contacts of the Panitsa family with the British intelligence continued with the previous intensity through commercial channels. Since Panitsa gladly invited to her home high-ranking German military officers, we suspected that it was done to collect intelligence information. The German counterintelligence warned all offices and staffs of the German Army in Bulgaria about their suspicion of the family. I requested many times from Bollmann facts about the transfer of intelligence data from Panitsa to the British, but he was only able to monitor her meetings with British spies and nothing more. With this information, I did not dare to ask the Bulgarian authorities to take repressive measures against Panitsa, because she was influential and had close ties with the Royal Palace, the Cabinet and other high-rank personalities" (Тайны дипломатии Третьего рейха, p. 65-66).

The person she warned about the deportations, Buko Levi, did the honorable thing and showed up at her trial to testify in her defense, despite the attempts of the prosecution to belittle her work and discredit Levi. The testimony covered his relations with Panitsa and her assistance in relaying information regarding the deportation plans for the Jews of Sofia in March 1943. It has been preserved in the archives:

"CHAIRMAN: Do you know Miss Panitsa?
"WITNESS DR. BUKO LEVI: Yes.
"C.: How do you know her?
"B.L.: Miss Panitsa did some favors to the Jews, that is how I know her. I was the Deputy Chairman of the Jewish Consistory in Sofia. Around the end of February 1943, we received information that the Jews in the Aegean region and Macedonia were going to be deported. The Commissariat for the Jewish Questions was hiding carefully from us and the public what was planned for those Jews. Something more, from the documents published recently, it became clear that the Commissariat tried deliberately to deceive the public opinion that the Jews were not going to Poland or elsewhere but were being moved within the old borders of Bulgaria. It was done to avoid a negative reaction from the Bulgarian public opinion, which could create obstacles to the work of the Commissariat. To us, the members of the Consistory, it was of enormous importance to learn the

intentions of the Commissariat. And we were able to get the information. A few days before March 10, 1943, a gentleman visited me with the message that the Jews of Thrace and Macedonia would be deported to Poland. The most interesting part was that he knew the exact time when the deportation was going to start, then he added that later the Jews in the old borders of Bulgaria would be sent to Poland as well.

"I asked him how he learned all that. He said he obtained the information from Miss Panitsa. Since our family, specifically my wife, knew Miss Panitsa, I decided one morning to check whether the rumors were true. They turned out to be true, I confirmed that the Commissariat actually planned to deport not only the Jewish population in the Aegean region and Macedonia, but also the Jews in old Bulgaria, including Sofia. The action would start at night, early in the morning of March 11, when several Jews in Sofia would be arrested, including me and my family. I reported the news to our Consistory. We exchanged thoughts and tried to find a way to avoid the blow against the Jews and do something, as much as our situation allowed.

"We had only one tool at our disposal: to mobilize the progressive public opinion, organize the progressive elements among the Bulgarian public to react against the Commissariat's measures. We found Bulgarians, who, for the sake of Bulgaria's honor, supported the Jewish minority. Ever since the mistreatment of the Bulgarian Jews began, the progressive elements among the Bulgarian public opinion proved and continued to prove that they did not share the position of the government. They joined the struggle against the mistreatment and that was the situation until March 10. Then the Jews from the Aegean region and Macedonia were sent to Poland.

"C.: We already know all that.

"B.L.: However, it is known that no Jews were deported to Poland from the old Bulgarian territory. I should say that in the period from March 10 to May 24, 1943, we were in a tense situation, because we did not know what the Commissariat was plotting against the Jews in Bulgaria. At that time, I contacted Miss Panitsa as a representative of the Consistory. I met her several times, five or six times. At every meeting I requested information about the plans of the Commissariat against us. And she told me that Commissar Belev intended to deport the Bulgarian Jews to solve the Jewish Question in Bulgaria in a radical way. He planned to send us to Poland.

"She already knew about some of our successes and said that we shouldn't think that the fight was over, because Belev, on the contrary, had even more radical plans to fight the Jewry and was not going to stay idle. She also told me something very important. She told me that Belev was working on the issue with the German police and that on behalf of the German police, the German Dannecker signed an agreement with the Commissariat to arrange our deportation. That was the first time I heard about that notorious agreement, which apparently demanded the deportation of 20,000 Jews to Poland. The news surprised us and that's why we made even more efforts to bring to our side the progressive public and fight strongly the planned measures. All that important information came from Miss Panitsa. She knew that I was the Deputy Chairman of the Consistory and her reports were of enormous help to us.

"C.: Did you know that she was an anti-Semite?

"B.L.: I told you that considering her actions, the way she treated us, and her ideas, she could not be an employee of the Commissariat for the Jewish Questions. She already made some confessions, but from her explanations at the time, I realized that her motivation for sharing the information with us was of personal nature and that other reasons, also personal, forced her to work at the Commissariat.

"COUNSEL STOENCHEV: Were you hiding at that time?

"B.L.: Since May 24, after some of the Sofia Jews were sent to provincial towns, I went into hiding, because we were convinced that the expulsion was just an early stage in the action for deporting the Jews to Poland. I lived underground for seven months.

"S.: Did Miss Panitsa know where you were hiding?

"B.L.: Yes, she knew.

"S.: She knew very well that you were living underground?

"B.L.: Yes.

"S.: And despite that, she didn't report you?

"B.L.: Of course, she didn't.

"S.: Did you know [Commissariat's agent Krustyu] Kozarov?

"B.L.: I was hiding for several months in different houses. At certain time, I was in the home of the parents of our colleague Haimov when the police raided it. They asked for everybody's address cards. Of course, I didn't have an address card, so Kozarov wanted to arrest me. However, I asked him not to arrest me and he let me go. I asked him not just for me, but also because of the old Haimov, who was in a very difficult situation at the time, moreover, if the authorities found out that he was sheltering a person without an address card, who was also in hiding, he could have been arrested and harassed.

"S.: Were you aware that Kozarov was sent to capture you?

"B.L.: I don't know the reason why he came to the house and how he found me, but what I know was that he came and wanted to know how many people lived in the house and asked for the address cards. Obviously, he was looking for people in hiding. Whether he was looking for me or somebody else, I don't know, but that's what he did at the time.

"S.: He was looking for you.

"B.L.: I wasn't aware of that.

"PEOPLE'S PROSECUTOR MANCHO RAHAMIMOV: When did you meet Miss Panitsa for the first time?

"B.L.: Long time ago, before the anti-Jewish law.

"M.R.: Was she paid for her favors?

"B.L.: She never asked me for any compensation. As far as I remember, she asked my wife once for a small purse, but we have never given her any money.

"M.R.: Did you ever hear that she was mistreating Jews?

"B.L.: There were complaints about bad behavior, but not against Miss Panitsa, they were against [her colleague at the Commissariat] Miss Pavlova. There was an enormous number of complaints against her.

"M.R.: Did Miss Panitsa do favors to the Jewish families or something else?

"B.L.: She did favors.

"M.R.: Were those favors to all Jewish families, to all Jews?

"B.L.: Beyond any doubt, she was helping everybody. It wasn't just about me. If she wasn't ready to help all Jews, I would not have been able to get help from her" (People's Court Session No.16, 1945, p. 1498-1503).

Lilyana Panitsa did the same again in May 1943, when she warned Jews about arrests, as it will become clear from the testimony of Dr. J. Benaroya at the People's Tribunal in the next chapter (People's Court Session No.16, 1945, p. 1577-1580). Despite the honest testimonies, both Panitsa and the Commissariat's agent Krustyu Kozarov, were punished.

Another alert came from an unlikely source. Dr. Iosif Vatev was an investigative physician who worked for the Commissariat; he also was a brother-in-law of the Minister of the Interior Peter Gabrovski, the notorious anti-Semite. "Vatev investigated medical complaints from Jews wishing to avoid expulsion from Sofia. He would verify medical disability only if given a bribe and presumably was not above fabricating medical excuses. When his assistant, Iordan Lazanov, a KEV agent, told Belev of the doctor's activity, the commissar dismissed both men. Vatev's connections with Gabrovski saved him from further punishment, and Belev threatened Lazanov if he went elsewhere with the story" (Chary, 1972, p. 68).

"On February 25, Haim Rahamim Behar of Kiustendil while in Sofia visiting relatives met Vatev, the commissariat doctor, near the consistory office. Vatev told him that he knew a great secret and asked Behar what it was worth to him. Behar bribed Vatev to talk and hence learned of the impending deportations." (Chary, 1972, p. 89) This is another proof of the strange ways of the Bulgarian politics, where secrets are impossible to keep and people, who are supposed to work against Jews, act in a totally unexpected way. It is hard to imagine something like that happening in Germany. However, this was one of the many factors that saved the Bulgarian Jews from deportation.

Another case of people with ties to the government getting involved in helping Jews, was presented in the book of the retired diplomat Christo Boyadjieff "Saving the Bulgarian Jews in World War II":

> "Richard Crampton from the University of Kent (U.K.) who is preparing the publication of the 'Archives and Memoirs of Ivan Stanchoff (a former Bulgarian diplomat and close friend of the Royal family) sent to the author, through the Stanchoff family, some excerpts from the book: 'Among Mrs. Marion Stanchoff's acquaintances in Sofia was Mrs. Mitzi Karakasheva, widow of a former very popular Director of the State Railways who, after the death of her husband, had maintained links with many railway employees. One afternoon in March 1943, Mrs. Karakasheva received a telephone call from one such employee, the Stationmaster at Kyustendil, who was in a state of distress. His message induced the same condition in Mrs. Karakasheva. The Stationmaster reported that there had recently arrived from Salonika a train which consisted of sealed cars heavily guarded by German soldiers; the train had been shunted into a siding not far from the town. Where the train was headed for was unknown, but it was thought to be Poland. If there was uncertainty as to the ultimate destination of the train, there was no doubt as to its contents: the shrieks and screams of the entombed Jews made that all too apparent. This appalling spectacle produced a most human but dangerous reaction on the part of the good peasants living near the siding. The populace was up in arms, peasants were coming with whatever they could find to break open the coaches. The German soldiers had orders to prevent this - an ugly battle could break out at

any moment. In despair the Stationmaster had turned to Mrs. Karakasheva in the hope that she would tell the King, who would then order the release of the poor deportees. In turn Mrs. Karakasheva had approached Mrs. Stanchoff who, she knew, was working closely with the Queen on certain welfare projects. Mrs. Stanchoff immediately telephoned the Queen who promised, in turn, to inform the King. The following afternoon, when Mrs. Stanchoff was at [palace] Vranya on welfare business, the King sought her out. His words, as recalled by Mrs. Stanchoff, were: 'Yes, it is all horrible. In this case there is nothing I can do. They are not my citizens. But it won't happen with ours. I am seeing to that. It will not be easy, though, and they will have it hard for a while. But they will not be taken, you'll see. In spite of appearances they will be safe. You'll see' (emphasis by the author)" (Boyadjieff, 1989, p 74-75).

Another person involved in the events of March 9-10, 1943, was the popular writer Elin Pelin, a close friend of the King. The Bulgarian historian Prof. Dinyu Sharlanov concludes from the testimony of Elin Pelin at the People's Tribunal, the diary of the King's adviser Sevov, and from the analysis of various documents, that the first signals for the imminent deportation of Jews from the old territories have been provided not by Dimitur Peshev, but by Elin Pelin. Seven hours before the meeting of Peshev with Gabrovski, the King had already told the Minister what to do. Sharlanov thinks that the big noise a few years ago to declare Peshev the only savior was not only false, but it also had the purpose to discredit King Boris III. On March 10, 1943, the German Ambassador in Sofia Beckerle wrote in his diary: "From Dannecker I learned that Gabrovski had ordered the release of all Jews from old Bulgaria and that the Commissar for the Jewish Questions had resigned. It happened exactly as I thought! My proposal to deport only the Jews from the occupied territories would have been much better" (Шарланов, 2009, p.133-135). Belev resigned after the failure of the March 1943 action, but Gabrovski did not accept his resignation.

Elin Pelin testified at the People's Tribunal in defense of his nephew, who worked for Belev's institution:

> "After Zachary Velkov [Elin Pelin's nephew. - M.M.] was hired by the Commissariat for the Jewish Questions, whenever Jews asked me for help, I contacted him. Often, he told me about bad plans against the Jews. For example, I heard from him the worst news [in March 1943] – that the Commissariat

had decided to send our Jews to Germany within ten days. I don't know whether the Commissariat made the decision or the government or the Minister of the Interior Gabrovski, but the decision for deportation was a fact. Since I had some connections with the King, I wrote to him and asked for a meeting. We met in the Palace. I shared my opinion with him.

As you know, I was one of those who signed the well-known letter in defense of the Jews from persecution. I am a member of the Writers' Union and on behalf of several colleagues I told the King that what was done to the Jews was despicable and inhumane. I told him that those people should be kept in the country at any price and shouldn't be handed to the Germans.

The King listened very carefully, then went to another room and phoned somebody. It was a long talk. I don't know who was on the other side, but the King came back upset and said: "Asses!" I didn't ask him whom he meant, because I never talked politics with him. We talked about other things. I told him of some bad cases related to me by Jewish friends. I even requested help for those people." The described meeting probably happened on March 9, 1943 (People's Court Session No.16, 1945, p. 1504-1505).

We owe another detailed description of the events to Yako Baruh who was a representative of the International Jewish Agency in Bulgaria. We have two versions of the events of March 1943, as seen by Mr. Baruh, an active participant.

In 1945, he testified at the People's Tribunal about the preparation of the Jewish deportation in Kyustendil and the measures that a few people took to prevent it from happening. According to Mr. Baruh's testimony, on March 7, he received a disturbing message from his brother, a pharmacist mobilized in Kyustendil, about a plan to deport the Jews to Poland. He asked Yako Baruh what he could do. At the time, the witness was a representative of the Jewish Agency for Bulgaria, arranging certificates for Jews who wanted to emigrate from Bulgaria. He couldn't find out anything from other Jews, so he had to reach out to his friends in the government – Dimitur Peshev, Deputy-Speaker of the Parliament, the Members of Parliament Peter Mihalev (Kyustendil) and Sotir Yanev, his classmate [later killed by communist terrorists – M.M.]. None of them knew anything and they even thought that such a deportation was unthinkable.

Peshev was confident that nothing like that would happen, but Baruh insisted to call the governor of the Kyustendil region. It was Sunday and the governor was out of town. Peshev decided to try again Monday morning and asked Baruh to come to his office in the Parliament at 8 a.m. This time, he talked to the governor and he confirmed that the deportation was scheduled for March 9.

Then Baruh visited again his friends Sotir Yanev, Peter Mihalev and Dimitur Ikonomov (all MPs). He also got in touch with his brother and learned that a delegation of five citizens from Kyustendil was about to leave the city for Sofia the same day and try to stop the plan. By that time, Peshev had already talked to the Minister of the Interior Gabrovski, who said that he didn't give an order for deportation of Jews. Peshev was confident that Gabrovski was lying, as he already knew that curfew was planned for Kyustendil for March 9 at 8 p.m. Nobody was supposed to go out and the Jews were to be collected in trucks and sent to the tobacco warehouse of the Fernandes Brothers. The MPs were worried by Gabrovski's lies and decided to wait for the delegation to start an action on March 9. Fortunately, that day the People's Assembly had a scheduled session. Three of the members of the delegation were stopped from leaving Kyustendil by the fascist youth from Ratnik and other organizations. The other two were barely able to board the train and arrived in Sofia at about 9:30 a.m.

The same day in the late afternoon, 3-4 hours before the action in Kyustendil, the delegates and a few MPs met again Gabrovski and insisted on cancelling the deportation; they knew for sure it was ordered. Gabrovski's replies were elusive and it appeared that he was conferring with Prime Minister Filov and other ministers. Meanwhile, the day before, Baruh had a meeting with the chairman of the International Red Cross in Hotel Bulgaria (he had to remove his Jewish star to enter). He told him that the Jews were scheduled for deportation on March 9. The chairman said that he was going to take the necessary steps but didn't give any details.

So, on the evening of March 9, after pressure from the delegation sent by the desperate Jews of Kyustendil, Gabrovski promised to order cancellation of the action by telegraph. Since he had a long history of lying, especially about Jewish issues, the visitors insisted that he deliver the order by phone in their presence. Gabrovski refused, but when they wanted to see Filov, it became clear that the latter agreed to stop the deportation; then Gabrovski took the phone and ordered the cancellation. [Actually, as others noted, the order most likely came from the King; Yako Baruh did not attend the meeting with Gabrovski. – M.M.] At that time, the Jews in Sliven, Plovdiv, Pazardjik and other cities had been already collected in schools and warehouses to be loaded on trains the next day. The order stopped the process.

After a question from the prosecutor, Baruh provided more details. Most people in Kyustendil knew that the tobacco warehouse was cleaned up to accommodate the Jews. There were 15 carriages on the railway station waiting, it was planned to load the Jews at midnight. Belev never forgot how Kyustendil ruined his plans, so in May 1943, he sent to the small city 3,500 Jews from Sofia to create tensions and accuse the Jews of fueling the black market (People's Court Session No.11, 1945, p. 912-919).

In the 1950s, Yako Baruh wrote memoirs that provided an even more detailed account of the events and his role in them. The manuscript is kept at the Yad Vashem archives.

He wrote that in early March, Belev's Commissariat was planning to deport the Jews from Kyustendil and other cities in Bulgaria. Despite the secrecy, it was clear what was being planned – there were trains already waiting in Kyustendil, Jewish women were forced to clean the carriages. One of the large tobacco warehouses was prepared for the Jews. Men were asked to bring food utensils and buy large casks for water. The Jews were desperate. The Bulgarians who felt compassion, formed a five-person delegation to go to Sofia. The difficulties of the communications between Jews, due to lack of telephones, made the organizing difficult. Baruh was visited by a Macedonian activist, whose name he didn't mention, but most likely that was Vladimir Kurtev, who told him that deportations were planned in many places; he even showed him a list with people included. It was supposed to start after midnight on March 9. The situation seemed hopeless.

Baruh wanted to do something but was aware that the decision was made by Belev, the government and the Germans. He went to the secretary of the government, Serafimov, who previously asked Baruh for help to arrange a Palestine visa for his Jewish friend. Serafimov was reluctant to get involved because he could be accused of taking bribes from Jews. He added that the Jewish deportation was a big political action, and nobody could cancel it. Then Baruh went to the secretary of the Minister of the Interior Gabrovski, "the worst anti-Semite in Bulgaria", named Golyubov, who previously also used Baruh's help for Palestine visas for his Jewish friends who had to leave urgently. The fact that those people, involved in the anti-Jewish policies, at the same time were soliciting the help of the Jewish Agency to assist their personal Jewish friends, shows once again the strange ways, in which the

Bulgarian political life functioned.

Baruh pleaded with Golyubov for cancellation of the horrible order. "**All my arguments were rejected by him, because that order did not come from the Bulgarian Government, but from the German authorities, which handled all issues related to Jews.** He made it clear that everything was already finished, and the Jews had to accept their fate." [Emphasis mine. – M.M.]

The next person to visit was the Minister of Agriculture Zahariev, who also used Baruh's assistance to get visas for his Jewish friends. Zahariev told him that the government was assisted in the deportations from Thrace and Macedonia but did not decide to deport the Jews from old Bulgaria. However, he refused to get involved, because he could be accused of taking bribes from Jews and could get into serious troubles with the Germans who oversaw the Jewish issues in Bulgaria.

Baruh's last hope was his classmate and friend from Kyustendil Dimitur Peshev, the Deputy Speaker of the People's Assembly. He managed to meet him on March 7 and had a two-hour talk in Peshev's office. He told him everything he knew and Peshev was shocked, he didn't know anything and even claimed that it was impossible. Baruh asked him to phone the Kyustendil District Police Chief, friend of Peshev. The Chief confirmed that the Jews were to be collected on March 9. Baruh told Peshev about the delegation from Kyustendil that was coming to Sofia. Both decided that they had to take some collective action at the session of the parliament, scheduled for March 9, which made it possible to talk to all MPs. Since it was already March 8, Baruh went to visit some MPs that he knew well and most of them promised to help. Meanwhile, he found out that only two members of the Kyustendil delegation reached Sofia – the rest were threatened with guns by the Legionnaires to be killed, if they went to Sofia to help Jews.

On March 9 at 11 a.m. Baruh and five MPs met in Peshev's office. It was decided that all MPs involved in the action would meet at the same office an hour before the session, and then as a group go to Gabrovski's office and demand cancellation of the order. If Gabrovski refused, they planned to go to the Prime Minister and state that they would debate the unjust order in the parliament and turn it into a scandal. Baruh went out, waiting for the decision in the park behind the parliament. At about 8 p.m. MP Mihalev came out and with an emotional voice told Baruh that the order was cancelled. He was later told that Peshev and the other MPs met Gabrovski and demanded the cancellation.

Initially, Gabrovski refused to acknowledge the existence of such an order, but when he was confronted with the proof, he told them that he had to confer with Prof. Filov before giving an answer. After his talk, Gabrovski reported that sadly the order could not be cancelled but postponed for an indefinite period. Since it was already late, and the police were about to start detaining the Jews in the province, the MPs demanded that Gabrovski give a phone order to stop the action. He refused but said that he already sent telegrams to all provincial towns to stop the action. However, for Kyustendil, Peshev phoned personally the police chief about the postponement.

Gabrovski's telegraphic order arrived with delay, so by midnight the Jews in many cities, like Plovdiv, Pazardjik, Samokov, Shumen and others, were forced into temporary camps, like schools and warehouses. Only the next day, after receiving the order, they were freed.

In the end, Baruh noted that the cancellation enraged Belev and he hatched a better plan. Baruh blamed King Boris III for the action against the Jews and claimed that the King, after the March failure, decided to deport the Jews quietly, by expelling them first to provincial towns. That happened but the Red Army saved the Jews" (Барух, Спомени 9 март 1943, p. 1-4). As we will see later, other documents refute Baruh's assumption about the negative role of the King and the supposed help by the Soviet Army.

In his memoirs, Baruh mentioned the delegation from Kyustendil, which initially included five people but only two of them reached Sofia. Maybe because he did not communicate with them directly, he did not know that actually four members managed to arrive in Sofia. Those were the MP Peter Mihalev, the lawyer Ivan Momchilov, the merchant Assen Suechmezov, and the Bulgarian Macedonian activist Vladimir Kurtev. Two of them, Mihalev and Momchilov, left memoirs about what happened (still in manuscript) that shed additional light on those fateful events.

The MP from the ruling coalition Peter Mihalev was one of the driving forces behind the saving of the Jews in March 1943. In his memoirs, written in 1973, he recalled the events.

After a few days of absence, Mihalev returned to Kyustendil on March 8, 1943, and found the town strangely empty. While wondering about what happened, he came across his friend Buko Lazarov who looked anxious when he approached Mihalev with the words: "It's all over for us." From the further details, Mihalev learned that for the last two days, a group of agents from Sofia had been preparing a deportation of the Jews, supposed to be detained by the police in the Fernandes Tobacco Warehouse and from there loaded on a train, already waiting at the railway station.

That was a real danger for the 800 Jews in the town. The idea that men, women, children and old people could be sent to their deaths, brought out his anger and Mihalev decided to do whatever was needed to spoil the plan. Mihalev told Lazarov that he was going to visit the district governor Lyuben Miltenov and get more information.

At the governor's office he saw Borislav Tassev, an agent from the Commissariat for the Jewish Questions, who told him that the deportation was imminent, planned to begin within hours. It turned out, Tassev was in charge of the agents who had to collect the Jews.

After confirming the rumors, Mihalev told the governor that it was people's duty to stop the atrocity, he was heading to Sofia and urged the governor not to do anything to help the police in their action until further notice. Buko Lazarov was waiting for him at his brother's home. After sharing the bad news, Mihalev was about to leave for Sofia to stop the deportation, but Lazarov informed him that about 40 other people wanted to go there with the same purpose. However, at 5 p.m., only four people showed up at the railway station – Ivan Momchilov, Assen Suechmezov, Vladimir Kurtev, and Peter Mihalev.

Upon his arrival in Sofia, Mihalev phoned Dimitur Peshev, the Deputy Speaker of the Parliament. The latter wasn't aware of the events in Kyustendil and they decided to meet the next day. On March 9, 1943, at about 10 a.m., Momchilov, Suechmezov and Mihalev visited Peshev's home and explained the situation. They decided to request a meeting with the Prime Minister the same afternoon in the People's Assembly building. At about noon, Peshev phoned Mihalev – he informed him that he spoke with the Minister of Interior Gabrovski who claimed that he never issued a deportation order. That denial was surprising after what Mihalev saw in Kyustendil. Shortly thereafter, he met at a café with Yako Baruh to tell him about the upcoming meeting with Prof. Filov.

At 3 p.m., Mihalev, Suechmezov and Momchilov went to Peshev's office and were told that the Prime Minister refused to see them. The refusal complicated the situation and they decided to see Gabrovski instead. Other than Peshev and Mihalev, six other MPs went to meet the Minister. As soon as they entered, he asked, "Mihalev, why are you all so worried in Kyustendil?" Mihalev told him what he knew about the preparations done by the agents. Gabrovski insisted that he knew nothing, so Mihalev asked him to call the governor. In the call that followed, the Minister was informed about the imminent deportations. Mihalev's impression was that Gabrovski was upset that the secret was out, yet he insisted again that he knew nothing.

That could be expected, now they had to push him to cancel the orders. They remained in the office for a long time and decided not to leave until a solution was provided. Finally, Gabrovski caved in and ordered the Kyustendil authorities to stop the action and send the agents back to Sofia. Suechmezov was waiting for them outside and when he heard the news, he rushed to Kyustendil to notify the people. Then Mihalev reported the news to Yako Baruch and Colonel Avram Tadjer.

Some of the young fascists in Kyustendil were not happy with the outcome, so they harassed the people involved with writings on their walls, breaking windows, threatening their relatives, etc.

That was the initial step in ruining those plans. Next came the protest letter of Dimitur Peshev and the other 42 MPs. As a revenge, on March 26, 1943, the Government dismissed Peshev from his position, despite the protests of his supporters. Still, the Bulgarian Jews were saved and Mihalev was satisfied that he fulfilled his human duty (Memoirs of Mihalev, p. 1-6).

The Kyustendil lawyer Ivan Momchilov left his own memoirs providing some unexpected information about the delegation's activities in Sofia. They were included in a letter to Haim Oliver, a leading journalist and writer in communist Bulgaria, in response to his article about saving the Bulgarian Jews, published in 1966. Oliver was a long-time member of the communist party, former partisan and a major perpetuator of the myth that the party and specifically the future dictator Todor Zhivkov played a crucial role in those events. In 1986, he even wrote the script for the film "The Echelons of Death", which provided a fantasy version of the saving, with Zhivkov as the main hero. It took courage for a former "bourgeois lawyer" like Momchilov to confront the powerful communist Oliver in 1966.

Momchilov attacked the cliché that the "Party, Soviet Army and the people" saved the Jews, which was central to Oliver's article published in the popular Bulgarian weekly "Pogled" [View]. The author listed many people who spoke against the anti-Jewish laws, but, as Momchilov noted, they had done nothing to stop the deportations.

He also noted some of Oliver's incorrect statements. The people in Kyustendil didn't "rise in protest against the local authorities". Nobody protested because the so-called "patriotic organizations" were ready to beat up people and break windows. It was not true that many people sent telegrams in protest, it didn't happen for the same reason. Oliver didn't mention that Vladimir Kurtev was in the delegation. [Kurtev, as a "Macedonian fascist", was killed shortly after the communist coup in 1944 and his name was taboo after that. – M.M.] Oliver didn't say what the delegation did and mentioned Dimitur Peshev only to try to humiliate him. He denied their role in the March 1943 events and at the same time claimed that the Jews saved the lives of Peshev and the delegates, which Momchilov found ironic – why should the Jews save their lives, if they had done nothing for them?

Then Momchilov explained why he was absent from the meetings in the parliament. He went to Knyazhevo [a cottage village near Sofia] to meet General Nikola Zhekov, former commander of the Bulgarian Army in World War I. The Kyustendil Jews relied on him because of his connections, specifically his friendship with Adolf Hitler. Zhekov received monthly allowance from Hitler, who also sent him an automobile as a gift and bought for him a large villa. So, the Jews thought, if Hitler valued the General, the German Ambassador Beckerle probably had the same attitude and would listen to him. Since Momchilov had friendly relations with Gen. Zhekov, the Jews insisted that he meet with him.

Both men met, Momchilov explained the horror the Jews felt and asked Gen. Zhekov whether he could help and told him that a delegation of four was to leave for Sofia. Zhekov sat silent for a moment and said, "Maybe the Jews are lucky. [The German] Marshall von Masow, who was a representative at my headquarters, is in Sofia now. He has a son in the German Embassy. He came here to see him. General Ganchev, the aide-de-camp of King Ferdinand is also here. Ambassador Beckerle is holding a lunch in their honor. I have been invited as well. A happy coincidence. I don't hate the Jews. I hate some of their character traits, against which I have spoken, so it would be inappropriate for me to talk to Beckerle, but I will tell Ganchev to raise the issue, he likes to talk."

Both went to Sofia in the General's car and parted ways. In the afternoon, the delegation went to the People's Assembly to meet the Prime Minister, but he refused to see them, then they left. [This is a discrepancy with the memoirs of Mihalev, who wrote that the delegation went to see Gabrovski but without Momchilov. – M.M.]

The Jews were impatient, they asked Momchilov to phone

Zhekov, but the latter said that such important questions are not discussed over the phone. Momchilov had to go to Sofia again. The Jews tried to send 40 delegates and hired 10 cars at 4,000 leva each but the governor Lyuben Miltenov refused to provide gas for the cars, so four people had to take the train. There were no angry citizens protesting. [This must have happened before the refusal of Filov to meet them, mentioned above. – M.M.] After the Prime Minister refused a meeting, Momchilov decided to leave, but at about 4 p.m. he met Zhekov who told him that the Jews were saved.

"How did this happen?" asked Momchilov.

"Ganchev did perfectly. We both supported him, Masow and me, but please keep my name out of this affair, at least as long as I am alive."

When he arrived at home the same night, Momchilov found all windows of his house shattered with rocks. That was the work of the National Legion. Every time he replaced the windows, they broke them again. In the morning he found writings on the walls: "Traitor, Bulgarian Jew, hireling, scum, etc.". He painted them over, but the Legionnaires did it again. The horror continued until September 9, 1944. The same happened to Assen Suechmezov.

Then he told Oliver that to understand who saved the Jews, it was necessary to answer several questions. Who ordered the cancellation of the deportation? This could do only the Prime Minister, but he wouldn't dare without Beckerle's approval, it is stupid to think that he would cancel his own initiative. Filov was forced to issue the order but by whom? It was said that the communist party did it, but it was too weak, many members were in jails, the party did nothing to save the Aegean Jews. Momchilov's group didn't mention the latter because they didn't know they were on trains and in tobacco warehouses, otherwise they could have asked for them as well. Then who forced Filov? It could have been only Beckerle and his intervention was a result of the actions described above.

The Soviet Army didn't play a role at the time. If it weren't for the delegation to Sofia, 9,000 Jews would have been dead. The delegation can be credited for the cancellation of the order, even though temporarily. The events slowed down the second order [in May 1943] and the Soviet Army eventually helped the Jews. Momchilov concluded: "I have shared this truth with your Chief Rabbi Hananel, but since I was mistreated by certain Jews, I didn't speak again. I wrote this for my sons to remember. We fulfilled a human duty under a grave danger and suffering. It is your business whether you will appreciate it" (Memoirs of Momchilov, p. 1-4).

The account of the events, presented by Momchilov, surely differs from most that the other participants recalled. However, the fact that he participated in the delegation and was actually involved in the struggle, lends credibility to his version. Besides, admitting in a letter to one of the dark figures of the Bulgarian communist totalitarianism like Chaim Oliver in 1966, that he had been friends with General Zhekov, required significant courage, it was like admitting to a friendship with Hitler, so it is unlikely that Momchilov made up the story. General Zhekov was a hero of World War I and although he was retired and old at the time (he was over 80), he was still sentenced to death by the People's Tribunal and would have been executed, if he didn't manage to escape in 1944.

Momchilov's rebuttal of Haim Oliver's version of the events brings us to the communist interpretation that was dominant during the communist control over Bulgaria. A typical example of communist myth creation is an essay about the events written from communist point of view. The picture was distorted after the communist takeover of Bulgaria by exaggerating the role of the Bulgarian Communist Party. You can get an idea about how this was done from the article "Who Saved the Bulgarian Jews from the Death Camps?" by Isaak Naimovich, a prominent Bulgarian communist of Jewish background, from 1966.

For example, he states that: "The completely secret negotiations between the two sadists Belev and Dannecker concluded with the signing on February 22, 1943, of a written agreement, which planned the deportation of all Jews from Bulgaria, regardless of sex and age." The agreement did not cover deportation of all Jews. This is followed by another false statement, that after Belev started to detain the Jews scheduled for deportation in March, "the Bulgarian Communist Party carried out among the broad masses of the people a huge campaign of resistance against the criminal intentions of the monarch-fascist gang." The communist party was too small and did not have the wide support necessary to organize a huge campaign.

"On March 8, shaken by the government decision to collect the Jews in temporary camps and send them to Danube ports to be handed over to the Gestapo, the citizens of Kyustendil spontaneously decided to react against that barbaric act by sending to Sofia a delegation to demand cancellation of the deportation. Under the pressure from his anxious and outraged fellow citizens, the Kyustendil MP Dimitur Peshev, Deputy Speaker of the People's Assembly, visited the Minister of the Interior and demanded a cancellation of the deportation. Afraid of inevitable further complications, if its criminal initiative were followed, the government retreated reluctantly and cancelled the order the same evening" (Two essays by Isaak Naimovich and Matey Yulzari, p. 18-20). As we saw from the testimonies, there was no mass protest in Kyustendil and the delegation was the result of the Zionists mobilizing their connections to pressure the government.

The sad part of the discussion was that the side that did most of the work was silenced after the communist coup in Bulgaria. All Zionists, who were over 95% of the Jewish population, left the country in 1948-1952. The arguments with communists over the issue of the survival continued even in Israel, but they were published in booklets and local newspapers in Bulgarian and Hebrew, so they never reached Bulgaria.

In 1961, the Zionists Albert Romano and Buko Levi published the booklet ""How Were the Jews in Bulgaria Saved? (Communists and Zionists; Regarding the Book of Nathan Grinberg "The Hitlerite Pressure to Destroy the Bulgarian Jews")". Unfortunately, since the discussion was in Bulgarian, the important questions raised in it remained unknown to most researchers.

Grinberg was a communist who, after the war, worked at the Commissariat for the Jewish Questions and published many papers he found there in his book "Documents", which revealed the attempts to deport the Bulgarian Jewry. His new book was also based on various documents and his goal was to prove that the authorities and especially King Boris III didn't play a role in saving the Jews (Романо, Леви, 1961, p. 3), thus confronting the opinion of Benjamin Arditti. His arguments were that even if the King felt some sympathy to the Jews, he still approved the anti-Semitic laws. Special attention from Romano received the admission that the deportation in March 1943 was stopped "from the highest place" (i.e. the Royal Palace). The author agreed with some of the arguments, concluding that the King acted under strong pressure from different directions.

However, he strongly disagreed with the main point of Grinberg, that the Jews were saved by the communists, and with his attempts to blackmail the Zionists and deny their role. After attacking the role or motives of every participant in the action, Peshev, the Holy Synod of the Orthodox Church, Metropolitans

Stefan and Kiril, the organizations of the lawyers, doctors, journalists, all that remained in Grinberg's explanation was the Bulgarian people, and that to him meant the Fatherland Front, and that was the communist party, the partisans. There was no place for the Consistory and the Zionists in that picture (Романо, Леви, 1961, р. 5).

In the second article in the same booklet, the author whom we already know, Buko Levi, also argued with the positions expressed by the communist Nathan Grinberg. The latter saw the King and the Government as mortal enemies of the Jews, who should be fought. The picture was not that simple, in black and white, there were many nuances, as Levi pointed out:

> "Regardless of what one thinks about the King and his role in saving the Bulgarian Jews, one thing is definitely true, and it is that the King hesitated how to act. On one hand, there was the strong pressure from the Germans and the homegrown fascists, who were a significant threat to him, on the other hand, he was pressured by the good Bulgarians, honest public figures, writers, etc. So, our task was to amplify the influence of the good factors to tip the balance to our benefit.
>
> "In the government there were also ministers, who would not surrender the Jews to the Germans. The same applied to the MPs from the majority, who, though loyal to their government, deep inside did not approve all that was done to us. These elements had to be strengthened. And they ensured the success of Dimitur Peshev, who managed to collect the signatures of over 40 MPs... The events proved that the strategy of the Consistory to connect with government and anti-government elements was correct.
>
> "I repeat, all actions of various organizations have been the result of persistent demands and requests made directly or indirectly by the Consistory or people close to it. However, the idea to act in that direction came solely from the Consistory. I will go even further. There were cases when certain actions required paying money, even though this sounds shocking. There are things, which should not be revealed at this point, but a day will come to discuss them openly and it will be seen that some things that are idealized now, were materialist in nature" (Романо, Леви, 1961, р. 24-25).

The cancellation of the expulsion from Bulgaria was met with joy by all Jews and those Bulgarians who supported them. An expression of that joy was a letter to the King written shortly after the events:

> "[Dated March 11, 1943, Plovdiv]
> Your Majesty,
> God's hand liberated us through you! We are grateful, grateful from the bottom of our hearts! God bless you and your family. God will protect and guide you in all difficulties and we will never forget what you did for us, the Jews...
> Here they wanted to do to us what neither Italy, nor Hungary, nor anti-Semitic Romania did. We never believed that you would let something like that happen! Now we cry for joy and gratitude. If you only saw how our innocent children were trembling in the cold - even an icy heart could feel pity. Thank you once again for saving my children!
> Let the Almighty always protect and guide you! Wishing you all the best, I kiss your hand.
> A grateful mother" (Благодарствено писмо, 1943)

A few days later, Dimitur Peshev wrote a letter of protest that was signed by 42 MPs from the government faction, he deliberately refused to accept signatures from the opposition to show that this was an inner disagreement. He accepted a signature only from Prof. Alexander Tsankov. Often, this letter is presented as a crucial part of the action to save the Jews. However, it was signed and delivered to the government on March 17, 1943, over a week after the Jewish issue was resolved, even though temporarily. The important thing to remember here is that the letter made it known officially that a significant number of Bulgarian politicians, who didn't hold leftist views, were openly opposed to the genocidal policies of Hitler and his high-ranked followers in Bulgaria.

The letter was addressed to Prime Minister Prof. Filov and stated in part the MPs' concern about the new measures taken against the Jews in Bulgaria:

> "The exact nature of those measures, their purpose and the reasons that forced them – there is no credible explanation for all that from the institutions in charge. Even the Minister of the Interior in his conversation with some MPs confirmed that some exceptional measures will affect totally the Jews in the old territories. In reality, a cancellation of all such orders took place.
> "Considering all that, as well as some new rumors, we decided to approach you, because similar measures will be

taken with the consent of the government.

"Our only request is that in taking any measures, only the real needs of the country and the people at the moment must be considered, and not to forget, however, the interests and moral positions of our people...

"The removal of all obstacles to the success of that policy is a right of the state and no one can argue against it, as long as its fulfilment does not go beyond the actual needs and does not go into excesses, which could be interpreted as unnecessary cruelty. But that is how we define all measures, which could affect women, children and the elderly, while individuals are not charged with specific transgressions.

"We cannot assume that the Bulgarian Government had the intention to deport those people from Bulgaria, as the malicious rumors say. Such a measure is unacceptable not only because those people, still Bulgarian citizens, cannot be kicked out of Bulgaria, but also because it would have harmful and politically devastating consequences...

"The small number of the Jews in Bulgaria, the power of the state, armed with so many legal tools and capabilities, make the neutralization of any dangerous and harmful element, regardless of its origin, so inevitable that, we believe, it is not necessary to take new, extraordinary and even cruel measures, which could bring up accusations of mass murder. It will be blamed on the government, but the blame will spill over Bulgaria as well. It is easy to predict the consequences of such a situation, so it should not be allowed" (Протест на Пешев и 42 парламентаристи, 1943).

Prof. Filov and Gabrovski did not like this disobedience. A few weeks later, they took steps to get rid of Peshev. It was proposed in the parliament to dismiss him from his position of Deputy Speaker. After a stormy parliamentary session, Bogdan Filov managed to get the necessary votes to remove Peshev. Over a year later, another cruel political joke was played on Peshev by the communists. At the People's Tribunal, he was sentenced to 15 years in prison for, among other things, "anti-Semitism". The same sentence received Yaroslav Kalitsin, Belev's deputy, one of the organizers of the Jewish deportation from Macedonia and Thrace. Many of the MPs who signed Peshev's letter were condemned to death by the same "court".

During those difficult days in March 1943, the Bulgarian Orthodox Church firmly maintained its policies of opposition to any type of cruelty against the Jews. At a meeting of the Holy

Synod that took place a few weeks later, on April 2, 1943, Metropolitan Kiril of Plovdiv shared his experiences of March 10, the day when many of the Plovdiv Jews were detained and waited for an order to board the trains:

> "I had the opportunity to tell the Metropolitans… what happened with the persecution of the Jews in the city of Plovdiv. I will provide again some information. At 3 a.m. on March 10, about 1,500-1,600 people from Plovdiv were arrested. They were detained in one of the schools, ready to be sent to Poland, as it happened with the Jews from the newly-liberated territories and Aegean Thrace. In the morning, I was notified about what happened. I did not have the exact information about what was going on and assumed that all Jews in the country had been captured that night. A special train was expected to arrive at the station to take them away. The indignation of the citizens was enormous. I could do nothing else but to act according to the decisions and the guidance of the Holy Synod and my own conscience. I sent a telegram to His Majesty the King, in which I pleaded with him in God's name to have mercy for these miserable people. After that, I asked to speak with the Director of the Police, who was in Plovdiv that day, but could not get in touch with him. I looked for the chief of the district police but was told that he was also absent. Then I summoned his deputy and asked him in a very respectful manner to notify the government that until that moment, I had always been loyal to the government, but with regard to this issue, I reserve for myself the freedom to act in a way determined by my conscience as a Metropolitan. Later, I was visited by a group of baptized Jews. I comforted them and told them that if they were under threat, they could find refuge in my home. Let the authorities take them from my own home. In this case, I was looking up to the example of the ancient Christians who not only protected their own kind, but also collected money among themselves to buy off the freedom of Christian slaves of other ethnicities. Later on, I found out that about noon, an order to release them had been received, which was met with joy by the detained. I must say that we should give credit to the Bulgarian police for treating well the Jews arrested in Plovdiv" (Свети синод, Протокол №4, 1943, p. 48).

There is something to be added here that would complete the picture. When I was a student at the University of Sofia in

Bulgaria, my professor of aesthetics, Prof. Isaac Passi, mentioned on several occasions the events in Plovdiv. At the time, he was 15 years old and he and his family were among the Jews detained in that school. He remembered how at certain point, Metropolitan Kiril showed up and addressed the crowd. He told the Jews that he was doing everything to help them and he was confident that none of them would leave the city. That's exactly what happened.

At the same meeting of the Holy Synod, Metropolitan Mikhail of Dorostol blamed the police in Plovdiv, which he thought had acted in an extreme way. He heard that there was an order to arrest the Jews in Russe as well (that was in his diocese), but the police chief did not do anything, he was waiting for clarification of the situation. Metropolitan Evlogi of Sliven added his observations. In Sliven, there were many Jews who came from Sofia, about 40-50 families. There were rumors that a deportation was considered. One morning, the Metropolitan was visited by a crying Jew who told him that all Jews in the city were supposed to be arrested and sent away. The Jewish men of ages from 17 to 70 received notices to go to a certain place. Everybody was afraid, and they expected that women and children would receive the same notices. Two hours later, a delegation of five prominent Bulgarian ladies visited the Metropolitan and begged for help from the Church to save the Jewish women and children. The Metropolitan inquired with the police commandant who confirmed the order to send the Jewish men to camps, but that didn't apply to women and children. By noon, a message came stating that the deportation order was cancelled. Later that day, another Jewish delegation visited him to express gratitude for the compassion of the Church (Свети синод, Протокол №4, 1943, p. 50-51).

Metropolitan Paissi of Vratsa raised the question of how the Church should treat the deportation of Jews from Bulgaria. The government measures for the safety of Bulgaria are one thing but deporting the Jewish minority and surrendering it to a foreign country did not comply with the Christian principles and the Church could not remain silent. In the past, when people were uprooted after the wars, such actions were considered cruel and unfair, and Bulgarians have suffered through such events. The expulsion of the Jews meant uprooting them from a country that was their homeland and sending them to a foreign state, where they can't find shelter and compassion. A Christian and truth-loving country like Bulgaria could not act like this (Свети синод, Протокол №4, 1943, p. 52-53).

Metropolitan Iosif of Varna noted that he didn't sign the initial letter in 1940 against the Law for Defense of the Nation. At the time, he thought the law was necessary to insulate Bulgaria from destructive foreign influence; it was expected to prevent the economic enslavement of Bulgarians by foreigners. However, it turned out that the law was directed exclusively against Jews, it took their properties without improving the economy of the country and it gave advantages to other ethnicities. The law didn't include the spiritual defense of the nation and was applied with cruelty and barbarism. The attempts to deport the Jews forced him to question even further the law. The law must be corrected to address real threats, not to persecute people just because they are Jews. The Jews must be protected (Свети синод, Протокол №4, 1943, p. 53-55).

Metropolitan Stefan of Sofia said:

> "The Bulgarian Orthodox Church must defend truth and bring comfort to those who suffer. When we ask the government, what wrongs the Jews in our country have done, they can't respond. They took everything from them, but when they tried to take their lives as well, the Jews sought the protection of the Church. We cannot reject them. Their suffering is unbearable. I could understand, if the government used the excuse to give them six months notice for expulsion with their property as elements, undesirable from government point of view, however, when a young guy enters your home to tell you to collect your belongings in two hours and be ready to be sent to an unknown place, this is something that our nation has neither heard nor seen. What happened with the Jews from Aegean Thrace was shocking. They were transported in sealed trains from Seres to Dupnitsa, without water and almost without air. The persecuted Jewish minority calls for our help and we cannot refuse to treat them with sincere Christian compassion. The Holy Synod cannot ignore the call of those unfortunate people. Let the government hear the advice of our Church, which has never provided a bad advice. We should insist for providing full freedom to the baptized Jews and providing them with all necessary conditions to feel as part of our Holy Church, and to also let them remove the Jewish stars and release them from paying tax to the Jewish community. Let us also pray for justice, humanism, and tolerance to those who are not baptized. Terror and robbery must be persecuted. Those who want to leave the Kingdom, should be helped. Those who are subject to moving to other areas of the country must be given time to do so in a free and peaceful way" (Свети синод,

Протокол №4, 1943, p. 60-62).

In the end of the meeting, the Holy Synod adopted a resolution proposed by Metropolitan Paissi:

> "The Bulgarian Church cannot support racist principles. It cannot accept the premise that certain race must be deprived from the human right of life, because that contradicts the basic ideas of the Christian faith.
>
> The Bulgarian Church states that it cannot refuse help to the persecuted and mistreated. If it refused such help, it would mean that it rejects itself. In this case, our Holy Church is approached by Jews asking for help and by Bulgarian Christians who want us to advocate for improving the fate of the Jews. Not only does not the Church deny, but it also emphasizes the duty and right of the government to take measures for defense of the nation and the state from aspirations against them, regardless of their source. However, at the same time, the Church emphasizes that the state should not deviate from the basic ideas of the Christian Gospel and justice.
>
> The Christians of Jewish background and the Jews in the country should not be deprived of their elementary rights as human beings and citizens and their rights to live in our country, work and have decent lives, should not be taken away. The restrictions of the Jews must be softened and applied without cruelty. The Bulgarian Church feels obliged to raise its voice in defense of the Jewish Christians, who have left the Jewish community and were accepted by the Orthodox Church. It can't bear the sight of Christian Jews carrying the sign of the Jewish faith, paying tax to the Jewish religious community, and forced out of their homeland" (Свети синод, Протокол №4, 1943, p. 63-64).

I have heard many people asking the question why the Bulgarian Orthodox Church opposed so consistently the mistreatment of the Jews, while churches in other countries did little to help. Perhaps, the answer should be sought in the unique structure of the Orthodox Church. It is not a monolithic entity like the Catholic Church, which is centralized under the Pope.

The key here is that there are fifteen Orthodox Churches, which follow exactly the same doctrine, unchanged since the 8th century, but they are independent from each other and reflect closely the character of the nations they dominate. That explains the differences in Russia, Romania and Bulgaria. In Russia and Romania, the Church supported silently or vocally the virulent anti-Semitism that was very common. As we saw in the previous chapter, the Bulgarians went through some horrible experiences during the 500 years of Turkish occupation. The Orthodox Church was a major factor in preserving the Bulgarian nation and had to deal with actual dangers and threats. When people go through such an intense collective experience, they learn what a real threat is. Jews were never such a threat, so imposing anti-Semitism was very difficult in Bulgaria, as opposed to Germany and Romania. Without going in detail through history, it is difficult to explain all that. In "Eichmann in Jerusalem", Hannah Arendt was pondering the same question – why Bulgaria, which had a culture so close to Romania and Russia treated Jews in such a different way.

Another touchy subject is why the Bulgarian Government followed the policies of Germany, though many politicians opposed them. Could the government resist openly the deportations?

In his testimony at the People's Tribunal, MP Georgi Lipovanski said that after Germany started a war against Russia, it was clear that everything was lost. Bulgaria should have stayed out of the war. However, in 1943, nobody could state openly those facts. Such a disagreement could result in a coup by pro-German politicians or direct occupation by Germany. The Bulgarian politicians were targets of spying. A top General told Lipovanski that in 1943 the Bulgarian Army could not support change in the policy, even the hint of change in Bulgaria's loyalties could activate the pro-German forces in the army. The same General mentioned that in 1944, when the government policies started to change, the Germans planned a coup, using as a potential leader Major Stoyanov, a Bulgarian military officer who fought for them on the Eastern Front. Lipovanski received the same warning from his friends in Hungary – that the Bulgarians and Hungarians were being watched carefully by the Germans who were ready to intervene, as it happened in Hungary (Народен съд, разпит на Георги Липовански, 1944, p. 254-255).

It should be added to this that, according to the confessions of the German Ambassador Beckerle during his detention in Moscow, Hitler considered twice imposing pro-German dictatorship in Bulgaria, led by Prof. Alexander Tsankov – after the death of King Boris III in August 1943 and just before the Soviet occupation of Bulgaria, in August 1944. The times were difficult; unlike Italy and Japan, Bulgaria was not big or important enough to act against the German wishes without suffering grave consequences.

The struggle to save the Bulgarian Jews did not end with the Royal order of March 9, 1943. The King needed a motive to explain to Hitler why he refused to deport the Jews. The labor duty became that motive. "On April 13, 1943, Prime Minister Filov wrote in his diary: "Then we talked about the Jewish Question. The King's opinion was to mobilize the able-bodied in labor groups, so that we can avoid the deportation of Jews from the old territories to Poland". The German intelligence in Sofia figured out that move of King Boris III. In a report of May 17, 1943, the Foreign Ministry in Berlin was notified of the following: "As the most important argument against their deportation to the East, King Boris III pointed out the necessity to use the Jews in the Bulgarian labor duty units… So far, about 5,000 Jews had been mobilized… In conclusion, it needs to be said that the Bulgarian Government very transparently uses the labor duty solely as an excuse to avoid the deportation that we want" (Ташев, p. 20-21).

Aware of the King's diplomatic games, the German authorities and their servants at Belev's Commissariat for the Jewish Questions continued to work on finding a way to send the Bulgarian Jews to the death camps.

A new clash was about to happen in May 1943…

12 SECOND DEPORTATION ATTEMPT – MAY 1943

The failure of the deportation of the Bulgarian Jews in March 1943, was seen by many as a temporary setback. The organizers of the atrocity were hoping that they would get a second chance. For Belev's fanatics and their German patrons, the fight wasn't over. They made another attempt in May 1943.

As it was the case with the March events, many participants left behind testimonies and memoirs describing what happened. That does not make the historian's efforts to build a truthful picture of the drama any easier. When reading the different versions of the events, one is reminded of the great short story "Rashomon" by the Japanese classic Akutagawa, where the same event is seen differently by the people who witnessed it.

Unlike March 1943, when most of the activities involved a relatively small number of people and the drama unfolded in the parliament, the Royal Palace and the offices of cabinet ministers, the May events spilled out of the top political venues into the streets and involved many people.

Let's provide a short summary of the visible events. Most of them unfolded on May 24, 1943, one of the most venerable Bulgarian holidays. It is the day of St. Cyril and Methodius, the two brothers who in 855 A.D. created the Slavic alphabet, which was adopted in Bulgaria and later spread to Russia, Serbia and other countries. This is the day when the Bulgarian culture is celebrated. On that day in 1943, the Jews in Sofia began to receive notices that they were going to be expelled from the city. With the macabre shadow of the Commissariat for the Jewish Questions behind that initiative, the Jews suspected with horror that this time they would be detained and sent to the concentration camps for real. Many of them, both leaders and ordinary people, were looking for help from the Orthodox Church and the politicians. A spontaneous demonstration of Jews started at one of the synagogues, although the Consistory didn't approve it - it could bring severe repercussions and deportations. A few hundred Jews wanted to protest at the royal palace but were stopped and dispersed by the police before they were able to leave the Jewish quarters. Many were arrested, all of them Jews. This event gradually grew in the communist mythology into an epic demonstration, organized by the communist party and specifically by the future dictator Todor Zhivkov, in which Jews and Bulgarians united and scared the authorities, forcing them to cancel the deportation.

Nobody knew that a few days earlier, the King was presented by the Commissariat with a deportation proposal, which included two options. Option A - deportation, and option B - expulsion to villages and provincial towns. The King chose option B. The Jews were supposed to leave Sofia within three days, but it took much longer. The Jews in mixed marriages were allowed to stay and so were the war heroes, widows and orphans. Though Belev was still hoping to bring his plans to a successful end, the dispersal of the Jews all over the country made the deportations much more difficult.

The outline of the events does not provide the various points of view, which were expressed by the participants years later. So, to clarify the situation, we have to evaluate those points of view. One of the most significant testimonies was provided by a major participant, the Chief Rabbi of Sofia Dr. Asher Isaac Hananel. In 1945, he was called to testify at the People's Tribunal and his testimony is a valuable source of information about the deportation attempt of May 1943.

In the beginning, he confirmed the fact that the Jews in Bulgaria, before Hitler's influence reached the country, were respected and had good connections with the ruling class. As a Chief Rabbi, Hananel managed to establish contacts with the Royal Palace through his books. Every time he published a new one, he thought his duty was to send a good copy to the King. And he always received a reply from King's office with thank you notes. This happened a few times, after he published "Talmud Legends", "Biblical Sermons", and "An Anthology of Biblical Words". Before the debates about the Law for Defense of the Nation, Hananel sent a personal letter to the King, asking him not to allow in Bulgaria the seeds of conflict. He also wrote that persecutions usually started with the Jews and nobody could predict where they would end. He meant that one day the King could be the target. This was the only letter the King didn't answer, it was clear the Rabbi lost the benevolence of the Palace. However, later, he met the King a few times in the cathedral "St. Alexander Nevsky". The King was always polite, shook his hand, waited for his blessing, thanked him sincerely, so the Rabbi thought that the King was the one of the best defenders of the Jews. However, he thought he was wrong.

When the expulsion on May 24 began, the situation was critical. The Central Synagogue was crowded. Hananel was the only one who comforted the masses, saying that God was merciful and will save the Jews from any evil, as He has always done. The next day, the holiday of St. Cyril and Methodius, the Jews decided to go to the Palace and cry for King's mercy. But someone ordered the synagogue to be closed the next day. Then he went to the other synagogue in Yuchbunar. It was crowded, and everybody was crying. His deputy, Rabbi Daniel Tsion was praying, and that made people cry even more. Right after the prayer, Rabbi Hananel took the pulpit and said: "Brothers! Why are you crying? Are you the people who are thought to be the descendants of the Maccabees? Was that how our fathers met misfortune – wailing and crying? Shame on you for disgracing yourselves! I know why you are crying – because you have no faith in yourselves and no faith in God – that's why you are crying. I know what expects us. I am telling you that the Sofia cemetery is more beautiful than the cemeteries in other places. You know what you have to do. Let the trains leave empty, we will remain here, we will not go to be slaughtered."

He said that, because he knew that the Jews would be killed in the fields of Poland. A woman from above yelled at him: "God bless you for giving us a soul!" Then he told them that he was going to knock on many doors, took with him Rabbi Tsion and drove to Metropolitan Stefan. They found in his office other Jews. Hananel told the Metropolitan: "Dear colleague, I and the Sofia Jewry state that the Jews of Sofia are determined to stay. We are ready to accept death. Tell His Majesty the King that we are ready to sacrifice our blood but here, in Bulgaria, and not abroad. Tell him that the Batak Massacre will pale when compared to what will happen today. The Sofia Jews will never leave."

The Metropolitan replied: "True, the situation is critical, but what shall we do, if His Majesty doesn't show up at the parade? I should leave now. I would advise you to see Mrs. Karavelova. She is the mother of the Palace, she can do something. Also, you can visit the Catholic priest Romanov, he is the spiritual father of the Queen, and we may influence the King through her, everything depends on him."

[Mrs. Karavelova was the widow of the prominent Bulgarian politician Petko Karavelov, former Prime Minister. She had close ties to the Royal Family. – M.M.]

So, the Rabbi and a few others visited Mrs. Karavelova. He explained the situation and the old lady started to cry, then she gave him a pen and asked him to write down everything he said in a letter that she would send to the King. He wrote: "Your Majesty, I beg you on behalf of the elderly, the women and the children, I beg you on my knees to extend you protection over all of us. In the name of the spirit of those of our fathers who fell on the battlefield and are reaching out to protect us in this moment. If it is necessary to spill our blood for this homeland, we are ready to spill it in Bulgaria and for Bulgaria, not abroad."

Mrs. Karavelova liked the letter and with a trembling hand added a line, addressing the King: "My son, you are also a father, don't harm anybody", and signed her name. At that moment, engineer Stanishev, a friend of Mrs. Karavelova, came and said that a few Jews visited him, all very scared. She asked the Rabbi to read the letter again and Stanishev added a few more lines. It was delivered to the Palace, to Princess Evdokia and read to the King. [It is not clear if it was read the same day, because on May 24 and the next few days, the King was not in Sofia. – M.M.]

Hananel thought that because of that letter, the police started to look for him. He phoned his wife before going home; she told him not to come back because the police were looking for him. They decided to meet at his mother's place. Not far from the house, he saw police agents leaving it. He stayed there all night and went home in the morning, only to be arrested there. He was held the whole day at the office of the Commandant of Sofia Chavdarov and the latter's aide Todorov was with him the whole time. They treated him well, even allowed his wife to bring food, but Todorov never left his side. Somebody called several times from the Ministry of the Interior asking for the Rabbi, Todorov confirmed that he was still there. At 6 p.m., they received an order to let him go on the condition to see first Commissar Alexander Belev. Hananel went to the Commissariat and Miss Panitsa took him to Belev's office. Belev started yelling at him right away, but the Rabbi was determined not to listen. The Commissar shouted: "Why are you Jews trying to influence the Crown and the Government? Don't you know that we are the Crown and the

Government, that we don't do anything without the Crown? You wanted Metropolitan Stefan to intervene. We don't care about him, we hate him, we don't like him. You, with the Anglo-Saxons, sabotage the existence of our homeland."

The Rabbi couldn't take it anymore: "Mr. Commissar, despite your position, you have no right to offend us in such a way. I am a Bulgarian Army officer, I took part in the wars, I spilled my blood for this country, I have wounds behind my ear, I was decorated with a cross for bravery, and you are telling me that I do harm; it is not just your homeland, but our homeland, because it is as much yours as it is mine." Belev said, "Stop that, it may be good for Metropolitan Stefan, but it doesn't work with us. You should be grateful that you have a strong support behind you, without it, I would have arrested you, as I will arrest tonight all of your activists and Rabbis and send them to Germany. For now, you are free, and I am warning you that I will hold you responsible for the black market that your Jews run." Hananel said: "I don't accept it, you, with all your agents, can't stop the black market, how can I be responsible that the Jews Avram or Shimon have bought eggs and butter?" Belev replied, "Look at the Jews in Pirot – 80 of them endangered the food supply for the whole town." The Rabbi shot back: "Those Jews must have been very hungry and greedy to do such thing."

Belev said, "You are free now, but I am warning you that you are under house arrest and cannot contact any authorities in any way, except through me and my institution." Hananel went home and another Rabbi visited him, "Congratulations, we have been saved." Hananel thought that he meant his release, but the Rabbi explained that the radio announced that the deportation was cancelled. Hananel countered, "Impossible – I just came from the Commissariat and Belev said that tonight he will send all activists to Germany." "It's not happening, people are already coming back from the railway station."

And there was such a rumor. Later, he found out that the communists were planning a demonstration. The police heard it and in order to prevent it, made that radio announcement.

When Hananel was detained, he sent his wife to Metropolitan Stefan to let him know what happened and get help, if possible. Stefan showed to her a telegram that he sent to the Palace: "Don't persecute, so that they don't persecute you. With the measure you use on others, they will measure you. Know, Boris, that God from heaven is watching over your deeds." At that moment, Dimo Kazasov showed up and started to comfort the Rabbi's wife. When she went back home, she was very happy to find him there. That was on May 25. On May 26, he remained home under house arrest and didn't want to go anywhere but people visited him, concerned about what was going to happen.

Hananel decided to act, despite Belev's threats. On May 27, he went to the Swiss Embassy. He walked around three times to make sure nobody was following him and went in (after a previous visit to the Soviet Embassy, the police called him for explanations). Then he asked the ambassador, as a representative of the Red Cross, to help now and later when the Jews are in concentration camps. The ambassador replied that during their meeting in March 1943, he promised Hananel that he would visit Prof. Filov and advocate for the Jews. He did so, but Filov told him that the Aegean and Macedonian Jews would be sent to Bulgaria. The ambassador knew he was lying and now he would lie again. The Rabbi was devastated and did not know what to do after that reply. That was on May 27. On May 28 and 29, a representative of the International Red Cross arrived in Sofia and the Swiss Ambassador arranged a meeting with Hananel. That meeting, thought the Rabbi, solved the Jewish problem. It seemed that the representative, after seeing the King, managed to convince him that what he was doing was a great crime and he could not take such a burden. The deportation to Poland was postponed. [Hananel is wrong, the order to send the Jews to the provincial towns and not Poland was signed by the King on May 20. – M.M.]

Then an order came that the Jews had to leave for the provincial towns, not with 30 kg of luggage, but with much more of their property. Hananel remained in Sofia and visited the Commissariat almost every day to ask for help for Rabbis and other Jews sent to the camp of Somovit. Among them was his sister and her whole family. There were rumors that by July 15 Belev was working on a new deportation initiative, this time seriously. But then Sicily fell, the King died, and that turned the things around (People's Court Session No.9, 1945, p. 805-816).

Also, on May 24, 1943, a group of Bulgarian Jews wrote a letter to Queen Ioanna, begging for her protection in their "hopeless and tragic situation". The Commissariat had taken all measures to start a mass expulsion of the Jews to the province on May 25, which they would accept with patience, but "this is just an excuse for the planned deportation of all Jews, regardless of sex and age, from Bulgaria, most likely to Poland". The authors of the letter explain their fears: the Jews of Thrace and Macedonia were asked to fill out declarations supposedly only for statistical purposes and a week later, they received notices for deportation to Bulgaria, "however, after they boarded the trains, they went to Poland, instead of Bulgaria". The Jews of Sofia were concerned, because they received the same notices. "We will suffer the same tragedy, if you, the mother of all Bulgarians, regardless of their religion, do not offer to us your compassion and support". The letter was signed: "Your loyal Bulgarian Jews" (Писмо от евреи до царица Йоанна, 1943).

The two most important issues at that time were the Jewish demonstration on May 24 and the behavior of King Boris III. There are many contradictory testimonies, misinformation and outright lies about the demonstration that have been spread over the years, so it is important to analyze the available information. Also, the behavior of the King in those days of May was very important, because again, he was the person who made the decision to cancel the deportation.

The Israeli historian of Bulgarian background Nir Baruh studied the events in the 1970-1980s, interviewing people in Bulgaria. He covered their version in his book "The Ransom". He writes that May 24, the day of the Bulgarian culture, was traditionally marked with a mass manifestation of school pupils, university students, youth organizations (including the Ratniks and the Legionnaires) and other cultural organizations, which usually included about 25,000 participants.

According to the information that Nir Baruh received in communist Bulgaria, upon hearing the news about the imminent expulsion of the Jews, the communist activist Metodi Shatorov decided to organize a Jewish demonstration that was supposed to clash with the regular manifestation and start a riot in front of the King who, as every year, was supposed to greet the students at the Royal Palace. The demonstration was planned to start from the area of the 3rd Regional Committee of the Bulgarian Communist Party, which had a Jewish population of about 10,000, concentrated in the quarters Yuchbunar, Konyovitsa and Banishora. Several other communist activists got involved in the preparation and were supposed to get help from the regional secretary of the BCP Todor Zhivkov, the future communist president of Bulgaria, but it was not clear if they reached him.

Shatorov and the other organizer, Vulka Goranova, were joined by three other women, Betty Danon, Berta Kalaora and Nastya Isaakova, all of them Jewish communists. The group decided to include in the demonstration Rabbi Daniel Tsion, who was the deputy of Chief Rabbi Hananel.

According to this version, Rabbi Tsion discussed the issue with Rabbi Hananel and decided to start the demonstration from the Great Sofia Synagogue, which was at five minutes walk from the Royal Palace. The communists claimed that Rabbi Tsion did not know that the BCP was behind the demonstration, he always believed that he organized it.

The Jewish Consistory and the leaders of the Zionist organizations heard about the planned event from Rabbi Tsion. They worried that such a demonstration could only speed up the deportation and tried to prevent it. Chief Rabbi Hananel was asked to lock the synagogue before the event.

Further, Nir Baruh presents Rabbi Hananel's version. He claimed that the demonstration was spontaneous. Early in the morning of May 24, about 100 Jews gathered in front of the Great Synagogue, which was locked. Rabbi Tsion and some young Jewish communists, most of whom have never entered a synagogue before, led the crowd to the smaller synagogue in Yuchbunar. There, he spoke to the people to comfort them and urged the crowd of about 1,500 people to march to the Royal Palace.

Most of them were women and children, they walked in silence to the palace, which was at about half an hour walk from the small synagogue. Several young people from the Zionist organizations tried to dissuade them from going to the palace. There were police officers in the nearby streets and about five minutes after it took off, the demonstration was attacked and dispersed by mounted police. Some people were lightly wounded. The number of the Bulgarian participants was insignificant, about 15, according to the early publications.

During the clashes, about 200 people were arrested and 12 hours later, 200 more Jews were arrested in their homes. Many of the second group did not take part in the event, but were activists known to the police, not only communists, but also rabbis, Zionists and even members of the Consistory. Initially, they were detained at a school and then sent to the newly-established camp for Jews, Somovit.

There were some benefits from the demonstration. It became a news in Bulgaria and was also covered in England, USA and Germany. It slowed down the expulsion of the Jews from Sofia to the provincial towns, which Belev wanted to finish within three days, but it was expanded to nearly a month. The Jews were allowed to take with them everything they could carry. A few hundred Jews remained in Sofia, mostly mobilized in essential industries, holders of temporary permits, and underground communists.

Then, Nir Baruh provides more information – according to the lists of the Commissariat, 25,743 Jews were expelled from Sofia, including men mobilized in labor groups, and were sent to 20 provincial towns. [According to other documents of the Commissariat, which I will quote further, the total number was lower, and the Jews were sent to 26 towns. – M.M.] The expelled Jews initially lived in schools, warehouses and gyms, later they were moved to Jewish houses, and those who had money to pay rent, were allowed to live in Bulgarian houses (Барух, 1991, p.98-100).

Another important source of information are the memoirs of Samuel Arditti. Though he was a young boy at the time, he came from a family that played important role in the events. His father was Benjamin Arditti, a Zionist leader of the Jewish community in Sofia. He remembers that the rumors of a new deportation and the notices received by the Jews in the Bulgarian capital caused panic. Everybody suspected that they would be detained and sent to Poland. The activists conferred in private offices and cafés, trying to find a solution.

The poorer Jews decided spontaneously to demonstrate in front of the palace and ask for the King's mercy. Mr. Arditti says that trusting the King was the correct attitude, after all, eventually he saved them and paid for that with his life.

The problem with the demonstration was that it was scheduled for May 24. The clash between the Jews and the students demonstrating in front of the Royal Palace could have negative consequences. Belev could use that as a proof that the Jews were saboteurs and troublemakers and demand their immediate deportation. That is why the Jewish leaders decided to lock the Great Synagogue and the protesters were sent to the distant small synagogue in Yuchbunar.

On the morning of May 24, Benjamin Arditti attended the meeting of the Jewish Committee, which included the Zionist organizations and also the Jewish groups that were part of the Fatherland Front (and anti-government organization). The Committee unanimously decided to stop the demonstration from entering downtown Sofia. However, a multitude of people already gathered near the synagogue. Rabbi Tsion was not there, he went to see Metropolitan Stefan, and when he came back, he told the crowd that the Metropolitan received assurances from the King that the Jews would not be expelled out of the Kingdom.

The Jewish Committee sent three leaders to Yuchbunar to convince the crowd to cancel the demonstration. One of them was Benjamin Arditti. His family, including the young Samuel, were waiting anxiously at home. They heard a strong noise and saw from the windows a platoon of mounted police galloping to Yuchbunar. They were horrified that something could happen to their father, but he came back a few hours later. The demonstration was attacked by the police and many people were arrested. Benjamin managed to escape through the back yards, jumping over fences.

Samuel Arditti notes that the Bulgarian Jews were proud of the demonstration – it was the only demonstration in Europe organized by Jews at the time. On the other hand, it was not necessary, because it was decided on May 20, 1943, to send the Jews to places within the country. If the demonstration reached the palace, the government could have changed the decision.

Further in his writing, Samuel Arditti noted another fact about the King's work. A friend of his told him of a visit to his home of the legendary Colonel Avram Tadjer. The Colonel told the friend's father how he visited the King together with other prominent people, writers, musicians, priests, Metropolitans, etc. and told him of the rumors that the Bulgarian Jews were going to be deported to Poland. The delegates told the King that if anybody tries to deport the Jews, they will lie on the rails to stop the trains. The King told them not to worry, he would not allow it as long as he was alive and if it was necessary, he would lie on the rails with them (Ардити, спомени).

In his book about King Boris and the Jews, Benjamin Arditti himself responded to a later article by Jacques Sabile, which claimed that there was a Bulgarian demonstration on May 24. Arditti flatly denied that such a protest took place. As a participant in the events, he confirmed that the arrested were Jews, all 412 of them, without a single Bulgarian. The claims of Sabile that the Bulgarians yelled "We want the Jews to stay!" and condemned the Axis; that the army got involved and protesters surrounded the Minister of the Interior, were not true (Ардити, 1952, p. 13-14).

Years later, in communist Bulgaria, the events of May 1943 were gradually distorted. The already quoted in Chapter 11 article by Isaac Naimovich shows how these events were misrepresented by the communist propaganda. After the plans for the second deportation became known, the leadership of the communist party decided to start a direct action in defense of the Sofia Jews. Naimovich quoted the memoirs of the communist functionary

Vulka Goranova, who wrote that the action organized by the Third Regional Committee of the BCP under the leadership of Todor Zhivkov was very broad and dramatic. The communists, led by Salis Tadjer, organized a rally at the synagogue in Yuchbunar with a speaker Rabbi Daniel Tsion. Then they started an impressive march of Jews and many Bulgarians, mostly communists, which had to merge with the student manifestation in downtown, from where they were supposed to continue to the Royal Palace for a protest. Goranova noted that the police attacked the march but were fought by "the Jewish militant groups" (Two essays by Isaak Naimovich and Matey Yulzari, p. 21).

> "The mass manifestation of the Sofia Jews on May 24, 1943, in which many Bulgarians took part, had an enormous impact in the country and abroad. It was the reason not to implement the plan to deport the Jews from the Bulgarian provincial towns to Poland. Under the pressure of the broad masses of people, afraid of more protests, the government and the Royal Palace were forced to kiss goodbye their plan for sending the Bulgarian Jews to extermination." Then the author quoted letters from Hoffman, the German military attaché in Sofia and Ambassador Beckerle about the events, in which they admitted that the process must slow down to avoid further problems due to "internal political difficulties" (Ibid., p. 22).

"What were the "internal political difficulties" that the dignitaries from the German Embassy lamented so strongly? That was the resistance of the people in cities and villages, organized by the Fatherland Front, the brave struggle to liberate the homeland from the yoke of the German and Bulgarian fascists. That was the powerful movement of more than 250,000 fearless patriots – people's partisans, helpers, and members of militant groups. Those were the mass strikes of the working class, the sabotage done by courageous sons and daughters of the people. That was the broad struggle of the Bulgarian Communist Party, which managed to unite all progressive and democratic forces for a fateful attack against the obscurantist, reactionary, people-hating ruling monarch-fascist gang" (Ibid., p. 23). Other than the fiery communist rhetoric, the article contains gross exaggerations of the resistance, the number of people involved in it was less than 8,000.

Even the Zionists, the nemesis of the communist Jews in Bulgaria, did not get off easily, the frothing Naimovich continued his attack against the Bulgarian Jews in Israel: "It is a shame and disgrace that there are Jews (not here in our homeland) whose lives were saved thanks to the selfless struggle of the Bulgarian people, who sing odes to the crowned murderer [King Boris III] and try to exonerate him for all the suffering and anxiety of the Jews in our country and excuse him for the horrible fate, which he planned for the Bulgarian Jews, and prove innocent that mean, cruel and deceptive inspirer of the ruling anti-Semitic Mafia. It is true, the official leaders of the Jews bowed, asked for quiet obedience, promoted the illusion that with slavish begging they could get the mercy of the government and the Royal Palace. However, the Jewish workers – communists and independent – did not rely on God's mercy, did not remain passive and distant from the great resistance of the people" (Ibid., p. 26).

A few years later, in the article of Donna Krispin "The Protest Demonstration of the Sofia Jews on May 24, 1943", published in 1970 in the annual of the pro-communist educational organization of the Bulgarian Jews, the communist version becomes more elaborate. Krispin wrote that Belev was planning a deportation of all Jews, but first wanted to send them to special camps in the Danube ports of Lom and Somovit. [That was incorrect, the Jews were sent to 26 towns. – M.M.] Krispin accused the King of ill intent – he could change the order, but he didn't want to and left Sofia for a few days. The District Committee of the Bulgarian Communist Party in Yuchbunar decided to act. Todor Zhivkov was the secretary of that committee.

According to this version, the communists led a demonstration on May 24, which started from the Yuchbunar Synagogue. A group of Zionists tried to stop them, but they were met with cries: "Traitors! Cowards!" At the next block, Zionist youths tried to stop the crowd again and the demonstrators fought them off. Then a large group of Bulgarians, mostly communists and communist youth, joined them. That was followed by a third attempt by the Zionists to stop them. A few minutes later, the police attacked the demonstration, beating people with batons. Finally, the demonstration dispersed, and many participants were arrested. Thousands of people took part in the event.

The author condemned the Zionists for their role in suppressing the revolutionary spirit. They were despicable traitors because they wanted help from the King and other government circles. Despite that, the demonstration had a significant political impact – it enraged the people of Sofia and influenced the King to change the decision to deport the Jews to Poland. Then the author quoted some communist leaflets and broadcasts of Radio Hristo Botev (communist station airing from the USSR), which actually had a very limited reach (Криспин, 1970, p. 36-41). There are a few lies in this version. The Zionists had neither the desire nor the manpower to confront the demonstration, other than sending a small group, which tried to persuade the participants. The King was not persuaded by the demonstration to change the decision – he made it a few days earlier, on May 20. Still, Todor Zhivkov did not receive in this article the ultimate credit for "leading" the protest. That came a few years later.

In a speech at a ceremonial meeting on the Victory Day, May 9, in 1975, Todor Zhivkov, already the General Secretary of the BCP, shamelessly took credit for organizing and leading in person the Jewish demonstration:

> "The older generations still remember vividly the dark years when the Hitlerists were seizing the Jewish population from the European countries occupied by or allied with Germany, loaded people like cattle in horse carriages and took them to the death camps. Despite the intentions and decisions of Hitler's fascists and the Bulgarian fascist government, the Bulgarian people, under the leadership of the BCP, did not allow the same to happen to their Jewish compatriots. [Continuous applause.] The people rose in their defense. One of the most powerful antifascist demonstrations with the participation of the Jews of Sofia took place in our capital. *It was my honor that the Central Committee of the Party asked me to organize and lead this demonstration, so I can personally attest to the internationalist feelings of our people and their humanism.* It is true that many Bulgarian Jews perished in those frightening years, but none of them died for being a Jew. Bulgarians and Bulgarian citizens of Jewish background fought together and sacrificed their lives for the freedom of their homeland, for socialist Bulgaria" [emphasis mine – M.M.] (Живков, p. 254-255).

The desire to lie and exaggerate is often a coverup of a lackluster and boring reality. In this case, the self-aggrandisement of Todor Zhivkov is just a part of overstating the importance of the Bulgarian communist movement. The latter had some very modest achievements and its activities were monitored closely by the police. In "Protocol of the interrogation of Obergruppenfuehrer of SA A. Beckerle, January 21, 1950", the former German ambassador in Bulgaria, held in a Soviet prison, recalls:

> "The Minister of the Interior Gabrovski told me that he managed to introduce into the underground communist movement several valuable agents, so he had good information about the plans of the underground leadership of the party and had the opportunity to liquidate the discovered underground communist centers at any moment. However, neither Gabrovski, nor [the police chief] Pavlov revealed to me their agents in the Bulgarian Communist Party and I did not receive any other materials from the Bulgarian police" (Тайны дипломатии Третьего рейха, p. 58).

The movement was not considered a threat serious enough to warrant a decisive action. The Bulgarian Communist Party rode to power a tide of cataclysmic events, over which Bulgaria had no control, it would have never been able to take control on its own.

After the fall of communism, the censorship restrictions on the historical research also fell and the newly-revealed information caused the collapse of the communist narrative about the events of May 1943. In the Bulgarian edition of his book, Nir Baruh added a conclusion, in which he expressed his disappointment of that colossal deception (even though, to those who lived under communism, government lies were part of the normal life):

> "Recently, I obtained new facts, related to the participation of Todor Zhivkov in the underground activities of the BCP. According to this new information, Zhivkov was not an underground activist in 1943, neither had he been the party secretary of the Yuchbunar region. If that is true, it means that at least four or five communist activists, Bulgarians and Jews, took part in building a colossal deception, published and filmed, describing the organization of the Jewish demonstration on May 24, 1943. Only now, 47 years later, was the version of the Chief Rabbi of Bulgaria Asher Hananel confirmed, who, in a conversation with the author, claimed that the communist party had no involvement in the demonstration of the Sofia Jews who rose spontaneously in the darkest period in the history of the Bulgarian Jews" (Барух, 1991, p. 144).

Far away in Israel, Buko Levi had the time to reflect on those fateful events. In an article published in Bulgarian, he examined the claims that mass action and especially the partisan movement played a significant role in saving the Bulgarian Jews. However, "if the partisan movement by itself puts its members and their families under a grave danger, the participation of Jews in those times was many times more dangerous. Often, the Polish partisans and the Warsaw Ghetto Uprising are given as examples. Those are truly glorious pages in our tragic history. The partisans in the Warsaw Ghetto knew that they were doomed in that place and they preferred to die with honor and take a revenge to the extent that was possible. The Warsaw uprising was an uprising of despair, uprising of people condemned to death. It provided to some at least a chance to escape.

> "Was the situation in Bulgaria the same? Was all hope lost? The circumstances proved that the opposite was true. So, the Consistory was correct in its actions. And even if it wanted to organize mass actions, demonstrations, riots or a partisan movement, the Consistory, which was constantly scrutinized as an official institution, was not the organization to do that" (Романо, Леви, 1961, p. 29-30).

In that difficult situation, though still different from the hopelessness of the Warsaw ghetto, many people had to use their limited options to fight the threat of deportation. The underground communist party was not a significant player, but politicians in high positions were able to do more. In a report of the Headquarters of Reich's Security of May 24, 1943, which reviews the situation of the Jewish Question in several European countries, the unwavering position of King Boris III to prevent the deportation of the Bulgarian Jews is clearly stated:

> "The expulsion of the Jews from Thrace and Macedonia for work in the East has been approved and completed. The agreement between the Commissar for the Jewish Questions (Belev) and the German adviser on the Jewish Questions (Dannecker) to deport 20,000 more Jews from the old territories of Bulgaria, was not fulfilled. While visiting the Fuehrer's Headquarters, King Boris stated that he intended to collect the Jews from the old territory of Bulgaria in labor camps and use them to build roads and so on. Considering the King's statement, Plenipotentiary Minister Beckerle does not think that the desired by the Reich's Security forceful solution of the Jewish Question could be fulfilled at this point, however, he intends to make some proposals, as soon as the situation changes" (Нойков, 1995, p. 50).

Another proof that the King was willing to prevent the

deportations, was a Secret Report No.267/43 of June 7, 1943, from the Police Attaché in Sofia Hoffmann to the Headquarters of the Reich's Security. He complained that the situation worsened, because according to the desire of the King, the government switched its policies to use the Jews only as labor force in the country. Further, Hoffmann reported that initially, the Minister of the Interior Gabrovski accepted Belev's proposal to deport all Bulgarian Jews, but the final proposal included two options:

a) To ensure the internal security of the state, all Bulgarian Jews must be deported to the German eastern regions;

b) If that is impossible, then the 25,000 Jews living in Sofia must be expelled to the provincial areas of Bulgaria.

However, when on May 20, 1943, Gabrovski visited the King at the Royal Palace with the request to approve the deportation, the King rejected the proposal and ordered that the Jews be used in public works within Bulgaria, even though Prime Minister Bogdan Filov continued to assure Beckerle that "he was determined to deport all Jews to the eastern regions."

Noykov concludes that: "To understand from a historical point of view the real value of King Boris's role in the struggle to save the Bulgarian Jews, it must be remembered that the reasons for the success were complex. The success became possible due to the resistance of large masses of the Bulgarian people, most of whom never had anti-Semitic feelings and were against racial discrimination and also to the work of King Boris, who relied on his authority and risked grave consequences but showed courage and did not hesitate to oppose the Nazi authorities and did not allow any Jews from the old territories of the Kingdom to be sent to the death camps" (Нойков, 1995, p. 51).

Some of the participants in the events of May 24, 1943, noted that it was impossible to reach the King on that day. As every year, he was expected to greet the student manifestation at the palace, but for the first time ever, he was not there. The mystery of the King's disappearance becomes clear from the memoirs of his personal driver Sava Djevrev, published in Bulgaria after the fall of communism. (Here I am using the quotes from them provided in Samuel Arditti's book "The Man Who Outsmarted Hitler").

Arditti quoted a newspaper interview of Djevrev, in which he described an encounter in 1942: "In 1942, on our way to Kurilo, we came across 50-60 workers who were paving the road. I stopped the car and His Majesty went to the group. The commander recognized him and stopped the work. The King talked to those people for over half an hour. When he boarded the car again, he sighed: "Those people were Jews. I hope they are lucky enough to get away, I don't like the situation now, but it is hard." And they were lucky, because he saved them. Because of that and the refusal to send troops to the Eastern Front, His Majesty lost his life."

In his book, Djevrev wrote that he recorded his memories, because he was tired of listening how the truth about King Boris III was distorted. There were plenty of lies under communism and they continued to spread even after its fall. He provided important details about the events of May 1943:

"During the action that the intellectuals started in defense of the Jews, His Majesty summoned me. As usual, he sat on the front seat of the car and [his valet] Svilen sat behind us. We headed to Chamkoria [in Rila Mountain]. We left the car at the Palace Tsarska Bistritsa and hiked to the cabin Yastrebets. It was His Majesty, me and another hunter. The Queen and the kids have been there before; that was the starting point to climb peak Musala. We reached the cabin. The King went to his room upstairs. Shortly after that, he came down and said: "Tonight we will be sleeping here. Make yourself comfortable." At the lower level, there were bunk beds for three people. I did not know what was in the King's room upstairs. That was my first trip to the cabin.

> "The King went to his room but warned us not to move too much, any passing people outside were not supposed to see us. Svilen remained at Chamkoria at the phone. As I said, there were three of us in the cabin, we brought food in soldiers' knapsacks. We were just sitting quietly. From time to time, the King talked with Svilen over the phone. The cabin was connected to Tsarska Bistritsa through a field telephone with cable. In the palace itself, there was a phone exchange that could transfer the calls to Sofia. On the third day, we went back to the palace and from there left for Sofia. Only then, I was told that a high-ranking military officer had arrived from Germany with a document from Hitler. The King was supposed to sign it to expel the Jews from Bulgaria. The Germans wanted them. We didn't know what they were going to do with them, but we, the Bulgarians, suspected what was going to happen to them. The Germans wanted to take the Jews from Bulgaria, the way they took them from Greece and then spread the rumor that the King gave the Greek Jews to Germany. The King went hiding, because he did not agree to deport the Bulgarian Jews, the way he did not agree to send troops on the Eastern Front, because we were in good relations with the USSR, until they occupied us

on September 8, 1944. Not many people knew about the high-ranked German who came to get the signature of His Majesty and deport the Jews. He arrived on a special airplane. However, as soon as the King learned about it, he left and hid in the Rila Mountain. Then the papers wrote that the delegation of intellectuals defending the Jews could not meet King Boris, because he went hunting. The truth was no one dared to go hunting. Even after one shot, everybody would have found out that we were at the cabin. There were many hikers and foresters passing by and they could try to find out who was shooting. That is how I learned that the King escaped to avoid signing of the document for deportation of the Jews."

Then Arditti quoted another part of Djevrev's memoirs, dealing with how the King handled the German spies and agents around him: "I found out that not everything that was happening in Bulgaria was reported to the King. One of the strong accusations against him was that he surrendered to the Germans the Jews, Bulgarian citizens, who lived abroad. It is true, pro-Nazi governments like in Italy and Spain did not surrender their Jews living outside, but they were big and strong countries. Maybe Bulgaria, as a small and weak country, could not afford that. Or maybe the clerks never asked the King. The only Jew sent from Bulgaria was Shaul Mezan, doctor, poet, public figure, fighter against fascism. If the King were notified, I don't believe he would have surrendered him. Dr. Mezan was expelled by Yaroslav Kalitsin, high official in the Commissariat for the Jewish Questions and a butcher of the Aegean Jews. After strong pressure, the People's Tribunal sentenced him to 15 years and Dimiter Peshev was also sentenced to 15 years. The so-called People's Tribunal had a strange logic" (Ардити, Човекът който изигра Хитлер).

When the threat of deportation to Poland was averted once again, the Jews from Sofia were sent to the province, which took a few weeks. As I noted before, they took anything that they could carry, and they kept their apartments and houses in Sofia.

In this situation, the secretary of Alexander Belev, Lilyana Panitsa, helped again prominent Jews threatened by arrests. The gynecologist Dr. J. Benaroyo described the situation in his testimony at the People's Tribunal on March 24, 1945, when he testified in her defense. During the events on May 24, he was arrested on the street and detained for a day. Then, Miss Panitsa whom he knew, sent him a message not to stay in his house, because he would be arrested again. He went hiding for a few days and avoided the arrest. A second warning came later; she notified him through an intermediary that the Jews, who wanted to avoid deportation by becoming Christians, would be at the top of Belev's deportation lists (People's Court Session No.16, 1945, p. 1577-1578). The prosecutor Eli Baruh tried hard to discredit Dr. Benaroyo by suggesting that he paid for Miss Panitsa's services. Despite the leading questions and pressure from Baruh, the doctor firmly defended her and refused to participate in the blackmail (Ibid., p. 1579-1580).

In his memoirs, Yako Baruh wrote that the expulsion of the Jews started on May 24, the day that celebrated St. Cyril and St. Methodius: "The Jews were taken by trains, free of charge, to their new places. The expulsion continued to June 7, 1943, when the last group left Sofia, according to the plan. After that date, only a few tens of Jews remained, mostly baptized with special privileges or civilly mobilized. The total of the Jews expelled from Sofia in that period was 25,743 [The same number was provided by Nir Baruh, but the Commissariat's number is different. – M.M.]. The Jews of Sofia started to come back after September 9, 1944, in small groups or individually. The mass return started in December 1944 and continued in the first half of 1945" (Барух, Спомени 1941-1943). Mr. Baruh's small number of remaining Jews is not confirmed by the statistics. The Commissariat stated in June 1943 that nearly 1,000 Jews were allowed to stay, but if those who lived underground were added, the number must have been even higher.

Information from the Commissariat regarding the Jews expelled from Sofia by June 8, 1943, provides some exact numbers. As of May 16, 1943, there have been 25,009 Jews registered in Sofia. 8,219 expulsion notices to families and individuals have been prepared; out of that number, 657 notices to 856 individuals have not been sent, because they were in mixed marriages (450), mobilized in labor groups (87), foreign citizens (184), under civil mobilization (29), persons residing temporarily in Sofia (87), for other reasons (19).

Notices were sent to 7,562 families (24,153 individuals). Out of that number, 6,789 families (19,156 individuals) have left the capital. In addition to the exempt categories mentioned in the previous paragraph, 773 families or 1,997 individuals have remained in Sofia, and 952 have been allowed to remain in the city (Сведение за евреи изселени от София, юни 1943).

Another document provides information from the

Commissariat about the Jews sent from Sofia to other cities and towns, as of June 10, 1943. Of the Jews in the capital, 19,153 have been sent to a total of 26 towns, in different numbers. Here are a few examples (the three numbers indicate the original number of Jews, followed by the number of the new arrivals and the total):

Berkovitsa (105, 395, 500), Vidin (1003, 1405, 2408), Vratsa (131, 730, 861), Dupnitsa (1050, 1388, 2438), Kyustendil (987, 1882, 2869), Lovech (39, 10, 49), Pazardjik (966, 1995, 2961), Plovdiv (5579, 3, 5582), Pleven (558, 1613, 2172), Razgrad (79, 577, 656), Russe (1914, 1912, 3826), Haskovo (652, 1213, 1865), etc. (Справка за броя на евреите, 1943).

In May 1943, the Jews from Sofia were forced to leave the city, which still wasn't considered the end of the plans for deportation. However, the way this was done creates the suspicion that the whole idea was somehow sabotaged. The Jews were sent to 26 cities and towns, almost equally distributed, and a very small number of politically active Jews were sent to camps, like Somovit. This made the future deportation practically impossible, because of the logistics of collecting the Jews. The action of dispersal contradicted the central idea of the Nazi Final Solution, which had to start with concentration of the Jews in compact groups in just a few areas. As early as September 1939, SS-Obergruppenführer Reinchard Heydrich, one of the chief architects of the "project", wrote a letter to the chiefs of all Einstatzgruppen of the Security Police concerning the Jewish question, where he stated: "The first preliminary measure for the final aim is the concentration of the Jews from the country into the larger towns. This has to be carried out with acceleration. It has to be distinguished, (1) between the area of Danzig and West-Prussia, Poznan, Eastern Upper Silesia, and (2) the remaining occupied territories." (Heydrich, 1939, p. 133). This directive was consistently applied wherever Germany was in charge, but in Bulgaria it wasn't realized. If the government sincerely planned to deport the Jews, it had to keep the 25,000 Sofia Jews in a separate area, instead of scattering them all over the country.

Additional documents concerning the fate of the Jews in Bulgaria and the occupied lands were presented years later, at the trial of Adolf Eichmann. The prosecution introduced several documents regarding the policies toward Jews in Bulgaria in 1943. Among them was the agreement between Belev and Dannecker, followed by a letter from Dannecker to Beckerle, where he said that the figures set out in the Agreement were too low and he would demand further deportations.

A report from the Attaché Hoffman addressed to the Attachés Group (April 5, 1943) specified that out of a transport of 11,343 Aegean Jews, 4,221 were sent by boat and 7,122 by train. It appears from it that Belev was in charge of the process and he would continue the deportations...

Another report signed by Hoffmann and countersigned by Beckerle (June 7, 1943) sent as information to Eichmann "says that in April the situation took a turn for the worse "because the Government of Bulgaria openly supports the attitude of the King as regards the Jews," and it speaks about the objections which have to be overcome concerning the deportation of the Jews from within the former borders of Bulgaria to the Reich."

The next letter from Hoffmann and Beckerle (June 24, 1943) stated that the deportation of 20,000 Jews from Sofia to the provincial towns had been completed. Here the prosecutor Bar-Or noted that it was clear from the documents the authorities used this action only to evade pressure from the Germans.

Another letter to Eichmann, dated July 28, 1943, mentioned among other things that Metropolitan Paissi, a high cleric in the Bulgarian Church with a positive attitude toward Germany, wanted a certain person to be sent to the camp Theresienstadt. The reply came a year later (June 31, 1944) stating that the request could not be accommodated.

A report form Beckerle, dated February 4, 1943, to the Foreign Ministry, forwarded to Eichmann, stated that the German Embassy in Sofia was "informed of an offer from England, through the Swiss Protecting Power, to accept 5,000 Jewish children [from Bulgaria] for Palestine." The German Foreign Ministry rejected the offer with the explanation that those "children will be educated under British influence to become 5,000 propagandists". In another document, Eichmann expressed the same opinion. [It should not be forgotten that at the same time, the Bulgarian Government sent to the British a proposal for sending all 60,000 Jews from the old and new territories to Palestine, but the British rejected it. – M.M.] That was followed by a general policy directive sent by the Foreign Ministry to all embassies. It stated that no negotiations about emigration of Jews were to be conducted with foreign governments. One of the arguments was that such negotiations would contradict the policies of the Axis toward the Arab nations. The prosecutor also presented two more letters, one, about further negotiations to send 4,000 Jewish children to Palestine, second, letter from Eichmann (May 4, 1943) to the Foreign Ministry that the authorities of Palestine had approved a large number of immigration certificates for Zionists with women and children. 8,000 of them were expected to go through Bulgaria and Eichmann wanted to prevent the passage (Trial of Adolf Eichmann, Session 47, part 3).

At a meeting of the Holy Synod, held on May 27, 1943, among other things, Metropolitan Stefan reported about his meeting with the Jews from Sofia. Early in the morning on May 24, 1943, he was surprised to see a large group of Jews in front of his office. They insisted on seeing him, he let them in, even though it was too early. They told him that the government decided to expel them from Sofia and they feared that it was even going to deport them from the country. They begged the Metropolitan to deliver to His Majesty the King their request for mercy and permission to remain in the country that was their only homeland. The Metropolitan could not deliver the request at the official Church service, because His Majesty was absent from the ceremony. However, he talked about it with the King's adviser Pavel Grouev and with the Prime Minister and the Minister of the Interior, asking for mercy for the Jewish minority. They could not promise anything positive. Later that day, he was visited by many groups of Jews and Christians, all asking for help from the Church. Metropolitan Stefan then sent a telegram to the provisional Chairman of the Holy Synod with information about the situation of the persecuted Jewish minority. He did what he could do: wrote to the Prime Minister and Pavel Grouev to pass the request of the Jewish minority for mercy to His Majesty.

Metropolitan Stefan's impression was that the Jews in Sofia were subjected to a difficult moral and physical persecution. He asked the Holy Synod to reaffirm its support for those who suffered. Since many Jews filed requests for baptism, he thought that the Church should speed up the process. The Holy Synod accepted his recommendations and asked for a meeting with the Prime Minister and the King's advisers (Свети синод, Протокол №19, 1943, p. 198-199).

However, these policies were resented by the anti-Semitic forces, who started to distribute libelous flyers against Metropolitan Stefan. The question was raised at a meeting of the Holy Synod on June 29, 1943. After the expulsion of the Jews to the provincial towns, the Church continued to baptize Jews. That caused a reaction of ridicule and slander in flyers spread anonymously against Metropolitan Stefan. Several Metropolitans complained that this was an unfortunate result of the disrespect shown by the Bulgarian press to the Orthodox Church. Some also blamed the recent baptisms of Jews, which were conducted in a hasty manner and were seen as having ulterior motives (Свети синод, Протокол №9, 1943, p. 118-121).

At another meeting on June 25, 1943, the Holy Synod discussed at length the situation after the expulsion of the Jews from Sofia in May-June 1943. Metropolitan Kiril of Plovdiv spoke:

> "The Holy Synod has already established its opinion about the Jewish question. Our current debates would hardly add anything, except the clarification of some specific facts. Before I start, I would like to discuss two thoughts, which have been persistently raised against the thesis of the Church.
>
> "One of them is that the Jewish question is not one of morality, but of security. We heard the same thought in the recent speech of the Reich's Minister of Propaganda, Dr. Goebbels. We do not know whether he meant the German social reality, and whether he was responding to it. It seems to me that the Jewish question in Germany had been resolved long ago. Its painful phase had long passed. It seems, Mr. Reich's Minister was responding to the moral reserves, which the Jewish question has caused in other countries.
>
> "How should the Church evaluate that thought? For the Church, the Jewish question is also a moral question. There is no security without morality. Security, which is not based on morality, does not last. So, the Jewish question should be not only a question of security but also of morality.
>
> "The second thought is that the Jewish question is European, not Bulgarian. I do not know how this thought should be understood, but it most likely does not mean that our attitude toward the Bulgarian Jews is not a Bulgarian issue. We admit that the Jewish question has a European character, but it has never ceased to be a Bulgarian question as well. Hence, in our country, it must be solved according to our national and social reality. Neither following others, nor rejection of the national sovereignty is recommended. We have in mind the different ways in which the European countries treat the Jews.
>
> It is more important to take a position on the specific situation of the Jews in our country after the latest expulsions from the capital. I think we must insist that they are not deprived of their right to work and support themselves. Otherwise, that would mean that they are deprived of the right of life. The Jews exiled to various cities must be moved to a few labor communities. At the same time, this would be a sign that the Jews will not be deported outside of the borders of Bulgaria.

The present undetermined situation should not continue. It is torturous to the Jews themselves and harmful to the country. The state will win from the labor communities. And after the war, the ultimate solution of the Jewish question could be initiated according to the circumstances" (Свети синод, Протокол №8, 1943, p.111-112).

An important event was the meeting of the Holy Synod with King Boris III and Prime Minister Bogdan Filov on June 22, 1943. The Synod requested the meeting after the expulsion of the Jews from Sofia, they wanted more information about issues they wrote about to the King but did not receive an answer. The ideas shared by the King at the meeting sound surprising and some use them as an argument that he was anti-Semitic. However, it is important to remember that the German agent Prof. Filov was at the meeting and, as Queen Ioanna noted in her memoirs, the King was extensively spied on and he had to play a double game (let's not forget the conversation with Goebbels mentioned in Chapter 7 of this book).

The King emphasized the speculative spirit of the world Jewry, which has been creating hostility toward Jews in many nations. That speculation was the source of many wars and conflicts. Many nations tried to liberate themselves from the influence and exploitation of the Jewry to strengthen their patriotism. This could be achieved when by law, the various economic, financial, commercial and industrial enterprises are taken away from Jewish hands. Such laws have been adopted in many countries in Europe. Nobody denied the right and duty of the Orthodox Church to advocate for the weak and comfort those who suffer, regardless of their ethnicity. However, by taking measures against the evils that the Jewry caused through propaganda and speculation, the government did its best to reduce the number of those who suffered in Bulgaria, and if possible, to avoid suffering completely...

The Church should not take all complaints from Jews at face value, upon inspection, many of them have been found to be groundless. If in the future it was proven that some institutions apply the law too harshly, the government would take correctional measures. The government would also decide how to ease the lives of the baptized Jews, if their conversion was sincere, some of them may reject their new faith, if things change...

Further in the meeting, Bogdan Filov agreed with the request of the Synod that the baptized Jews must not be forced to carry

Jewish stars, although the change should be done quietly, without too much attention. Filov also agreed that there were certain excesses in the application of the law, however, in other cases, the Jews exaggerated the incidents. Still, the government would strive for fairness in the treatment of the Jews (Свети синод, Протокол №6, 1943, p. 89).

Why did the King deliver such a hostile monolog? First of all, the punishment of the Jews had ended, they were out of Sofia, dispersed in different towns and a deportation was unlikely. Like in the case of the conversation with Goebbels, the King probably pretended to agree with the main German points without supporting them with deeds. If he deeply believed what he said at the meeting, he would have deported the Jews long time ago. As the secret reports showed, the Germans suspected him that he was not sincere in dealing with the Jewish Question. It was impossible to take an open and confrontational position, delays were the only way to proceed. Besides, at the meeting he had Prof. Filov, a staunch supporter of Germany and possible German agent, who would report anything the King said. And let's not forget the admission of the Security Police Attaché at the German Embassy Friedrich Panzinger (quoted in Chapter 10), that he maintained a spy network of 40 high-level Bulgarian politicians and other prominent people.

At least one of the Metropolitans, members of the Holy Synod, was a strong supporter of Germany – it was Paissi of Vratsa. As I already noted, at the trial of Eichmann, among the documents presented by the prosecution (Trial of Adolf Eichmann, Session 47, part 3) was a letter to Eichmann, dated July 28, 1943, which mentioned that Metropolitan Paissi, a high cleric in the Bulgarian Church with a pro-German attitude, wanted a certain person to be sent to Theresienstadt. Eichmann replied a year later that the request could not be accommodated. The King, who survived 25 years on the throne, with several coup d'état and assassination attempts, and had to be always one step ahead of his enemies, most likely knew the Metropolitan's priorities and spoke in a way that didn't jeopardize his policies.

The complexity of the Bulgarian policies toward Jews that resulted in their rescue, was caught by the philosopher Hannah Arendt who attended Eichmann's trial and covered it in her book "Eichmann in Jerusalem". In Chapter 11 of the book, she noted that no Jews were deported from Bulgaria and by August 1944, the anti-Jewish laws were revoked. She found that paradoxical, considering the fact that Bulgaria "received considerable territorial aggrandizement" thanks to Nazi Germany. She saw some of the reasons in the weakness of the local fascist movement, which did not create a serious threat to the monarchy and the parliament. Bulgaria didn't send troops to the Eastern front and refused to sever its diplomatic relationships with the USSR.

She was puzzled by the lack of anti-Semitism: "But most surprising of all, in the belt of mixed populations where anti-Semitism was rampant among all ethnic groups and had become official governmental policy long before Hitler's arrival, the Bulgarians had no "understanding of the Jewish problem" whatever. It is true that the Bulgarian Army had agreed to have all the Jews – they numbered about fifteen thousand – deported from the newly annexed territories, which were under military government and whose population was anti-Semitic; but it is doubtful that they knew what "resettlement in the East" actually signified. Somewhat earlier, in January 1941, the government had also agreed to introduce some anti-Jewish legislation, but that, from the Nazi viewpoint, was simply ridiculous: some six thousand able-bodied men were mobilized for work; all baptized Jews, regardless of the date of their conversion, were exempted, with the result that an epidemic of conversions broke out; five thousand more Jews – out of a total of approximately fifty thousand – received special privileges; and for Jewish physicians and businessmen a numerus clausus was introduced that was rather high, since it was based on the percentage of Jews in the cities, rather than in the country at large. When these measures had been put into effect, Bulgarian government officials declared publicly that things were now stabilized to everybody's satisfaction. Clearly, the Nazis would not only have to enlighten them about the requirements for a "solution of the Jewish problem," but also to teach them that legal stability and a totalitarian movement could not be reconciled."

Hannah Arendt suspected that the unorthodox Bulgarian policies made the Germans realize the difficulties involved in applying the "final solution" in Bulgaria. "In January 1942, Eichmann wrote a letter to the Foreign Office in which he declared that "sufficient possibilities exist for the reception of Jews from Bulgaria"; he proposed that the Bulgarian government be approached and assured the Foreign Office that the police attaché in Sofia would "take care of the technical implementation of the deportation." (This police attaché seems not to have been very enthusiastic about his work either, for shortly thereafter Eichmann sent one of his own men, Theodor Dannecker, from

Paris to Sofia as "adviser.") It is quite interesting to note that this letter ran directly contrary to the notification Eichmann had sent to Serbia only a few months earlier, stating that no facilities for the reception of Jews were yet available and that even Jews from the Reich could not be deported. The high priority given to the task of making Bulgaria judenrein can be explained only by Berlin's having received accurate information that great speed was necessary then in order to achieve anything at all. Well, the Bulgarians were approached by the German embassy, but not until about six months later did they take the first step in the direction of "radical" measures - the introduction of the Jewish badge. For the Nazis, even this turned out to be a great disappointment. In the first place, as they dutifully reported, the badge was only a "very little star"; second, most Jews simply did not wear it; and, third, those who did wear it received "so many manifestations of sympathy from the misled population that they actually are proud of their sign" - as Walter Schellenberg, Chief of Counterintelligence in the R.S.H.A., wrote in an S.D. report transmitted to the Foreign Office in November, 1942."

Arendt also realized that the decision to send the Jews from Sofia to numerous provincial towns in Bulgaria created even more difficulties for the future German plans for deportation: "Under great German pressure, the Bulgarian government finally decided to expel all Jews from Sofia to rural areas, but this measure was definitely not what the Germans demanded, since it dispersed the Jews instead of concentrating them. This expulsion actually marked an important turning point in the whole situation, because the population of Sofia tried to stop Jews from going to the railroad station and subsequently demonstrated before the King's palace. [The demonstration was dispersed before reaching King's palace. – M.M.] The Germans were under the illusion that King Boris was primarily responsible for keeping Bulgaria's Jews safe, and it is reasonably certain that German Intelligence agents murdered him. But neither the death of the monarch nor the arrival of Dannecker, early in 1943, changed the situation in the slightest, because both Parliament and the population remained clearly on the side of the Jews. Dannecker succeeded in arriving at an agreement with the Bulgarian Commissar for Jewish Affairs to deport six thousand "leading Jews" to Treblinka, but none of these Jews ever left the country. The agreement itself is noteworthy because it shows that the Nazis had no hope of enlisting the Jewish leadership for their own purposes. The Chief Rabbi of Sofia was unavailable, having been hidden by Metropolitan Stephan of

Sofia, who had declared publicly that "God had determined the Jewish fate, and men had no right to torture Jews, and to persecute them" (Hilberg) – which was considerably more than the Vatican had ever done. Finally, the same thing happened in Bulgaria as was to happen in Denmark a few months later – the local German officials became unsure of themselves and were no longer reliable. This was true of both the police attaché, a member of the S.S., who was supposed to round up and arrest the Jews, and the German Ambassador in Sofia, Adolf Beckerle, who in June, 1943, had advised the Foreign Office that the situation was hopeless, because "the Bulgarians had lived for too long with peoples like Armenians, Greeks, and Gypsies to appreciate the Jewish problem" – which, of course, was sheer nonsense, since the same could be said mutatis mutandis for all countries of Eastern and Southeastern Europe. It was Beckerle too who informed the R.S.H.A., in a clearly irritated tone, that nothing more could be done. And the result was that not a single Bulgarian Jew had been deported or had died an unnatural death when, in August 1944, with the approach of the Red Army, the anti-Jewish laws were revoked. I know of no attempt to explain the conduct of the Bulgarian people, which is unique in the belt of mixed populations. But one is reminded of Georgi Dimitrov, a Bulgarian Communist who happened to be in Germany when the Nazis came to power, and whom they chose to accuse of the Reichstagsbrand, the mysterious fire in the Berlin Parliament of February 27, 1933. He was tried by the German Supreme Court and confronted with Göring, whom he questioned as though he were in charge of the proceedings; and it was thanks to him that all those accused, except van der Lubbe, had to be acquitted. His conduct was such that it won him the admiration of the whole world, Germany not excluded. "There is one man left in Germany," people used to say, "and he is a Bulgarian" (Arendt, 2006, ch. XI).

The "Hero of Leipzig" will play later a disastrous role in the communist terror in Bulgaria, whose victims became many of the people who helped to save the Bulgarian Jews.

By June 1943, the situation seemed settled and despite the rumors of new deportation plans, there were no visible actions taken of the magnitude of March and May 1943. Still, the prevention of the catastrophe did not mean that the bad treatment was over. The Bulgarian Jews still lived under the anti-Jewish laws that restricted their rights.

As we saw in the introduction, this situation is still used to claim that the Bulgarian Jews lived through a Holocaust, only with "different dynamics". The next chapter is dedicated to an analysis of that situation. Based on the available documents and testimonies, I will explore the conditions under which the Jews lived, mostly in three major spheres of existence – camps, labor groups, and forced settlement in provincial towns.

13 EXILED – BULGARIAN JEWS IN CAMPS AND LABOR GROUPS

The second deportation attempt of May 1943 failed and eventually contributed to the fall of Alexander Belev as a Commissar for the Jewish Questions and one of the main architects of the deportation proposals. The Bulgarian Jews avoided the total catastrophe of extermination, but that did not mean an end to their tribulations. Their lives changed drastically in 1943 due to the exile from Sofia, which affected half of the Jewish population in Bulgaria.

As we saw in the introduction, there are people who are willing to equate the Jewish experience in Bulgaria with the Holocaust experience of the Jews in other European countries. On the surface, such an approach has its merits, because in both cases we can observe the loss of civil rights, forceful confinement in camps and labor groups, and other forms of mistreatment. However, if we go deeper and compare the two realities, we will see substantial differences that cannot justify their equalization.

There is a vast historical literature that has documented the Holocaust in Eastern Europe, specifically in countries that are similar to Bulgaria culturally and historically. An honest comparison between the events in those countries and in Bulgaria (where we also have testimonies and documents) shows clearly the drastic difference in the treatment of the Jews.

Let's begin with the major tragedy of the Holocaust, the physical extermination of the Jews, which was completely avoided in Bulgaria. In his book "The Destruction of the Jewish Population in Ukraine in 1941-1944" (in Russian), the historian Alexander Kruglov provides shocking numbers. At the beginning of the war in 1941, there were about 2.7 million Jews in Ukraine, living in all regions of the republic. Many of them lived in the urban areas, but there were also many farmers in Jewish kolkhozes in four Jewish national districts. By the time of the liberation in 1944, about 1.5 million of them had been slaughtered. If the killed in battle and the evacuees, sent to Caucasus in 1941 and killed by Germans there, are added, the total number rises to 1.6 million. For example, in Lvov Region out of 355,000 Jews, 266,500 were killed; in Ternopol Region out of 136,000 Jews, 126,000 perished; for Ivano-Frankov Region the numbers were 140,000 and 109,500; Volyn Region – 123,000 and 102,500; Rovno Region – 112,000 and 98,000 and so on (Круглов, 1997).

However, mass murder on such an enormous scale wasn't possible without the participation of helpers recruited from the local population. In his book "Holocaust in Rovno", J. Burds wrote that the German effort to recruit locals into service in the occupation authority was by all measures enormously successful. The ratio of Germans to local collaborators in many departments and police organizations ran from one to five in 1941, to 1 to 20 or more by 1943. Figures from the Reichskommissariat Ukraine show that the SS (Schutzstaffel, Protection Squad) employed some 15,000 Germans and 238,000 native police at the end of 1942, reflecting a ratio of nearly 1 to 16, a rate that rose to 1:25 or even 1:50 in some eastern regions by 1944. Romanichev found that the size of the Schuma (police auxiliary) units in German police forces throughout the occupied zones in the East grew more than ten times between late 1941 and early 1943 (Burds, 2013).

If we move further to the south, to a country that is even closer to Bulgaria culturally, Romania, we will see that things were not much better. At least 250,000 Romanian Jews were killed during the Holocaust. A minimum of 55,000 Jews perished during the summer of 1941 in Southern Moldavia, Bessarabia and Bukovina at the hands of Romanian and German military units, and at least another 70,000 Romanian Jews were killed or died in the deportation to Transnistria by the Romanian fascist authorities. In 1944 the Hungarian authorities and the Germans deported 150,000 Jews from Northern Transylvania to Auschwitz-Birkenau in Poland. Only 15,000 of these deportees survived (Ioanid, January 1992).

The Romanian practices were so bad that even the German anti-Semites criticized them. In October 1941, the Chief of the Security Police Mueller sent a letter to the Foreign Minister Joachim von Ribbentrop, reporting on the "progress" in the extermination of the Jews, one of the areas covered was Romania:

> "There is no system in the way in which the Rumanians are dealing with the Jews. No objections could be raised against the numerous executions of Jews if the technical preparations and the execution itself were not totally inadequate. The Ru¬manians usually leave the executed persons where they have been shot without burying them. The Einsatzkommando has issued instructions to the Rumanian police to proceed somewhat more systematically in this direction" (Letter to Ribbentrop on Einsatzgruppen, 1941, p. 180).

Later, at the People's Tribunal, one of whose sections was supposed to condemn anti-Semitism in Bulgaria, the "People's Prosecutor" tried to shame Bulgaria that Romania was better because its Jews were not deported. It was a rather hypocritical statement, because the Romanians themselves did the dirty extermination job.

One of the horrific moments of the Holocaust in Romania was the Iasi pogrom of June 1941, committed entirely by Romanians. The Jews in the city were accused of collaboration with the Soviet Union. Many were shot, and the rest rounded up and on June 29 loaded on two trains to be transported to another city. The first train had about 39 cattle carriages with about 2,500 Jews transported without food or water, despite the heat. The next day, when it stopped at a railway station, it became clear that in each carriage containing 140-145 people, 80-90 were dead. Those who tried to escape or looked for water, were killed on the spot. The train stopped at two more spots to unload the corpses. On July 6, at the final station, there were only 1,076 survivors, many of whom were already dying.

> "The number of victims of the Iasi pogrom cannot be established with certainty. While the number of victims on the trains is known and relatively accurate, we do not know how many Jews in Iasi were buried in communal graves, how many such graves there were, and how many corpses were simply thrown on rubbish heaps or in the Bahlui River. German diplomats in Bucharest estimated at least 4,000 victims, and Raul Hilberg accepted this figure. Curzio Malaparte mentioned 7,000 victims. The most reliable source seems to be documents from the archives of the Ministry of the Interior which, according to Gheorghe Zaharia, place the number of dead at over 8,000 victims" (Ioanid, 1993, p. 143).

Lithuania was a small country, in which, under German

occupation, over 95% of the local Jews were killed. Documents of eyewitnesses describe those horrors. Kazimierz Sakowicz left behind records, later published as "Ponary Diary 1941-1943: A Bystander's Account of a Mass Murder". The author lived in a small cottage in Ponary, suburb of Vilno, Lithuania. That was in the woods, near a place where the Russians planned to build a fuel storage facility for an air base. It was never completed because of the German invasion in 1941. All that remained were large pits for fuel tanks – 12 to 32 m in diameter and 5 to 8 m deep. The Germans used the pits to exterminate up to 60,000 people, most of them Jews, but also many Poles perished there. They were brought from the Jewish ghetto in Vilno. From his attic Sakowicz could observe the pits and witness the killings. He counted the victims and recorded everything he saw or heard. Women, children and men were brought every day to the pits, undressed and placed at the edge of the pits to be shot by the German SS and Lithuanian police. This continued from 1941 to 1944; when the pits started to fill up and it was necessary to move the corpses around to avoid overflowing, the murderers placed the victims so that they could fall in the desired spot that didn't need rearrangement of the corpses (Sakowicz, 2005).

Another diary from the same era was "The Jews in Vilno: 1941-1944 Chronicle" (in Russian), the diary of Grigory Shur, which documented the everyday horror of the Jews who were locked in the ghetto in Vilno (Vilnius). About 40,000 Jews were driven inside and locked. It looked like a normal town, though with overcrowded houses, with its own theater and workers who went to work in an outside factory every day. But it was an extermination place – the Germans frequently demanded various numbers of people to be selected and taken out to be shot; often that "work" was done by the ghetto Jewish police. Shur recalls how those policemen were sent to a nearby village to shoot 1,500 Jews. They managed to negotiate with the Germans and shot only 406, so they were very proud. Thus, by 1944, all inhabitants of the Vilno ghetto were dead, including the police. One of the last "actions" was the shooting of nearly two hundred children (Шур, 2000). It is important to note that in Bulgaria, neither the Consistory nor other Jewish leaders were involved in such activities. On the contrary, through their connections and ingenuity, they managed to improve consistently the conditions of the Jews.

Since thousands of Bulgarian Jews were mobilized in labor groups, it will be useful to compare their treatment with that of similar units in other countries. In "Nazi Empire-Building and the

Holocaust in Ukraine", Wendy Lower provides information about the Jewish labor in the occupied Ukraine. The Nazi policy of using Jewish laborers, in projects such as road construction, was officially endorsed by Heydrich at the Wannsee Conference in January 1942. But what Heydrich revealed at Wannsee had been put into practice months earlier in Zhytomyr (and before that in eastern Galicia). In August 1941, while stationed at Zhytomyr, Otto Rasch, chief of Einsatzgruppe C, reported that "until the Final Solution of the Jewish problem is achieved across the continent, Jews can be used up in the cultivating of swampy areas around the Pripiat', the Dnepr, and the Volga." A month later he reiterated that instead of following the common procedure, the Jews in Ukraine should be killed through the kind of hard labor that was so desperately needed (Lower, 2005, p. 143).

At Mykhailivka, twelve kilometers west of Haisyn, about 500 Jews from Ukraine and Romania were crammed into a stable along with the horses. In such abominable conditions, as the survivor Arnold Daghani wrote in his wartime diary, disease was rampant, and those who could not get up to work were eventually separated and shot. Besides children, there were a number of women among the laborers. Starvation was perhaps the workers' greatest form of suffering. A rare and revealing source, Daghani's diary presented the odd mix and interaction of perpetrators at the road construction sites in Ukraine: German engineers and their families, lowly power-seeking SS men, Lithuanian non-commissioned officers, and high-ranking SS officers. Despite their diverse backgrounds, they devised a brutal system for selecting and killing the "unfit" laborers (mostly women, children, and the infirm); they seemed to relish their power over the laborers, beating them as they worked on the road and in the gravel pits. Their inhumane approach thrived on routine as well as random acts of humiliation, and on murder, which had the desired effect of terrorizing the workers and curbing resistance. Daghani related that at Haisyn, for example, the Lithuanian guards convinced German inspectors to kill two elderly women working on the road. The women (who were friends) appeared to be healthy, but one of them possessed a pair of sturdy snow boots, which the guards wanted. They were simply ordered to march a few hundred yards from the site and were then shot by one of the guards (Lower, 2005, p. 146-147).

The added presence of SS-policemen assigned to the DG IV project meant that Zhytomyr's Jewish population faced yet another concentrated effort to "clear" the areas along the highways. For most Jews who were assigned to the project, their suffering was merely prolonged, and their fate remained the same as their Jewish relatives who had perished earlier in 1941 and 1942. Upon the liquidation of the DG IV camps in late 1943-early 1944, the German SD, Order Police, and non-German auxiliaries had killed, according to one scholar's estimate, as many as 25,000 Jewish laborers in Ukraine. At the DG IV labor camps in Haisyn, about 7,000 Jews were worked to death and killed when the camps were liquidated. Thousands were killed in June 1943 and October 1943 at the former Khmil'nyk ghetto. A recent quantitative analysis of the Holocaust in Vinnytsia estimates that 10,000 Jews died in the labor camps during 1942-43 (Lower, 2005, p. 149).

As we will see, the situation in Bulgaria was quite different. Despite the harsh problems many Jews faced, nothing came close to the treatment experienced in those countries. Declaring moral equivalency between these two different developments is morally dishonest.

LABOR GROUPS

The labor mobilization played an important role in the lives of the Jews in Bulgaria during World War II. As it happened with everything related to that period, the interpretations vary widely, and it takes some careful research to restore the truth.

In his article "The Jewish Labor Camps in Bulgaria" (in Bulgarian), the Jewish Bulgarian historian Dr. David Cohen gives his take of the problem by painting a dark picture. The groups were a direct consequence of the Law for Defense of the Nation, which deprived the Jews from many rights. "Through mobilization of the men beyond conscription age, and the clerks, their families were completely destroyed, especially the families expelled to other cities."

Then, Dr. Cohen provides some details. Government Decree No.48 of July 17, 1941, started civil mobilization of all Jews with foreign citizenship (?) from 20 to 46-years old by the Commandment of the Labor Army for construction work at state, communal and other public projects. They were supposed to work without pay, only for food, and work clothes are not provided. [Not true.] Those who had families, received wages of 50 leva. A month later, on August 12, all Jews, subject to military conscription, as well as the retired officers and soldiers, were included in labor groups under the Ministry of Public Works under the same conditions. Each group included 100 to 300 people and worked on a specific project. They were expected to bring their own clothes, shoes, blankets, and utensils. [Not true]

"The working conditions were very difficult. The mobilized were expected to dig four cubic meters of soil and sand, usually mixed with stones. The norm included digging, loading on a wheelbarrow and moving it at a distance of 50 meters. Compared to the usual norms of the Ministry, it meant that the mobilized had to do twice as much work in an 8-hour workday or to work 12 to 16 hours daily." [The workload is exaggerated, we will see that despite some excesses, the workers were treated mostly fairly.]

September 9, 1944 [the day of the communist coup] found the productive part of the Bulgarian Jewry in labor groups, skinnier, sick, in torn clothes, barefoot, with lice, without work or means for survival in the coming winter. The Muraviev Government did not listen to the call to release them. [Another exaggeration, the Jews, like all other mobilized, worked only when the weather was good.]

Dr. Cohen concludes that the claim that sending the Jews to labor groups was the King's way of saving the Jews from deportation, was a lie. Among the people, who hold that "wrong" view, he includes Guenter (Eichmann's deputy), the Police Attaché at the German Embassy in Sofia Hoffmann, Benjamin Arditti, Pashanko Dimitrov, and Hans Joachim Hoppe. Dr. Cohen's argument is that the labor groups were created in January 1941, a year before the confirmation of the Nazi plans for destruction of the Jews at the Wannsee Conference (January 20, 1942) and two years before the events of March 10, 1943 (Коен, 2004).

Some of Dr. Cohen's points are exaggerated, others are plainly wrong, I will go over them in detail further in this chapter.

In his book "The Ransom – King Boris and the Fate of the Bulgarian Jews", Nir Baruh provides his opinion about the labor groups. In 1941, the Jews were pulled out of the military and transferred to the Labor Army. Usually people whom the government considered "unreliable" served in those units, like Turks, Gypsies and political activists. They worked on paving roads, building fortifications, bridges and other public structures.

Because of their high qualifications and intelligence, the Jews were used in the Labor Army for planning, surveying, accounting, and so on. Few of them were involved in physical work. In 1942, following a proposal by Commissar Belev, the government established special Jewish labor groups under the control of the Ministry of Public Works. Most of these groups were building roads near the Yugoslavian and Greek borders, some worked in the mountainous regions of Bulgaria.

The commanders of the groups included one retired non-Jewish officer, Lieutenant or Captain, and 3 to 4 non-Jewish Sergeants, each group included 100 to 120 people. "In 1942, about 3,000 Jews, 20 to 40 years old, were mobilized in 12 labor camps. In 1943 and 1944 the camps doubled to 24. At the top of this system was the retired Colonel Rogozarov, an anti-Semite. The government provided only tools and food, often insufficient; blankets, clothes and medicines had to be provided by the mobilized. Every Jew in a labor group had to display on his sleeve a 12-cm wide yellow ribbon, but this order was not observed. The labor groups were concentration camps with hard physical labor. Officially, there were no leaves, the mobilized could get away only when sent to hospital by the Jewish doctors, where they could see their families. A large number of the families suffered economic difficulties, which caused the suffering of fathers and sons who could not take care of them" (Барух, 1991, p.59-60).

This presentation is more balanced, but it still contains questionable claims. Leaves for the mobilized were allowed. Besides, as we saw in Chapter 11, with the activities of Dr. Vatev, it was possible to get away from mobilization for medical reasons.

In a comment to the online publication of Dr. Cohen's article, the Bulgarian journalist Daniela Gorcheva raises objections to some of his claims. "The age of the mobilized varied from 20 to 44 and the sick were excluded. Many Jews were able to obtain false medical certificates and did not go to work. They were mobilized from the spring to the fall and had the right to leaves. The labor groups were completely different from the communist concentration camps, where the forced labor was extremely hard, and many people died of hunger, sickness, and beatings, and many were even shot. The Jewish labor groups were created under German pressure. By the way, the communists mobilized people for work in the same way, even children." Further, she notes that Dr. Cohen's claim that the labor groups were not a tool for saving the Jews from deportation is wrong. The people he mentioned were high Nazi officials or historians who knew very well what King Boris was doing.

From the writings of Dr. Cohen and Nir Baruh, the reader remains with the idea that the Jewish labor groups were created specifically to punish Jews. This simply is not true. As we saw, in the labor groups in Ukraine, everybody, including women and children, was forced to work to death, while that was never the case in Bulgaria. Besides, the Labor Army in Bulgaria was much older than the Jewish groups.

I already mentioned that the Jews in Bulgaria were proud to serve in the Bulgarian Army and, as the Consistory pointed out during the debates over the Law for Defense of the Nation, over 900 Jews gave their lives serving in the army. The Bulgarian Labor Army was a direct result from the Treaty of Neuilly of 1919.

The treaties with the defeated nations after World War I, severely restricted the number of the soldiers in their armies, such was the case with Germany as well. The tradition to serve in the army was considered a matter of honor by the Bulgarian citizens. Alexander Stamboliyski, the Prime Minister who signed the Neuilly Treaty, created on June 14, 1920, the so-called Labor Duty, which gave the opportunity to men and women to serve the country by working for it, mostly on projects involving construction and other public works. The institution survived Prof. Alexander Tsankov's coup d'etat, which reversed many other policies of Stamboliyski's Agrarian Party.

> "As a substitute for conscription he [Stamboliyski] introduced a compulsory labour law which required a physically fit male to undertake at some time between his 20th and 40th birthdays an eight-month period of manual labour for the benefit of the state and to be liable to perform in his district up to 21 days of labour for the state every year until the age of 50 (the requirement for unmarried women was less and married women were exempt from the service). The physical and psychological results achieved were considerable. By the end of 1925 about 800 bridges had been constructed, 600–700 miles of railway track laid, 1,800–1,900 miles of road built, swamps drained, canals dug, telephones strung, and forests planted" (Gallagher, 2001, p. 96-97).

The institution was viewed with suspicion by the foreign powers; it was considered an attempt to circumvent the strict clauses of the treaty by creating an underground army. The construction industry also saw a threat in it, since the state was competing with them with cheap labor. Nevertheless, it continued and later it was transformed into a Labor Army, under the control of the Ministry of War. Bulgarians could be mobilized in either of the two armies, regular or labor.

After the 1944 coup, the communists kept the Labor Army. It is not clear how strictly the rule to recruit "unreliable" people in it was observed in the Kingdom of Bulgaria, but the Bulgarian communists enforced it strictly, mostly from ideological point of view. Most Bulgarians, including citizens from "reliable" minorities like Jews, Greeks and Armenians, were conscripted in the regular army. On the other hand, people with politically unreliable views (of even related to such people) and minorities perceived as potential threats, like Turks and Gypsies, were recruited in the Labor Army. On the bright side, the experience in construction gave to those who served there the chance to learn useful trades.

The communists went much further than the Kingdom in using low-paid or free labor. The mass Youth Brigades movement after 1944, included many thousands of young people working for free on government construction projects, forced by enthusiasm or peer pressure. Later, the industrialization reduced significantly the labor force in the agriculture. The solution was to use child and student free labor to pick the harvest or work in the rural construction. The writer of this book was also part of this "glorious" movement. The school year in Bulgaria used to start on September 15, but the first month wasn't dedicated to study, we had to go every day to work in the agriculture. We were picking hops, plums, raspberries, cucumbers, etc. and this started at the age of 12. Starting from Grade 8, at age 15, we were supposed to work for an additional month during the summer vacation. We had to provide our work clothes and shoes.

These "labor brigades" were mandatory for university students as well. The government took them so seriously that if somebody did not show up or was kicked out for poor performance, he or she could be expelled from the university. If we consider the textbook definition of "slave" as a person who is forced to work with no pay, it is safe to state that communism was built to a great degree on slave labor. And that is before we consider the communist concentration camps, where inmates were subjected to excruciating labor, malnourishment and often death, in conditions worse than anything seen in the Kingdom of Bulgaria. As an element of that free-labor system, the Labor Army survived even the fall of communism, to be disbanded only in the year 2000.

So, the issue here is that he Jewish labor groups cannot be analysed outside of the historical context of the times and seen as a sinister punishment established specifically to make the lives of the Jews difficult.

The collection of documents of the Bulgarian State Archives "Jewish Labor Groups in Labor Duty 1941-1945", published in 2008, traces the history of that institution. After the approval of the Law for Defense of the Nation in 1940, the Jewish youth was required to serve "in labor brigades, part of the Labor Duty, the latter was included with a King's Decree No.15 of June 13, 1940, in the Bulgarian Army as a separate unit under the name "Labor Army". The Minister of War issued a special decree arranging the service of the Jewish youth in the Labor Army, which was confirmed with Order No. 195 of May 15, 1941. The same order determined the conditions for service of people of the age of 17 and the mobilization of the retired army personnel up to the age of 46 in those labor units. The mobilized were required to wear uniforms and their commanders were Jewish officers. The only exception were the Jews with medical education; following an order of the General Staff, they served in military medical institutions.

> "After Bulgaria signed the Tri-Partite Pact on March 1, 1941, the Third Reich's pressure to increase the repressions against Jews, became even stronger. In the summer of 1941, the German Plenipotentiary Minister in Sofia [Ambassador] Adolf-Heinz Beckerle protested against the service of young Jews in the Labor Army and the order that allowed it. He saw it as liberal treatment of the Jews. The government backed off after the German demand and on August 12, 1941, approved a Government Decree No.53, which detached the labor brigades from the Ministry of War and placed under the control of the Ministry for Public Buildings, Roads and Development [a.k.a. Ministry of Public Works]. The mobilized Jews were deprived of their uniforms and Bulgarian officers were appointed as commanders of their units" (Еврейски работни групи, 2008, p. 7-8).

A protocol that followed the decree of August 12, 1941, outlined the changes:

> "Protocol 132 of August 12, 1941 of the Ministers' Council regarding a verbal report by the Minister for Public Buildings, Roads and Development. Decisions based on the Law for Defense of the Nation:
> - persons of Jewish background, subject to regular labor service, will be mobilized in separate labor groups under the jurisdiction of the Ministry for PBRD
> - during their service, the Jews will receive free of charge food and work clothes
> - all retired military personnel of Jewish background, as well

as those who fulfilled their labor service obligations in the past, are subject to civil mobilization for government or community works; the Jews under civil mobilization will form labor groups under the Ministry of PBRD

- those of them who have family obligations, are to be considered needy and will be paid a salary of up to 60 leva

- both groups, those who fulfill their labor service and those who are civilly mobilized, are to carry specific signs that make it clear that they are Jews" (Labor Battalions 1941-1943).

As we can see in the testimonies and surviving documents, the Jews in the labor groups had varied experiences. Some were treated harshly, others had much better lives, but it is clear that the negativity was the result of personal biases of some commanders. There was no official policy to mistreat Jews or work them to death, as it happened in many German-controlled areas. A letter from Yaroslav Kalitsin of July 28, 1943, the deputy of Belev in the Commissariat for Jewish Questions, stated that the Jews mobilized in labor groups were allowed to receive parcels from their families once a month (Labor Battalions 1941-1943).

At the Seventh Section of the People's Tribunal in 1945, which dealt with the anti-Semitic crimes, there were several testimonies against the commander of a Jewish labor group, Lieutenant Pavlov, who forced the Jews to work for over 12 hours digging, so they often had to sleep outside. He used to beat them and regularly threatened them that he was going to send them to Poland (People's Court Session No.15, 1945, p. 1450-1462).

In his memoirs, Samuel Arditti shares the experience in labor groups of people he knew: "Our landlord had four sons. Three of them were mobilized in the Labor Duty. All Jews of the ages from 20 to 40 were mobilized. My father was older. [Our friend] Nisso also remained "civilly mobilized" at the pub to serve wine and sell kebapcheta [grilled ground meat] and fried potatoes. In the early stage of the war in 1941, the Jewish officers preserved their epaulets and honor. They were appointed commanders of the labor groups. The results of their work were good and that enraged the Germans, because the Jewish officers kept their ranks and the Jewish privates remained Bulgarian soldiers serving in the Labor Duty. The Germans issued a threat – if that continued, they would sever their ties with the Labor Army, so in 1942, the Jews were sent to do heavy physical labor.

"Our landlord's sons were telling us about the bad conditions of the Jews in the labor groups. They used to build bridges, lay new roads, hammer gravel, raise embankments, push wheelbarrows and do other heavy work. Their food was not good – cabbage soup, onions, white beans, potatoes. They slept in torn tents in sunny and cold weather. They did not receive salaries; their clothes were old. The guards and the officers were sadists, anti-Semites, bullies and grafters, but there were also humane people, true Bulgarians.

> "My friend Harry told me different things. After his family was expelled to Pazardjik, he spent a few days at the camp where his father was mobilized. The workers bribed the sergeant to let them play poker instead of working. The sergeant regularly received a percentage of the profits and also sold them tea and coffee" (Ардити, спомени).

In his testimony, Leon Anzhel, mobilized in the labor camp in the village of Rudnik, recalled: "The first mobilization of Jews took place in 1941 along the Iskar River from Kurilo to Lukatnik. They were building the railway tracks. At every railway station there were Jewish groups, they were given labor uniforms, and military officers were appointed. And in every labor group there were one or two Bulgarian military officers. Another labor group was created that same year. They weren't a military group; they were like us and worked in a place called Trunska Klisura.

> "I left in 1942. Before that I was called upon to appear before a military commission to decide whether I was fit for military service. And when they decided that you were fit for military service, you received a call-up order and they mobilized you. You took only the most necessary clothes.
> "I was in the labor camps from 1942 until 1944. I received four call-up orders. I was in the village of Rudnik, the village of Chuchuligovo near our border with Greece, Belitsa, Vratsa, Svishtov. We were working during the summer; in November they would let us go home for the winter period and in January would mobilize us again. We would sleep in tents and cabins. We worked hard everywhere. We mainly built roads and railroad tracks. In Varna district our group was taking out and crashing rocks in a quarry in the forest. We loaded the stones on a cart drawn by oxen. The mobilized Bulgarians would take the cart to the road Varna - Burgas. The other laborers from other groups covered the road with the broken stones" (Anzhel, 2006).

Among other things, the testimony shows that Bulgarians were also mobilized for labor duty.

Another one of the mobilized, Mayer Rafael Alhalel, shared his experiences as comments to a photo showing him and other workers in a Jewish labor camp in 1943.

"This photo was taken in the second labor camp I was in at the village of Sveti Vrach in 1943. I'm the third man from right to left, dressed in a white vest and even smiling. The man with the peak cap, dark clothes and white band first on the right was our smart supervisor, who at first treated us badly and later turned out to be on our side and just putting up a show for his superiors. He is dressed like that here because he was giving away quinine to the people suffering from malaria. I was also down with tropical malaria and was waiting to be given a portion of quinine. I remember that we were around 300-400 people in the first and second camp. We were divided into groups: a Vidin one, a Vratsa one and a more general one including workers of Jewish origin born in Northwest Bulgaria. Of course, each group had its platoon commander, something like a supervisor. Our group, the Vidin one, had a very vicious and cruel supervisor. In the first days of spring 1942, he humiliated us a lot: he hit us, shouted at us, swore at us, called us anti-Semitic names like 'chifuti'. He always punished someone who had stolen the bread of a fellow worker. The psychological attack discontinued after a month.

"We worked there for around ten months. He made us sweat our guts out, we were his slaves. We had to haul 15 wagons of stones from the excavation site we were digging. It was only after we made it so deep that we couldn't be seen from outside when the strange supervisor gathered us all and said, 'Guys, the sweating was up to here. I trust you now. From now on I will protect you and you will protect me.' So now we worked very slowly and leisurely in the big excavation site because no one from the outside could see what we were doing.

"When one of us noticed that the chief of our supervisor was approaching, he would make a signal and we would all start working very hard, while our supervisor started swearing at us and calling us names. When his boss would leave, we would stop working and start playing belote with the supervisor. But that story doesn't have a happy ending. In summer 1942 we were given five to six days of leave to visit out families. During that time the camp was moved from Sveti Vrach to the nearby village called Belitsa. Many of us were absent and there weren't enough Jews to carry the baggage of the others as well as the common tents. So, our 'rude' supervisor also helped them move the camp. Naturally, at that time his action was more than strange and unforgivable. His chiefs started suspecting him and fired him. He had incidentally revealed his sympathies towards us. That was the end of our holiday. It was only after 9th September that we learnt that our strict supervisor was also a UYW member, just like us. But he became a supervisor in a Jewish labor camp, because he was very poor and needed the money" (Alhalel).

Years later, Buko Levi, in an article published in Israel in 1961, admitted that the labor groups were one of the factors that helped the Jews to avoid the deportation:

"We knew that as long as the Jews served, even in the labor force, not everything was lost. On the contrary, we could always refer to that service. And if we fulfilled well that heavy duty, we had the right and reasons to demand our rights. We also knew that even in 1941, when no one knew about deportations and mass murders of Jews, the labor service would be a good argument in the hands of King, government or anybody else to refuse the expulsion of Jews from Bulgaria. We were interested in serving, even though it was hard, because we knew that this could be the price of saving the Bulgarian Jews...

"And the events proved we were right when we thought the labor service was a factor in our salvation. I don't want to say that the labor service itself saved us. However, everybody will admit, and that is seen in the documents quoted by Grinberg, that every time when the Bulgarian King or government refused to surrender us to the Germans, their main argument was that the labor service of the Jews provided great benefits to Bulgaria" (Романо, Леви, 1961, p. 31).

This position is echoed in the memoirs of Yako Baruh, who also acknowledged the changing conditions in the Jewish labor groups:

"The first Jewish labor groups established on May 1, 1941, when Jews of up to 40 years of age were mobilized. Their job was to build roads to the Greek border or fix and expand existing roads. The orders allowed exemption only in serious cases of physical of mental illness, which left in the groups people not suited for physical labor. At that time, the life of these groups was not different from the life in the Bulgarian labor groups. Both received clothes and food in the same amounts, the difference was the attitude of the commanders who often treated the Jews differently. The situation worsened when in August 1941, the administration of the Jewish labor groups was transferred from the military to the Labor Army [under the Ministry of Public Works]. They were allowed leaves and family visits. It was difficult because most of the mobilized had never done physical work before, but despite that, many showed creativity and ingenuity. The term of mobilization was 150 days, after that the workers were sent home" (Барух, Спомени 1941-1943, p.8).

Later, the labor service was a source of hope when the deportation seemed to be imminent: "In 1943, the mobilizations increased, and the Jews thought that the labor mobilization would prevent the deportation of their families. The conditions were harsh, the food insufficient. The Jews worked only when the weather allowed outside work, they were sent home for the winter. The only ray of light were the visits of prominent Bulgarian public figures. For example, the group working on the road Plovdiv-Sofia was visited consequently by Metropolitan Kiril and [former Prime Mnister] Nikola Mushanov. Both of them told the workers that the worst has passed and there was no danger of deportation anymore" (Ibid., p.24). By 1944, the situation in those groups became chaotic. The food supply did not improve, but the work was not taken seriously, there was little control, many of the mobilized routinely ran away to their homes (Ibid. p.29).

As you may recall, Nir Baruh mentioned in his book "The Ransom", quoted earlier, that at the top of the Jewish labor system "was the retired Colonel Rogozarov, an anti-Semite". Reports by Rogozarov, preserved at Yad Vashem, cast doubt in that blanket accusation. In his report of April 12, 1943, Lieutenant-Colonel Rogozarov covered his inspection of the 8th Jewish Labor Group regarding complaints against its commander Lieutenant Parashkev Yurdanov.

Rogozarov discovered many violations. The Lieutenant treated the Jewish laborers badly. Many of them complained that he swore at them and beat them with sticks or his pistol because of various transgressions: he beat with a stick a worker because the latter walked too slowly. He ordered the worker Hertzel Eshkenasi to bring a thick stick to beat other workers, but when Eshkenasi brought a thinner stick, the Lieutenant was so upset that he beat him until the stick broke. The Lieutenant beat several workers of the group with his pistol for giving bread to the Aegean Jews passing by in trains to be deported.

He confiscated workers' parcels with the excuse that he distributed them among the poor but kept the content for the commanders. Still, the Lieutenant insisted that he re-distributed the content into 25 small parcels, which he gave away to the poorest workers. He confiscated the camera of one of the workers and asked him to buy it back. He allowed a private courier among the workers who demanded 15 leva to send or deliver a letter. The Lieutenant allowed 1-day home leaves to three workers, though he was not authorized to do that.

The auditor found that the bean soup served for lunch was tasty and nutritious. The kitchen was staffed sufficiently. The discipline and order were very good and workmanship - excellent.

The next day, April 13, 1943, Lieut.-Col. Rogozarov wrote another letter - he fired the person in charge of the food for the 8th Labor Group due to systematic drunkenness. "Lieut. Yurdanov receives a last warning to stop the beatings, if not he would be criminally charged" (Labor Battalions 1941-1943).

During a later inspection of 11th Labor Group, conducted on August 16, 1944, Lieut.-Col. Rogozarov reported to the Ministry significant violations. The area was not clean enough, the kitchen was located too far from the dormitory, which made it difficult to go for lunch or dinner in bad weather; that was also a security issue, because the food storage could be robbed. After weighing 5 loaves of bread, he found out that each of them weighed 200 g less than required. That size of bread had been distributed among 600 people for 60 days. Before the inspection, nobody measured the bread. If it were to be assumed that within the 60 days the bread weighed 200 g less, it meant that about 3,500 kg of flour had been stolen. He ordered an investigation to punish the guilty. The commanders had given leaves to the Jewish workers, which was a violation of the rule that only the Ministry could do that. He ordered an investigation to charge criminally the violators. The group was expected to clean the road and handle landslides and ditches. The work was performed poorly, probably due to close relations between commanders and workers. He attributed it to poor control, because the work of the group hasn't been inspected before (Labor Battalions 1941-1943).

One of the higher commanders of labor groups, Colonel Moumdjiev, was among the accused at the People's Tribunal in 1945. The testimonies described him as a reasonable and humane person. In 1943, when inspecting the Jewish labor groups in the

Sveti Vrach area (southern Bulgaria), he gathered workers and commanders to tell them that their relations should be respectful, no fights and beatings were allowed. That was the only way to have the job done. He sent to the medical commission all sick or infirm workers, about 150-169, and about 120-130 of them were allowed to go home. Colonel Moumdjiev regularly gave leaves of over 10 days (which he had no right to do) to many people, including students, who were not entitled to leaves. A witness said that he was not an anti-Semite and he helped the Jews without getting any material benefits. He also knew many of the parents of the mobilized, who used to come to him to ask for help (People's Court Session No.16, 1945, p. 1531-1532).

Despite the harsh conditions, the Jews in the labor groups in Bulgaria managed to survive, unlike the Jews under German occupation.

JEWISH CAMPS

Unlike the mass mobilization in labor groups, the number of Jews sent to concentration camps was much smaller. Those were mostly perceived violators of the restrictions imposed by the Law for Defense of the Nation; the internment to the camps was considered an administrative measure, applied at the discretion of the local police chiefs and approved by the Commissariat for the Jewish Questions. For example, most of the people arrested during the Jewish demonstration on May 24, 1943, were sent to the newly-established camp Somovit. The inmates were not kept for a fixed term, many were released due to different factors after a few months in the camps. The more serious crimes, like speculation and participation in the partisan resistance or in communist terrorist groups, had to be handled by the courts and involved prison sentences.

The term "concentration camp", when describing the World War II phenomenon, evokes the horrible memories of people gassed to death or the piles of starved corpses seen in the haunting photographs from Auschwitz and Dachau. The extermination of millions of people in those camps is a well-documented fact.

However, the situation in Bulgaria was quite different. The Jewish camps in Bulgaria were not extermination camps. In his speech at the Seventh Section of the People's Tribunal, which dealt with the anti-Semitic crimes, the "People's Prosecutor" Mancho Rahamimov provided a breakdown of the Jews who perished during the fight against the government in 1941-1944 (I will get back to it later). In his list, he included 10 Jewish inmates killed in concentration camps. Those were the 10 people who died in the fire in camp Kailuka on July 10, 1944 (People's Court Session No.18, 1945, p. 1918). The circumstances of that fire will be covered in detail in the next chapter. What I need to mention here is that the tribunal was not called to deliver justice, it was created to punish anybody who could become a competitor of the communists in the control over Bulgaria. So, often the prosecutors provided biased interpretations or "invented" crimes to push their agenda.

The fact that, with all the bias, they could not find even a single death in a Bulgarian concentration camps beyond the fire victims, tells us clearly that the attempts to equate those camps with the German or Romanian Jewish camps are impossible to defend. It is understandable that people, who have had all the rights of Bulgarian citizens and lived quiet lives, would have a strong emotional reaction after finding themselves in a camp. We can see such a reaction in the testimony of Eli Chaim Eshkenasi, sent from Sofia to Somovit, immediately after the demonstration on May 24, 1943, in which he claimed: "It was like the camps described in the books about Maidanek, Lublin, etc., for people who are about to be sent to their deaths" (People's Court Session No.10, 1945, p. 854-859).

The differences remind me of the case of Prof. Todor Pavlov, a Marxist philosopher who in the last years of his life was the Director of the Institute of Philosophy at the Bulgarian Academy of Sciences (where I used to work). He lived for years in the Soviet Union. In 1936-1937, Stalin started his infamous purges, in which many Bulgarian communist emigrants were either shot or died in the Gulag. Prof. Pavlov avoided that fate by returning to Bulgaria; he spent time in the concentration camp Gonda Voda, where he had no problem surviving. While visiting Queen Ioanna as a regent, after the coup in 1944, he told her that King Boris III pardoned him three times. In "gratitude", he later joined the communist ruling forces that destroyed hundreds of Bulgarian intellectuals.

This does not mean that the conditions were not harsh, but extermination was never part of the government plans. Again, it is important to analyze testimonies and documents to build an objective picture of the Jewish concentration camps in Bulgaria.

In his book "The Ransom", Nir Baruh mentions the Jewish camp Ignatievo: "In the second half of the 1930s, the Bulgarian Government decided to expel from the country the Jews with foreign citizenship. All of them who have not found a refuge by the deadline, were taken to a concentration camp near the village of Ignatievo, Varna region. The location of the camp betrays the intention of the authorities to load the inmates on boats and expel them from the country. This temporary camp was closed after expelling of all inmates to countries that agreed to take them" (Барух, 1991, p. 61). Mr. Baruh may have a few things wrong because in the second half of the 1930s, until the Law for Defense of the Nation, no measures of any kind were taken against Jews, local or foreign.

The largest Jewish camp was located in the village of Somovit, in northern Bulgaria, which was a small port on the south bank of the Danube. The camp was established on May 26, 1943, shortly after the expulsion of the Jews from Sofia. Most of the people arrested at the demonstration on May 24 were sent there. It is assumed that Belev's Commissariat wanted to concentrate there the most "dangerous" Jews who would be deported by boats from the port. The camp did not have its own buildings, so the inmates were kept in the local school (the students were already in summer break). Later, barracks and sheds were built in the nearby Tabakova Cheshma area and the inmates were moved there on January 17, 1944. The camp closed in June 1944 and the remaining inmates were released.

Somovit was the largest camp but it is difficult to determine its size – inmates were constantly arriving, while others were being released. It is estimated that at its peak, the camp housed between 500 and 600 people. Somovit was also known as the camp with the harshest order and living conditions. Due to these facts, we have more information about this camp than about the smaller Jewish camps.

As it was mentioned before, the Jewish Zionist leaders and other activists never severed their connections with the different levels of the government and never stopped the attempts to help the detained Jews. Whether they used bribes or direct help from sympathetic people, they managed to achieve their goals most of the time. Camp Somovit was not an exception. The Jewish community in the city of Pleven, the center of the region where Somovit was located, tirelessly worked to improve the living conditions in the camp. In his memoirs, Heskia Finzi from Pleven outlined the activities of David Iosifov, a prominent local leader.

He and other leaders maintained contacts with the camp. In the early months, the Jews from the camp sent a message that one of the sergeants serving there was too cruel. Iosifov started negotiations with the police commissioner of Pleven and promised a great gift, if the sergeant was transferred, and it worked. Then he focused on improving the living conditions and managed to increase the bread ration in Somovit from 200 to 500 g per day. He got a permission to send the sick inmates to the Pleven hospital, then to allow the inmates to receive parcels with food, medicines, and clothes. After that, he arranged a visit of a local Jewish delegation to the camp to investigate the needs of the inmates (Memoirs of Heskia Finzi).

There are many memoirs describing the life in Somovit, but the best source appears to be the unpublished book of Albert Varsano, an intellectual with literary talent and good power of observation, who covered every aspect of the camp existence, the political situation, and the anxieties and hopes of the inmates in a 250-page typewritten manuscript. Its title is "Evlag", short for the Bulgarian words Evreiski Lager (Jewish Camp). Varsano started writing when the deportation seemed imminent and his idea was to drop the manuscript from the train, so that he could leave a testimony about the ordeal of the Jews.

That didn't happen, so he took his secret notes with him after he was released and continued to work on the book in the city of Haskovo in 1944. He finished the manuscript in 1956, after he emigrated to Israel.

After providing some information about the camp, initially a final stop before deportation, later a place for administrative punishment of the violators of the anti-Jewish laws, Varsano tried to answer the question why things turned so bad in Bulgaria. Before Hitler's ascend to power, Bulgaria was tolerant to the Zionist idea, the Jews had their organizations, charities, press. After Hitler took over, fascist organizations like the National Legions and the Ratniks popped up and gained some influence. The Bulgarian elites were encouraged by the early successes of Germany in Poland. The masses were impressed with the pact between Ribbentrop and Molotov, seen as a sign of good friendship between Russia and Germany. The Jewish community felt isolated, withdrew within itself and tried to speed up the emigration to Eretz Israel. The community also helped thousands escaping through the Danube from Germany, Poland, Austria, and Hungary to reach Palestine. The Law for Defense of the Nation was a turning point. It was met with outrage by Jews and Bulgarians alike and even though the Bulgarian and Jewish organizations couldn't stop the law, the common actions were the start of the future collaboration that eventually was successful

(Varsano, p. 2-6).

Further, Varsano noted that on March 2, 1941, Bulgaria was occupied by Germany. The government created the labor battalions for Jews, involving hard work in building roads and bridges. The units worked only from the spring to the late fall, after that the mobilized Jews were free for the winter. Even more restrictions were imposed on the Jews, though parliamentarians, the Orthodox Church, and the Macedonian organization, all took the side of the Jews and tried to help. The far left was hesitant to get involved because of the agreement between Germany and the USSR, which treated the Nazi country as a friend of communist Russia. Another bad development was the law for giving unlimited powers to the government to resolve the Jewish question, which was followed by the creation of the Commissariat for the Jewish Questions (Varsano, p. 6-8).

Then Varsano shared his experience with the deportation attempts in 1943. The German pressure on the Bulgarian government over the Jewish issue increased immensely after in early 1943 the German representative Dannecker was sent to Bulgaria to prepare the deportation, which led to the Dannecker-Belev agreement, and the Jews from Macedonia and Thrace were sent to Poland. When they tried to do the same in Bulgaria, the attempt was resisted by the Church, Macedonian activists, the people and the King, so the plan was cancelled. The second attempt in May 1943, failed, but the Jews had to leave Sofia. At the demonstration on May 24, 1943, a few hundred Jews were arrested, and many were freed later, but that led to the idea to send the most prominent Jews to a camp, like Somovit, the "Evlag". On May 25, 1943, the expulsion began. It was a horrible experience for the victims, because they didn't know where they were going. Many started selling their property at very low prices before leaving. Varsano witnessed ugly pictures of greedy buyers, many of them farmers from the villages around Sofia, pushing the prices down (Varsano, p. 9-11).

Varsano was arrested on May 27, 1943, and held at a police station in Sofia. In the same room, he saw a Jewish friend of his who was a lawyer. The latter told him that his wife was sick, and his neighbor, friend of Gabrovski, had already petitioned the minister to free him. While Varsano was still awaiting his fate, the lawyer was freed. A few days later, Varsano and a few other people were placed on a regular train heading to Somovit, but with a police guard. The group bribed their police guard to buy them food and a large bottle of wine and they talked for hours. A lawyer, whose wife had good government connections, told them about the serious conflicts in the highest levels of government concerning the Jewish Question. In his opinion, these disagreements and conflicts were the most important cracks in the government position that had to be used by people in Bulgaria and from outside with access to the Palace to lobby for a solution, because the parliamentary opposition and the Church were too weak to make a difference on their own. Another person argued that the mass action of Jews, Bulgarians, the Church and the opposition was still important and couldn't be ignored (Varsano, p. 21-28).

When they arrived in the camp, they were searched and the excessive luggage, as well as their money, were taken from them. The luggage was placed in a special storage in the camp, but the inmates suspected that the guards were stealing items from there. In the beginning, the conditions were restrictive, they had to sit in the rooms and avoid talking to each other. The food was insufficient, the daily ration of bread was 75 g, received at lunch with bean soup (without fat). For dinner they had only bean soup. The inmates were allowed to go out for half an hour for lunch and for another hour at dinner time.

The building of the Somovit village school was used for the camp. When the author arrived, there were 190 people, about 100 arrested at the demonstration, 60 were prominent community activists, and 10 were rabbis. He saw a few families, some with children, the youngest inmate was a 10-month old girl, brought to the camp with her mother, because they stayed in Sofia beyond the expulsion deadline, while her husband was mobilized in a labor group. All people were from various social backgrounds, it was "the most fantastic mix that a person could imagine" - lawyers, doctors, industrialists, merchants, etc., together with peddlers, butchers, craftsmen, porters and even one beggar, all of them mixed in different school rooms. The guards were officers and soldiers from the army. One of the rooms was allocated to the families. The place was overcrowded, and it was hard to move around (Varsano, p. 31-43).

The camp commandant was demanding and rude, some guards were harsh, but others felt compassion for the inmates. The commandant told them that they were hostages to be shot if the Jews in Bulgaria started a big riot and at the same time, they were supposed to be the first to be deported to Poland. The everyday routine in the camp included: waking up at six, washing, going back to the rooms, where they had to sit quietly on the floor. At noon, the inmates formed lines to go out for lunch for less than half hour, at six in the evening came the dinner, for half an hour, followed by walking, when they were allowed to talk. A camp committee was organized immediately to handle the communication between the guards and the inmates. That is when Varsano decided to keep records about the everyday life. The first week was the week of great hunger (Varsano, p. 44-50).

The first important "breakthrough" in improving the conditions came when an experienced Jewish doctor – "Dr. Roz" – was asked to treat the little daughter of the mayor of Somovit. She had been sick for a while and the young local doctor couldn't diagnose the condition. Dr. Roz found out that she was suffering from pneumonia and, with the correct treatment, she recovered. Then the doctor was called for other cases, in return, he was allowed to bring to the camp food and its amounts gradually increased. He also managed to get from the mayor a liter of milk daily for the woman with the baby. Meanwhile, the diverse social status of the inmates caused frictions and internal fights. The committee of the intellectuals was "overthrown" by the newly-formed "raya" committee ["raya" is a derogatory term used in the Ottoman Empire for Christians, Jews, and other "infidels" – M.M.], which established links with the commandant and accused the intellectuals that their activities against the anti-Jewish laws have brought innocent Jews to the camp.

In the first month, a group of young people from Aegean Thrace were brought. They were mobilized in Jewish labor groups in Bulgaria, but the Commissariat was planning to send them to Poland. They were never deported and a few months later, they were released. A serious problem was the lack of running water. The water had to be brought in containers daily by the inmates, but still there was not enough water for washing and laundry, which caused parasites (Varsano, p. 52-69).

When the camp was established, the local authorities told the peasants in the area that the Jews were brought there, because they wanted to kill the King. The peasants were forbidden from communicating with the Jews, but some did it anyway. The guards chased them away and even beat some inmates for the interaction. One of the worst soldiers, Stanyu, one night tried to take out of the camp a woman, a ballerina, probably to rape her. A Jewish man, who was out to use the toilet, tried to stop the soldier and was beaten, while the girl ran back to her room. Stanyu yelled that the Jews had been abusing for years Bulgarian girl servants. The Jew fired back that he never had a servant but was still forced to stand at the wall without moving as a punishment. When Stanyu's duty for the night ended, the next soldier freed him (Varsano, p. 70-79).

The next month, June 1943, the conditions in the camp started to improve. The daily amount of bread increased from 75 g to 120 g. The inmates received new underwear. They were also allowed to walk freely from room to room. From the fifth week, more parcels were allowed into the camp, soap was distributed to do laundry. The lunch walk increases to one hour. The people could play chess with self-made sets. The quality of the soup improved - instead of only beans, they added onions, tomatoes and peppers. Machine for treating lice infestation was brought to the camp (Varsano, p. 70-79). All these changes were probably the result of the work of David Iosifov and the other Jewish activists in Pleven, who were mentioned in Heskia Finzi's memoirs.

An interesting episode from the camp's life was the attempt of the commandant to use the differences in social status to create tension among inmates. The commandant gave one of his suits to a poor Jewish porter, whom he started calling "The Lord" (like the British title). He also started to give him some of the food and other things from the parcels and used to tell the Lord often that now he amounted to something. Before, people like him were ignored and exploited by the rich Jews (Varsano, p. 97).

Also, in June, a young survivor from the Greek deportations was brought to the camp. He told Varsano his tragic story. The captured Jews were loaded on trains, packed like sardines, with little food, beaten, and brought to a temporary camp in the town of Dupnitsa. On March 19, they were packed in locked carriages, with little air, on the way to the Danube port of Lom. There, he and another man escaped and hid at a Jewish family in Vratsa. Later, he was captured and brought to Somovit (he was freed a few months later). On June 30, the military guards were changed with police. Most of the soldiers went to the rooms to say goodbye, many of them felt pain that the Jews were still there. Some of the restrictions were lifted again – the inmates were allowed to move freely in the rooms and the yard. The new commandant, a drunkard, rarely showed up in the camp, so his deputy, a sergeant, with anti-Semitic views, ran the camp (Varsano, p. 100-106).

By July, Dr. Roz was already allowed to go freely to the village and back and practice his profession. He used his privileges to bring more food, better soup and more soap. The inmates arranged with a policeman to buy food and bring it to the camp. A camp inmate cooperation was created; it sold the food to the inmates. Soon, most of the policemen got involved in the deliveries, only the sergeant didn't know anything. The tensions between rich and poor inmates continued. Varsano described how some women got involved in prostitution, serving the rich inmates to get more food. In another incident in July, a few policemen tried to take a few women at night to the office for "interrogation", possibly to be raped, but a few men woke up and convinced them to leave the women alone. After an inspection by the Pleven police commissioner, the bread amount increased to 200 g a day (Varsano, p. 110-120).

On July 11, Commissar Alexander Belev visited the camp. Doctor Roz requested that he meet the camp prisoners. Belev made bad impression on Varsano, he had a snotty behavior and avoided looking people in the eyes. Belev said that a large group would be freed, mostly Jews with lower social status, the prominent ones were staying, because they conspired against the government, they deserved to be sent to Poland. The ominous threat caused panic. The camp committee planned a riot, if a deportation to Poland was announced; they thought it would be easy for 300 men to disarm about 30 policemen. Meanwhile, more inmates were brought in, mostly for smaller violations of the anti-Jewish laws. The camp seemed to turn into a jail (Varsano, p. 122-126).

On July 16, the author received a message from the Jewish community in Pleven that Belev tried again to organize a deportation to Poland. Zahary Velkov, an assistant to Belev, told Pisanov, the police commissioner of Pleven, that the Commissariat tried a new deportation, but it was derailed by high people in the government, a new failure for Belev. Thus, Somovit was changed to a concentration camp, where all Jewish criminals would be sent, to be kept until the end of the war. The same month, the sergeant introduces bathing in Danube, which was to take place 2-3 times a week. Men and women were led to the river in separate groups; when was the women's turn, the police guards were supposed to stay behind the bushes to provide privacy.

On July 21, a large group of 44 people was brought from Russe, mostly relatives of communists and partisans. The next day, a group of 24, which included families, was released from the camp. The sergeant continued his attempts to confiscate the money of the Jews and called them a dirty and lying tribe for hiding money (Varsano, p. 130-141).

Since there were many children in the camp, a total of 25, with the permission of the guards, a study group was created, where the kids could learn, play and tell stories. On July 27, 38 of the poorest inmates, who never received parcels, were released, the next day, another 8 people were freed. On July 30, another 100 new people were brought in. By July 31, there were already over 500 inmates in the camp and the number of intellectuals increased. With so many educated people in the camp, they managed to get a permission to organize lectures and presentations on various topics (Varsano, p. 142-149).

By August 5, the mayor of the village started to use the inmates for public works, building a road. They did not like that and the work was stopped soon. However, while they were working, they had contacts with the local people. Varsano recalls how, after finishing the work for the day, the Jewish group was sitting and relaxing in the field. They were approached by a group of children from the village who brought baskets with fruit. Initially, they looked at the Jews with fear and curiosity but in minutes got used to them and sat with the group:

> "The kids started asking strange questions, a ten-year old boy asked, "You are Jews, what does that mean, aren't you Bulgarians like us?"
> "We are people, just like you," I said with a calm and slow voice, "but from a different tribe."
> "But you speak Bulgarian," interrupted me a twelve-year old kid.
> "We speak Bulgarian as well," I tried to explain, "besides, we studied at Bulgarian schools."
> "And why are there kids in your camp?" asked a third little boy.
> "Because they came with their parents..."
> "Did your kids also want to kill the King?" hurriedly asked the first kid.
> "None of us wanted to kill the King."
> The kids didn't say anything else. They couldn't figure out that riddle. One of the police guards was standing nearby, listening to our conversation with astonishment.
> After the short pause, one of the kids asked again, "And how long are you going to stay here?"
> "Until the end of the war."
> One of the kids couldn't keep quiet and heatedly added, "But in a month, we will start school again, give us back our school..."
> Nobody answered. What answer could we give to such an insistent demand from a child? The policeman was following quietly our talk and it was sure he was going to report it to the

sergeant." (Varsano, p. 152).

In early August, the daily amount of bread was increased to 250 g. The Pleven police commissioner visited the camp again. He told one of the inmates that the deportation to Poland had been cancelled for good. Another large group of inmates was freed, about 20 intellectuals. On August 18, another 26 people were freed, it became clear many of those were released by bribes. The cruel sergeant who was abusing the inmates, was transferred and the new one looked more intelligent and with good character. The authorities kept bringing more people, mostly for administrative violations. The new guards agreed to collaborate with the committee to bring food and other products (Varsano, p. 155-170).

On August 29, the news about the death of King Boris III reached the camp, along with the rumors that he was poisoned by Hitler because of his refusal to send troops to the Eastern Front. One rich Jewish merchant confirmed that the situation of the Jews may worsen after his death – in March, the order to stop the deportation came from the palace, now Filov's government could proceed with it. Another inmate argued that there would be no change – the King acted under an external pressure and that was not going to change. A few days later, the regents of the 6-year old new King Simeon II were sworn; the Jews feared that they were anti-Semitic and had the same fear of the new government, worried that the new Prime Minister Bozhilov would follow Filov's policies, and the new Minister of the Interior Docho Christov seemed even scarier than Gabrovski (Varsano, p. 176-192).

On September 15, the camp guards allowed card gambling, mostly poker. Varsano saw people playing for hours, with large sums involved. The social tensions didn't decrease. More and more money was arriving in the camp, but not for everyone, the poor used to sell their clothes to the rich inmates to get more food (Varsano, p. 176-192).

On September 24, 1943, the police commissioner visited the camp again, and shared the news that Docho Christov told him that the situation of the Jews was going to improve. In the end of the month, more and more people were being released. The guards allowed Jewish prayers. The committee started to collect money for the poor. In October, Yom Kippur was celebrated officially. On October 10, the inmates were moved into newly-built barracks, there were about 170 people left at the time.

An incident happened on October 13 – while building the new kitchen, a policeman who was drunk, insisted on piling up more soil on the roof, but because the beams were thin, the roof collapsed on the eight people working in the kitchen. A few were injured but nobody died, two of the victims were sent to a hospital in Pleven and recovered.

On October 15, Varsano was released. In November 1943, friends in the camp wrote to him that a delegation of Jews from Pleven visited the camp and requested more access and more food to be brought in (Varsano, p. 202-235).

The testimony of Eli Chaim Eshkenasi, whose comparison of Somovit to Maidanek was quoted earlier, provides a more negative picture. He confirmed the confiscation of money and the bad living conditions, with 70 g bread daily and bean soup (he claims no dinner was provided). He also claims that in the Bulgarian concentration camps they could receive parcels, but not in the Jewish, which could have been true in the beginning, but it changed, as Varsano noted. Further, Eshkenasi wrote that there were a few good soldiers, but the commander was bad. Among the inmates, there were disabled people and babies. The peasants there were told that the Jews were big criminals, but finally realized they were not and started to help the inmates (People's Court Session No.10, 1945, p. 854-859).

Another inmate, Albert Adroki, left a short description of his life in Somovit. His family arrived in the camp on August 1, 1943. It was not clear why he was sent there, he thought he was innocent. The sergeant was rude but didn't mistreat Adroki. Only his wife was affected when one day the sergeant blamed her, along with other women, that they didn't clean properly the hallway. He shouted at them and forced them to clean it for a week.

Adroki also noticed the problems created by placing people with different social status in the same place. The young people whom he called "gavroche" (after Hugo's character in the novel "The Misérables") – poor, disrespectful and rude, acted like wolves and took control over the other inmates. He was in the fourth family room, size 3 by 4 m, with 50 people inside, on 3 bed rows with 17 beds, which made it hard to move around. The food was bad. The underwear was insufficient, in the beginning soap for washing was lacking, all that caused lice infestation.

The bad sergeant liked to mistreat people. He told the Jews that all of them were equal in the camp, if they tried to run away, they would be punished. He was beating people over small violations. Adroki met Albert Varsano, whom he called the "commentator of the camp", loved for his wisdom. Dr. Rosenfeld (Roz) was helping everybody. The tensions caused theft – once a camp inmate washed his pants and left them out to dry, but someone stole them. The sergeant demanded that the pants be found within an hour or else he would punish everybody. Somebody brought a pair of pants before the hour was up, though not the stolen pair, to avoid further trouble (Адроки, p. 1-6).

Neither the memoirs, nor the documents about Somovit report any deaths in the camp.

From the preserved archival documents, we can learn who, how and for what reasons sent Jews to Somovit. A document from the authorities of the town of Dupnitsa, issued in early 1944, listed the number of the Jews from the town sent to Somovit in 1944, along with the reasons (the totals are in the parentheses): 5 families of underground activists (16); 4 families of political prisoners (14); participants in an unauthorized picture taken 5 years ago during hiking (22); suspected in communist activities (1); professionals who worked without permit (2); caught without Jewish stars (3); female worker who left a factory for 12 hours (1) (Данни за Сомовит).

On August 10, 1943, the Nova Zagora Police Department reported that Jacques Nisimov Shoev, a Turkish citizen from Odrin, was caught spreading leftist propaganda and was suspected of being a foreign agent. He was sent to Somovit (Донесение за Жак Нисимов Шоев).

On September 23, 1943, the Dupnitsa District Government reported that Hanna Nisim Mordehai, 24 years old, collaborated and was friends with Jewish communists. On September 13, she was caught at a secret meeting with a communist activist, previously jailed for 5 years for conspiratorial activities. It was discovered that she was communist in the past. She was sent to Somovit (Донесение за Хана Нисим Мордехай).

On September 7, 1943, the Gorna Jumaya Police, sent a report about Engineer Davidov, living in a Bulgarian house with a radio. He had listened regularly to Radio London and shared the news with fellow Jews with the words: "Be strong, England will be victorious, just a bit more patience, etc." It was requested to send him to Somovit. Belev's resolution on the report was: "Yes, Somovit" (Донесение за инж. Давидов).

In the monthly report for July from Division State Security of the Plovdiv Police, dated August 4, 1943, it was mentioned that after the Allied gains in the Mediterranean, the local Jewish minority felt relieved and uplifted. Many of them started to spread malicious rumors about hopes for further success of the Anglo-American armed forces. Due to such activities that harmed the state security, on July 28, 1943, the police sent to the camp Somovit 37 Jewish families for indefinite time (Месечен доклад, август 1943, p. 5).

As you can see, the police had a high level of discretion in determining who should be sent to Somovit and the cases did not go through the courts. The only necessary permit was the approval by Belev's Commissariat.

The food shortages in Somovit and other camps in Bulgaria were bad and they affected the Jews who were sent to a smaller town in the province. However, we should consider the situation in the context of the conditions in Bulgaria at the time. The country experienced shortages due to the increased exports to Germany, which caused a large trade deficit.

As Albert Varsano wrote in his memoirs, the bread ration in Somovit during the first week, was the tiny amount of 70 g, which soon increased to 120 g, then to 250 g, and even more after his release. That was not sufficient, but the civil population in Bulgaria suffered food shortages everywhere. In Chapter 15, I will cover the bombings of Sofia and other cities by the American and British Air Forces in 1943-1944, but it should be mentioned here that these atrocities caused a mass exodus from Sofia, hundreds of thousands of people left the capital, evacuated to the smaller towns and villages. The new people in the province caused food shortages, which affected Bulgarians and Jews alike, with the Jews suffering more, because of the restrictions imposed on them.

In October 1943, the US Army intelligence published a secret report evaluating the situation in Bulgaria, "Joint Army-Navy Intelligence Study of Bulgaria, Janis No.38, Volume 2, October 1943". Later, the report was declassified. It was written with the future occupation of Bulgaria by the US military forces in mind. The report tried to estimate the supplies necessary to extract from the country to support the occupation.

It indicated that by 1942, the average consumption of various food stuffs dropped, compared to the pre-war period (and it was probably even lower by 1943). The wheat flour ration dropped from 548 g daily to 432 g; rye flour, from 68 g to 44 g; vegetables, from 99 g to 77 g; fruit, from 110 g to 99 g; meat, from 129 g to 112 g, etc.

The nutritive value of the average diet dropped from 3,666 calories before the war to 3,212 calories in 1942-1943. However, the writers noted that the different groups differed in their consumption. "Although some of their dietary habits have shifted, most rural Bulgarians, 80 per cent of the population, have almost as much food as in pre-war years, since it is almost impossible to limit the food supply of producers. Although there has been an attempt to limit the amount of grain that peasants may retain, they are adept at hoarding, not only for their own needs but for sale through the black markets in the cities. Most urban consumers are less well-off than their rural countrymen. The rationing system, applied only to the city and town populations (roughly 1,700,000 people), was introduced in October 1940. This was later than in most European countries because of the high degree of self-sufficiency in food production of the country as a whole."

From the findings in the intelligence report, it is safe to assume that the Bulgarian government lacked the ingenuity and cruelty in collecting and redistributing the food produced by farmers that Stalin's Russia possessed in abundance. Another bad news regarding the topic of this book is that the Jews, as entirely urban population, were disproportionately affected by that food distribution in a negative way. As you may recall, in the breakdown by professions, presented by the Central Consistory during the campaign against the Law for Defense of the Nation, it was stated that only 75 Jews were involved in the agriculture.

To ensure sufficient food rations, the government introduced group breakdown of the population, depending on physical activities. The diet of a normal consumer was supposed to include 1,588 calories, for the heavy worker – 2,284 calories, very heavy worker – 2,618 calories, farmer – 3,594 calories.

The report clarifies that "different food allowances are made to five groups: children under one, children from one to five years of age, normal consumers, heavy workers, and very heavy workers. Children, who receive supplemental milk rations, are probably receiving an adequate diet. All adult consumers receive about two-thirds of their caloric requirements, if it is assumed that rations are available. However, full rations are not always available through legal markets. Low-income consumers who cannot afford black market prices and cannot secure food from country relatives or friends have less food than legal rations permit. Bread has always formed a staple food for the Bulgarian consumer, and the most important wartime change in the diet has been the decrease in bread consumption and the decline in quality. As yet there are no reports of wide-spread disease or deterioration of health due directly to food conditions.

"The amount of food surplus available to occupying forces would depend on the methods of food collection. At present the Bulgarian peasantry has undoubtedly hoarded substantial stocks of food for a number of reasons: dislike for government requisitioning; fear of further requisitioning by the armed forces; and ease of sale at high prices in the black markets of the cities. Most peasants would be willing to sell their produce at fixed prices if it were possible to secure farm equipment and other manufactured goods. If such psychological factors could be overcome by the occupying forces, large stocks of food would undoubtedly be released for the market" (Intelligence Study of Bulgaria, 1943, p. VI-23).

The Americans didn't get to apply these plans. However, the Soviet Union did – the food was collected from the farmers in a brutal way during the Russian occupation in the mid-1940s.

LIFE IN THE PROVINCE

The food shortages were a serious problem in Bulgaria during the war. After the Jews were expelled from Sofia, the German Ambassador Beckerle hoped that they will take control over the black market in the province that would cause hostility among farmers, most of whom have never seen Jews before. That, in his opinion, could make the next deportation attempt more successful. However, nothing of that happened, the rural food producers were in control of the black market, as the American report above stated.

The Jews were supposed to be accommodated in Jewish houses and only if they were not available, other options were considered. This becomes clear from a letter of the head of the administrative division of the Commissariat for the Jewish Questions Yaroslav Kalitsin to his representative in the Jewish community in Razgrad. It stated that in July 1943, 400 Jews from Stara Zagora would be sent to Razgrad. The accommodation for them should be provided in the following order: Jewish houses; if not available, other foreign houses; as an extreme measure, they could be accommodated in Bulgarian houses without common hallways like in schools (Писмо от Калицин, 1943). Stara Zagora was considered a strategic city at the time, so the Jews were sent to the smaller Razgrad. The foreign houses mentioned by Kalitsin were probably Turkish, there is a large Turkish minority in the town.

Once the Jews arrived in the cities or towns, they were expected to create a local consistory, in which there was a representative – "delegate" – of Belev's Commissariat. Unlike the "Judenrat", a Jewish administrative body, created by the Germans in their occupied territories, which was often involved in activities that harmed Jews, the local consistories in Bulgaria provided significant help to the Jews that they represented.

In the memoirs of Heskia Finzi about David Iosifov and his activities, we see how the Jewish administration in the province operated. Often, they had to act discretely or in secret to help without causing confrontations. David Iosifov was from Pleven. He was a Zionist and he left for Palestine in the end of 1944. At the railway station when he was leaving, he expressed to Finzi his regret that all he did for the Jews in 1941-1943 was buried, because it was done in secret and even members of the Consistory didn't know everything. After the Jewish communists took over in 1944, they didn't want to talk about anybody but Stalin. Iosifov's main contributions were organizational – he often managed to ease the impact of the anti-Jewish orders and make life easier for Jews in camps.

After the Jews were expelled from Sofia, he met them at the railway station in Pleven, found accommodation and helped to create: 1) housing commission; 2) financial commission; 3) Jewish police; 4) free kitchen. Everything worked smoothly, and the kitchen provided two meals daily to 800 people.

Every day he visited the local representative of the Commissar for the Jewish Questions and received orders introducing more limitations. That made him sad, but he kept working around the orders. The local police started to arrest Jews for small violations like curfew, going to prohibited areas, shopping in prohibited hours, etc. Iosifov worked every day to release those people. In most cases it was done by paying bribes according to the "guilt". There was a case of four young Jews from Aegean Thrace – they lived in Sofia and were sent to Pleven, then the Commissariat in Sofia tried to arrest them. The local commissar in Pleven initially looked for them, but after receiving a large bribe from Iosifov, notified the central office that they were not in Pleven. After the war, they returned to Yugoslavia (Memoirs of Heskia Finzi).

Samuel Arditti recalls that his father managed to postpone the expulsion of his family from Sofia by several months. Their relatives were leaving one by one, not knowing if they will see each other again. The majority of the shirt makers in Sofia were Jews, his father Benjamin Arditti was one of them. When most Jews left the city, his workshop had no competition. At the time, shirts were custom-made. His "monopoly" let him earn a lot of money that the family had to use when they moved to Russe. Because of the inflation, Benjamin Arditti had to buy at great risk 40 gold coins.

In Russe, the problems of the family didn't end. They had to share accommodations with relatives. His father got into trouble with the numerous restrictions and there was a danger to be sent to a camp. He tried to ask the Police Commissioner of Russe Stefan Simeonov not to send him there, but Simeonov yelled: "Get out of here! Your fellow Jew Anna Ventura tried to kill me in front of my own house! Besides, I don't like your dossier." In the end, with some friends' help, the family managed to leave Russe for a few days.

It was hard to find somebody to host a Jewish family in 1943, but Benjamin Arditti remembered his employee Boyka, she worked in his shirt workshop. Her father owned a small farm in a village south of Russe. They sent him a telegram, and he gladly agreed to take them in. They took the train to the nearby town and from there, the farmers took them in two buggies for the next 20 kilometers to the village. It was raining, and by the time they arrived, everybody was wet and looked pathetic. Later, Samuel Arditti learned that the peasants were skeptical whether a Jewish city family could survive on a farm. However, they adapted well, started to help with the work. His mother was sewing clothes in exchange for eggs, meat, flour and other food. His father also worked; they never lacked food at the farm.

Other families had much harder lives. At the People's Tribunal, Isac Rozanes described the lives of the Jews sent to Vidin, a city in north-west Bulgaria on the Danube. He was a long-time chairman of the Jewish community when some of the Jews from Sofia arrived in Vidin.

They had to be accommodated in Jewish houses, but since the largest ones were sold, the limited space caused housing problems. Three, four, even five families had to share one room. The ration for the Jews was smaller than that for the general population – every citizen was getting 500 g bread, while the Sofia Jews received 300 g per person. They rarely received oil and rice; Rozanes complained to the local authorities, but they showed him documents that they were following the orders of Commissar Belev. Some organizations, like the union of retired military officers, spread rumors that the shortage of food in the city was due to Jews who controlled the black market. That wasn't true because very few of the 1,700 newcomers had enough money. Rozanes thought that the low rations were part of a plan to destroy the Jews. Some former officials in Vidin were sentenced to death because of that after the communist coup. The German troops stationed in the city wanted all Jews deported as spies. Many members of the fascist organizations "Ratnik" and "Brannik" wanted to organize a pogrom as a revenge after the Allied bombings. They even vandalized the Jewish cemetery. The Jewish leaders went to the police, which managed to restore order.

It was difficult to maintain cleanliness; the soap was not enough; a typhus epidemic started and was stopped through enormous efforts. There were many restrictions – Jews were allowed out for only two hours daily (from 10 to 12). That lasted for about 2 months, from February 1, 1944. The Commissariat never gave a straight answer why those limitations were imposed. The families were followed to see what they buy and where – they had to go only to certain stores. The Commissariat threatened the Jews with collective punishments, if one did something wrong (People's Court Session No.14, 1945, p. 1281-1288).

The "house arrest" the Jews were subjected to in many places, was fought by their leaders. In his testimony at the People's Tribunal, the Chief Rabbi of Sofia Dr. Asher Isac Hananel recalled that after the dismissal of Belev, he met the new Commissar Stomanyakov to ask for help for the Jews in Plovdiv and Vratsa, where the local authorities allowed them to leave home for only two hours per day. Stomanyakov was surprised that something like that would be done without his knowledge. He cancelled those orders, but Hananel thought it took him too long to do it (People's Court Session No.9, 1945, p. 805-816).

In Lom, the Jews were allowed to leave homes only between 10 a.m. and 4 p.m. Nadezhda Vasileva, who had helped the Jews in the town in many ways, supplied them with food that she bought. Her 7-year old grandson delivered it in a knapsack (she was followed and had to avoid going in person to the Jewish homes). The Jews paid what she paid for the food, but she was still accused by some people of running a black-market scheme with the Jews. And many of her accusers made a lot of money by overcharging Jews. One day, at about 5 a.m., a Bulgarian woman she knew, came to buy milk from the distribution place. She brought her tenant Nastya Isakova, a prominent communist, just released from a camp, with whom even the Jews were afraid to communicate. Vasileva whispered to Isakova that she had to conceal her Jewish star when going out so early, or else she could be arrested. Then she yelled to the landlady, if she wanted to help she could have brought the milk container herself. While they were waiting, a man with military pants and boots, an engineer working for the Germans, showed up and got immediately 5 liters of milk, while the others had to wait for hours to get 1-2 liters (Спомени на Надежда Василева, p.17-19).

In these hard times, people in high positions who did not agree with the government policies, continued to provide help, as much as they could. Metropolitan Kiril helped Jews in 1944, as explained in this confidential report from the Chief of Staff of Second Division District in Plovdiv, dated May 28, 1944:

> "Information collected in May:
> On May 11, 1944, the Plovdiv police arrested 5 young communists, who were planning to go underground. Related to their arrests, a certain number of Jewish families were detained at Second Police Station.
> Upon learning about the case, the Plovdiv Metropolitan Kiril, accompanied by Archimandrite Gorazd, went to the station and demanded an explanation for the reason for the arrest of the Jews. Moreover, he requested the release of the Jew Nisim Avram Madjar.
> The Metropolitan's trip to the station took place between 8 and 10 in the morning, when Jews are allowed to leave their houses. All Bulgarians noticed that while he was walking the streets, the Jews started to bow and greet him. Immediately after that, rumors were spread among the Jews in the city that Metropolitan Kiril will order the release of the detained" (Донесение за Митрополит Кирил, 1944).

Even members of the parliament from the government majority tried to help. The witness Matilda Jacques Vradjali testified at the People's Tribunal about the help she received from Georgi Lipovanski, MP from the government majority, representing the town of Byala Slatina. She said that Lipovanski had many Jewish friends. The witness and her family were sent to Vidin in 1943, but the climate was not good for her and her children. Her husband thought of moving to Byala Slatina and wrote to the Chairman of the Jewish Consistory there. The chairman replied that it would be easy, because Lipovanski was in the town at the time. The MP even found housing for them and told the local authority to treat the family well. Lipovanski even received a thank-you letter from the Consistory for helping all Jews in the town. He always treated Jews well (Народен съд, свидетел Матилда Жак Враджали, 1945, p. 2040-2041). Despite the help, Lipovanski was sentenced to death and executed.

The Bulgarian Jews in those difficult times got also some assistance from abroad. Yako Baruh remembers that they were helped by two international organizations. "The Joint, with headquarters in Switzerland, which sent through its representative in Bulgaria Moritz Markus the sum of 3 million leva to help the community kitchens, and the Jewish Agency in Istanbul, which sent 9,500 British pounds in credit and separately the sum in support of the community kitchens, youth organizations, as well as public figures and the Zionists. By the way, this sum was used mostly by the kitchens and by all Jews regardless of their convictions, as long as the commissions decided that the individual Jews needed help. From that sum was helped even the Zionist-hater Jacques Nathan [a communist] in Pazardjik and possibly all of his followers and opponents of Zionism after September 9, 1944. Actually, it doesn't matter. The goal was to help every Jew and the Bulgarian Zionists are proud that they didn't differentiate between communists and Zionists, between Jews and Jews" (Барух, Спомени 1941-1943, p.22).

14 THE FIRE IN CAMP KAILUKA – ARSON OR ACCIDENT?

It is important to cover the fire incident in camp Kailuka to understand better the events that happened in Bulgaria during World War II. As I explained in the previous chapter, the Commissariat for the Jewish Questions maintained several concentration camps specifically for Jews. Similar camps existed for Bulgarians, but they were under the direct jurisdiction of the Ministry of the Interior. Both types of camps housed people who were known for their anti-government political activities but had not committed serious crimes under the laws that would require trials and more severe punishments.

It is safe to assume that initially, the Jewish camps were planned by the Commissariat as temporary stops on the way to the Eastern occupied territories of Germany. Since the deportation attempts failed, the camps became detention centers. A significant difference from the camps maintained elsewhere in Europe was that those in Bulgaria were neither intended, nor functioned as extermination camps. Most of the camps established by Germany or "inspired" by it in Austria, Poland, Croatia, and Romania, had the task to either directly exterminate their inmates or to destroy them through heavy work and malnourishment. Nothing like that happened in Bulgaria. Other than the 10 people who perished in the fire in camp Kailuka, there are no other deaths recorded in other camps. More Jews were killed because of the Anglo-American bombing of Bulgaria and in the sinking of the boat Struma by the Russians in 1942.

This is confirmed by the People's Prosecutor Mancho Rahamimov in his speech at the beginning of the hearings held by the Seventh Section of the People's Tribunal. He provided a breakdown of the Jews who took part or perished in the political confrontations with the government in 1941-1944:

1. Killed underground functionaries – 4
2. Killed concentration camp inmates – 10
3. Killed political prisoners – 9
4. Concentration camp inmates – 233
5. Political prisoners – 177
6. Partisans – 131
7. Killed partisans – 54 (People's Court Session No.18, 1945, p. 1918).

The tribunal was mostly a tool of revenge, created to punish everybody who was actively involved with the governments that ruled Bulgaria from the late 1930s to September 9, 1944. The deaths in concentration camps are only 10. There is no doubt that if the communists, who organized the tribunal, had even the slightest chance to claim more victims, they would have done it.

How was camp Kailuka established?

It was a new location of camp Somovit, covered in the previous chapter, which initially provided temporary detention in the buildings of the village school. In his book "The Ransom", Nir Baruh explains:

> "The Somovit facilities were not suitable for many inmates (there were 500 in July 1943), that is why the camp was transferred close to village Tabakova Cheshma, 4 kilometers from Pleven. Here the conditions were "better", there were only 120 people in the camp. Later, they were moved to a new camp at the Kailuka area near Pleven, to long barracks, 12 by 1.20 m, where men, women, children and babies were held.
>
> "The camp commandant, Lyuben Zamerliev, a young man of 23, member of the anti-Semitic organization Ratnik, treated the inmates in a brutal way and told them that they were supposed to be sent for extermination to Poland. In a fire that started in the camp on July 11, 1944, ten inmates were burned to death and a few tens suffered serious burns. There are two versions regarding the causes of the fire.
>
> "According to the first version, the fire was started by one of the camp guards. It was based on the fact that containers with flammable liquid were brought to the camp. The second version was that a candle left burning by one of the women with a baby started the fire. In 1945, the commandant was charged by the People's Tribunal, but he was acquitted for the lack of evidence"

(Барух, 1991, p. 59-60).

There are a few corrections I should make to Nir Baruh's description. I hope that the width of the barracks of 1.20 m is an honest mistake or a misprint, because it is physically impossible to accommodate beds and any other amenities in such a narrow building. Also, in the protocols of the hearings of the People's Tribunal regarding the fire, where the accused was present, he was called Zimriev and not Zamerliev, so I will use that name. From the testimonies, it becomes clear that Zimriev was not the commandant of the camp. He had the lower position of "domakin", which was neither police nor military position. In Bulgarian, "domakin" means something like a steward, a person who takes care of supplying food and other necessities for a company, school or other establishment.

It is clear, that the barrack was long and narrow, with two rows of bunk beds. The walking space in the middle was less than 1 m, some said about 50 cm. There was only one exit, but it had windows without bars. Regardless of the reasons for the fire, the building was poorly designed to hold so many people, and in an emergency, it could turn into a trap. That is exactly what happened. Even if this was not an arson, the authorities in charge of the camp should have been convicted of criminal negligence for violating the fire safety regulations.

Instead, both in memoirs and in the witness accounts at the trial, the focus was on the role of Lyuben Zimriev.

In his memoirs, Robert Rubenov described the incident. He was a communist and a brother of the well-known partisan Mati Rubenova. His sister was killed in 1944 in a fight with the police. On April 1, 1944, he was taken from Yambol with his parents, other family members and others, 28 people in total, and sent to Tabakova Cheshma (the former camp Somovit), near Pleven. They were held there until the end of June 1944, then moved to camp Kailuka. There were 120 people in a barrack probably designed for 50. They slept in two-level bunk beds.

The commander was Lyubcho Zemirliev [at People's Tribunal called Zimriev; Lyubcho is the diminutive form of the Bulgarian name Lyuben], a young 20-year old fascist. He was rude, loved to punish people, ripped letters received by the inmates, and sometimes harassed women. Rubenov called him a beast in human image. Once, in the presence of the Pleven District Director and the Commissar for the Jewish Questions, Zimriev said that one match was enough to start a fire in that shed. When he realized the inmates heard him, he added, that's why we need to fix it (Rubenov, p. 1).

Further, the author claimed that the high officials came to the camp to design a sinister plan to get rid of the inmates, which they put into action. On July 10, 1944, the inmates celebrated the release of a young man who was being freed to take care of his mother. After the celebration ended, around midnight, when everyone was sleeping, the fire started. The people screamed and tried to escape. They saw at the only door Zimriev with a gun yelling that nobody should leave. The author and two others pushed the commandant to the ground, so the rest were able to get out. Rubenov was injured along with other people, the doctors among them helped. The heavy rain that started during the fire, extinguished the flames and many were saved (Rubenov, p. 2).

According to the author, 10 people died in the fire, including his old grandfather and the man about to be released. Rubenov ran to the city in his torn clothes to seek help and was surprised to see on the road Zimriev who reached the fire station before the author. The latter tried to wrestle down Zimriev to take his gun on the way but couldn't do it. At the station, the author was surprised to hear Zimriev complaining about 100,000 leva that he lost in the fire but didn't say anything about the victims. At that time, the author recalled that he saw near the shed a few containers with gas, which were probably used to start the fire. Rubenov continued into the city and went to the home of a Jewish roentgenologist to ask for help. The doctor took him to the hospital the next day, where the author spent two months. After that, the district director ordered the author and his family back to Yambol (Rubenov, p. 3-4).

Several witnesses testified about the case at the People's Tribunal. Mariyka Behar, an inmate at the camp, testified to implicate Zimriev as the arsonist. She saw him standing with a gun at the door when the fire started, and he tried to stop the people from running away. One of the inmates slapped Zimriev and he fell. She jumped from a window. When the defense counsel confronted her that Zimriev was seen to run for the fire brigade, she corrected herself – after he was pushed, he ran to reach the fire brigade.

The lawyer added that Zimriev may have taken out the gun in the panic when everybody was running around. She said she thought that he did it to make all Jews burn inside. The lawyer countered, if Zimriev had bad intentions, he could have locked the small door, instead of standing there with a gun, exposed to the angry people running out. She added that he didn't take out the gun but was holding it. The same night, Zimriev slept in the barrack with the inmates, later he told them that 100,000 leva ($1,200) of his money burned in the fire, along with his clothes. He stayed there because the same night the inmates had a party for one of them, supposed to be released the next day (that person was killed in the fire). Behar admitted that there was a candle inside, used by a mother while giving medicine to her sick child. There was a small flame near the ceiling before the fire broke out, but she didn't think the candle started it.

After she managed to escape, she saw that the roof was burning. What was the general behavior of Zimriev, asked the lawyer. Behar replied that he liked to dance with the girls; after the fire, he felt guilty, he was sorry for the inmates. She spent 3 months in the camp with him. Zimriev had a bad attitude, he tore letters delivered to the camp. Replying to the question whether Zimriev was anti-Semitic or just rude, Behar said that she couldn't tell. She provided more details – some people tried to bring water to extinguish the fire. From her testimony it looked like Zimriev was the only one present, no guards were mentioned. Behar said that there were 110 people in the shed. It was raining until the fire started and everything around was wet (People's Court Session No.14, 1945, p.1271-1280).

According to another witness, Nisim Bohor Alfandari, the fire started at about 1 a.m., everybody tried to get out, but the door was too narrow, and people got stuck. He heard after that that Zimriev was at the door, but he didn't see him. Most people escaped from the windows, which were low. The fire probably started from the inside and before that it was raining (People's Court Session No.15, 1945, p. 1405).

Leon Samuel Levi explained the circumstances surrounding his behavior and that of Zimriev during the fire. Zimriev was a young, emotionally unstable guy. The first day in the camp, he asked the young girls and boys to sing and when they refused, he got mad. At the fire, Levi saw a flame in one of the corners of the shed. The witness ran to the city for help and Zimriev was with him. On the way, Zimriev complained that a bag with 80,000 leva of his money was destroyed in the fire. The witness tried to take Zimriev's gun. Eventually they reached the fire brigade, and their trucks went to the camp. That night Zimriev slept in the shed and participated in the party. He was wearing pajamas (People's Court Session No.15, 1945, p. 1407).

The witness Chelebi Eshkenazi suspected an arson, since the barrack was too big to burn that fast. Besides, it was raining at the time. Zimriev slept inside that night, and did the same before, even though the inmates didn't want him there. The prosecutor interrupted him that other witnesses and Zimriev said that he slept there for the first time. The witness replied that it was not true, Zimriev had a devious plan to start a fire.

"CHAIRMAN: How do you know that?
"ESHKENAZI: It took 3 to 7 minutes to burn.
"C: Did you have a watch?
"E: No.
"C: Three minutes is a very short time to cause such a damage, even if gasoline is used.
"E: Zimriev stood at the door and swore at us, holding his gun and didn't want to let anybody out. Somebody grabbed him and when I saw that Zimriev may shoot that person, I jumped on him and punched him to allow people to leave.
"PROSECUTOR: In your preliminary testimony you didn't mention that he stood at the door swearing.
"E: I thought that it wasn't moral to write such things when I could discuss them here at the court.
"C: There is nothing immoral in that. If it were immoral at the time, it would still be immoral here.
"E: I am sorry.
"C: Did this really happen, or you made it up?
"E: I really saw him at the door.
"Ch: What was he wearing?
"E: Pants and shirt.
"C: Didn't he wear pajamas?
"E: No.
"C: At which door was he standing?
"E: At the outer door.
"DEFENSE COUNSEL: How long did the altercation with Zimriev continue?
"E: About a minute."

In the end, the witness said that he helped the victims and wasn't aware that Zimriev went to look for help (People's Court Session No.15, 1945, p. 1412).

Robert Mois Rubenov, whose memoirs were quoted above, also testified against Zimriev, saying that Zimriev was standing at the door but didn't hold a gun. Someone hit him. The witness ran to Pleven with Zimriev and the other witness. Zimriev complained that several hundred thousand leva of his money burned in the fire. Several people were injured, especially from his family. Since the food was insufficient, the witness used to go every day to the city to buy more. Zimriev wanted every night to have a party with the inmates. Arson was suspected because it was impossible to start a fire with a candle (People's Court Session No.15, 1945, p. 1420).

An important witness was Valdemar Robert Meerson, a young, 21-year old inmate of Danish background. That night, he spent most of the time in the bed next to Zimriev's bed:

> "CHAIRMAN: Were you at the camp when it burned down?
> "MEERSON: Yes, I arrived two days before the fire.
> "C: How did the fire happen?
> "M: I would like to share some details.
> "C: There is no need of details.
> "M: I slept next to Lyubcho Zimriev's bed. We were awake until after midnight. You already know that. Some people told me not to leave Lyubcho alone. It so happened that the whole time from midnight until the moment the fire started, I was with him. We were already in bed by 2 a.m.
> "COUNSEL: Were you in the same bed?
> "M: We had parallel beds. We were awake for a while. Then we saw a candle in the corner of the barrack. The candle attracted my attention, because I knew that there was a sick kid in the corner and assumed that the mother had to take care of the kid and left the candle burning.
> "C: Then?
> "M: Then, I don't know if the candle fell down or finished burning and when. I didn't know, I wasn't watching, but at certain moment I saw a small flame, bigger than normal.
> "C: At the same spot?
> "M: Yes. Then I jumped from the bed and headed to the fire, to the flame. Halfway from my bed to the candle, there was already a lot of smoke and I was suffocating. At that point, I saw Nisso Pinkas trying to extinguish the flame.
> "C: Who was he and where was the candle?
> "M: He was there.
> "C: Was his child sick?
> "M: I don't know.
> "PEOPLE'S PROSECUTOR ELI BARUH: When you saw the flame, was Zimriev sleeping?
> "M: Yes, he was.
> "EB: So, you left him sleeping and went to the flame?
> "M: Yes.
> "EB: Why?

"M: I did not expect such a big fire, as it happened afterward. It is natural when a person sees a flame to get up and walk to it.

"EB: So, he was in bed?

"M: He was in bed in his pajamas.

"EB: When he left, did you see how he left?

"M: When the flame became bigger, I got scared, grabbed my coat and ran out. Lyubcho was still inside and I stood at the left side of the door, the barrack was burning gradually. There was no fire started in several places, as some witnesses claimed, the barrack was burning in a natural way, from top to bottom. The flames were advancing toward the river, near which the barrack was built. Before the door caught fire, that area was not crowded, and the people could leave without problems. So, you see that the claim of some that Lyubcho was standing at the door and did not let them go out may not be true. I did not see such thing and cannot confirm it. At that moment, I wasn't watching the fire, because the picture was too scary.

"EB: So, you were already outside?

"M: Yes.

"EB: Did he leave before the door caught fire or after that?

"M: I didn't see.

"EB: Can you assume that he was slow to leave, and he got out only after the fire reached the door and scared him?

"M: I don't know what to tell you.

"EB: Some witnesses said that he stood at the door preventing people from leaving the barrack, and even was holding his revolver.

"M: Yes, I heard that.

"EB: Are these claims true?

"M: I think, no.

"C: So, how did it happen?

"M: Before the flames reached the door, something like that could not happen. After that, I saw that everybody was horrified, because some escaped from inside with burns and were screaming. So, I can't tell you what exactly happened at that time near the door. If Lyubcho was standing at the door when it was already burning, which is unlikely, he could have prevented people from leaving. But, as I said, it seems to me unlikely.

"C: You think it was impossible for him to stand at the burning door and stop people from leaving?

"M: Yes.

"C: Did you leave before he did, or he left before you?

"M: No, he was sleeping when I left, and I did not see him

after that.

"C: Where did the fire start? From top to bottom, or from the spot where the candle was?

"M: When I left, the flame was small.

"C: Was the candle close to the ceiling?

"M: I can give you some details to explain the fire. Since it was raining heavily, some people covered with tarred paper the lower part of the windows and parts of the ceiling. As you know, tar burns well. So, that candle could have set the paper on fire.

"COUNCEL: Did people in the barrack have a lot of luggage?

"M: Yes, there was a lot of luggage.

"C: After you left the barrack, did you see Zimriev leaving?

"M: [no answer]

"C: You left before him?

"M: Yes.

"C: Did you realize that he went to bring the fire brigade?

"M: I was told so, they said he ran with one of the inmates to reach the fire brigade and I found him there.

"C: You were lying next to him, but you didn't notice when Zimriev left the barrack.

"M: No.

"C: Did you sleep until the fire started?

"M: I was awake.

"C: So, you are saying that Zimriev did not go out from the moment you went to bed to the moment of the fire.

"M: I didn't see him going out.

"C: Everybody says that in the camp he behaved like a person who hated Jews and wanted to harass them. Isolated incidents are understandable, but didn't you have the impression that he acted like a sadist?

"M: I would rather say that, at least in my view, in the camp he made the impression of a mentally unstable little boy.

"C: Were you sure about that?

"M: Yes.

"C: What do you mean under "Mentally unstable young man"?

"M: Just young man...

"C: Punk.

"M: Yes.

"COUNSEL: When the fire started, what was he wearing?

"M: Red striped pajamas.

"C: Was that the first time he slept there?

"M: Somebody told me that he often expressed the desire to sleep in the barrack. But that was not the first time he came there.

"C: Did you have a party there?

"M: Yes, I am sure he had no fault for the fire.

"PEOPLE'S PROSECUTOR ELI BARUH: You were there at the moment of the fire, weren't you?

"M: Yes.

"EB: And only you were awake?

"M: Yes.

"EB: Nobody else was awake?

"M: Nobody.

"EB: When did the rest fall asleep?

"M: At about 12:00-12:15 a.m.

"EB: When did the fire start?

"M: 2:15 a.m.

"EB: Why were you awake?

"M: I was awake, because I was used to going late to bed. And I was nervous the first two days.

"EB: Was the candle burning from 12 to 2:15?

"M: I don't know if it was burning or not, but it definitely burned for a long time.

"EB: Was it burning when you fell asleep?

"M: I didn't sleep.

"EB: Until the fire started?

"M: When the fire started, the candle had already fallen down.

"EB: Where did the first flame appear?

"M: At the same place.

"CHAIRMAN: Wasn't it at a different place?

"M: It was the same.

"EB: How did you go out and from where?

"M: Through the door.

"EB: How far was your bed from the door?

"M: It was just against the door.

"EB: Where did you sleep?

"M: On the top bed.

"EB: What was the distance from the door?

"M: About a meter.

"EB: And you escaped through the door?

"M: No.

"EB: Then what did you do?

"M: First, I went to extinguish the fire.

"EB: And what happened?

"M: Other people also tried to extinguish it.

"EB: Who gave the first signal for the fire?

"M: Nobody.

"EB: What do you mean, nobody?

"M: We lost our minds.
"EB: So, you were awake, and the rest were sleeping?
"M: Yes.
"EB: Did anybody start an alarm?
"M: No.
"EB: Didn't you alarm the people?
"M: I think, Mr. Polikar yelled, but it seemed nobody heard him.
"EB: Did you hear him?
"M: Yes.
"EB: You said you were awake, the rest were sleeping, but Mr. Polikar gave the signal?
"M: Yes.
"EB: But you were the first one to see the fire, weren't you?
"M: Yes, but in the beginning, it didn't look like a big fire that needed an alarm.
"EB: And what did it look like?
"M: Like a small flame.
"EB: A little flame that burned the barrack within a minute. Strange observation!
"M: It didn't happen in a minute, the barrack burned in about fifteen minutes. [exclamations and laughter in the courtroom]
"EB: How long did it take for the fire to intensify?
"M: In four minutes, the fire became very strong.
"EB: How did you leave unharmed?
"M: I just left...
"EB: The fire intensified in four minutes, you left, and those who followed you immediately, were burned!
"M: I left right away.
"CHAIRMAN: What is the meaning of these questions?
"EB: Was the door open for the people to go out?
"M: Everybody left through the door.
"EB: And the whole barrack burned down in four minutes.
"CHAIRMAN: He said fifteen minutes.
"COUNSEL: Did some of those who left, go back inside to retrieve their stuff?
"M: Yes, I think the child of Polikar was outside and went back in again.
"COUNSEL: Did you see other people who managed to save their luggage, but came back with burns?
"M: Yes.
"COUNSEL: Did you see people leaving through the windows?
"M: Yes, some jumped through the windows.

"COUNSEL: When the fire brigade arrived, was the barrack still burning?

"M: No, there were only debris left.

"CHAIRMAN: You are free to go" (People's Court Session No.16, 1945, p. 1602-1610).

The odd thing about the memoirs and the cross-examination of witnesses is that they are focused entirely on the personality of Lyuben Zimriev. It sounds as if he was the only representative of the authorities in the camp. No other guards are mentioned. Even more unusual is his behavior – he treated the Jews in a bad way, insulting them and ripping letters, yet he spent the night at their party (Mariyka Behar used the Bulgarian word "veselie" to describe the event, which could be translated as "merriment") and even slept in the barrack with the inmates, whom he supposedly disliked.

The confusing testimonies make it difficult to believe that he could do all that, then sneak out and use gasoline to start the fire and come back. If his alleged goal was to cause maximum damage, he could have locked the only door or at least his unnamed collaborators could have stood with him at the door. Besides, this was happened in the summer of 1944 when the Bulgarian Government, under a rapidly deteriorating international situation, was gradually removing the restrictions imposed on Jews. Such an atrocity, like burning 120 people, would have severely damaged the attempts to exit the war. The event could benefit the Germans, but neither the court, nor the witnesses explored the version of possible German interference.

Another odd episode was the attempt of Rubenov to wrestle Zimriev out of his gun while both of them were running to Pleven. Something like would have been a crime and, if Zimriev were the person described in the testimonies, he could have easily arrested Rubenov, after they reached the city. However, it did not happen, and we are left guessing why.

I am inclined to think that, most likely, the fire was an incident turned deadly due to the criminal negligence of the authorities, who ignored the possibility that the wooden building could turn into a trap. The people responsible could have been easily convicted, but the issue never came up during the trial. It is one more proof that the People's Tribunal was focused exclusively on removing the political competition of the rising communist power and not on delivering objective and fair justice.

The confusion around the case was covered well in the closing arguments of Counsel Filchev, the voluntary defender of Lyuben Zimriev. The case was investigated three times – by the office of the Governor of the Pleven Region, by the Commissariat for the Jewish Questions, and by the clerk Petkov who was there immediately after the fire. All three presented reports that the fire was an accident. Nobody argued about that, except Chelebi Polikar who deposited a statement at the police that Zimriev was the arsonist, to remove the suspicion of negligence from his son Nissim Pinhas and his wife, who left the candle burning.

Later, he repeated that accusation at a session of the People's Tribunal, which caused the outrage of the lawyer Vasil H. Datsev, who investigated the fire, using his connections with the Jews in Pleven, and concluded that it was caused accidentally by the candle of the Pinhas family.

Filchev said further that the only ground for the accusations was the testimony of Zimriev during his detention at the Directorate of the People's Militia. Zimriev got the job of a steward thanks to a general, who was at the time a representative of the Commissariat in Pleven, but later was removed. His functions were assumed by the mayor of Pleven Vulchev, who did not like Zimriev and tried to replace him.

Yet Zimriev said in his deposition that one day Vulchev called him to his office and said: "Set the Jews on fire, destroy them, this is the only way to save yourself from the crimes you had committed, which can send you to jail." Then he pointed at a jerrycan with gasoline in his office and told Zimriev to take it and start the fire.

However, when his trial started, Zimriev rejected his confession. Filchev could not mention it, but the confession was probably extracted with torture, which was a common method of interrogation of the People's Militia. The whole interaction did not make sense – Vulchev was an educated and clever man, a lawyer, who had under his control a large police apparatus. It was unlikely that he would use a young boy to take the gasoline for the fire from his own office.

At the trial, Zimriev was confident that the fire was started by Mrs. Pinhas, who was allowed by the doctor to keep the candle burning, because her child was sick. She fell asleep; the candle was on a flammable wicker basket, and it started the fire. In the beginning, people ignored the flame and later, it was out of control.

The testimonies were contradictory – some saw Zimriev at the door, near the door, holding the door; he was pointing his revolver at the people, held the revolver or had no revolver; he was wearing a military coat, pajamas or shirt and pants, etc. He might have stood at the door when he realized that his bag with money and documents was inside but could not get in because people were running out.

Also, about Zimriev's attitude – some said it was bad, others found him friendly, in good relations with the inmates. As of the torn letters, he said that a few times he found letters with political content and destroyed them, because he could get in trouble for delivering them.

Finally, Filchev said that there was no evidence to convict Zimriev and to refute the more credible hypothesis of the candle fire caused by the Pinhas family. (People's Court Session No.20, 1945, p. 2098-2101).

Zimriev was acquitted.

15 BULGARIAN JEWS ON THE EVE OF THE SOVIET INVASION

You may remember than in his memoirs, "Evlag", Albert Varsano expressed his own and other Somovit inmates' anxiety over the political changes after the death of King Boris III on August 28, 1943. The ascension to the throne of his 6-year old son Simeon, as King Simeon II, required the selection of a three-member Regency Council. Prof. Bogdan Filov resigned from his post of Prime Minister and became head of the council. The Constitution required a Grand People's Assembly to appoint the regents but holding new elections in war time was deemed impractical. The other two regents were Prince Kiril, King Boris's younger brother, and General Nikola Mihov, former Minister of War. According to the entry in the diary of Dr. Goebbels, quoted in Chapter 7, the top Nazis were satisfied with the regents and believed in their loyalty to Germany.

A new government was formed with Prime Minister Dobri Bozhilov. Probably because of the quickly changing international situation, the fears of the Jews of harsher policies after King's death proved wrong. Bozhilov tried to ease the tensions in Bulgaria. "In an endeavor to appease and deradicalize the country, in the fall of 1943 the Bozhilov government granted a broad political amnesty. The detention camps were closed. All persons detained without trial since mid-1941 were thus released. The great majority were communists or suspected communists. They were asked to sign written statements to the effect that in the future they would undertake no political activities. The same procedure was applied to political prisoners serving short-term sentences in state prisons. In October 1943, therefore, the communist intellectual elite found itself free, even though in some cases prominent communists were not allowed to reside in the capital. Only a few joined the resistance movement. The great majority, who had never accepted the idea of an armed rebellion, remained inactive and awaited developments" (Oren, 1971, p. 233). Still, though many Jews were freed from their special detention camps, the latter continued to function but the conditions in them improved.

The new 1944 brought even more problems to the Bulgarian ruling circles. The steady advancement of the Soviet Army on the Eastern Front brought the war battles closer to the Balkan Peninsula. On April 8, 1944, the Russians reached the Romanian border and a few days later, liberated Odessa. The unstable situation in Romania made the ports and other facilities provided in the cities of Varna and Burgas, on the Bulgarian Black Sea coast, even more important to Germany. To counter that, the Soviet Government protested on April 17 against the German military presence in those ports. "The Bulgarians denied the charges, saying that the Black Sea bases were not being employed for offensive purposes. To this, the Soviets responded on April 26 by requesting the reopening of the Soviet consulate in Varna, which the Bulgarians had closed down in 1942, and the establishment of two new consulates in Burgas and Russe in order to verify the Bulgarian contentions. Afraid to offend the Russians, but unwilling to agree, the government postponed its reply" (Oren, 1971, p. 234). As it was already mentioned, Bulgaria, despite the German pressure, did not declare war on the Soviet Union and kept its embassy in Sofia open throughout the war. Moreover, the Bulgarian Embassy in Moscow also presented the interests of Germany, Hungary, and Romania.

Bozhilov's government proved incapable of handling the increased pressure. On May 18, the Cabinet resigned. Prof. Filov did not want to give the power to the opposition, which included pro-Western and pro-communist elements. Instead, he selected Ivan Bagrianov, a career politician from one of the agrarian parties.

A major change for the Jews in that period was the dismissal of Alexander Belev as the Commissar for the Jewish Questions in October 1943. However, this did not change the functions and goals of the Commissariat. The new Commissar Hristo Stomanyakov lacked the zeal and fanaticism of Belev, but he did little to change the general conditions of the Jews, though he interfered positively in many specific cases. Only the new government of Bagrianov, seeing the coming defeat of Germany and concerned about its political future, started to make changes in the Jewish policies. Bagrianov saw the restrictive laws as contrary to truth and justice. Yako Baruh recalls that in a speech on July 27, 1944, Bagrianov practically annulled the Law for Defense of the Nation and all decrees that followed it. The Jewish stars were removed, the restrictions of movement lifted, etc. The next step had to be the restoration of the economic positions of the Jews, from which the law deprived them. Before that speech, however, Bagrianov restored the supreme Jewish institution in Bulgaria, the Jewish Consistory, which was shut down after the Jews were expelled from Sofia in May 1943. Chairman of the Consistory became Dr. Israel Moisey Kalmi, with members Colonel Avram Tadjer, David Lidji, Eng. Eliezer Isaac Levi, Mancho Rahamimov and Fiko Levi from Russe (Барух, Спомени 1941-1943, p.28).

Their first demand was the dismissal of Commissar Hristo Stomanyakov and his replacement with a person who would liquidate the Commissariat. They wanted that person to be Judge Protich. The latter received an order from the Minister of Justice Staliyski to prepare a law that cancels all laws and orders against Jews. Judge Protich worked for a month with the members of the Consistory and presented the proposal to the Minister of the Interior Prof. Stanishev for approval. The Minister rejected it and requested certain changes that harmed Jews, which were rejected by the Jewish Consistory. The commission at the Ministry of Justice, which worked on that issue, took the side of the Consistory and the original version was accepted. However, the interference of Prof. Stanishev slowed down the process and even though the new law was approved before the fall of the Bagrianov Government, it was published only on September 4, 1944, under the Muraviev Government. The latter ruled for only seven days before it was overthrown by force by the coalition of the Fatherland Front (Барух, Спомени 1941-1943, p.28-29).

In his memoirs, Mr. Baruh also mentions rumors about a planned anti-Jewish pogrom in Russe and other cities for the night of September 7, 1944, by "Bulgarian fascist forces". The pogrom had been foiled in some unknown way, but even the plan of such an event was not confirmed (Ibid., p.29). It is a strange development, for which there is no more information, especially considering the fact that there were no pogroms in Bulgaria before that.

The internal fight and arguments within the different levels of the Bulgarian Government, combined with the German suspicions, made the situation of the Jews complicated. In 1944, some government circles continued to distrust the Jews. In the Bulgarian State Archives, I found a letter of a colonel from the Military Intelligence to the Directorate of the Police, sent out on May 27, 1944, warning that the Jews leaving the country become foreign spies. He claimed that all of them were expected to go to the "Bureau for Jews Leaving Europe", ran by the British intelligence service in Istanbul, where the Jews were expected to provide detailed information about Bulgaria. That included the locations of German troops, consequences of the Allied bombings, locations of factories, persons in important government positions, activities of communists, etc. The colonel recommended listing all Jews coming to Bulgaria as enemies (Преписка за евреи напускащи България, 1944, p.12). Despite that, in a letter to the Director of the Police (June 1944), the Commissar for the Jewish Questions Stomanyakov, stated that the police should issue exit visas to all Jews who want to leave the country, except those convicted of crime (Ibid., p.20).

Despite the easing of the procedures for leaving the country and issuing transit visas in 1944, the Jews, who had to go through Bulgaria and cross Turkey on their way to Palestine, were endangered by the Germans. Bulgaria had no control over the situation, but it tried to warn the Jews who had Bulgarian transit visas, as it becomes clear in the following letter from the Consul Directory of the Ministry of the Foreign Affairs to the Directorate of the Police:

> "The Ministry of the Foreign Affairs notified the Embassy in Bucharest that the persons travelling from Bulgaria to Turkey, after leaving Svilengrad [Bulgarian town on the Turkish border. – M.M.], must pass through a former Greek territory controlled by the German authorities; they inspect again the passports and prevent some travellers from continuing their trip. The Embassy must warn the travellers, especially the Jews, who have a transit visa, that if they have not obtained in advance a pass for the mentioned territory, they could be stopped by the German authorities. To preserve the reputation of our country, the Ministry requests that the Directory of the Police warn the travellers in the same way and tell them that the additional inspection, though conducted in Svilengrad, is related to the non-Bulgarian territory, occupied by the Germans, who exercise that control" (Преписка за евреи напускащи България, 1944, p.21).

The problem was serious, and the Germans created obstacles for Jews passing through Bulgaria. This was covered in a letter from the Passport Bureau of the Russe police to the Directorate of the Police in Sofia (June 1944):

> "According to information from the German Secret Police, Jews passing through Bulgaria to Turkey will not be allowed to enter Turkey and at Svilengrad, they will be stopped and sent back. Since the countries, from which the Jews come, have no interest in allowing them to come back, those countries create obstacles and don't accept them. Please order our embassies not to issue visas to Jews travelling to Turkey and also warn the crossing points not to allow in Jews with transit visas to Turkey, even if their visas are legitimate" (Преписка за евреи напускащи България, 1944, p.23).

The Bulgarian authorities simplified the procedure for Jews leaving the country, according to the order of the Directorate of the Police to the regional police directors of August 25, 1944. It stated that passports to persons of Jewish background should be issued after presenting certificate for citizenship and local residence, bank statement, and statements from the state and local tax authorities. For the exit visa, they still needed statement from the regional military office, but a certificate from the Commissariat for the Jewish Questions was no longer required. Also, for the exit visa, the permission of the Central Police Directorate was not necessary anymore. The Jewish foreigners living in Bulgaria, who did not have passports, would be provided with Nansen passports [travel documents for refugees. – M.M.] (Ред за напускане на България от евреи, 22 юни-25 август 1944, p.4)

Leaving the country by boat was also made easier, according to a letter from the Commissariat for the Jewish Questions to the local consistories, dated July 8, 1944, and signed by Maria Pavlova: "Notify the Chairman of the Consistory at the Jewish community, who is in charge of the voluntary emigration of the Jews from Bulgaria, that with letter No. 792 of July 3, 1944, the General Staff of the Army declares the city of Burgas an exit port, from where the boats with Jews emigrating from Bulgaria will be leaving the country" (Ред за напускане на България от евреи, 22 юни-25 август 1944, p.6). In addition to this, Bulgarian boats started to transport thousands of Jews from Romania to Palestine.

Despite the British White Paper, which reduced the Jewish immigration to Palestine, many Bulgarian Jews were allowed by the government to leave. For example, from January 1 to September 9, 1944 (the day Bulgaria was occupied by the Russians) 958 Jews left Bulgaria, the majority from Plovdiv (544), Russe (165) and Sofia (175) (Справка за броя на еврейските изселници, 1944). The same document indicates that even after the new government took over, by December 27, 1944, another 341 Jews left for Palestine.

No coverage of that period of the Bulgarian history would be full without telling the story of the Allied air raids against the country. In 1941, under strong pressure from Germany after signing the Tri-Partite Pact, Bulgaria declared war on the USA and Great Britain. At the time, that was considered a "symbolic war" with no real consequences for Bulgaria. However, by late 1943, Mussolini was ousted from power, Germany occupied Italy only to be pushed back by the Allied forces, which established bases in southern Italy. This made it possible to bomb the allies of Germany, including Bulgaria.

Bulgaria had a modest participation in the war and did not have major military installations on its territory. Those facts did not deter the Allies, because the bombings were seen as a form of psychological (and real) terror, whose victims were predominantly civilians.

The situation was covered in the communications between the Allies and the Bulgarian authorities. In March 1944, the Bulgarian Ambassador to Turkey N. Balabanov held talks with representatives of the US State Department. The intimidation tactics of the American diplomats are on clear display in a telegram sent from Hull (US State Department) to the War Refugee Board (Washington, D.C.), which covers the talks of Hirschmann from the War Refugee Board with representatives of Romania and Bulgaria. The same diplomats met representatives of Romania and Bulgaria and stated the importance of the treatment of the Jews for the future relations but did not make any distinction between the policies of the two countries.

Hirschmann warned Cretzianu, the representative of Marshal Antonescu, about the brutal treatment of Jews and other minorities in Romania. "Our Government, Hirschmann warned, would remember in the future any continuation by the Rumanian Government of the execution of the policies of Hitlerite persecution and that, in its own interest, the Rumanian Government would be well advised to take advantage of those opportunities to permit refugees to depart across its borders which may become available to it in the future... Cretzianu assured Hirschmann no bodily harm would come to any of the many Jews in Transnistria, provided the Germans had not taken over from Rumania the administration of Transnistria, which lies directly in the path of the retreating German Army and where many thousands of Jews were held in Rumanian concentration camps..." (Reports by US diplomatic representations, 1944, p. 1-5). It is important to remind the readers that the Romanian brutality in the extermination of the Jews rivalled that of Nazi Germany. Over 250,000 Jews were killed on Romanian territory, mostly by the Romanian authorities.

The Americans decided to treat Bulgaria in the same way:

> "The conspicuous success of this direct approach to the Rumanian Government decided Hirschmann, with Steinhardt's approval, to make a similar approach to the Bulgarian Government. A conference between Hirschmann and Minister Balabanoff [Balabanov] of Bulgaria at he home of the Intercross representative at Ankara was arranged about March 20. This meeting opened by Hirschmann in same manner as that with Cretzianu, stating that **reports of the brutal treatment accorded to minorities in Bulgaria, especially the Jews, had outraged the Government** and the people of the United States and that Bulgaria would be called upon to answer therefor in the near future. Hirschmann warned, after advising Balabanoff of this Government's determination to save refugees, that any continuation of execution of these Nazi persecution policies would be remembered by our Government in the future and that in its own interests the Bulgarian Government would be well advised to take advantage of whatever opportunities present themselves in the future, which will permit the departure of refugees... Balabanoff stated in reply that the maltreatment of minorities in Bulgaria was result of policies of Gabrovski, former Minister of Interior, who, according to Balabanoff was a German tool and no longer was a member of the Government. The Jews lately, Balabanoff stated, had been accorded much better treatment in Bulgaria and he believed that relaxation of pressure against them would continue. Immediate dispatch of a telegram by Balabanoff to his Government recommending that identical treatment be accorded Jews and all other minorities in Bulgaria to that given Bulgarian citizens, that the deplorable conditions under which the Jews and other minorities are living in concentration camps

be ameliorated immediately and finally that the Bulgarian Government take immediate steps to authorize granting of visas and to provide transportation for all refugees wishing to leave for Palestine or Turkey was suggested by Hirschmann" (Ibid.). [Emphasis mine. – M.M.]

Aside of the one-size-fits-all intimidation applied to both countries, Hirschmann's mentioning of the brutal treatment of minorities (twice!) is puzzling. The Jews were the only persecuted minority, a situation due exclusively to the German demands. None of the other minorities, like Turks, Gypsies, Armenians, Greeks, Tatars, Gagauz or Wallachians was persecuted. The Gypsies, who elsewhere were rounded up and sent to death camps by Germans, were not touched in Bulgaria. It is not clear whether this was arrogance or simple ignorance, especially when Hirschmann didn't make a difference between the mass murder of Jews in Romania and saving every Jews in Bulgaria, but such an uncompromising tone made further talks difficult.

The telegram continued:

"Hirschmann arranged a second meeting with Balabanoff about April 6. No reply had apparently been received by the latter to the telegram and long memorandum he claimed had been dispatched to his Government after the first conference. Receipt of indirect word that the Bulgarian Government was relaxing its attitude toward minorities, especially Jews, and that Jews were being allowed to leave Bulgaria by both ship and train was claimed however. The bombing of Sofia, as the possible reason for nonreceipt of a reply, was mentioned... The failure of the Bulgarian Government to reply to Balabanoff's telegram and memorandum has created an unfavorable impression on this Government, as indicative that Bulgaria has not (repeat not) yet determined to discard the Nazi ideology of race and minority persecution and that such a stand will be taken into consideration in the final reckoning" (Ibid.).

On June 28, 1944, Herschel V. Johnson from the US Embassy in Stockholm, forwarded to the US Secretary a State an informal statement by the Bulgarian Ambassador in Turkey N. Balabanov, who was in contact with the Americans. Among other things, he covered the Jewish situation in Bulgaria and the continuous bombing of the country:

"Measures taken against the Jews by Bulgaria have been

applied without harshness by all organizations of the administration. It is no secret – and the Bulgarian Jews themselves know it very well – that the late King Boris, as well as the supreme authority of the Bulgarian Orthodox Church have always taken care to see that the Jews were treated without harshness. As for the Bulgarian town and rural populations, these have declared a sympathy for the Jews which the Jews themselves have recognized. At this moment the Jews are living in much better conditions than those enjoyed by the majority of the Bulgarian citizens who have been forced to abandon their towns destroyed by American air raids and have lost everything they possessed...

"The American Air Forces have carried out acts of the greatest and most arbitrary cruelty against the civilian population of the cities of Sofia, Plovdiv, Skopje, Dupnitsa, Velles, Vratsa, and others. They have done violence to the chateau of Vrana, residence of the Queen, a widow of barely six months' standing, and of her two orphan children, aged 12 and 7. The chateau has been totally destroyed, although it is far from any military objective, far from any other habitation.

"If the Bulgarian people were to learn that there are still to be found in the United States of America noble souls who deplore these cruelties; if those who preside over the destinies of the great American nation, instead of addressing threats, were to promise to repair the damage that their cruel military leaders have already done, and never again to permit their Air Force to kill and ruin a harmless and guiltless population, then without a doubt the Bulgarian Government would recognize the moral right of the USA to give humanitarian advice and then the Bulgarian people would fully approve action which conforms to such advice" (Reports by US diplomatic representations, 1944, p. 19-20).

As it often happened in the Bulgarian history, the appeal to a higher morality was futile, because once again, the country has turned into a pawn in the strategic games of the Great Powers. The subject of the bombing of Bulgaria was discussed in the secret correspondence between Roosevelt and Churchill during World War II. In a clarification of those letters in the second volume of "Churchill & Roosevelt: The Complete Correspondence", the commentator and editor of the edition Warren F. Kimball explains that Churchill showed clear hostility toward Bulgaria. He resented the fact that Bulgaria was at war with the USA and Great Britain, but not with the Soviet Union. Besides, if his country started negotiations with Bulgaria, that could damage the British interests in Greece and Turkey, traditional enemies of Bulgaria. Churchill thought that the heavy raids over Bulgaria could force it to accept his conditions. He did not like Roosevelt's idea to get Bulgaria to join the fight against Germany, because that could prevent the punishment of the country for being a German ally (Churchill & Roosevelt, Vol.2, p. 714).

In February 1944, Roosevelt wrote to Churchill:

> "Washington [via U.S. Navy]
> Feb. 9, 1944, 12:35 P.M.
> R-463
> Personal and Secret for the Former Naval Person from the President. I have received an unconfirmed report that the Bulgarian Government desires to send a mission to Istanbul to discuss conditions under which Bulgarian Army would joint the Allies. If this report should prove to be true it appears to me that it would be worth while for us to make some concessions such as suspending the bombing attacks on Bulgaria for a limited period and with your sending representatives to meet the Bulgarian Mission at Istanbul. Probably the Russians should be in on this too. It is assumed that your sources of information in Turkey have heard the same story if it has any validity. I am repeating this to you only for what it is worth in anticipation of possible future developments.
> Roosevelt [WDL]" (Ibid., p. 714).

Churchill sent out his cynical reply the next day (the emphasis is mine):

> "C-575
> London [via U.S. Army]
> Feb. 10, 1944, 2320 Z / TOR 0045 Z, Feb. 11
> Prime Minister to President. Personal.
> Eden and I are agreed here that the bombing of Bulgarian targets as weather permits should not be stopped because of the peace overtures. If the medicine has done good, let them have more of it" (Ibid., p. 715).

In a new letter, a few days later, Churchill outlined the "benefits" of the bombings:

> "C-576
> London [via U.S. Army]

Feb. 12, 1944/TOR 1355 Z
Prime Minister to President Roosevelt. Personal and Most Secret.

1. Many thanks for your telegram number 463 of February 9th.

2. It seems to me most undesirable that a Bulgarian Mission should open conversations in Constantinople. If the Bulgarian Government really mean business, they should be told to send a fully qualified mission to meet representatives of the Three Powers at a place which will be indicated and might be Cyprus or Cairo. Cyprus is absolutely secret and nearer.

3. Our bombing of Sofia appears in fact to have had exactly the effect we hoped for, in that the Bulgarians are falling over each other in their haste to make contact with us. That being so, would it not be a mistake to suspend it at the request of the firstcomer who no doubt hopes for a respite during protracted conversations..." (Ibid., p.724).

Churchill then contacted Roosevelt again with a proposal to arrange negotiations, while continuing the air raids against Bulgaria:

"C-580
London [via U.S. Army]
Feb. 15, 1944, 1631 Z / TOR 1850 Z
Prime Minister to President Roosevelt. Personal and Most Secret.

1. I would propose to telegraph as follows to Ambassador Clark Kerr:
..."These proposals have been considered by the President and the Prime Minister whose views are as follows: It is undesirable that a Bulgarian mission should open conversations in Constantinople. If the Bulgarian Government really mean business, it would be a mistake to rebuff them because they do not at the outset offer unconditional surrender. They should be told to send a fully qualified mission to meet United States, Soviet and British representatives at a place which will be indicated, and which might be Cyprus or Cairo. Advantage of Cyprus is that it is nearer to Bulgaria and absolutely secret.

"This Bulgarian peace feeler shows that the air bombing of Sofia appears to have had exactly the effect which was hoped for. In these circumstances it would be a mistake to suspend it at the request of the Bulgarian Minister to Turkey before it is known whether the Bulgarian proposals really are serious ones and when it is probable that the Bulgarian Government hope for a respite from bombing during protracted conversations. It is therefore proposed to continue with the bombing of Bulgarian targets." (Ibid., p.729-730).

Sir Winston was known for his sarcastic and cynical language. But this goes beyond language. The "medicine" he had in mind was the brutal bombing of Bulgaria and those letters were exchanged just before the most devastating air raids in the country. They were already mentioned in the quoted letter from Ambassador N. Balabanov and I will provide more details. However, here I want to mention another controversy related to the Anglo-American air forces.

Shortly after the magnitude of the Jewish destruction became clear in the 1940s, various Jewish leaders and organizations called the Allies for intervention. A very large number of Jews were brought to concentration camps by trains, so the proposals were to bomb the railways or the gas chambers and crematoria in the large camps like Auschwitz.

On August 9, 1944, A. Leon Kubowitzki from the World Jewish Congress wrote to the American official John J. McCloy: "I believe that destruction of gas chambers and crematoria in Oswiecim [Auschwitz] by bombing would have a certain effect now. Germans are now exhuming and burning corpses in an effort to conceal their crimes. This could be prevented by destruction of crematoria and then Germans might possibly stop further mass exterminations especially since so little time is left to them. Bombing of railway communications in this same area would also be of importance and of military interest." McCloy responded a few days later: "After a study it became apparent that such an operation could be executed only by the diversion of considerable air support essential to the success of our forces now engaged in decisive operations elsewhere and would in any case be of such doubtful efficacy that it would not warrant the use of our resources. There has been considerable opinion to the effect that such an effort, even if practicable, might provoke even more vindictive action by the Germans." (Auschwitz Bombing Controversy, August 1944).

So, what were those "decisive operations elsewhere"? One of their targets was Bulgaria, a country that didn't fight against England and the USA. The military airplanes were delivering Churchill's "medicine" to Bulgaria. The bombing there was credited for sparing the Jews from deportation, but the Americans were not concerned at all that their assault "might provoke even more vindictive action" by the Bulgarians, especially when the whole Jewish population of over 48,000 was living intact in Bulgaria. It is hard to believe that some of the 45,000 bombs dropped on Bulgarian civilians could not be diverted to stop the Germans from killing Jews in the concentration camps.

Here are the details about the bomb "medicine" that Sir Winston delivered to the Bulgarian people.

After the Allies got the opportunity to start air raids from the occupied southern part of Italy, the first air raid on Sofia took place on November 14, 1943. 91 bombers B-25 Mitchell dropped 141 tons of bombs, destroying 47 buildings and damaging 129. The number of the killed was 59 and 128 were wounded. The first three planes used machine guns to shoot people running in the streets. The small shelters proved insufficient. Three more raids followed – on November 24, and December 10 and 20.

On January 10, 1944, Bulgaria became the target of a large devastating raid. Sofia was attacked twice, during the day, and later at night. At about 1:30 p.m., 330 American airplanes attacked – 220 bombers, B-24 and B-17 Flying Fortress and 110 fighter jets Lightning. They were confronted by 73 airplanes – 43 Bulgarian and 30 German fighter jets, which managed to shoot down 6 Flying Fortresses and 5 fighter jets; 2 Bulgarian and 5 German pilots died in the counter-attack. At 10:00 p.m., the capital was raided by 80 British airplanes, but despite the anti-aircraft artillery, they managed to cause damage.

As a result of the two raids, 947 people were killed and 710 wounded. 93 government and 3,211 private buildings were destroyed and 427 badly damaged. The communications and water supply networks were interrupted. A total of 1784 bombs were dropped. The attacks disrupted the life in the capital and caused mass evacuation, by January 16, 300,000 people left Sofia.

Another attack was attempted on January 24 but was prevented by the thick fog that covered Sofia and the surrounding field. The American bombers circled the area for 45 minutes and then dispersed. Some of them bombed Skopje, another 84 hit the city of Vratsa (not a military target), killing 124 and wounding 250. Some fighter jets flew low to shoot people with their machine guns, then they bombed neighboring villages as well.

On March 16, 1944, a flock of British bombers attacked downtown Sofia, dropping flammable magnesium bombs, which started 70 fires. There was another attack the same night, which destroyed 45 and damaged 13 buildings, killing 19 and wounding 76.

The worst bombing happened on March 30, 1944. Sofia was attacked by 450 bombers Liberator, Flying Fortress, Mitchell, and Halifax, accompanied by 150 fighter jets Lightning. They dropped over 3,000 destructive and flammable bombs, which destroyed 3,575 buildings and killed 139. The evacuation was to be credited for the lower number of victims. Among the destroyed or severely damaged buildings were the National Theater, the Ministry of Justice, the National Library, the Holy Synod of the Bulgarian Orthodox Church, the Catholic Cathedral, the Russian Church, the State Printing Company, the Parliament building, schools, etc. (72 години от бомбардировките над София).

During the bombing campaigns, 187 villages and towns were attacked with 45,000 destroying and flammable bombs. The killed numbered 4,208 people, the wounded – 4,744. About 12,000 buildings and houses were destroyed, the total damage was estimated at 24 billion leva. Bulgaria lost 19 military pilots, but the attackers lost 147 airplanes and about 200 pilots, 329 crew members were captured and held in the POW prison in the city of Shumen until the end of the war (Тенчев, 2008).

Even the widow of King Boris III and his children were not spared in those attacks. The summer palace, where they lived, was heavily bombed on March 24, 1944. Queen Ioanna recalls:

> "The Allied bomb attacks, American and English, continued almost every day and every night. That incident was organized and executed deliberately, when on March 24, 1944, the park of the palace Vrana was bombed at night, with two interruptions, with over 500 flammable bombs, 36 of which started a fire in the upper two floors of the palace. Eleven heavy bombs hit the park. One of them made a crater, seven meters in diameter and three meters deep, which filled with water. We put red fish in it and called it Lake Churchill.
>
> "The bombings continued for nearly two months over the whole Bulgaria. As they did elsewhere, the British used fewer airplanes and aimed with accuracy. The Americans, on the other hand, came in numbers, even with 600 planes at a time, bombing indiscriminately from high level even at day time. It was clear, they sought psychological and not tactical damage" (Царица Йоанна, Спомени, p. 132).

The methods of the Anglo-American air forces are covered in

the testimony of Krikor Aslanyan (Bulgarian of Armenian background) "Sofia and the War through the Eyes of a Child Witness":

> "Many died in Sofia during the bombings, many became homeless, many remained under the ruins of the houses. The American Air Forces used to drop small bombs shaped like toys, which exploded when handled. Who were the victims of these "toy" mines? Naturally, the kids. What inhumanity, what cynicism, it is to use the natural interest of the innocent children in toys to kill them. To kill children, instead of soldiers, to mock the future of mankind and to boast today that you were a savior and peacemaker. That was a war, some may say. But is it so? I think that in the war there must be morals. Not a single Bulgarian government wanted to place a small memorial of the thousands of innocent victims of those senseless bombings in Sofia. No military objects were bombed for the simple reason that such did not exist in Sofia" (София и войната).

Ivan Petrinski, in an article about the bombings, states that while bombing the large Bulgarian cities, the Anglo-American airplanes were involved in numerous attacks on smaller towns and villages, home to many evacuees. There were no troops or military installations in the tiny villages, so the only reason must have been to cause maximum casualties among the women, children and elderly, who had found refuge there (Петрински, 2015).

He also confirmed the testimony of Aslanyan:

> "From April 1943, information emerges that over the German positions, small items for personal use were being dropped, for example, match boxes that upon opening, explode in the hands of the soldiers. Soon, the initiative expands, and the Anglo-American airplanes start to drop in many places in Bulgaria exploding children's toys or tempting items like watches, fancy pens, chocolate boxes. The choice of the exploding items shows that the kids and the youth were targeted in this action. The goal was to maim the "recipient" of the exploding toy, not to kill him. Suffering was the aim of this idea.
>
> "Despite the warnings, on June 16, 1943, the 17-year old Kiril Stamenov found near village Kiselitsa, Kyustendil area, a luxury chocolate box, which exploded in his hands, tearing all his fingers. Ten days later, the 14-year old Ghero Vutov found a

nice pen, which exploded when he tried to open it; he lost all fingers of both hands and his face was disfigured... The psychosis of the exploding toys kept the Bulgarian children on their toes nearly two decades after the end of World War II" (Ibid.).

Even a town like Lom, with no military importance, home of thousands of evacuees, was bombed regularly by the Anglo-American air forces. Nadezhda Vasileva, the nurse who helped the Jews in March 1943, did not stop her good work. She recalls in her memoirs that after every bombing, she was always running to the Turkish quarter, where many Jews expelled from Sofia lived. Many houses were destroyed and often she had to pull survivors from the debris. A few times, she managed to provide first aid to people who were badly injured. After one of the bombings, she found in a half-destroyed house a young Jewish woman who was giving birth. Vasileva remained with her, and after two hours of labor, twins, a boy and a girl, were born. Vasileva and the familuny tried to find transportation to take the mother and the babies out of town to the hills and save her from death. However, the town was empty, everybody was hiding from the next bombing that could come. She saw the police chief in the street, but he refused to help - he did not care if a Jewish woman died. Then she saw that the pharmacy was open, but Dr. Koeva, who was inside, said that she had no time for Jews. Finally, the chief doctor of the State Hospital helped by giving her a stretcher and the people who started to come back from hiding provided a buggy to take the mother and her children to safety. The family survived and later returned to Sofia (Спомени на Надежда Василева, p. 13-16). In a letter clarifying some points of her memoirs, she noted that the bombing on the day the twins were born, happened on August 18, 1944 (Надежда Василева, писмо, 1947), just a few weeks before the Soviet occupation. At the time, Bulgaria was on its way out of the war that it did not even fight, so there was neither strategic nor tactical justification for the barbaric bombing of civilians in Lom.

Initially, the number of the Jews in Lom was 251, and, according to information from the Commissariat for the Jewish Questions of June 10, 1943, 909 Jews from Sofia were sent to Lom, which brought the total to 1,160 (Справка за броя на евреите, 1943). A few more were added after that. So, at the time of the bombings, there were over a thousand Jews in Lom; there are no official records about how many Jews and Bulgarians were killed by bombs.

Decades later, the air raids issue resurfaced in 2010, when the USA decided to erect a monument in Sofia, honoring the pilots who died while bombing the city. The initiative was met with almost universal outrage. Many expressed the opinion that maintaining war cemeteries of foreign soldiers was acceptable, but a monument to people, who killed thousands of civilians, was immoral. Some asked if Japan would agree to a monument in Hiroshima to the pilots who dropped the atomic bomb. Eventually, the memorial was placed on the territory of the US Embassy in Sofia.

Meanwhile, in 1944, the Bagrianov government was looking for ways to pull Bulgaria out of the war. Several different approaches were tried to connect with individual members of the Allied powers. The situation was deteriorating quickly and the opportunities – slipping away. A hostile speech of Sir Winston Churchill, delivered in the British parliament, worried the Bulgarian politicians. The speech showed his reluctance to engage in negotiations with Bulgaria:

> "Thrice thrown into wars on the wrong side by a miserable set of criminal politicians, who seem to be available for their country's ruin generation after generation [said the British Prime Minister in his speech before the House of Commons], three times in my life has this wretched Bulgaria subjected a peasant population to all the pangs of war and chastisements of defeat. For them also, the moment for repentance has not passed, but it is passing swiftly. The whole of Europe is heading, irresistibly, into new and secure foundations. What would be the place of Bulgaria at the judgment seat, when the petty and cowardly part she has played in this war is revealed, and when the entire Yugoslav and Greek nations, through their representatives, will reveal at the Allies' armistice table the dismal tale of the work the Bulgarian Army has done in their countries as the cruel lackeys of the fallen Nazi power?" (Oren, 1971, p. 241).

Still, Prime Minister Bagrianov sent to Ankara his negotiator Moshanov the day after the speech to try to establish contacts with the British diplomats in Turkey. He also tried to continue with the reforms. The People's Assembly had a session on August 17, where Bagrianov revealed a broad program for "democratic reconstruction". He announced the end of the anti-Jewish persecutions and promised a broad amnesty for political prisoners. "The Prime Minister's declaration was wildly applauded. The very same deputies who in December 1941, applauded Filov when he announced Bulgaria's entry into the war were now happy with Bagrianov for trying to bring an end to the conflict" (Oren, 1971, p. 242).

A new blow came on August 23, when Rumania capitulated. The German Embassy in Bucharest was taken, and the ambassador committed suicide. The new development emboldened the leftist forces united in the Fatherland Front and they demanded a say in the government policies.

The Germans were watching anxiously the events, willing to prepare for the worst. There was a real possibility that Bulgaria may withdraw from the territories it occupied in Macedonia. The German Ambassador to Bulgaria Adolf Beckerle was later, after the occupation, arrested by the Russians and sent to Moscow. In a protocol from an interrogation on March 23, 1945, we learn that the Germans were planning to establish a puppet state in Macedonia under the rule of the Bulgarian-Macedonian revolutionary Ivan Mihailov:

> "Shortly before the departure of the German Embassy from Sofia, due to the imminent invasion of the Red Army, Obermeier introduced me to one of the leaders of the SS, whose name I don't remember. The latter said that he was the leader of an organization created following a personal order from Himmler to maintain close ties with the right-wing nationalist circles. From my talks with that SS leader, I found out that his organization was preparing to declare the independence of Macedonia with the participation of right-wing nationalists. He told me that within days, he would meet the leader of the movement for independence of Macedonia, [Ivan] Mihailov, the organizer of the murder of the Yugoslavian King Alexander in Marseille in 1934. And Mihailov actually arrived on a plane from Zagreb (Croatia), with his wife and other political supporters, and was sent to Skopje by Obermeier. Then, the SS leader told me that he transfers under my control himself and the organization of courageous young Bulgarian nationalists that he created. However, I was not able to use the help of the organization, it was too late. The Red Army invaded Bulgaria" (Тайны дипломатии Третьего рейха, p. 52-53).

The panic over the future of the German interests in Bulgaria prompted an urgent meeting between Ambassador Beckerle, Foreign Minister Ribbentrop, and Adolf Hitler. Beckerle described the events during an interrogation in Moscow on November 2, 1950, when he was asked about his last visit to Hitler's headquarters.

> "Beckerle: On August 23, 1944, I received the news of a coup d'état in Romania and the suicide of the German Ambassador in Bucharest, Manfred von Killinger... The same day Ribbentrop called me, and I flew from Sofia to Berlin and from there, on a special train, I reached Hitler's headquarters in East Prussia... Ribbentrop, as usual, was calm and only his deadly pale face gave up his confusion over the defeat of the German Army on the south of the Eastern Front. He listened absentmindedly to my report about the situation in Bulgaria. He looked like he did not expect good news from me. He made a few small remarks that I had to prevent the disorderly withdrawal of the Germans from Bulgaria to avoid panic among our supporters, and then he just said hopelessly: "Actually, the solution of the Bulgarian question is entirely in the Fuehrer's competence. We all rely on his providence." I figured out that the situation was hopeless..."

Then Beckerle and Ribbentrop went to Hitler's office. They found Hitler sitting at a large table, with a few generals around. Ribbentrop and Beckerle sat aside from them:

> "For about 8-10 minutes, Hitler did not pay any attention to me. He was dictating loudly his orders to [Field Marshal] Keitel and from time to time asked for information the other officers sitting around the table. I was shocked that at the headquarters they were discussing whether to give to certain commanders on the Eastern Front this or that reserve battalion. Later, I found out that without Hitler's permission, no general on the Eastern Front could use any unit from the reserve army. I was troubled by that..."

Then, an air raid alarm sounded, so everybody headed toward the underground bunker. In his bunker's office, Hitler "asked Ribbentrop what he wanted to report. Ribbentrop introduced me and said that Beckerle wanted to report in person the situation in Bulgaria. Here I had the chance to look at Hitler closely. He sat hunched over, his shaking hands on his knees, staring into space past me with motionless gaze. I was just in the beginning of my report, when Hitler interrupted me, saying to his aide-de-camp: "Bring me the letter from the Bulgarian regents. Ambassador Beckerle will take to them my answer."

"From the expression of Ribbentrop, I realized that he heard for the first time about the letter. The aide-de-camp returned with the letter and Hitler asked Ribbentrop to read it out loud. It was signed by the regents Prince Kiril, Filov and Mihov, who assured Hitler of their loyalty, but said that Bulgaria was not able to endure anymore the hardships of the war. The regents requested a permission for Bulgaria to exit the war, which would give them the opportunity to put under control the unruly elements and "heal" Bulgaria.

"As soon as Ribbentrop finished, Hitler dictated his reply to the stenographer. It was filled with the usual for him demagogic statements about the power of the Third Reich, which will fight until the final victory. He warned the regents that they were surrendering themselves and their collaborators to the Russian Bolsheviks.

"The stenographer left, and Hitler turned to me. Raising his unpleasant raspy voice, he ordered me to put pressure on the regents and if that did not help, to organize a coup d'état and install a military dictatorship. He right away ordered Fegelein to send to the Skopje mountain a division of SS troops. Then he signed the letter and gave it to me.

"It was quiet for a couple of minutes. Then, still gazing with a heavy unmovable stare, Hitler started to talk in a monotonous voice. He talked for two hours without interruption. It was a rambling monolog, in which Hitler either complained that his generals hid the truth from him or threatened all dissatisfied with retribution. From time to time, he yelled about the future victory, and suddenly, with a lower voice, said that he had rockets, with which he could destroy the enemy...

"In 2:30 in the morning, Hitler noticed that the people were not listening. He suddenly ended his speech, rose up, and took his hat and gloves, indicating that the meeting was over. Everybody got up. Hitler shook my hand silently, looked me straight in the face and, without saying a word, left the bunker. I left with Ribbentrop, who invited me in his car, and went to his residence. That was my last meeting with Hitler...

"When we reached the castle, Ribbentrop did not invite me in and only said in the car: "So, the most important thing now is to immediately fly back to Sofia. The Fuehrer gave you the instructions."

"...I argued that I did not receive specific instructions. He shot back with an angry voice: "How can you say that? If you can't influence the regents, organize a coup and install Tsankov as the dictator. You can trust him." Then he asked if I had enough military power for the coup. I told him that I did not have anything like that. Ribbentrop advised me to maneuver, build up strength, and most importantly, keep the government under control to avoid what happened in Romania" (Тайны дипломатии Третьего рейха, p. 69-72).

Beckerle returned to Bulgaria and delivered Hitler's letter to the regents on August 28. Since that was the first anniversary of the death of King Boris, the regents were with the Queen at the King's grave in the Rila Monastery. Beckerle travelled all the way to the mountain to meet them. In her memoirs, Queen Ioanna wrote about the meeting and her narrative about the content of the letter differs from that of Beckerle:

> "The Germans had already lost the war. Hitler knew it better than anyone else and on August 28, 1944, I was told that he had sent through Ambassador Beckerle a letter to the regents, in which he accepted the offer of the regents to appoint a government of personalities able to withdraw Bulgaria from the conflict. The letter was brought by Beckerle to the Rila Monastery, because the regents were visiting with me the grave of Boris. Hitler wanted only guarantees for the retreating German troops and preservation of the German interests" (Царица Йоанна, Спомени, p. 133).

Bagrianov's government continued to look for ways to leave the war, so it focused its activities on establishing the neutrality of the country. On August 25, it ordered the disarmament of the German troops in Bulgaria. The Foreign Ministry notified the Soviet Union about the decision. On August 27, the government issued an official statement about its readiness to leave the war and announced that it was negotiating with the countries Bulgaria was at war with. The Allies responded that they were ready for talks, but they had to be moved from Turkey to Cairo, Egypt. Moshanov, the Bulgarian negotiator, requested changes in the government to include people from the oppositions, who would be acceptable to the Allies. He was confident that the new faces would improve the outcome.

On August 29, Moshanov left for Cairo, but Bagrianov did not follow up with the promised appointments. "On August 30, the government's basic assumption that the Soviet Union would respect Bulgaria's neutrality suffered a blow. On that day, the Soviet news agency TASS categorically denied rumors to the effect that the Soviet government had officially recognized Bulgaria's neutrality. Bagrianov attempted to offset the Soviet statement by announcing that the Bulgarian occupation corps was being withdrawn from the occupied territories. This proved of no avail. The regents at last decided to drop Bagrianov, bringing his political career to a close" (Oren, 1971, p. 244).

The regents gave the mandate to the Agrarian Party of Dimiter Gichev, part of the opposition, so politically, this was a step to the left. The second party that agreed to participate was the Democratic Party, but all other forces that were approached, communists, Social-Democrats, and leftist Agrarians refused to take part. They were willing to be a part only of a government of the Fatherland Front. The cabinet was formed on September 2, with Konstantin Muraviev as the Prime Minister.

Pressed for time, it approached again the Soviet Government and expressed its determination to keep strict neutrality in the war. Muraviev tried to expel the German troops from Bulgaria and threatened to break the diplomatic relations with Germany is case of resistance. Bulgaria left the Tri-Partite Pact and continued the withdrawal of the army from Macedonia.

On September 7, new reforms were announced – the government decided to dissolve the 25th People's Assembly. It also issued a Decree-Law for Amnesty. All convicted under the following several laws were covered by the amnesty: Law for Defense of the State, Law for Defense of the Nation, Law for the One-Time Tax on Jewish Properties, Law for Dissolving the Political Organizations, Decree Regarding the Press, Law for Temporary Control of the Press (Шарланов, 2009, p. 188).

Despite the changes, the USSR was not satisfied, they wanted from Bulgaria to join the war on the side of the Allies. Molotov summoned the Bulgarian Ambassador in Moscow and handed him a note that the Soviet Government had tolerated the Bulgarian militarist behavior for three years, but it had decided to declare war on Bulgaria.

The news reached Muraviev during a meeting of the government. It was a total surprise; the ministers debated the situation until the early morning and sent a delegation to the Soviet diplomatic representative in Sofia. They told him that Bulgaria had broken up with Germany and wanted immediate peace. On September 6, the government made two important decisions: it prohibited any resistance against the invading Soviet Army and declared war on Germany.

However, the decisions were not announced immediately.

General Marinov, the Minister of War, wanted the Bulgarian Army to get prepared for military action. The Bulgarian occupation corps in Macedonia was outnumbered by the Germans and any clash could end badly for the Bulgarians. The same day, the government, after prolonged pressure, managed to convince Prof. Filov to resign as a regent.

The official announcement of the war with Germany came on September 8, when the Soviet Army had already invaded the north-east part of the country. For a few days, Bulgaria found itself in the unusual situation of being at war with the major world powers – Germany, the Soviet Union, USA and Great Britain.

The leftist forces, which so far refused to take part in any government, were encouraged by the Russian invasion and took immediate steps to overthrow the government. Under normal circumstances, they would not have been able to do so, because the armed communist resistance was quite small and poorly armed, but in the conditions of government disarray and Russian presence, they proceeded successfully with their coup d'état. "The blow came in the early hours of September 9. The main effort was directed against the Ministry of War, where much of the government was concentrated. The building was taken at 2:15 A.M. without a shot. This action was made possible by a group of junior officers led by Captain Petur Iliev (later General) who, as employees of the ministry, were able to unlock the back doors from the inside. Vranchev, who concluded the agreement with the police chiefs, led a unit into the ministry. The Minister of War [General Marinov], placing himself openly at the disposal of the Fatherland Front, telephoned the Sofia garrison to secure its cooperation... The Regency Council was dismissed, and its members arrested. Three new regents were appointed: Venelin Ganev, a distinguished law professor; Tsvetko Boboshevski, an affiliate of Zveno; and Todor Pavlov, the well-known Communist theoretician" (Oren, 1971, p.252).

In the morning of September 9, 1944, Bulgaria learned that it had a new government of the Fatherland Front, with Prime Minister Colonel Kimon Georgiev. Kimon, Bulgaria's most distinguished "coup specialist", successfully managed another violent power takeover. Later, in the communist mythology, the coup became known as the "Socialist Revolution of September 9".

It is important to give credit to the governments of Bozhilov, Bagrianov and Muraviev for ensuring the smooth peaceful transition in the months before the occupation. Elsewhere, this transition turned into a bloodbath, with Germans and Allies fighting on the territories of several countries. Had Beckerle been successful in taking control of Bulgaria with the puppet dictatorship of Prof. Tsankov, as Hitler demanded, Bulgaria would have been turned into a war theater with numerous fatalities. In such a situation, a grim fate would have expected the Bulgarian Jews.

However, the peace ended on September 9. The communists, Bulgaria's new masters, did not have full control, but were already supported by the Soviet Union, so they unleashed a horrible campaign of terror against their own people. Nothing like that was seen in the newer history of Bulgaria, even under the "fascist" government of Prof. Alexander Tsankov in 1923. Even after the mass riots that followed his coup against Prime Minister Stamboliyski, parliamentary elections were held on November 18, 1923, and the communist party won 8 seats, the Agrarian Union – 30, both were able to form parliamentary groups (Шарланов, 2009, p. 59). In contrast, within a few short years after 1944, the communists managed to destroy completely their opposition.

That difficult time in the Bulgarian history, which eventually brought the exodus of about 90% of the Bulgarian Jews, will be covered in the next chapter.

Here, I just want to provide a few numbers to emphasize the magnitude of this disaster. "From September 9, 1944 to November 1989 [the fall of communism], in Bulgaria have been exterminated by the communists 31,000 people from the social and cultural elites of the nation. And just in the days from September 9 to October 20, 1944, 40 days, 26,850 have been killed. In those days, Bulgaria turned into a "valley of tears" ...Bulgarian communists, after taking power, organized a brutal purge unmatched to anything that happened in the other Balkan countries. While for the time from June 1923 to September 1944, 21 years, 3,246 people perished in political clashes, i.e. 9 times less" (Шарланов, 2009, p. 9-10).

The previous political class, which was formed on the basis of education, business and other abilities, was practically exterminated and replaced with people of low education but with "working class consciousness" and "unshakeable faith in the bright communist future". "The people who imposed the Soviet model in Bulgaria lacked national dignity, intelligence and spirituality. At the 5th Congress of the BCP in December 1948, it was revealed that the Party had 464,000 members, 52% of whom had rudimentary education (7% illiterate, 45% with Grade 4)" (Шарланов, 2009, p. 35).

Queen Ioanna got acquainted quickly with the new masters of the country:

> "The old regency was replaced by a new one, a sign that for the time being, the Fatherland Front Government intended to keep the monarchy in Bulgaria. The regency included two representatives of the left-wing parties and one from the communist party: Venelin Ganev, professor of commercial law at Sofia University, Tsviatko Boboshevski, former minister from the People's Party, and Todor Pavlov, publicist and Marxist writer.
>
> "The three new regents arrived in Tsarska Bistritsa, where [King] Simeon resided, each in a "personal" car, confiscated from the 11 vehicles, which comprised the whole car park of the old government. Three more vehicles followed them, packed with men and women with red handkerchiefs, armed to the teeth. It was September 14, the name-day of Simeon. They looked pretentious and confused. I hoped to get news about [Prince] Kiril and the other two regents, who disappeared, so I invited them for a breakfast. All three knew nothing. At the table, Prof. Pavlov told me: "Don't be afraid. I have been pardoned three times by King Boris. If it weren't for him, I would not be sitting here." Pavlov and Ganev were true intellectuals. Still, I realized that everybody in Sofia, including the cabinet ministers, lived paralyzed with horror... The communist government maintained some formalities but was trying slowly to isolate me and my children. All friends and people dear to me had disappeared in jails or were killed in the purges. I couldn't even ask for my brother-in-law without causing suspicion" (Царица Йоанна, Спомени, p. 135).

The people on the opposite end of the social ladder also felt uneasy about the drastic changes. I quoted in a previous chapter the memoirs of Samuel Arditti, which covered the ordeal of his family in Sofia and Russe during the persecutions of the Jews. When the family was living in a village in the Russe area, there were no hateful intellectuals, clerks of the Commissariat for the Jewish Questions, Ratniks or Legionnaires.

> "After we arrived, we visited the mayor. He said: "Welcome to our village, here I am the king and my order is that you remove your yellow stars. I will not restrict you in any way. I will be happy, if you become friends with the local people and feel like ordinary citizens." There were three other Jewish

families in the village. The villagers treated us with warmth and friendship and helped us any chance they had. After September 9, 1944, we learned that the mayor was sent to prison. From a practical point of view, the Bulgarian Communist Party was not able to save the Jews. The Bulgarian Jews were saved as a result of the quarrels among the top echelons of the fascist administration. The prosecutors of the People's Tribunal noticed that fact. The Bulgarian "fascists", who saved the Jews, were punished most severely. Today everybody sings odes to Dimitur Peshev, but at that time, he was sentenced to fifteen years in prison. Even after he was released, he didn't get back his house and he was not allowed to practice law. Let's remember that Peshev was the person who defeated Hitler and preserved the honor of Bulgaria for the future. Twenty of the 42 members of the parliament, who signed his petition, were executed. Even Prime Minister Ivan Bagrianov, who cancelled the Law for Defense of the Nation, was executed. Lilyana Panitsa, who revealed Belev's secrets to the Jewish leaders, was sentenced to a year in prison. Even the people's leader, defender of the Jews, Nikola Mushanov, was sent to prison. On the other hand, the real anti-Semites received very lenient sentences" (Ардити, спомени).

The "revolution" of September 9, 1944, did not improve significantly the lives of the Jews in Bulgaria. Even though the restrictions were lifted, they remained poor and the new communist rules against private initiative liquidated many of the trades that the Jews were involved in. Only the relatively small number of Jews, who took part in the Bulgarian communist movement, could embark on a "career path" in the communist bureaucracy, which was closed to the rest. Besides, the communists started to introduce their own Jewish restrictions and "Zionist" gradually became a dirty word. Although the increase of the emigration to Mandate Palestine increased after 1944, after the restoration of the Jewish state in 1948 it turned into a real flood.

16 COMMUNIST TERROR AND JEWISH EXODUS

The Soviet occupation brought a new kind of totalitarian oppression. Before that, Germany imposed on Bulgaria totalitarianism based on racial superiority, which, though not supported by the population, was accepted by a small group of politicians who managed to introduce laws and take actions that were foreign to the traditions and nature of the Bulgarian people. Among them were the anti-Jewish laws and the secretly provided help for the deportation of the Jews from Thrace and Macedonia, organized by the Germans, which many politicians and historians with agenda want to present as an expression of an inherently evil streak of the Bulgarian people.

The new totalitarianism was based on class and was as brutal to the people that belonged to the wrong class, as the first one to members of the wrong race. The war on the private initiative and success changed profoundly the Bulgarian society. You may find many flaws in the industrialists and capitalists in general, but they helped the society to develop. When they were replaced with the semi-literate communist bureaucrats, things turned out much worse. The social transition was imposed with unseen cruelty. Just like in the case of the German influence, the new terror, inspired by Russians, was implemented by Bulgarians who benefited from the collaboration. Since the October Revolution in Russia, Jews are often accused of playing a major role in communist dictatorship. It is hard to accept it as a fact, because even there, most of the Jews suffered under the communist dictatorship. Such an anti-Semitic accusation, although maintained by some, is even less credible in Bulgaria, where the Jewish participation in the communist resistance was very small and the Jews were much more interested in the Zionist movement, which dominated their community in Bulgaria.

The Nazi control in Bulgaria shattered the traditional life of the Bulgarian Jews, although their community managed to survive in its entirety. The Soviet occupation and the forcing of the new communist order managed to destroy completely their traditional life. They understood that there was no place for them in the new egalitarian society. Through a favorable combination of events, the majority of the Jews managed to leave the country from 1945-1952.

"Bolshevization" was the dark vision of King Boris for the future of his country, a vision, which he tried to avoid at any cost. But after his death, the nightmare materialized in 1944. The new rulers, in Sofia and in the provincial towns, were not restrained by any moral principles and neither were their protectors from the Soviet Army. The looting and killing started immediately after the communist takeover. Officially, the Fatherland Front and its government were a broad coalition of "progressive forces", but the communists controlled the army and the police, now called "People's Militia".

The demands of the Russian occupiers and their atrocities urged the Bulgarian communists' leader Georgi Dimitrov, who still lived in Moscow, to send a letter to Stalin and Molotov on September 22, 1944. He begged the dictator to let the new Bulgarian authorities fulfil their obligations in the occupied by the Red Army regions. He complained of the violence of Soviet military personnel against Bulgarian civilians. For example, they arbitrarily confiscated from the locals working animals, buggies, food and other items without notifying the local authorities or providing any authorization. They also confiscated state and private motor vehicles and machine oil, which would make impossible to collect the fall harvest. Some drunk soldiers broke at night into private homes and robbed them and in some cases raped women and killed the men. In the village of Divdiadovo, Shumen region, among others, was killed the oldest member of the communist party (Шарланов, 2009, p. 229-230).

It is not clear whether Stalin responded, but the government-sanctioned looting continued. In another document outlining the demands of the Soviet Army, dated October 21, 1944, the Bulgarian authorities stated that they could not provide the demanded amounts of 17 out of 21 types of supplies. That included flour, dried bread, rice, macaroni, potatoes and other legumes, and sugar, and they could provide only 55% of the requested cheese. As of meat, the document noted that the asked for 15,000 tons could not be provided, because the urban population received 0.5 kg of meat per week, the peasants – 0.4 kg, and the soldiers – 0.45 kg, and still the government was short 45,204 tons of meat. However, the Soviet military kept pushing and the Bulgarian government had to cut the rations, which affected mostly the urban population. The government still promised to deliver 5 million litres of wine the Russians asked for, if their army provided the necessary containers (Шарланов, 2009, p. 232).

Bulgaria's fate was sealed – the Allies agreed to leave the country in the Soviet region of interest. On October 8, 1944, Sir Winston Churchill and his Foreign Minister Sir Anthony Eden, visited Moscow. They discussed with Stalin and Molotov, among other things, the division of the Balkans into spheres of interest. Churchill offered 75% Soviet influence in Bulgaria and 25% of the other Allies, Stalin demanded 90%. As we will see soon, the final result was 100% Russian communist control.

It is not clear how many people had been killed by the Russian military. Probably much fewer than in Germany and Poland, where the Russian atrocities are memorable, but it should be remembered that there was no fighting in Bulgaria and its citizens did not resist the Russians. However, at certain point, the Bulgarian government started to pay compensations to the victims' families. According to a list found in the Bulgarian Ministry of Foreign Affairs by Dinyu Sharlanov, by September 1946, the "Allied troops", meaning Soviet soldiers and officers (the only allied army in the country), had killed 123 Bulgarian children, women and men. The number is probably much higher, according to additional sources. The break up of the victims is: killed by Soviet motor vehicles, killed during military drills, raped and killed women, mostly young, and people shot under various circumstances. Here are a few examples of victims. Ivanka Bakalova of Topolcha village was killed by a Soviet soldier who broke into her home in February 1946; the same happened to Sultana Krasteva from Burgas died in April 1945 and Atche Mehmedova from Vetren, Provadia region, in July 1946. Lilyana Mihailova from Sofia was killed with a knife by a Soviet soldier in 1946. Kuna Stoikova was shot in November 1946 in Metlichina, Provadia region; Avaneya Mesronova from Varna was shot by a Soviet officer in May 1946. A Soviet officer shot on the street in broad daylight Alexander Alexiev in 1946, and so on. Most of the killed women were between 18 and 23 years old.

The families of the killed received compensations from 20 to 40 thousand leva, modest sums in the conditions of high inflation.

The total number of the victims of the Soviet Army is unknown, it was either not recorded or the documents were destroyed (Шарланов, 2009, p. 244-245).

The Bulgarian terror was not unlike the Red Terror unleashed by Lenin and his fellow communists in the years after the revolution. It was a time of revenge, when the former partisans and members of communist terrorist groups wanted to crush any opposition. The memoirs of the early chiefs of the People's Militia carefully avoided this topic (the future communist dictator Todor Zhivkov was one of them). More information began to emerge after the fall of communism. According to a testimony of R. Hristozov, who worked at the militia headquarters in 1944, killings happened regularly. He mentioned how a large group of former police officers were brought to the building and when the next day the higher ranks wanted to interrogate them, it turned out that one of the lower officers took out the policemen the previous night and shot them. According to another employee, before the start of the People's Tribunal in December 1944, two teams of executioners, led by Mircho Spasov and Lev Glavinchev, loaded on trucks every night functionaries and supporters of the old governments to be shot. The Soviet representative in the Allied Commission complained to the Minister of the Interior Anton Yugov that the measures were excessive. Yugov summoned Spasov and Glavinchev for an explanation. They said, "Guilty as charged, but let us kill a few more this night and we will stop tomorrow" (Шарланов, 2009, p. 263-264).

Even people with enormous contributions to Bulgaria were not spared. The national heroine Grandma Tonka Obretenova from Russe and her whole family played a very important role in the fight against the Ottoman yoke in 1860-1870s. Her granddaughter Tonka's husband Niko Prosenichkov was a high school principal in Russe. He was arrested in November 1944, because he was considered "fascist" for writing articles in support of the national unification. During the arrest, his wife reminded the militiamen that she was from Grandma Tonka's family. Because of her "arrogance", she was taken with her husband and both were shot outside of Russe on November 3, 1944. Later, their daughter Lilyana recalled that after her parents did not return, the rest of the family started to look for them. With some connections, they were shown a house where arrested "enemies of the people" were kept. The guards told them Tonka and Niko were in the house, but they could not see them. However, they needed some things, so the family started to bring food, clothes, and cigarettes, feeling happy that they helped their parents. The charade continued for three months. Eventually, the heirs of Grandma Tonka were evicted from their house to provide accommodation to Soviet officers, who also looted their belongings. The younger daughter of Tonka and Niko Prosenichkov, Milkana, became insane and soon died. The other daughter, Lilyana, spent years in a communist concentration camp (Шарланов, 2009, p. 267-268).

This was a time of violent transition and concentration of power in the hands of the communist party. The repressive apparatus, later known as Committee for State Security (the Bulgarian equivalent of NKVD or KGB) was accountable only to the Central Committee of the Bulgarian Communist Party and its Politburo. There was an order in the murderous chaos – on December 17, 1944, the CC of the BCP authorized State Security to arrest at its discretion any person suspected of "pro-fascist" or "reactionary" views, regardless of status or party affiliation. Over 28,000 people were arrested – the regents, cabinet ministers, members of the parliament, judges, clerics, journalists and others. 12,122 of them were handed to the People's Tribunal (Шарланов, 2009, p. 272).

Dinyu Sharlanov states that no official diplomatic protests were made by representatives of the Allied Commission over the mass killings, although they were aware of the atrocities. At an official dinner at the British Embassy in Sofia in 1944, in the presence of one of the new regents, the ambassador said that if Bulgaria continues the violent Bolshevization, the government would need to be changed. In a report in the New York Times of January 16, 1945, it was mentioned that everything was done by the Bulgarian communist politicians with the silent support of the Russian occupational army, which did not interfere directly in the Bulgarian affairs (Шарланов, 2009, p. 289-290).

In those times of looting and universal misery, the fate of the Bulgarian Jews was not on the radar of the new authorities. While during the war the communists exploited the Jewish misfortune by urging the Jews to join their struggle against the government, once they gained power, the communists adopted the Stalinist policies of suspicion toward Jews. Apart from the relatively small number of privileged communists, the rest of the Jewish population continued to live in poverty after returning from the forced evacuation.

The reality contradicted the rosy picture painted by the party functionaries and the "official communist Jews" of Bulgaria. In the end of 1944, the American journalist Joseph Levy visited several quarters in Sofia, where many Jews lived. He reported in the Bulletin of the American Embassy in Moscow for January 17, 1945 that the Jews were starving, without clothes or shoes. He considered a farce the statement of the Fatherland Front government that the Bulgarian Jews had equal rights. The government promised to return the confiscated Jewish homes, factories, etc., but failed to do it. He also noted the suspicions of the communist party about the Bulgarian Zionists, they were considered agents of London (Шарланов, 2009, p. 145). As we will see later, the hostility between Jewish communists and Zionists will only deepen with the strengthening of the communist government.

The sad situation of the Jews was also observed by David Ben-Gurion during his visit to Bulgaria in October 1944:

> "The one incident that, he claimed, moved and shocked him more than anything else was his visit to the Jewish poor of Sofia. There he met Jews who had been destitute even before the war and who were left, after their expulsion to the countryside, completely bereft. Nor had they been able to recover what had been theirs when they returned to Sofia. They were given shelter in public buildings no longer in use, many people packed into each room, with no furniture, no heat, and not even the minimal sanitary facilities. Among the inmates were many children, barefoot and practically naked, despite the December temperatures" (Ofer, 1990, p. 310).

The dire situation was confirmed by the surveys conducted by the Jewish Fatherland Front in the end of 1944. The unemployment among the Jewish craftsmen and merchants in Sofia was 90.4% and 90% respectively, and in the province – 70.8% and 80%. Of the stores and workshops of the 1,320 surveyed, 343 were sold voluntarily, and 704 taken under pressure. About 33% of the new owners were not merchants or craftsmen. By the end of 1945, in the whole country, 7,520 houses and buildings were returned. In Sofia, 443 apartments were returned, valued at 17,460,664 leva... Out of the confiscated 3,400 radios, 1,200 were returned, for the rest, the government demanded a payment, though at lower prices (Василева, 1992, p. 22-23).

The neglect of the Jewish issues did not stop the communist authorities from profiting from the Jewish exodus a few years later. In 1956, Stefan Bogdanov, chief of the counterintelligence section of State Security, testified at the commission for investigation of the excesses in the time of Stalinism: "Among other things, we let the Jews emigrate and made a lot of money, regardless of political considerations, because the Jews had a fund in US dollars, and we demanded for each émigré, leaving the country, a certain amount of dollars for leaving the country. This was the condition to let them go" (Шарланов, 2009, p.145).

Bogdanov's statement is confirmed in a protocol of a meeting at the Ministry of the Interior, on May 18, 1949, discussing the money collected from Jews with transit visas or emigrating from Bulgaria to Israel. Stefan Bogdanov was one of the participants. 14,565 Jews from Rumania with transit visas entered Bulgaria and were charged $20 each, with 451 children, at $10 each, total – $295,810. The emigrants from Bulgaria leaving through the Consistory were 28,095, charged $30 each, with a total of $842,850, and so on. The amount collected for 1947, 1948, and 1949, was $1,615,995 (State Security, 2012, p. 253).

The next step in legitimizing the new authorities was the establishment of special courts to prosecute the "enemies of the people". The indiscriminate mass murder did little to raise the moral standing of the new rulers. The People's Tribunal (Naroden Sud in Bulgarian) had to deal with the enemies in a "lawful" manner. It is often lauded as the first court, organized while the war was still raging on, to put on trial fascists and anti-Semites, so it was a predecessor of the Nuremberg Trials and the Tokyo Tribunal. While some of the legal statutes of the latter are still questioned, the People's Tribunal in Bulgaria totally contradicted the Constitution and the common decency, because it was a tool of revenge with little respect for justice.

Nikola Dolapchiev was a prominent Bulgarian jurist in the field of criminal law. At the People's Tribunal, he served as a defender of Prince Kiril, regent and King Boris's brother. Later, he was sent as a diplomat to London, were he defected. In 1952, he held a lecture on the history of law in communist Bulgaria at Chatham House, England, published in the journal "International Affairs" in 1953.

Dolapchiev pointed out that after the mass terror, which followed the coup of September 9, 1944, the communists needed to consolidate their power by destroying all political forces outside of the mass organization they controlled, the Fatherland Front. Thus, they organized the so-called People's Tribunal, which was a violation of some basic judicial principles. The decree that established it, charged the accused retroactively for acts that were not crimes when they took place. That was also an exceptional court, and as such, prohibited by the Constitution of Bulgaria, which allowed only regular courts. The chosen judges and members were selected from people, who lacked impartiality and were even hostile toward the defendants. They were also under pressure from mass rallies and media propaganda to deliver harsh sentences. [Only after the communist archives were opened in 1990s, it became clear that most sentences were determined at meetings of the Politburo of the Bulgarian Communist Party. – M.M.]

There was no genuine defense, the counsels didn't have the right to present proper evidence. "The main defendants, the former Regents and the leading Ministers, were detained in Moscow and were presented to the court nearly a month after the trial began. Thus, the principle that judicial proceedings should take place only in the presence of the defendant, was bluntly set aside." The lawyers were threatened that by defending "enemies of the people", they became complicit in their crimes. They were not able to speak privately to their clients. Some of them were appointed in the last minute by the court to create the illusion that the judicial process was followed. Many people saw this as a horrific preview of what was to come under the influence of the Soviet Union (Dolapchiev, 1953, p. 59-68).

Another "innovation" of the People's Tribunal was that dead people were put on trial. Thousands were killed by the People's Militia without investigation and trial, but they were still prosecuted, because the government wanted to confiscate their belongings and evict the surviving family members from their houses. Even one of the saviors of the Bulgarian Jews, Dimitur Peshev, received 15 years and many of his colleagues, who signed the letter against the deportation, received death sentences.

Dinyu Sharlanov, in his book "History of the Communism in Bulgaria" (Volume 1), provides documents that the sentences had been determined in advance by Politburo of the BCP. On December 19, 1944, a day before the start of the trials, the member of Politburo Traicho Kostov informed Georgi Dimitrov in Moscow with a telegram that Politburo has already formed an opinion about the sentences: "The People's Tribunal starts tomorrow. Todor Pavlov proposed death sentences for all ministers of the cabinets of Filov and Bozhilov, Bagrianov and company should get life in prison, and some of Muraviev's ministers could even be acquitted. We haven't made our final decision, but we would like to be harsh. What do you think?"

Dimitrov did not reply immediately, so Traicho Kostov sent a reminder that since the trials were about to begin, the judges had to receive instructions from the BCP. Dimitrov replied on December 22, 1944: "I think that nobody should be acquitted. All of them are responsible and must be punished. Of course, the level of punishment must depend on the degree of responsibility. For example, the ministers from the first two cabinets [of Bogdan Filov. – M.M.] and the third cabinet [of Dobri Bozhilov. – M.M.], who are directly responsible for murderous actions, should be sentenced to death. The rest of them from the third [of Ivan Bagrianov. – M.M.] and the fourth [of Konstantin Muraviev. – M.M.] cabinets must receive life in prison or 15 years. All this should be agreed with the most important political partners [of the Fatherland Front] and justified in the sentences" (Шарланов, 2009, p. 298). However, the communists failed to consult their "partners" and only two years later, destroyed them through another fake trial.

The tribunal was divided into several sections that tried different crimes. For example, Section One tried the regents and the cabinet ministers. Important for the topic of this book is Section Seven, which dealt with the anti-Semitic crimes. Later, it received attention as the first court that analyzed the reasons and consequences of the Holocaust, even before the end of World War II. However, the main goal of the People's Tribunal was to liquidate the potential opposition to the new communist order, so the anti-Semitic crimes were not investigated thoroughly. Very little attention was paid to the actions of some of the accused who helped Jews, and, at the same time, officials involved in serious crimes were not even charged (like most of the officers that took part in the arrests of the Jews in Thrace and Macedonia).

The People's Tribunal's prosecutors, during the trial against the Commissariat for the Jewish Questions, attempted to blame King Boris III for all crimes against the Jews, claiming that his support for them was just a legend. As Benjamin Arditti noted in his book, the prosecutors found many documents and testimonies against the Commissariat's staff, many of them published in Nathan Grinberg's book "Documents" (see Гринберг, 1945), but could not present a single document to prove any wrongdoing by the King, even though they claimed they had such evidence (Ардити, 1952, p. 9-10).

Most of the top employees of the Commissariat for the Jewish Questions stood trial, including Lilyana Panitsa, who, as we already know, informed the Jewish leadership about the secret plan for deportation. Her trial was an example of the farcical character of the accusations against many people. Despite her substantial help to the Jews, she still was put on trial. Her lawyer Simeonov was puzzled that the prosecution did not present any specific accusation, neither did it provide any specific information about deeds punishable by the People's Tribunal. Disturbed by the lack of evidence, the prosecutor tried to use her membership in the organization Ratnik, which was not a crime in Bulgaria. Further, the prosecutor tried to use her position of secretary at the Commissariat, which kept her informed about everything that was going on. However, continued Simeonov, working at the institution, without any proof that she was prosecuting Jews, is not a valid accusation. Her real views and behavior were pointed out in the testimonies of Buko Levi and Dr. Benaroya. She came from a progressive democratic family and that background guided her activities. That would be enough to acquit her (People's Court Session No.20, 1945, p. 2175-2176). Despite that, it was too late, after the torture she endured at the People's Militia, Miss Panitsa died about a year after the trial.

Commissar Alexander Belev was tried in absentia, the court either did not know or hid the fact that he was killed by partisans in September 1944, after they caught him trying to leave the country. Belev and the police chief of Dupnitsa, known for his harsh treatment of Jews, were sentenced to death. According to Nir Baruh, four of the accused received life sentences, but three of them were missing. Two received 15 years, one of them was Belev's deputy Yaroslav Kalitsin, and his sentence was the same as that of Dimitur Peshev, the savior of Jews. The rest of the sentences were: 3 people got 5 years; 4 people – 3 years; 1 person – 1 year; 37 people – even lesser punishment. Two of the accused were acquitted and for nine, the prosecutors did not even file charges, so they were freed before the trial.

The light sentences caused an outcry, so the court revised them and announced its final verdict on April 3, 1945. There were no changes in the death, life in prison and 15-year sentences. Of the rest, one person got 8 years, another one – 6 years, six received 5 years, another six – 2 years, three people – 1 year, and eight received suspended sentences of 1 year. Out of 64 accused, 40 were acquitted. The sentences were much lighter than those of the top politicians (Барух, 1991, p.120-122).

The farce becomes even worse when we consider the fact that it had a special section that was supposed to punish journalists, editors and publishers of media (newspapers, magazines and radio). That was the Sixth Section, which, in the early 1945, dealt with the intellectuals who had already spent several months in custody. On November 4, 1944, the future communist dictator of Bulgaria Georgi Dimitrov sent to the new government special instructions regarding censorship: "Disturbing news and cartoons are published in the press... The government should issue a decree determining what newspapers must be published, with the explanation that it is necessary for rational use of the available print paper for the benefit of people's causes. Under the guise of military censorship, it is necessary to apply strict political censorship that would not allow anything that could harm the work of the Fatherland Front..."

Some of the accused, like Raiko Alexiev, had already been killed before the trial by the militia and communist terrorists, but were sued anyway to confiscate their properties. Among the accused were five prominent cartoonists – along with the killed Alexiev, the other four were Alexander Bozhinov, Alexander Dobrinov, Konstantin Kutsev and An. Andreev.

The accusations included blackmail and mockery of Soviet Russia and its government, especially Stalin, in their cartoons, published in newspapers and books. One of them likened Soviet Russia to a "giant prison, where few get in and even fewer can get out". Other artists, afraid for their safety, testified against the accused with the common opinion that they lacked artistic talent and used the help of the "fascist press" to get ahead. That was a blatant lie, because those cartoonists had a firmly established presence in the Bulgarian art. Only a few of the witnesses supported them. The court decided to teach the artists a lesson and show what the limits will be under the new social order. Like the most accused intellectuals, the cartoonists were found guilty and spent years in prison (Златева, p. 277-293).

In addition to that state-sanctioned court lawlessness, we can find in the memoirs of Queen Ioanna haunting images of the extermination of Bulgarian journalists, editors and writers:

> "It is difficult to make a full list of the condemned to death in the trial of "bloody Thursday" [the day of the People's Tribunal executions. – M.M.]. After what I said about the executions, I must add that after the trial of the regents, ministers, diplomats and members of the parliament, came a large trial of journalists. The only accusation was that they "supported with their written materials the governments that brought Bulgaria to a catastrophe". I want to remind you:

Danail Krapchev, the publisher of [newspaper] "Zora" [Dawn, Bulgaria's largest newspaper], a national liberal, was sentenced to death and found strangled with his socks in his cell. All editors of "Zora" were sentenced to death and shot, including the sports editor, shot in the street. The latter travelled on a streetcar, which was stopped by a red patrol for ID inspection. After the poor man showed them an ID from "Zora", they dragged him out and shot him on the spot. The administrator of the paper Nikolaev, its literary critic [Iordan] Badev and even a proof-reader, were also killed. Also prosecuted and killed were Raiko Alexiev, the director of the satirical paper "Shturets" [Cricket], Boris Rumenov, writer for the humor section; Damianov, the director of two Sofia dailies, "Dnevnik" [Diary] and "Utro" [Morning]; the journalist from the opposition Kozharov, director of "Slovo" [Word], and Anton Nikolov. In the provincial towns, the purge was even worse. There were seven dailies in Sofia, all of them more or less anti-communist. In the province, they shot in Plovdiv the director of "Yug" [South] Govedarov; in Varna, Luka Konstantinov, director of "Varnenska Poshta" [Varna Mail] was also killed, and so on... After the killings of the politicians, the communists tried to win the support of scientists, intellectuals, actors, writers, etc. Elin Pelin, a personal friend of King Boris, was celebrated as a "people's writer"." (Царица Йоанна, Спомени, p. 147-148).

The surviving artists were scrutinized. A curious example of restriction of the individual rights under the new totalitarianism was the case of David Peretz, the Jewish artist, highly praised by Andrei Nikolov in B. Piti's survey (quoted in Chapter 8). On May 19, 1945, Peretz applied to the Director of the People's Militia to be granted the right to paint freely within the borders of Bulgaria, including the Black Sea coast. On May 21, 1945, the management of the Artists' Union vouched that he had not been a fascist. After a thorough investigation of his past and his current financial situation, on May 28, 1945, he received the permit:

> "The Directorate of the People's Militia, section State Security, allows David Avram Peretz, an artist from Sofia, to paint landscapes and people in the whole country and on the Black Sea coast, if the drawings do not depict objects of interest to the foreign intelligence services. He has the obligation, upon visiting a place to paint, to report to the local militia authorities with this permit, so that they can observe his work. The permit is valid until the end of 1946" (State Secirity, 2012, p. 67-68).

The People's Tribunal affected the whole country, court sessions were held in most towns and even villages. Thousands of people were dragged to courts, often on false charges, and sentenced. On July 3, 1945, the Chief People's Prosecutor Georgi Petrov sent to the CC of the BCP a detailed information report about the results by regions and towns. In the end, he provided a recapitulation of all sentences. A total of 10,919 people had been charged and 2,618 sentenced to death, with 1,046 executions carried out. The difference means that 1,572 people had been already killed, and they were tried for confiscation of their property. Life in prison received 1,226 people; 20 years – 28; 15 years – 946; 12 years – 41; 10 years – 627; 8 years – 134; 7 years – 134; 6 years and 6 months – 1; 6 years – 48; 5 years – 1,006; 4 years – 7; 3 years – 332; 1 year – 724; 8 months – 4; 6 months – 5; 1 year suspended – 652. Only 1,485 people were acquitted; the proceedings against 104 were stopped; 202 died during the trials; 1 person was sent to the front [the Bulgarian government sent troops to fight Germany. – M.M.] (Мешкова, Шарланов, 1994, p.190-191).

The tribunal also targeted the Bulgarian Royal Family. King Boris's brother, Prince Kiril, was tried by Section One of the People's Tribunal. He was sentenced to death and executed on February 3, 1945. Their sister, Princess Evdokia, was arrested and investigated. The communists were looking for proof to incriminate her for "fascist" activities. They couldn't find anything – she was known for her anti-German convictions and supported Great Britain. Eventually, she was released.

Queen Ioanna recalls how on the day after the execution of her brother-in-law, the communist regents showed up in the palace (against her wishes) to express their "condolences". After listening to them, she told them that she could not accept what was happening and she wanted to leave the country. Then she wrote: "If they had found any proof to fabricate a trial against me, they would have been happy. That is why the secret police was searching my trunks with such fervor" (Царица Йоанна, Спомени, p. 144-145).

Her request was rejected, the communists still wanted to maintain the illusion that Bulgaria was ruled by law. Later, she heard that the US General Robertson warned the Bulgarian Government and the Soviet authorities that, if she and her children "disappear" in Russia, there will be repercussions. The Queen, and her children King Simeon II and Princess Maria

Louisa were allowed to leave only after the illegal referendum, held on September 8, 1946, abolished the monarchy. Very few bulletins for keeping the monarchy were distributed, and in some places, there were none. Even then, there were problems: "About a month before leaving, a commissar from the [Bulgarian] political police came to see me, and it seemed he had the assignment to convince me to use an airplane. He emphasized the convenience, speed, etc. I knew very well the danger of choosing an airplane, which could be no other but Soviet. We could easily end up on the territory of the USSR, pushed into a dark future. So, we were able to leave, because the people would not have accepted our destruction. And it wasn't just that – in Sofia, there were many offices of the Allies, who were watching" (Царица Йоанна, Спомени, p. 149-150). The Royal Family left on a boat that took them to Alexandria, Egypt.

The People's Tribunal was not the last word of the communist repressive order. Under the guidance of the Soviet Government, Bulgaria adopted its forced labor camps. Unlike the camps in the times of King Boris, the new ones were designed to break people's will through harsh treatment, heavy labor and brainwashing. The largest camp was on the Danube island of Belene. The number of the inmates in 1957 was 782, increasing by April 1959 to 1,896, with 254 women. Many were kept there for political reasons, without sentences, but there were also criminal inmates, mostly accused of "hooliganism". Many people died of poor nutrition and regular beating. The corpses were placed in bags and buried in hidden locations (Шарланов, 2009, p. 391-392).

It is not clear how many non-communist Jews had perished in the murderous purges, because, just like in the cases of ordinary Bulgarians, no records were kept. In his book "The Ransom", Nir Baruh mentions a few cases of prosecutions of Jews during the early years of communist terror.

In those years, the suffering Jews in Sofia were receiving help from other countries, especially from the USA. The Joint was sending medications, food, clothes and other items. At the same time, representatives of the Soviet secret services scoured the country for "enemies of the people", often fabricating evidence; two colonels, Filatov and Chernyaev, were in charge. It was done according to Stalin's plans for repressions against Jews in leading positions (though in Bulgaria no Jews were in key party of government positions).

Since 1948, the Joint was represented in Bulgaria by the Levy family from the USA. They had good relations with the Zionist organizations and also with the leaders of the Jewish community, who were communists. A well-known activist was Nisim Aladjem from Kyustendil, former owner of a glass factory, nationalized by the authorities. In 1952, Aladjem met "accidentally" on a train a young Bulgarian woman, twenty years his junior. They developed a relationship and she told him that she knew a German industrialist willing to buy the shares of Aladjem's nationalized business, because the end of communism was near. Since the German couldn't come to Bulgaria, they decided that he could give the money to a relative of Aladjem living in France. After the transaction, the relative was supposed to send a telegram with the text "We had a baby". The telegram came, and Aladjem handed the shares to the young woman.

A few days later, he was summoned by the State Security office in Sofia. He was told that they knew about the telegram and the whole "deal". They were ready to show leniency and waive the prosecution, if he signed a document stating that the Chairman of the Jewish Consistory Fransez (a communist), the Chairman of the Jewish Community Yosef Baruh and some of their assistants have spied for the American intelligence through the Levy family and other representatives of the Joint. Aladjem was told that, if they charge him, he will get the death penalty. They were also ready to prepare the declaration, he only had to sign it. That was in the times of the Doctors' Trial in the Soviet Union, Stalin's last purge, when many prominent Jews were charged with treason and sabotage. Aladjem knew that the situation was serious.

On March 27, 1953, Nisim Aladjem hanged himself from a tree in the Sofia Jewish Cemetery, near the grave of his sister. He left with friends two letters, to the First Secretary of the BCP Vulko Chervenkov and to the Minster of the Interior. He never signed the declaration (Барух, 1991, p.130-131).

These persecutions were part of a wised investigation. A letter from the Ministry of the Interior of 1952, preserved in the archives, ordered an investigation of all people who worked for the Joint until 1949. It has a resolution on it, added on March 19, 1952, that the investigation was not needed anymore. That was after the death of Stalin in the early March, which put an end to the anti-Jewish trials (State Security, 2012, p. 287).

Another case involved Momchilov, the lawyer from Kyustendil who took part in the delegation to save the Jews from deportation in March 1943 (his memoirs were quoted in Chapter 11). Nir Baruh learned about it in 1990 from Buko Beraha, a Jew from Kyustendil living in Israel.

Beraha visited Momchilov's home after he came back from Sofia on March 10, 1943. All windows were broken and the Ratniks wrote obscenities on the walls. Beraha called two workers from Nisim Aladjem's factory to fix the windows. After that, the whole Momchilov family had problems for years, but they did not disappear after the 1944 "revolution". Momchilov and Suichmezov (another member of the Kyustendil delegation) were mobilized in the army and sent to Dupnitsa. One evening, Momchilov's wife came to Beraha's home to tell him that peasants from a village near Dupnitsa blamed Momchilov for the murder of a member of the Agrarian Party in the 1923 riots (that could mean a death penalty). Beraha went to the village and found the son of the killed person, but he denied Momchilov's participation. Then he went to the local chief of the People's Militia to defend Momchilov. The chief advised him not to get involved, because they had credible information. Beraha replied that this could become a huge scandal and asked the chief to interview the son of the person who was killed. He wasn't sure if that was done, but Momchilov was not prosecuted (Барух, 1991, p.170).

The third incident mentioned by Nir Baruh involved Dr. Baruch Konfino who was an ophthalmologist, prominent Zionist and the head of the Zionist Theodor Herzl Club in Sofia. He organized ships to transport European Jews to Palestine. He did this from February 1939 to December 1940. Through his efforts, 3,683 people reached Palestine on eight separate transports (Ofer, 1990, p. 91-93). However, in the 1945 Sofia, few people cared about Dr. Konfino's contributions.

Nir Baruh quoted the memoirs of his friend, the State Security official Stefan Bogdanov, who was sympathetic to the Jews. At the time Bogdanov worked for the counterintelligence unit of the Directorate of the People's Militia:

> "In 1945, we conducted at State Security illegal "purges" of class enemies and sometimes innocent people suffered as well. One day, [the housekeeper of the Directorate] Angel [Paskalev] came to my office and told me with distressed voice that Dr. Konfino was put on the truck that took the detained "enemies" away to be shot. A well-known officer from the section of Georgi Ganev saw Dr. Konfino (of the emigration boats fame) on the street and decided by himself to add him to the group scheduled for shooting. By accident, Angel Paskalev saw the doctor in the truck. At the time, I was a big chief, so I went to the inner yard of the Directorate, pulled the doctor from the

truck and released him. This incident impressed me deeply and we became friends until his death at 94 in Israel" (Барух, 1991, p.177).

It's a feel-good story, but it raises the question of the monstrous amorality of the communist authorities. The people, who claimed to be superior to the Nazis, had no problem killing people for no reason. Even Alexander Belev did not dare to shoot randomly prominent Jewish leaders, but the communists had no ethical constraints that could stop them. Bogdanov doesn't say what happened to the rest of the passengers in the horrific truck, who had been detained randomly and condemned to death without any trial. And he doesn't say either how many such executions of "class enemies", as he called them, were conducted with his consent and participation. The most outrageous fact is that after the fall of communism, none of those sadistic communists was ever tried and convicted.

One of the demands of the Jewish community was to abolish the dreaded Commissariat for the Jewish Questions. The communist authorities kept the institution, with the main difference that they appointed in most positions Jewish communists, receiving generous salaries, while the majority of the Jews suffered in poverty. There was enough money to cover the salaries. On September 9, 1944, the fund "Jewish Communities", controlled by the Commissariat, had at its disposal 187,000,000 leva. The money was not returned to the ordinary Jews, from whom it was taken; the new staff continued to manage the money the way Alexander Belev did, for covering some needs of the Jewish communities. According to the information provided later, from September 9, 1944, to January 1, 1945, the fund spent about 60 million leva. At the same time, it continued to collect money from various sources to a total of 29, 074,000 leva (Майер, 1969, p.65-77).

None of the problems from that post-war period was covered objectively in the Bulgarian communist historiography. The common approach was to cover up the bad and exaggerate the good. A good example is the article of Israel Meyer "Benefits to the Bulgarian Jews from the People's Government", published in 1969 in the annual of the Jewish Cultural-Educational Organization of the Jews in People's Republic of Bulgaria. Meyer writes that the new government had the intention to continue recruiting Jews in labor groups, only this time they were brought back under the control of the Ministry of War. The Jews' right to serve in the regular army was also restored. In March 1945, the Ministry of War, in collaboration with the Ministry of Public Works, sent 700 conscription notices for special labor groups. "The Central Consistory opposed that and cancelled all notices, which had to go eventually to 3,000 Jews."

He also emphasized the help received from the Sofia city authorities by Jewish schools and needy families, the students' kitchen provided food for 350 children, with an annual budget of 2,100,000 leva. The social services provided additional food, like walnuts, jams, butter, etc. Meyer did not mention the financial and other aid received from international Jewish organizations.

Another Jewish "benefit" was the reform of the Jewish schools. The national education program, introduced by the government, became mandatory for those schools as well. Traditionally, the Jewish schools offered courses in Hebrew and Jewish history, but these two subjects, wrote Meyer, took too much time and efforts from the students. That forced parents to enroll kids in Bulgarian schools. The new educators changed the curriculum: "Hebraization must be abolished. Hebrew needs to be included only as far as it is necessary to study Jewish history and research of the artifacts of the Jewish culture."

Nowhere in the article did Meyer say that after all the help and reforms, over 90% of the Bulgarian Jews left the country within a few short years. Instead, he ends it with the obligatory communist slogans:

> "United and joined into a steel fist, under the banner of Marxism-Leninism, under the leadership of the Bulgarian Communist Party, in brotherly friendship and cooperation with the great Soviet Union and the rest of the socialist countries, the Bulgarian Jews, together with the whole Bulgarian people, work tirelessly for the prosperity of our dear socialist homeland" (Майер, 1969, p. 57-64).

The better access to information after the end of communism, allows us to recover the real story of confrontations and problems that plagued the Jews after the "socialist revolution" in Bulgaria. A good chronology is provided in the book of Boika Vasileva "The Jews in Bulgaria 1944-1952".

Immediately after the September 9 coup, restrictions on Jewish emigration were introduced. In a letter, the Palestine Office in Bulgaria complained to the Prime Minister that on November 8, 1944, the government stopped issuing passports to emigrating

Jews. A few weeks later, the process was renewed but with many restrictions – the most offensive was the declaration that upon leaving, the Jews were required to liquidate their properties and surrender their rights over them. The Office protested that, since the central bank did not provide any currency to export capitals, the Jews had to leave everything to the state or other institutions without any compensation and rights in the future. The obstacles created a feeling of hopelessness and anger among Jews (State Security, 2012, p. 40-45).

Despite the restoration of the civil rights of the Jews, we can see from the first moves of the communist-controlled government that it was reluctant to allow the old autonomy of the Jewish organizations. The goal was to put under communist control all citizens and their actions, regardless of ethnicity.

On September 17, 1944, under government pressure was established the Jewish Fatherland Front (JFF). It is not clear how it differed from the regular Fatherland Front, but it included Jews from various political parties and movements, under the undisputed leadership of the communists. The Central Jewish Consistory was restored; it included D. Yeroham, Jacques Nathan, Mancho Rahamimiov, Nastya Isakova, S. Tadjer, E. Arie, Israel Meyer, Y. Alkalai, and N. Mashiah. Again, the communists dominated the institution (Василева, 1992, p. 14).

The government tightened its control over citizens' initiatives. For example, on March 15, 1945 was created the Bulgarian-Palestinian and Middle East Economic Institute with the goal to establish economic and cultural ties with Mandate Palestine and other countries. On May 23, 1945, the Ministry of the Interior refuses to register it, because a private organization could not pursue the declared goals; they were under the control of government institutions (State Security, 2012, p. 61-66).

The big "losers" under the new order were the Zionists. Most of their organizations never came back to life. They created the United Zionist Organization (UZO), which held its first conference on October 7-8, 1944, with 12 delegates. Though tolerated for the time being, they were treated with suspicion and often ignored. On November 12, 1944, a conference of the Fatherland Front Jews took place in Sofia. It was declared the "first legal Jewish conference", a statement that ignored the priority of the Zionist event in October. Israel Meyer reported that the first priority for the Jews was to take part in the war against Germany, started by the new government. The Zionists found that war meaningless and thought that dragging Jews into it after years of persecutions was unfair (Василева, 1992, p. 17-19).

This was just the beginning of the conflict between JFF and UZO. At a meeting of JFF in November 1944, the communist J. Nathan opposed the inclusion of any Zionists. Isaac Fransez accused them that they worked only for emigration of the Jews and were not interested in the Bulgarian problems. In December 1944, David Ben-Gurion visited Bulgaria; he had meetings with Prime Minister Kimon Georgiev, ministers and leaders of the Bulgarian Orthodox Church. His passionate speech at a big Jewish rally emphasized the creation of a Jewish state as the most important task. The visit gave a boost to UZO, which continued to work on the preparation for emigration (Василева, 1992, p. 22-23).

The Zionist organizations in Bulgaria were the object of constant monitoring. In a collection of declassified documents, "State Security and the Jewish Community in Bulgaria, Documentary Volume", published in 2012, we can find many reports of State Security agents attending meetings of the Zionists. One of the most closely scrutinized organizations was Poale Zion, see (State Security, 2012, p. 120-151), which was strange – the group was an official supporter of the Marxist ideas. Perhaps, the communist party did not want to allow any "competition" in the interpretation of Marxism.

On April 25, 1945, the Sofia Committee of the BCP held a conference of the Jewish communists, with the participation of Todor Zhivkov. It was called specifically to oppose the Zionists and to analyze the tactical "errors" made after September 9, 1944. The participants tried to clarify the nature of Zionism and the reasons for its strong influence in Bulgaria. It was noted that the economic situation of the Bulgarian Jews was difficult, and Ben-Gurion offered them good opportunities, if they emigrated to Palestine. The provincial delegates worried about the advancement of the Zionist organizations through their women and youth sections. The two main subjects of conflict were the emigration and the study of Hebrew at school. Chaim Benadov proposed to increase the influence of the communist party by establishing new mass organizations, capable of confronting the Zionists. Baruh Shamli recommended to organize at city level a special group to fight Zionism, which could use the help of other institutions. In his closing speech, Todor Zhivkov called for caution in the pressure against the Zionist organizations, because they, unlike the Turkish groups, were not isolated and had a strong support abroad (Василева, 1992, p. 24).

The differences were becoming irreconcilable. Despite the praise of the new government, the report at the conference of the United Zionist Organization that took place in January 1946, showed an uneasy co-existence with the Jewish Fatherland Front, controlled by the communists (Доклад ЕЦО, 1946).

Both ideological wings of the Bulgarian Jewry tried to make a good use of the international support mentioned by Todor Zhivkov. As early as the end of 1944, the Consistory prepared a delegation for a meeting of the World Jewish Congress in New York, which included J. Nathan, D. Yeroham, Y. Alkalai and N. Isakova. At the rally before boarding the train in Sofia, Yeroham stated: "The vast majority of the Bulgarian Jews, under the new government, are reluctant to follow the chimerical idea of emigration. They will remain in Bulgaria and their desire is to live and work here in peace." The delegation could not reach New York on time, they were stuck in Istanbul waiting for US visas. At the same time, a delegation of the UZO reached the USA. Still, the Consistory informed the WJC that the Jews received all rights available to Bulgarian citizens and that their properties, taken by the previous regime, were given back. The WJC expressed skepticism and recommended to expand the time for returning the properties and to make sure that the right of emigration to Palestine was not violated (Василева, 1992, p. 50).

In the early years, the government allowed contacts between Bulgarian Jews and international Jewish organizations, because Bulgaria was in the process of negotiating the peace treaty with the Allies and the fair treatment of Jews was one of the scrutinized issues. In June 1945, the Joint sent 221 trunks with various items – shoes, coats, medicines, cotton clothes. The Consistory managed to waive the import tax. These shipments created tensions between Bulgarians and Jews, because many Bulgarian children were in similar situation, but they didn't receive help from the government or external sources. In response, the Consistory arranged some of the received items to be distributed among Bulgarian children (Василева, 1992, p. 59-60).

Another step toward improving the economic situation of the Bulgarian Jews was the creation of cooperatives. The large factories and businesses, Jewish and Bulgarian, were expropriated without compensation by the communists. The craftsmen were united in 38 Jewish cooperatives, which employed 2,697 people. However, the poor organization and lack of raw materials prevented those enterprises from growing, so they did not bring substantial improvement of the living standards.

In 1946-1947, the international activities of the Bulgarian Zionists increased. They took part in various conferences, but they were pressured by the government to prevent and condemn the illegal emigration from Bulgaria to Palestine.

The Jews in the communist leadership, following the Bulgarian and Soviet party line, raised voices against collaboration with foreign Jewish organizations. For example, after the meeting of the WJC in November 1946, one of the Bulgarian communist delegates, A. Arie, reported to the top leadership of the Bulgarian communists that the WJC was a "second edition" of the World Zionist Organization. Although the WJC worked on the issue of reparations, its leadership was "reactionary" and the Bulgarian membership made sense only if it helped to organize the "progressive forces" in the Congress. A strong argument was the fact that the Soviet Union had no contacts with the WJC and criticized its activities. The ties between Bulgaria and the World Jewish Congress were severed in 1948 (Василева, 1992, p. 97-98).

The communist grip on the Jewish organizations tightened more and more. One of the top Jewish communists in Bulgaria, J. Nathan, recommended that the Zionists elect a new leadership of "progressive elements" and limit its activities only within Bulgaria, because external contacts invited guests "who are agents of the Anglo-American imperialism". Those were the conditions to allow the Zionist conference of November 1947. The Zionists surrendered – in their resolution, they said that the Zionists must join the progressive forces, led by the USSR. Despite that, the voices demanding the liquidation of the Zionist organizations became stronger. In December 1947, the Jewish communists proposed to the CC of the BCP to create an organization to unite all Jews – the Jewish Democratic Front. Once created, it was supposed to replace all other groups, so the Jewish youth and women's organizations, B'nai Brith, the National Fund, the Palestine Committee, the Jewish Agency, and so on, had to be liquidated. Politburo of the BCP discussed the proposal. Vulko Chervenkov wrote that the Jews should not have separate organizations. Others proposed to modify the existing Jewish Fatherland Front into a Jewish Democratic Committee (Василева, 1992, p. 102-103).

Zionists were not the only targets, the political climate in Bulgaria was deteriorating by the day. In February 1947, the peace treaty with Bulgaria was signed in Paris. With this out of their way, the communists decided to consolidate their power and turn the country into a full-fledged pro-Soviet dictatorship. The last "free" elections were held on October 27, 1946; despite the enormous pressure and threats against the opposition parties, many people voted for them. The communists won 53.14% of the popular vote and 277 of the 465 seats in the People's Assembly. The other pro-communist organizations of the Fatherland Front received 89 seats and the opposition – 99. A new government with Georgi Dimitrov as a Prime Minister was formed. The Agrarian Party of Nikola Petkov became the face of the fight against communism in the parliament. On June 5, 1947, the American Senate ratified the peace treaty with Bulgaria. The same day, Nikola Petkov was arrested in the parliament, which was followed by expulsion of all members of the opposition. Some of them were tried and sentenced to death for spying, most of the others received lengthy prison sentences. The USA protested the death sentence of Nikola Petkov, but that did not stop them from recognizing the dictatorship of Georgi Dimitrov.

Religious organizations were also persecuted. In 1949, 15 pastors of the Protestant Organization United Evangelist Churches were accused of spying for the USA, illegal currency exchange and amoral lifestyle. All were convicted, with 4 receiving life sentences, the rest – various prison terms. Especially cruel was the persecution of the small Catholic minority in Bulgaria. In 1950-1952, the communist government organized a series of trials against 2 Catholic bishops, 38 priests, 1 nun and 15 members of the church, with the standard accusations of spying and sabotaging the "people's government". Six of the accused were sentenced to death and executed, two died during interrogation and the rest received prison sentences with confiscation of their property. Special advisers from Stalin's secret services took part in the preparation of the trials against the political opposition and the clerics.

Even the Bulgarian Orthodox Church lost its independence under communism, while it was able to keep it under the "fascist" rule. Most Metropolitans followed blindly BCP's policies despite the destruction of churches and persecution of priests, and several of them became secret agents of the State Security. In an interview for the Israeli newspaper "Naroden Glas" (People's Voice) during his visit to Israel in 1962, quoted in (САЩ искали), Patriarch Kiril attacked the Royal Family and presented himself as a martyr of the regime. He even slandered Queen Ioanna, who did so much to help the Bulgarian Jews through her connections with the Catholic Church:

"My relations with the palace have always been bad and the King's people were not friendly to me. On one hand, it happened, because of my relations with the Queen, who saw in me somebody who fought actively against her attempts to introduce Catholic influence in Bulgaria. On the other hand, the palace did not trust me, because of my past." [In his youth, Kiril was anarchist. – M.M.]

Claiming that the tiny Catholic community in Bulgaria (they were fewer than the Jews) conspired with the Queen to impose its influence over the country was as absurd as the claim that the Jews controlled the Bulgarian economy and culture during the debates about the Law for Defense of the Nation. Probably, the thirty pieces of communist silver made Kiril blind and deaf when in the 1950s Bulgarian Catholic priests were murdered and jailed by the communist regime.

In these conditions, it was just a matter of time before the active Zionists received similar "attention". However, a turning point in the situation became the restoration of the Jewish state on May 14, 1948. The lukewarm approval of the action by the Soviet Union, gave the Bulgarian Zionists a chance to leave.

The Emigration Commission started its work in September 1948. It included four members from the Consistory and three Zionists, with chairman the communist J. Nathan. Dr. Konfino was in charge of arranging the passports. The Jewish organizations covered all expenses and, as we saw earlier, the Bulgarian Government was charging a fee for every Jewish emigrant and was also limiting the amount of luggage the Jews could take with them. The government wanted the emigration to be done in perfect order to avoid the impression that the Jews were expelled from Bulgaria. The initial number included 10,000 people. The Zionists proposed half of them to be families with children, 30% young people aged 18 to 25 (70% of them young men), and 20% children from 14 to 18. The government strongly opposed the emigration of children. By the end of October 1948, the first group left for Israel. A month later, a second group of 2,903 people was sent, and a third one of 2,857 left in the end of 1948 (Василева, 1992, р. 120-122).

Despite the desire to create a good impression, the government could not help but reveal its dictatorial nature, even before the mass emigration of 1948. In his book "Saving the Bulgarian Jews in World War II", Christo Boyadjieff quoted the memoirs of the well-known Bulgarian writer Atanas Slavov, who lived in Sofia, near a railway station, from where the Jews took the trains to the Black Sea ports: "A trainload of Jews, officially emigrating to Palestine in 1946, circled the city and was brought into the station cloaked by a forest. The passengers were given food and drink at the canteen, tables having been set for them in the open under the sombre oak trees. Every double-bottom suitcase was opened, every doll taken from children's hands (their heads plucked off), every girl was stripped naked and searched, and hidden gold was confiscated before the poor emigrants — stripped of their better chances — were transferred further to the Black Sea coast where the ships for Israel awaited them. There was something very brutal in the way those emigrants were trapped" (Boyadjieff, 1989, p. 137). During the mass emigration campaign, the Consistory specifically warned the Jews not to take with them gold, wool fabric, leather, musical instruments and so on.

Further, the government limited the emigration of young people without families; in a circular of January 1949, the Consistory announced that Jews under 18 had no right to emigrate and orphans could leave only with a special permission from the Emigration Commission.

Another problem emerged from the communization of the economic life in Bulgaria. The strict control over industrial production and commerce, criminalized some traditional Jewish activities. A large number of Jews were small merchants and peddlers, however, under the Law on Prices and Supply these ways to make a living became criminal activities. The situation was not that different from the ban on speculation under the old Law for Defense of the Nation and the derivative decrees, only this time all Bulgarian citizens were targeted. Jews, whose families wanted to emigrate, were convicted under the law. The punishments were harsh, 10 to 15 years in prison. On July 31, 1950, a delegation of Jewish women visited the Speaker of the People's Assembly and deposited a request for pardoning their husbands and other relatives, so that they could leave for Israel. The presented list included 35 people. Most of the requests were approved (Василева, 1992, p. 122).

From October 25, 1948, to May 16, 1949, a total of 32,106 Jews left Bulgaria for Israel in several groups (Ibid., p.125). The difficult conditions in Israel in the first years, forced some Jews to reconsider their decision to leave Bulgaria. They wanted to go back, but the Bulgarian government refused to take them. In a few cases, such permits were granted, especially if the returning Jews could be used in the communist propaganda against Israel, whose pro-Western orientation was getting stronger. I remember the case of the poet David Ovadia, a devout communist, who returned and became known for his condemnation of Israel.

An interesting document about the emigration was a confidential report of the CIA, presented on June 11, 1948 (its full declassified but redacted text is in Appendix B of this book). It dealt with the migration before the official Emigration Commission was established. The CIA estimated that "there are approximately 46,000 Jews in Bulgaria, of whom 44,000 are Sephardic (Spanish) Jews and 2,000 are Ashkenazic (German, Austrian, Polish) Jews." Three main reasons for emigration were listed in the report. First, religious motives; second, desire to join relatives in Palestine who have been there since the 1920's; third, opposition to communism.

The CIA also assumed that communist agents could be among the emigres. It was thought that in the group that at the time was still in Bulgaria, there were about 40 agents. No more than 2% of the Bulgarian Zionists desiring to move to Palestine were communists. About half of that percentage were idealists who were communists before the coup of September 9, 1944, and the rest were "opportunists who still wanted to do business".

The report stated further that "the Bulgarian government considered the Jews anti-communist and non-assimilable, and that their opposition to communism cancelled any economic value they might have had". It was very likely that soon Bulgaria could stop further emigration, following the example of Romania and Czechoslovakia, which had already made it difficult for the Jews to leave (CIA Report, Bulgaria 1948).

The mass exodus forced the liquidation of the properties of the Jewish communities – most of them were sold or transferred to the Consistory. It also eased the tensions between communists and Zionists in the Jewish communities. With the Zionists gone, the communists became the undisputed rulers, but only over a fraction of the once-vibrant Jewish community of Bulgaria. From an important player, the Consistory was reduced to one of the minority institutions, like those of Armenians, Turks and Gypsies.

By the end of 1951, there were only 7,676 Jews left in Bulgaria. The larger part – 4,259 – lived in Sofia, 3,417 – in the province. About 90% of them worked for government institutions and industries. In less than five years, 42,000 Jews emigrated, most them from Sofia. The core of the emigrant wave were small property owners who did not fit in the new communist economic order (Василева, 1992, p. 138-143).

The remaining Jewish leaders, exclusively communist, called for assimilation. At a conference in 1952, Dr. Goldstein from Russe stated that Jews should not differ from Bulgarians, the differences had to be liquidated as soon as possible and that was the best way to fight anti-Semitism. Others said that Israel was the cause for turning the Jews into such a small minority, they could still keep their holidays, but should not be treated any differently than Bulgarians (Ibid., p. 144).

The profound ideological differences between Bulgaria and Israel made the contacts more and more difficult. In 1955, a decree of the CC of the BCP took further steps to eliminate Jewish institutions: "The representation of the Bulgarian Jews by the Consistory must be abolished. The real representative of the Jews in Bulgaria is our people's government, not the Consistory". It was another blow to the distinct Jewish culture. There were even symptoms of political anti-Semitism that emerged during the anti-communist riots in Hungary in 1956. The secretary of the CC of the BCP Georgi Chankov stated at a few meetings that the riots were caused by the Jews that dominated the leadership of the Hungarian Socialist Workers Party, it was regrettable that in 12 years, the leaders did not attract enough Hungarians. Similar statements were made by Vulko Chervenkov (Ibid., p.144).

By that time, the communist party had already assumed full control over the Jewish life in Bulgaria. The Consistory had been reduced to educational and cultural institution without any social influence. The events in Hungary and the Suez Crisis in 1956 brought more hostility toward the Jews and Israel in the communist countries.

A tragedy that happened in July 1955, worsened the relations between Bulgaria and Israel. A passenger jet operated by the Israeli airlines El-Al took off from London on its way to Vienna and Istanbul with final destination Tel Aviv. However, the plane strayed from its itinerary and entered the Bulgarian airspace. It was shot down by two Bulgarian fighter jets and all 58 people onboard perished. Despite the strong protests of the Israeli Government and the Israeli Embassy in Sofia, followed by a 9-year investigation and trial, the incident did not bring an end to the relations between the two countries (Маринова-Христиди).

However, the Six-Day War of 1967 had fatal consequences for those relations. Almost all European communist countries (except Romania) severed their diplomatic relations with Israel, Bulgaria was one of them. The communist countries wanted to show their support for the unsuccessful aggression of the Arab states, because the Arab world at the time was seen as the next big hope of the socialist revolution. The eradication of real or imaginary Zionism and Zionists became an urgent task in those countries, which was noticeable during the crises in Poland and Czechoslovakia in 1968.

> "In Bulgaria, this trend found an expression in policies of the CC of the BCP, which aimed at removal of Jews from leading positions on the "ideological front" – mostly in radio and television, section "Agitation and Propaganda" of the CC of BCP, Committee for State Security, Bulgarian People's Army, etc. The Jews who held positions in those structures, were moved to other places, mostly in the economic sphere. Even though no repressive measures were taken against the Jews in Bulgaria after 1967, in general, the times were not good for them" (Ibid.).

Another incident in 1973 brought new problems between Israel and Bulgaria, the trial of the Bulgarian citizen of Jewish background Heinrich Nathan Spetter. He worked at the Institute of Economics at the Bulgarian Academy of Sciences and also was an adviser of the government. Before that, from 1966 to 1972, he was an expert at the UN Center for Industrial Development in New York and Vienna. The Committee for State Security, with the help of the KGB and intelligence services of other communist countries, received information that Spetter was recruited by the MOSSAD in Vienna and got his job at the UN with the help of the CIA. He was arrested by the Bulgarian secret services in November 1973, attempting to leave the country with over 1,500 pages of secret analytical materials with economic information about the European communist countries. He was charged with spying for the USA and Israel and sentenced to death. The execution was postponed and later, he was exchanged for a top Soviet spy caught in the West. Spetter lived until old age in Israel (Маринова-Христиди).

The relations between Israel and the Soviet Union after 1967 were limited to a fierce propaganda war. Russian academics and propagandists (sometimes, it was difficult to tell the difference) produced a never-ending flow of anti-Semitic writings, disguised as criticism of Zionism. I still remember the numerous books (in Russian) on Zionism as a "lackey of imperialism" and the "fascist nature" of modern Israel, clogging the display racks at the Sofia bookstores, which were complemented by daily newspaper articles on the same topic. The culmination of that war was reached in

1975, when the communist and Arab countries managed to pass through the UN a resolution condemning Zionism as a form of racism and racial discrimination. Along with the ideological war, the Western countries were trying to get the Soviet Jews out of the country, where they were trapped.

Although Bulgaria copied almost everything from the Soviet Union, its Jewish policies were less extreme. Still, you were not supposed to say anything good about Israel. However, the large number of Bulgarian Jews in Israel, their stories and, most importantly, the made-up glory of the General Secretary of the BCP Todor Zhivkov as the savior of the Jews, delivered some unadvertised benefits. Bulgaria still maintained unofficial contacts with Israel.

The dark period after the victory of communism in Bulgaria was marked in the Jewish community by the relentless confrontation between communists and Zionists. As it happened during World War II, the Zionists did much more for their community than the communists. For many years, very few people knew it, because information was purged, facts were distorted and the writings of the Zionists, living in Israel, never reached Bulgaria.

In an article published in Israel in 1961, the Zionist Albert Romano argued with the communist Nathan Grinberg over the latter's book that exaggerated the role of the communists in saving the Bulgarian Jews. He strongly criticized the Jewish communists, especially in Bulgaria:

> "Why were the Jewish communists silent when Stalin, with anti-Semitic intentions, started the monstrous trial against the Jewish doctors and when he was killing the Yiddish writers?
>
> "Weren't the Jewish communists those who, after September 9, 1944, took over the Consistory, grabbed the money from the Jewish one-time property tax and paid fat salaries to their friends, even though they knew that most of the money came from poor craftsmen who needed it, because fascists took everything from them?
>
> "Weren't the Jewish communists those who threatened the Zionists with death for their work on the emigration to Palestine?
>
> "Weren't the Jewish communists running around like devils to deprive the large majority of the Bulgarian Jews from the opportunity to leave for Eretz-Israel and breathe freely and work in peace?

"Weren't the Jewish communists around the Consistory those who insisted that the Jews emigrating to Israel carry only a few tens of kilograms of luggage?

"Didn't Grinberg find refuge in Israel and the freedom to follow and preach communism and nobody threatened him with death or other consequences, when he used this freedom to trash Zionists?

"As of his sermons about the importance of the Bulgarian people, they are totally unnecessary – the Bulgarian Olim remember everything and are ready to express their gratitude to all who contributed to their salvation.

"However, the Bulgarian Olim have only bitter memories from the Jewish communists, which Grinberg's book is not going to sweeten.

"The Bulgarian Jews know that they were born and grew up in that country, they breathed its air, admired its beauty, benefited from its freedom and especially from the freedom to work for its people and ideals, inspired by its heroes. Even without the biased theorizing of Grinberg, they will always remember Bulgaria and its people, will follow its progress and wish it all the best" (Романо, Леви, 1961, p. 15).

17 EPILOGUE – SAINTLY DANES AND LOWLY BULGARIANS

"Why do you look at the speck of sawdust in your brother's eye and pay no attention to the plank in your own eye?"

Matthew 7:3
(NIV)

From the documents, memoirs and historical analysis in the preceding chapters, we can conclude that the fate of the Bulgarian Jews was closely linked to the shared history of two ethnicities that co-existed in Bulgaria, moving together through the good and bad events of their history. The lack of anti-Semitism was a serious obstacle to the discriminatory measures imposed by a powerful external force. Even the political class was divided, and those measures were sabotaged, mostly silently, but sometimes with vocal opposition. That opposition succeeded in stopping the deportation of the Jews from Bulgaria but failed in the occupied territories. I think it became clear from documents and opinions of Bulgarian politicians, leading communists and Jewish activists, that those were lands under strong German control, where the Reich had the final word, and the agreement for deportation had to be signed and put into action in secrecy, without the knowledge of the parliament and the people.

I will try to answer the question about who made the specific contributions to the survival of the Bulgarian Jews, but let me first address another important issue, which I mentioned in the introduction, the silence surrounding those events.

In the times of communism, it was difficult to maintain a

rational discussion, especially under the imposed false narrative about the crucial role of the Bulgarian Communist Party. Although the fall of communism somewhat relaxed the discussions, those events of World War II are still little known. And when attempts are made to promote the role of Bulgaria and its people, their contributions usually are attacked with accusations of their evil intent in the deportations in Thrace and Macedonia. The latter are seen as events, for which Bulgarians are solely responsible and should be ashamed forever, because what was done in those territories cancels anything good that happened to the 50,000 Bulgarian Jews.

Even in the comprehensive Yad Vashem annuals of Holocaust studies, there is mostly silence about the events. I reviewed the volumes from 1957 to 1990, where the only article about the Bulgarian case was "The Bulgaria Exception – a Reassessment of the Salvation of the Community" by Nissan Oren (in volume VII for 1968). Another one was the partial translation of the memoirs of Nadezhda Vasileva, which I quoted in Chapter 10; the translated part included only her work during the deportation in 1943, but omitted other important events, including the Allied bombing of the Jewish quarter. A third article by Alexandar Matkovski about the Thracian-Macedonian deportations blamed Bulgaria about the events.

The situation is aggravated by the strong pro-communist elements that survived the changes in Eastern Europe in 1989-1990 when the Bulgarian Communist Party transformed itself overnight into a "socialist party" but kept most of its old ideas, including its hostility toward many events in the Bulgarian history. A recent article (see, САЩ искали) in their party newspaper "Duma" (Word), published on February 22, 2018, under the title "The USA Wanted to Save the Bulgarian Jews by Sending Them to Turkey", promised to reveal sensational unknown documents, "which demolish the myth of the Savior King [Boris III] and his monarcho-fascist government, soaked in blood up to its elbows. Because the December Declaration of 1942 of the three great powers – USA, USSR and Great Britain – and the notes of the American Government to the Bulgarian Government from the early 1943 (which the latter refused to accept!) indicate that the Allies were aware of the role, which the Bulgarian authorities played in the Holocaust of our Jews... The USA had the sensational idea to save over 30,000 Bulgarian Jews by transferring them to camps in Turkey, with resources provided by the American and British Governments" (САЩ искали).

The article maintained the myth of the role of the communist party in saving the Jews and the documents attached to it did not prove much. They included the declaration read by Sir Anthony Eden at the House of Commons on December 17, 1942, recognizing the extermination of the Jews, but did not name Bulgaria. (As we will see later, the Allies did nothing to prevent it.) Another document was a telegram from Secretary of State Hull (August 8, 1941), which threatened Bulgaria with consequences, if the Law for Defense of the Nation was applied to American citizens residing in the country but did not object to its application to other Jews. Another telegram from the Secretary of State to the Bulgarian Government protested the deportations of Jews, but was dated March 27, when the Jews were already deported from Macedonia and the deportation from Bulgaria was cancelled. The telegram of March 29, 1943, explored the possibility to transfer to Turkey 30,000 Jews from "Bulgaria and the territories occupied by Bulgarian troops", but that could not be considered a serious offer, after the refusal of Great Britain to allow Jews from the same area to immigrate to Palestine, announced earlier that month.

The Bulgarian "socialists" are not the only ones to downplay the historical role of Bulgaria. The trend is also noticeable in the Western historical literature. A recent book by Waitman Wade Beorn, "The Holocaust in Eastern Europe: At the Epicenter of the Final Solution", which I read after I finished the main text, maintains the view that Bulgaria does not deserve recognition due to its "guilt" in Thrace and Macedonia:

> "It [Bulgaria] also managed to refuse implementation of the Final Solution more successfully than either Romania or Hungary. **As a result, some have attempted to compare Bulgaria favorably to Denmark, which through extraordinary efforts rescued most of its Jewish population.** One Bulgarian historian went so far as to claim that his country could recall its "history with pride, thanks to the collective protection they provided the Jews under the control." He refers to this as a "miraculous occurrence of goodness." This "miracle" would be cold comfort to the over 11,000 Macedonian and Thracian Jews the Bulgarians deported in the Dannecker-Belev Agreement above, the majority of whom died in the gas chambers of Treblinka and Auschwitz" [Emphasis mine. – M.M.] (Beorn, 2018, p. 195).

The important point in this paragraph was the juxtaposition

between Denmark and Bulgaria, as two countries and cultures at the opposite ends of the moral scale. I will return to the "extraordinary efforts" of Denmark, as opposed to the "lowly" role of Bulgaria but let me say that such approach reveals deeply rooted cultural differences between Eastern and Western Europe.

Eastern Europe is seen from the point of view of the West as the clueless younger brother (or sister) that adheres to some childish views, which need to be overcome or eradicated to become equal to the "enlightened" elder sibling. Perhaps, the different paths of historical development are to blame for those differences. While Western Europe was developing science and philosophy, the East was suffocating under the yoke of a backward power, the Ottoman Empire, which brutally suppressed any attempt for freedom and progress. It didn't help that centuries later, the Islamist rule was replaced by the equally suffocating grip of the Stalinist communism, which survived in various local versions until 1990 and even beyond. When the western students and intellectuals were free to engage in "play communism" and cheer Chairman Mao before returning to their luxurious lives, their eastern counterparts could only dream about escaping from the dreary communist reality.

These deep cultural differences established a certain pecking order among the countries – at the top were the great powers, followed by the developed western countries, with most of Eastern Europe at the bottom. The order was not only based on industrial and military power, but also on perceived moral authority. When a country at the bottom, like Bulgaria, does something good, that is embarrassing to the rest. It is seen as an inappropriate leap that violates the order, so the deed must be either covered up or discredited. That attitude ignores the fact that during World War II, Bulgaria did the maximum it could do under impossible circumstances – the choice at the time was to be nimble and covert to accomplish anything or to risk a catastrophe in an open confrontation (as it happened in Greece and Yugoslavia).

An interesting feature of that divide was that it was maintained by different ideologies in different periods of history. For example, in the racist ideology of Adolf Hitler, the Westerners were still privileged, most of them considered "Aryans", with all benefits derived from that. Hitler and his henchmen acted there with care; they never revealed their true plans for the Holocaust and tried to implement the extermination discretely. In the "savage" East, populated by lowly Slavs, just one rung above the Jews in Hitler's racial scale, all moral considerations were off, and the extermination was conducted in the open. The Slavic Bulgarians were one rung above the Slavic bottom, thanks to Hitler's definition of them as "Turkomans"; if they went for a conflict, they could have been treated just like the other Slavic people.

Years later, we see the same divide even in the Holocaust revisionism. While its major proponents debate fiercely the existence of gas chambers and crematoria in Auschwitz and other Nazi concentration camps, they mostly ignore the events in Eastern Europe. It is hard to question the mass exterminations conducted at plain sight, with thousands of witnesses and irrefutable evidence. Finally, even in the "New Europe" embodied in the European Union, we have the elites in Germany and France trying to impose questionable polices on the eastern part of the continent. That was the case with the disastrous mass immigration to Germany of people who don't fit there, whom the leading powers try to redistribute to other countries, like Poland, Hungary, Slovakia, etc., and shamelessly threaten them with sanctions, if they don't comply. The West is oblivious to the fact that most of the new immigrants come from cultures that are profoundly anti-Western and anti-Semitic and in the environment of encouraged multiculturalism, which allows them to keep their views, that would spell disaster not only for the Jews, but also for Europe at large.

So, all this begs the question: was Bulgaria that reprehensible morally in its policies that it did not deserve any praise for its efforts to help Jews?

If the existing pecking order has any basis in reality, we should expect that the policies of the Great Powers, followed by those of the superior Westerners, treated Jews in a morally superior way during the same time in history. A closer look reveals a different picture. The USA and Great Britain had an atrocious record during the Holocaust. Despite the claims of the revisionists about conspiracies, the documents revealing that record are not hidden in dusty boxes in hidden archives; most of them are readily available in official publications and only the human indifference keeps them "secret".

Denmark's record of moral superiority over Bulgaria crumbles under closer scrutiny. Jews are known for their reluctance to rock the boat when something involves large or influential countries. You can't blame them – it is a lesson learned in their long and horrible history of persecution, although they are more assertive now, after Israel's creation. However, it is dishonest to attack a country like Bulgaria, which did more than the great powers, just because it is safe to do so.

As I mentioned earlier, Great Britain was under the obligation to run the Mandate for Palestine, a task bestowed upon it by the League of Nations in the 1920s in order to prepare the land to be a "national home" of the Jews, as it was stated in the Balfour Declaration in 1917. The task was handled with a spectacular incompetence. Uncontrolled Arab immigration and redrawing the territory by the British created internal conflicts and made the Jewish state practically impossible. The Peel Commission in 1937 granted a few hundred square miles in northern Palestine for that state, far away from all traditional Jewish towns and holy places. The desperate Jews agreed to that partition, but the Arabs rejected it.

The next blow came with the White Paper of 1939. This British document restricted severely the Jewish immigration to Palestine at a time when the persecutions in Germany and its occupied territories worsened. As a party of a treaty of 1925, the USA had the obligation to ensure the proper implementation of the Balfour Declaration, but Roosevelt decided not to object to the White Paper (Groth, 2014, p. 124).

Things deteriorated even further – the "Memorandum by the Assistant Chief of the Division of Near Eastern Affairs (Merriam)", which I quoted in Chapter 10, stated that the total number of Jews to be allowed in Palestine was capped at 500,000, a number that was not to exceed the number of Arabs. It was also justified by the "absorption limit" of Palestine, which, according to the British, could not sustain more people. The arbitrary decision ignored the ingenuity and industriousness of the Jewish people, which were mentioned in Chapter 8 by Bulgarian politicians who visited Palestine in the 1930s and were impressed by the Jewish agriculture. As of this writing, there are over 6,000,000 Jews in Israel and other minorities, yet the land can still sustain them.

The memorandum revealed the British plans to change profoundly the Mandate, which were supported by Roosevelt, by turning the land into a trusteeship under the rule of the three major religions. Roosevelt's opinion was quoted, "it might be difficult to get the agreement of the Jews to such a plan but if Moslems and Christians of the world were agreed he hoped the Jews could also be persuaded". The reason for change was attributed to the strong nationalistic movements that were out of control. Palestine had to be removed form the jurisdiction of the League of Nations and ruled by a religious body: "Considering that there are in the world some 585,000,000 Christians, 220,000,000

Moslems, and 15,000,000 Jews, the body might have a membership of 6, consisting of 3 Christians, 2 Moslems, and 1 Jew" (Foreign Relations US, Vol. 4, 1943, p. 818). Thus, the Jews were to be turned into a marginal minority in the land, where they were supposed to re-establish their state. And that was happening in the most dangerous period of the Jewish history.

Symbol of that policy of indifference became the German steamship St. Louis, which left Germany with 930 Jewish immigrants in May 1939, and sailed to Cuba. Hitler wanted to test the "compassion" of the West for the people he persecuted. "In a speech to his parliament on January 30, 1939, Hitler employed bitter sarcasm as he noted the obvious discrepancy between the complaints about his persecution of the Jews and the paucity of offers to accept Jewish refugees. "It is a shameful example to observe today how the entire democratic world dissolves in tears of pity but then, in spite of its obvious duty to help, closes its heart to the poor, tortured people," the Fuhrer declared. The Nazi publication Der Weltkampf echoed Hitler's theme: "We are saying openly that we do not want the Jews, while the democracies keep on claiming that they are willing to receive them—and then leave them out in the cold." The time had come to call Roosevelt's bluff" (Medoff, 1987, p. 59-60).

The West failed spectacularly. Upon arrival in Cuba, only 30 passengers were allowed to disembark, though all of them had valid Cuban visas. People were desperate, there was a suicide attempt, but the ship was turned away. It attempted to reach Miami Beach, but it was confronted by Coast Guard planes and a boat. The ordeal was not a secret, it even made the front page of the New York Times, but that did not change the mind of the US Government. "Yet none of the leaders of the major American Jewish organizations called for the Roosevelt administration to grant sanctuary to the refugees. None of the publications of the major Jewish groups demanded American intervention. In his private correspondence at the time, [the leader of the American Jewish Congress] Stephen Wise implied that his fear of what he called "the really rising tide of anti-Semitism" helped shape his reluctance to demand that the Dinted States take in more refugees" (Ibid., 1987, p. 59-60).

The final blow was delivered by Canada, where the ship headed after the US rejection. Prime Minister William Lyon Mackenzie King stated that this was not a Canadian problem, despite the pleas of many influential Canadians. Eventually, the ship sailed back to Germany and the lives of most of her passengers ended in concentration camps.

The restrictions of Jewish immigration were imposed consistently in the 1930s and 1940s not only in Palestine, but also in most western countries. As early as March 1933, Rep. Samuel Dickstein planned to introduce a resolution recommending admission into the USA of German Jews, "free of quota restrictions". Many Jewish leaders opposed such special amendments and the motion failed (Ibid., p.22-23).

The Evian Conference in July 1938 was organized to resolve the problem with the Jewish refugees. It was attended by 32 countries and 24 international organizations. It was a failure – other than the Dominican Republic, willing to accept a few thousand Jews, no other country expressed willingness to help. In the early 1939, Sen. Robert Wagner and Rep. Edith Rogers introduced a legislation to admit 20,000 German refugee children to the USA over two years. It was vehemently opposed by restrictionist groups. The Jewish leaders already knew that the situation in Germany was bad, but their reaction was lukewarm, they still did want a special treatment for Jews (Ibid., p. 56-57).

Other proposals included housing European Jews in the Virgin Islands, a US territory, rejected by the Secretary of State Cordell Hull, and providing refuge in Alaska. Roosevelt was interested in the Alaskan scheme but wanted only 10,000 per year admitted – 5,000 of them from the continental USA and the rest from other parts of the world, according to the existing quotas. The Jews had to be restricted to no more than 10% of the total to avoid criticism (Ibid., p. 65-66). Neither of the proposals was implemented.

An unexpected offer came from Japan in early 1940. Its government wanted to provide the occupied Manchuria, in northern China, as a Jewish refuge, hoping to use the assumed political and financial power of the Jews to influence the US Government to provide economic assistance to Japan. A representative of Japan met the Jewish leader Stephen Wise, but he scoffed at the proposal (Ibid., p. 70). It was a mistake, because Japan fulfilled its promise – tens of thousands of Jews were protected and survived the war in the occupied Manchuria, Shanghai and other places, including on the territory of Japan.

Meanwhile, the persecution in Europe was quickly turning into extermination. Rafael Medoff quoted the gruesome description of the pogroms in Romania in January 1941, reported by the Jewish Telegraphic Agency:

"Jewish leaders believe their dead throughout the country

would exceed 2,000... Unknown hundreds of Jews will never be found, however, because of the manner in which they were put to death... Dozens of Jews—women and children as well as men—were literally burned alive... beaten senseless in the streets, robbed, doused with gasoline and set afire. Trusted friends have told me, and officials have confirmed, numerous cases of Jewish women whose breasts were cut off, not to mention sadistic mutilations like gouged-out eyes, brandings and bone-breakings. Perhaps the most horrifying single episode of the pogrom was the "kosher butchering" last Wednesday night of more than 200 Jews in the municipal slaughterhouse" (Ibid., p. 73-74).

With the invasion of the Soviet Union on June 22, 1941, such horrific news became part of the everyday routine. Thousands of Jews were shot daily in Belarus, Ukraine, Lithuania, Russia and elsewhere. It was beyond clear that a plan for mass extermination of the Jews was put into practice. However, the horror failed to shock the Western governments into action. Even the reports about the massacres in the Jewish press in the USA became shorter and shorter. Yet the Jewish leaders were still reluctant to ask for an immediate and decisive action. "None of the featured speakers at the AJ Congress rally demanded specific American action on behalf of the Jews in Europe. Stephen Wise, for example, stressed that Europe's Jews would be redeemed only "through a victory speedy and complete of the United Nations." The theory that Europe's Jews should be rescued not through Allied intervention on their behalf but rather solely through Allied military victory over the Nazis was put forward by Roosevelt administration officials as an excuse for their failure to save the Jews" (Ibid., p.97).

The news was passed to Roosevelt, but his only reaction was to express outrage and solidarity with the Jews. The USA was not prepared to deal with a crisis of these horrific proportions. Another half-hearted attempt to solve the Jewish refugee problem was the Bermuda Conference in April 1943, between the USA and Great Britain. It did not go beyond vague discussions of unnamed safe havens, but the most important issues, like lifting the immigration quotas in the USA or opening of the Mandate Palestine for the Jews, were not covered at all. The only tangible measure to help Jews was the establishment of the War Refugee Board by Roosevelt in January 1944, ironically, at a time when over 90% of the victims of the Holocaust were already dead.

The commonly used excuse that the Allies lacked knowledge about the Holocaust is difficult to maintain, considering the available documents. As early as September 1942, President Roosevelt sent his representative to the Holy See, Myron C. Taylor, to meet Pope Pius XII in Rome. Mr. Taylor brought a letter, which contained several paragraphs of a vivid description of the liquidation of the Warsaw Ghetto by the Nazis and other atrocities in Poland. The letter, along with other documents, has been publicly available since 1961 in the multivolume edition "Foreign Relations of the United States, Diplomatic Papers" (Groth, 2014, p. 115-117).

It is difficult to explain such a prolonged inaction in the face of mass extermination. Almost every attempt to help and provide some solutions had been crushed. It makes you wander, if the entry of December 13, 1942, in Dr. Goebbels's diary about the hidden hatred for Jews had some merit:

> "The question of Jewish persecution in Europe is being given top news priority by the English and the Americans. ... At bottom, however, I believe both the English and the Americans are happy that we are exterminating the Jewish riff-raff. But the Jews will go on and on and turn the heat on the British-American press" (Goebbels, 1948, p. 241).

The inaction in Europe looked strange, when it was known that the Polish Government-in-Exile was hosted in London, just a few blocks from Sir Winston Churchill's residence at 10 Downing St. Its staff maintained continuous communications with Poland and could provide valuable information about countering the Nazis. The lack of military action against the units and locations involved in extermination of Jews is justified with logistics, mainly the perceived long distances.

Prof. Alexander Groth shows convincingly that until the occupation of southern Italy and using its airfield in Foggia for bombing actions against Eastern Europe, the Allies had at their disposal the airfield of Lowestoft in southeast England.

> "An airplane flying from Lowestoft to the extermination camp in Chelmno would only need to travel 703 miles. But from Foggia, it would require no less than 840 miles. The distance from Lowestoft to Treblinka is 859 miles; from Foggia it is 819 miles. Now, with respect to the most important extermination camp, Auschwitz (Oswiecim), the distance from Foggia was 646

miles. The distance from Lowestoft would have been 770 miles. Even had the Allies attempted to reach the more distant (from Lowestoft) camps at Belzec, Majdanek and Sobibór, most of these flights would have actually been shorter than the June 12, 1942 and the August 1, 1943 US bomber flights from North Africa to Ploiesti, Romania and back" (Groth, 2014, p. 119).

Prof. Groth is convinced that factors other than technical issues had been involved when he compares two identical events – the uprising in the Warsaw Ghetto in May 1943 and the Warsaw Uprising of August-September 1944. The second one received substantial Allied aid by air, while the first one was mostly ignored. The common explanation that the Allies had no other remedies than "the ultimate threat of retribution" was hard to accept. "But during the entire course of the war, and especially after this threshold date, was there a single instance of Allied attack, or Allied-sponsored attack, against a single Nazi agent of the Final Solution? Did a single guard on one of the hundreds of trains rolling in Europe lose a fingernail in consequence of any Allied attack? Did the Allies look for Eichmann when they knew exactly what he was doing and when and where he was doing it in Hungary, for example?" (Ibid., p. 122-125).

The indifference of the Great Powers to the fate of the Jews during the Holocaust, which bordered on complicity, made practically impossible the attempts of a lesser countries to help. On September 23, 1942, the British Home Secretary Herbert Morrison opposed any further Jewish immigration into Britain, fearing that it would encourage the French Vichy government to dump Jewish children into Britain. On December 7, 1942, "a British Official, John Cecil Sterndale Bennett, was upset because Bulgarian Jewish children might "be allowed into Palestine based on Jewish Agency requests..." A horrifying prospect!" (Groth, 2011, p. 140). According a report in the New York Times of February 16, 1943, "the Rumanian government was offering the Allies Rumanian ships to transport 70,000 Jews anywhere the Allies wished. A departure tax to cover the transportation costs was all that was required. Both the U.S. State Department and the British Foreign Office rejected this offer, "fearing that it [was] a piece of blackmail...unloading all their unwanted nationals (i.e. Jews) on other countries (i.e. the Allies). To Britain, Palestine [was] out of the question as a destination. The only way to help the Jews, the Allies maintained, [was] by an Allied victory" (Groth, 2011, p. 172).

Let's summarize the situation. Here we have the mighty

Franklin Delano Roosevelt, the Slayer of the Great Depression, a World Humanist, who had a vast power, weapons better than those of Hitler, large territories at his disposal, yet he did not move a finger to prevent the slaughter of millions of Jews. Despite that, he is still revered and that dark side of his is kept under cover by generations of historians. Sir Winston Churchill, whose country was entrusted with the establishment of the Jewish state, did everything possible to keep Jews away from the Mandate Palestine.

On the other hand, the little Bulgaria, with only a fraction of those powers, under the constant threat of destruction by Hitler, Stalin and the Allies, saved its own Jews and is still constantly demonized by some Jews, Westerners and "postmodern" Bulgarian historians that it did not do the impossible by sabotaging the German action of deporting the Jews in Thrace and Macedonia. It is true that history is written or rather routinely distorted by the victorious powers.

Let's now compare the deeds of Bulgaria and Denmark, a comparison that caused Mr. Beorn's indignation, quoted earlier: "...Some have attempted to compare Bulgaria favorably to Denmark, which through extraordinary efforts rescued most of its Jewish population." What were the extraordinary efforts of Denmark that superseded the lowly Bulgarian actions?

I do not want to denigrate the efforts of many Danes to help the Jews in their country, but they are not in any way superior to the similar efforts of politicians, intellectuals and ordinary citizens in Bulgaria. What cannot be accepted is the mythologization of those efforts and turning them into a wide movement that rescued the Danish Jews by overcoming insurmounlicetable obstacles.

Probably everybody has heard the story about the Danish Royal Family, who upon hearing that the Germans wanted to register the Jews, started to stroll in Copenhagen wearing yellow Jewish stars to show their solidarity with their Jewish subjects. The story is false, but like any myth, it stubbornly refuses to go away.

The Germans never introduced anti-Jewish legislations in Denmark, because of its officially adopted policy of "negotiation", a sort of compromise that kept both sides happy to a degree. Let's not forget that from Hitler's point of view, the Danes were Aryans and the occupation in April 1940 was nothing like the occupation of the Soviet Union in June 1941. ""Negotiation" no doubt saved the lives of countless Danes, Jew and Gentile alike. But the policy, often regarded as the lesser of two evils, only worked because it brought Denmark into the service of the German war effort. The policy of negotiation—which Denmark only gave up when prospects of a German victory grew slim, and then, for reasons having nothing to do with welfare of the country's Jews—thus contributed—indirectly, but not insignificantly—to the suffering of Europeans elsewhere on the continent" (Hollander, 2013, p. 42). Denmark surrendered hours after the German invasion, in exchange, Germany provided it with a broad autonomy. The country kept its government, election system and the monarchy.

The Danish agriculture and industries contributed significantly to the German war effort. Most of the agricultural surplus, especially meat and butter, went to Germany. Over 124,000 Danes were recruited in Germany as foreign workers. The Danish military provided to the Wehrmacht 60,000 rifles and bayonets, almost 1,000 machine guns, mortars, munitions, and a host of other goods necessary for the war. The Danish industries supplied to Germany military boats and other ships. The Danish Army was in charge of the fight against saboteurs, partisans and "traitors", which in other occupied countries was the job of the Germans. 2,000 Danes were working for the Luftwaffe directly (Ibid., p. 47).

Another dark fact in the Danish war history is that about 6,000 men joined the dreaded Waffen-SS and fought, partly encouraged by the Danish authorities (as opposed to zero Bulgarian soldiers in the Waffen-SS). The Danish SS soldiers were not more humane or morally elevated than their German counterparts. "In July 1941 in Galicia, units from the Waffen-SS division Wiking, which consisted of Danish, Norwegian, Swedish, and later Icelandic members, the alleged finest of the "Aryan race", perpetrated together with Ukrainians the horrific massacres of six hundred Jews in Ternopol and of two to three thousand in Zloczow. The latter massacre was stopped by a German Wehrmacht officer who was shocked by the cruelty and the methods of execution used by the Ukrainians and the Scandinavians. According to a message dated 3-4 July 1941 from the chief of the Third Army squadron in the area, members of Wiking blocked the escape routes from Zloczow and some went "hunting for Jews" and plundering" (Vilhjalmsson, Bludnikow, 2006, p. 7-8).

The Danish Government was also known for expelling "undesirable" elements. For example, 21 stateless Jewish refugees were deported to Germany, without any demand from Germany. They perished in concentration camps. Since the 1930s, Denmark acted like many other European countries, closing its borders to Jewish refugees. In 1943, the country expelled 72 non-Jewish German socialist and communist refugees in 1943. An interesting fact is that the documents describing these actions, were kept secret by the Danish Government until 1997 (Ibid., p. 5-6).

In the 1940s, many Danish companies started to "Aryanize" by expelling their Jewish board members, without any objections from the government. Many "inconvenient" records about the time of the Holocaust are still kept secret in Denmark. "To this day it is impossible to access information from the Bovrup Index, a book published in 1946 disclosing the names of twenty-eight thousand members of the Danish Nazi Party (DNSAP). The Danish authorities banned both access and possession of this list in 1946. It seems that all things reprehensible in Denmark were to be concealed as long as possible" (Ibid., p. 12-13). In contrast, Bulgaria not only disclosed the names of the members of such organizations, but also put them on trial after the war.

The success of the saving of the Danish Jews in October 1943 was predetermined by various factors. There was a noticeable apathy of the Nazi administration in charge of the deportation. The different methods applied in Western and Eastern Europe are part of the explanation. Brutality was generally avoided in the West and the Germans were eager to find a solution that would merely expel the Jews from Denmark. The negotiations with Sweden, which agreed to accept the Danish Jews, were an open secret and the Germans were aware of the plan. The smuggling from Denmark was done with done with many small boats and it was impossible to hide. Yet, during the smuggling operation, that took place in the narrow strait with enormous strategic importance, the entire fleet of German patrol boats was grounded, supposedly for repairs (Hollander, 2013, p. 55). The few Danes who were arrested during the smuggling were not prosecuted by the Germans but handed to the Danish authorities and did not suffer any consequences.

During the attempted arrests of the 8,000 Danish Jews, the German authorities managed to detain only 284 Jews the first night, bringing the total to 475 the next few days. "Some Jews crossed the Oresund legally, with exit visas furnished by the German authorities; and in reality, finally, the handful of Jews who were caught (some, it must be added, because they were betrayed by Danes) were sent not to Auschwitz but to Theresienstadt, that Potemkin village of Nazi concentration camps, where 90 per cent of them survived the war" (Paulsson, 1995, p. 435).

The rest were hiding but the danger forced them to take advantage of the opportunity to move to Sweden. The Danes involved in the transportation were not very charitable. "In the early days of the flight, before routes and prices became regularized, fares ranged from 1,000 to 10,000 kroner per person, while some captains took advantage of the situation and the fear, extorting much higher sums from those who were rich and desperate enough to pay. In the end, however, the average fare came to about 500 kroner ($100 per person), something that most at the time considered reasonable" (Hollander, 2013, p. 54).

Though officially the deportation action was considered a failure, there were no punishments imposed on the local Nazi authorities. On the contrary, it seemed that the whole event was covered up and forgotten. This development created the hypothesis that the events were staged – the Nazis caused panic with their intended deportation, which "outed" all hiding Jews, forcing them to flee to Sweden, which complied with the regular solution in the West, expulsion, especially when the total number was so small. A "regular" detention campaign would not have been able to round so many of them.

> "The expulsion policy as it was actually implemented resulted in removing from Denmark not only the 6,000 Jews about whom the Nazis knew, but also some 1,500 whose existence they had not suspected. It was thus the only anti-Jewish action undertaken by the Nazis that was more than 100 per cent successful in attaining its objective. The term 'abortive' therefore seems somewhat misplaced" (Paulsson, 1995, p. 455).

The involvement of the high-ranked Nazis in the escape is confirmed by a telegram of an American diplomat in Sweden to the State Department of January 10, 1944. He summarized a conversation he had with Dr. Felix Kersten, a medical doctor of Finnish background, who treated Heinrich Himmler and other SS leaders. Himmler shared with the doctor his willingness to oust Hitler and arrange an armistice with the Allies and gave as an example of his new thinking the Danish events: "As illustration of this changed point of view Doctor cited Denmark where Himmler gave his men orders to allow Jews to escape to Sweden without injury" (Foreign Relations US, Vol. 1, 1944, p. 492).

When he summarizes the official narrative about the rescue of the Jews in Denmark, Gunnar S. Paulsson writes: "Three themes can be discerned here: first, that the Danish Jews were rescued, from a determined Nazi effort to murder them, against fearsome odds and at great risk; second, that the primary reason for the success of the venture was the virtuous nature, not only of the few thousand people who were directly involved, but of the whole Danish nation; and, third, that the Danish case stands as an accusation against other nations, which could have done the same thing if they had only had, to cite the title of the collection from which the above passage is quoted, 'The Courage to Care'." (Paulsson, 1995, p. 431).

The reality does not match the morally elevated narrative. Denmark had its dark sides and secrets and its authorities were from being a beacon of high ethics. The special treatment of the "Aryan" Danes and the German reluctance to get deeply involved, combined with the willingness of the neutral neighbor Sweden to accept the Jews, helped the latter to get away. Of course, without a few thousand Danish citizens, who got involved in the practical side of arranging the transportation, even at exorbitant prices, things could have been much more complicated.

But regardless of what the Danes have done, it does not put them above the Bulgarian people who were in a much worse situation, scrutinized and even occupied by the Germans without the benefits that Denmark enjoyed.

So, who prevented the deportation of the Bulgarian Jews? Was it the abstract "people", "the masses", which in Marxism are the driving force behind the historical events?

That is what the People's Prosecutor Mancho Rahamimov wants us to believe in his speech at the People's Tribunal in 1945: "Thanks to the energetic involvement of the Bulgarian public, of the Fatherland Front, which, while operating underground, was preparing the Bulgarian workers and peasants to defend the Jews; thanks to the democratic Bulgarian people, who felt good about the Front, we were saved" (People's Court Session No.18, 1945).

Similar view about the role of the ordinary people (though without the communist rhetoric) expressed the former President of Israel Shimon Peres in a speech at a Bulgarian exhibition in the European Parliament in Brussels:

> "The Israeli President thanked not only our country but also the thousands of ordinary people who had the courage, while risking their own lives, to save another life and thus to preserve the entire Jewish community in Bulgaria. We are gathered here to celebrate history, but also to look into the future and into everything that we will pass to our children, said Shimon Peres. The most precious lesson for them is never to surrender, to

think like heroes and act with courage" (Шимон Перес).

In his memoirs, Yako Baruh addresses the issue by delving into the complicated realities of that tumultuous period. "If you ask the Chief Rabbi of Bulgaria, he will tell you that God saved the Bulgarian Jews. It is possible, but why did not God save the other six and a half million? Or maybe he will answer that those six and a half million Jews redeemed the sins of the fifty thousand Bulgarian Jews who received God's blessing.

> "If you ask the Jewish communists in Bulgaria, they will tell you that the Red Army, the partisans, and the Fatherland Front Government saved the Jews. It's possible, but then why didn't the partisans and the underground Fatherland Front rescue the 12,000 Jews of Thrace and Macedonia or didn't make at least an attempt to destroy the railway or sabotage the action in other ways? Their voices were nowhere to be heard in those tense days of March 1943. And was the Red Army able to save the Bulgarian Jews when at the time it was not capable of rescuing its own Jews in the territories occupied by German troops? No matter what the Jewish communists say, if the Red Army did not cross the border in September 1944, the Germans could have had enough time to destroy the Bulgarian Jews. We can accept that its fast offensive at the time helped to save the Jews, but it was also possible that in the case of a delay, the German troops could act in the way they did in Hungary in 1944, dragging the Jews to their territory to be destroyed" (Барух, Спомени 1941-1943, p.30).

Mr. Baruh then discusses the reasons for the rescue of the Bulgarian Jews and sees them in a series of accidental events. In the beginning, in 1940, Hitler wanted to create a Jewish reservation in Eastern Poland, but by 1942, the plan changed to annihilation. The possibility of a second front in southern Europe in 1943, alarmed the Nazis and they decided to eliminate the Jews in Thrace and Macedonia that they saw as a security risk. That is why the original agreement Belev-Dannecker mentioned only those Jews. It did not matter to the German Ambassador to Bulgaria, Beckerle, when the Bulgarian Jews were to be deported, so he accepted the amendment, adding 8,000 from old Bulgaria. Mr. Baruh thinks that the lower number of 20,000 was accepted due to the lower capacity of the ovens and other tools of destruction. As of the personalities involved, he thinks that people like Dimo Kazasov, Nikola Mushanov, Trifon Kunev, and the Metropolitans Kiril and Stefan contributed most to the rescue. The intervention of outside institutions like the Swiss Embassy and the US Government was not successful in other countries or in Bulgaria. The disagreement of the Bulgarian people with the Jewish policies of Gabrovski forced him to take a step back and delay the action, but the later events made it impossible to implement. That is what Mr. Baruh understands under the term "series of chances" (Ibid., p.31-32).

Samuel Arditti decisively points at King Boris III as the main reason for saving the Bulgarian Jews:

> "The survival of the Bulgarian Jews bothers many researchers. Their theory is that the deportations from the new lands were a preparation for deportation from Bulgaria. Something is wrong with this theory. The Bulgarian Jews were eventually saved, which shows that King Boris did not arrange the deportation from Thrace and Macedonia. So, these historians have to prove that the Jews were saved not because of the King, but despite him. And they create the legend that the rescue was due to something vague, like the "Bulgarian people" ... King Boris fought for the lives of the Jews in Sofia, Plovdiv, Dupnitsa, Pazardjik and many other places in old Bulgaria. He was victorious, not a single Jews was handed to the Germans. It was clear that King Boris did not initiate the deportation of my brothers. Everything was done under the strong pressure of Nazi Germany, with the help of its agents in Bulgaria. The claim that the King had to prevent the demise of the 12,000 Jews comes after the fact. It's like with a critic who sits on the fence, and after everything is done, says, you had to do this and that" (Ардити, Човекът който изигра Хитлер).

He criticizes all other forces that did little to prevent the Holocaust or even aggravated it:

> "I can say many other things: the responsibility of Great Britain, which issued the White Paper and stopped the immigration of the East European Jews to Palestine, is covered up. If free movement was allowed, millions of Jews could have been saved. Hundreds of Jews who reached the shores of America were sent back to Europe. The Americans and the British found enough airplanes and bombs to destroy Sofia and kill plenty of innocent citizens, but when the Jewish organizations requested from the USA to bomb the Auschwitz

death camp and the railways that led to it, the request was rejected. Yet places near the camp were bombed. Why did not the Tito partisans blow up the railways used to transport the Macedonian Jews? What did Greece do to save its Jews? Why did not [the partisan commander] Slavcho Trunski attack camp Monopol in Skopje? Why did not the resistance send and armed group to kill Belev, the way they killed [General] Lukov, Pantev, Sotir Yanev and the radio engineer Yanakiev? There are many more questions but probably none will be answered" (Ibid.).

Our long journey through books, documents, memoirs and archives brought us to the question, from which we started. I think that It would be dishonest to deny the role of Bulgaria in saving the Jews or to claim that their ordeal was as bad as the ordeal of the Jews in other countries.

The most important condition that made the survival possible was the lack of anti-Semitism, which prevented the pro-German politicians from imposing and exploiting anti-Jewish hostilities, as it happened in other countries. Thanks to that tradition, the Nazi theories and practices remained foreign to the way of thinking of the vast majority of Bulgarians.

The role of King Boris III was crucial. He was in a difficult situation – maneuvering between two disastrous options, Hitler and Stalin, while being offered only imaginary help from the USA and Great Britain, he did not have many choices. But he never considered deporting his own citizens as a viable choice. Besides, his position as the holder of the real power in Kingdom, helped him made the ultimate decision in preserving the lives of the Bulgarian Jews.

The Bulgarian political class also contributed. The small anti-Semitic minority, despite the help from Germany, its army and a network of agents, was never popular. The "progressive" members of the parliament and the other government institutions were not the only ones who resented those policies; in the difficult situation, politicians with more conservative convictions, like Dimitur Peshev and his group, were also involved. As we saw, the silent opposing majority included even the people surrounding Gabrovski and Belev, who helped Jews in various ways. There were also diplomats issuing transit visas.

All of that would not have happened without the Jewish organizations, and first of all, the Zionists. The Jews in Bulgaria were never seen as a foreign group and that view did not change even after the introduction of the discriminatory laws, which were met with universal outrage. The bonds of the Zionists with politicians and intellectuals helped to maintain the pressure on the government to avoid a catastrophe. Thus, the Jewish leaders in Bulgaria were always able to help the other Jews and were never forced to make the tragic choices imposed by the Nazis in other occupied countries, like Poland and Lithuania.

Unfortunately, the Jewish communists, despite their good intentions, proposed a solution that could have been disastrous, if followed by all Jews. Mass armed struggle against the government could only bring more repressions, especially in Bulgaria, where the communist resistance was poorly armed and lacked wide support. And let's not forget that even the idealists in the movement were working for the victory of the macabre Stalinist order, which changed Bulgaria for the worse and chased away most of the Bulgarian Jews.

The role of the Bulgarian Orthodox Church was also remarkable. They did not support Judaism as a religious doctrine, but they stood up for the Jews as an inseparable part of the Bulgarian people, from the time when the Law for Defense of the Nation was proposed to the end of the Bulgarian Kingdom. The Metropolitans and the priests maintained the same position throughout the whole ordeal.

We must also add the thousands of ordinary and mostly unknown people who helped every day in big and small ways. None of the actors in that drama could have been successful on their own. Their combined efforts delivered a result of a high moral value, and I can confidently state that they, "through extraordinary efforts, rescued" the Jews, a praise that Mr. Beorn had reserved only for the Danish people.

History is always complicated. Using it to confirm or reject current political opinions often means to place the facts on the Procrustean bed of prejudice and distorts them. Jews have been the targets of such treatment for thousands of years. An objective view of the historical events, with all of their complexity, would help us understand better our past and make sense of our present, and in the process, we for once may even learn something from history.

APPENDIX A: CIRCULAR OF THE RATNIK ORGANIZATION ON THE JEWISH QUESTION

This is a circular of one of the anti-Semitic organizations in Bulgaria; among its members were Minister of the Interior Petur Gabrovsky and the head of the Comissariat for the Jewish Questions Alexander Belev. The Ratniks were known for their blind faith in Adolf Hitler and his anti-Jewish ideas. The document is very valuable, because it criticizes the inconsistencies in the government's Jewish policies, as they were happening; the Ratniks' "sensitivity" helped them notice things that were missed by others. As you can see, there was no will to go all the way on the path that Germany followed and tried to impose on all satellite countries.

The suspicions of the Ratniks prove that forces in high positions, even probably the King, sabotaged the full implementation of the anti-Jewish measures. That is consistent with the opinions of various historians.

Some of the claims, for example the behavior of the deported Jews, are doubtful because they were placed in boxcars that had no windows. Also, the ability of the Kyustendil Jews to collect 100,000,000 leva overnight is hard to take seriously. Other facts, especially the under-collected amounts from the one-time Jewish tax, are credible because many Ratniks worked for the Commissariat and even controlled banks. Finally, the rage of the Ratniks, who saw that the policies they found so dear were failing, is a good testimony about the failure of extreme anti-Semitism in

Bulgaria. (The document is included in the collection "Documentation on antisemitism in Bulgaria, 1918-1943" at Yad Vashem, item 4060292, file 148. The original is in Bulgarian. Translated by Miroslav Marinov.)

Situation of the Jewish Question in Bulgaria in the Beginning of April 1943 (No.57, April 3, 1943)

In Talk No.30 of 1942, titled "What is presented in the order of August 29, 1942, regarding the Jewish Question in Bulgaria", we described the situation of the Jewish Question in September 1942.

In it, we showed how from 1940 on, the pro-Jewish rootless rulers, on one hand were warning, facilitating, letting loose and immunizing Jews against the half-measures that they were forced to take, and on the other hand, put on an anti-Semitic mask to be liked both in and out of the country.

Let's see what happened since then.

In October 1942, the Press Control directorate was ordered to block anything in the press covering the Jewish Question in Bulgaria, because the Bulgarian people found it irritating (!) and was outraged by the extreme measures, which the authorities supposedly took against the Jews. There was a publication ban even for orders of the Commissariat for Jewish Questions, so their orders are known only to a few state agencies, while the society remains ignorant about them and there is nobody to control their applications.

Even until now, nothing has been done to educate the Bulgarian people about the importance of the Jewish Question and the meaning of the measures that must be taken.

Jews are the only ones who spread propaganda about the Jewish Question and, naturally, it works for their own benefit. The Bulgarian society was deliberately abandoned to the influence of the Jewish propaganda with the purpose to create Judeophilic feelings, which should justify the half-measures and their deliberately loose application. This situation didn't last because of the Ratnik propaganda and the arrogant and provocative behavior of the Jews.

The Jews, whose factories were to be confiscated, got the opportunity to hide behind various screens.

And the authorities gave the opportunity to countless Jews to practice their professions and trades even today, under the guise of "civic mobilization".

It was announced with great fanfare that the one-time tax on Jewish properties would bring billions of leva, but little was collected. Until today, under 15% of the announced amount has been collected.

In the end of March, the Law of the People's Loan passed, it will collect money from Bulgarians by force, but none of the Jewish money blocked by the state is taken, of course, they hope to keep it and return it tomorrow to the Jews.

The order of August 29, 1942, prescribed the separation of Bulgarians and Jews by distance and in dwellings. It was never applied. Some insignificant measures were taken in a few provincial places, but no one controls their fulfillment. On the contrary, civically mobilized Jewish doctors, dentists and others were sent all over the country to villages and towns that didn't have a single Jew before. There, the Jews under strict conditions win the sympathies of the gullible and have become centers for their Marxist and Anglophilic collaborators.

The only measure taken in Sofia are the Jewish stars, but its application has been left to the good will of the Jews, since nobody controls if and how those stars are worn. Now, over a third of the Sofia Jews don't wear the stars.

The same applies to the Jewish curfew, a high administrative agency even demanded a written clarification from the Sofia Military Commandant why the latter has requested written explanations from two Jews because they disregarded the curfew.

The Academic Council of the State University refused the order of the Commissariat to expel the Jewish students and jealously protected them, while admission to the university is denied to Bulgarians. Fifth Sofia Secondary School refused to admit the brother of a worthy sergeant from a Sofia battalion, but admitted ten little Jews, while the little Bulgarian remained out because the sergeant couldn't support him with his small salary.

And so on, and so on...

However, something very unexpected happened and even the most gullible saw behind the masks.

Since the rulers were pretending in front of Germany that they were concerned about the Jewish question, in early February, Germany sent a specialist in Jewish deportations and offered to deport to Poland in 3 months all Bulgarian Jews. So, the long-dreamed about opportunity to purify Bulgaria of all Jews became a reality! And others are willing to pay for it! But what happened?

Didn't the rulers just sign an agreement with England through Switzerland to move 8,000 Jews to Palestine? And what now?

Instead of exporting soldiers and workers for the English in Palestine, they were offered to send all Bulgarian Jews to a different destination.

And they decided to protect the Bulgarian Jews. They agreed to deport only the Jews from Thrace and Macedonia, who belonged to Germany anyway, because that country conquered those lands with blood and handed them to us. Since they assumed that those Jews were 20,000, the agreement was for 20,000 people.

Then the collection in camps began. But it turned out, there were only 13,000 Thracian and Macedonian Jews. So, 7,000 Jews from the old territories had to be deported. The Commissariat ordered the collection of Jews in special buildings with their luggage in Kyustendil, Plovdiv, Yambol, Burgas and other places. But the next day, telegrams flew from the highest places and those Jews were freed. The society was scandalized and when it opened its eyes, saw a clear evidence of the truth!

The rulers don't want to give away the Jewish leaders (who are the most important). In the last month and a half, the Sofia Telephone Service has been overloaded by Jews and Bulgarians can barely get the chance to talk. Why and who are those Jews calling in Bulgaria and Istanbul? The escaped and captured chairman of the Bitola Jews admitted that he was warned by a call from Sofia. High administrative agencies in Skopje warned the Jews in the city and when the Jews were collected, it turned out that hundreds of the most influential have fled to Albania. And from Sofia and elsewhere, every day Jews are leaving for Istanbul. Who and why is letting them go?

Next came the disgraceful comedy in the National Assembly. The Deputy Speakers D. Peshev and P. Kyoseivanov submitted on March 16 a written protest against the treatment of the Jews, signed originally by 42 members, among whom were P. Kyoseivanov, D. Peshev, Sirko Stanchev, Sotir Yanev, from the majority, and from the opposition, Prof. Alexander Tsankov, Todor Kozuharov and others. And after parliamentary "magic", they only demoted D. Peshev, while Dr. N. Nikolaev and Dr. Hikola Minkov and others left to avoid the vote. And the director of that comedy, P. Kyoseivanov, who followed an order from the top, was not touched. The purpose of this comedy was, on one hand, to convince Germany that the rulers did their best, even going against the feelings of the Bulgarian people, who supposedly were great friends of the Jews, and on the other hand, to look good in the eyes of the international Jewry.

And what about the Jews? All residents of Lom know and that's why there somebody distributed a leaflet saying that when the Jewish deportation train arrived in Lom, Jews were throwing out from the windows the already unnecessary Bulgarian bills, on which the King's image was covered with excrements, shouting: "Only this remain for you in Bulgaria!" Ask the people of Kyustendil, and they will tell you how the windows of Peshev were shattered.

When the Jews from the old territories saw that they were being collected, the B'nai Brith lodge in Kyustendil called for help the central B'nai Brith lodge in Sofia (supposedly already shut down) and in different ways collected overnight 100,000,000 leva, gave them away for bribes and did other things – not only the telegrams that freed the Jews, but also the dirty comedy in the National Assembly...

This way, the military important Thrace and Macedonia were cleared from Jews only with the great efforts of Germany.

What does today's official Bulgaria look like when it refuses to deport the Jews from the old territories? It looks like a man with lice who was offered delousing, and he fights to keep his lice...

It is true that the persecution of Jews causes temporary suffering but if someone gets soft because of that, he is an idiot. The question is clear – US or THEM. Can you imagine what they will be doing, if Germany loses the war? Will anyone feel sorry for us?

Maybe Germany wants to collect all Jews in Poland, not only to protect the inner front from these enemies, but also to have at its disposal 7 million Jews, i.e. half of the international Jewry, if necessary.

Who and what are harming those who keep by all means the Jews in Bulgaria?

They harm the Bulgarian national spirit, they harm the victory of Germany and Italy, as well as everybody who fights the world Judeo-capitalism...

If only we could publish details with names and evidence! But the time for that is coming!

Yes! The rootless rulers have unbreakable ties with the Jews! Both are so intertwined with the state that should be swept away together. No more half-measures.

Comrades Ratniks! You know that the rootless plutocrats persecute us with a vengeance because of our fight against the Jews. They have been ready to overlook anything, but that!

Time, events, and the struggle remove the masks. And they have been already removed. Therefore, with unwavering persistence, let's continue to our inevitable VICTORY!

APPENDIX B: CIA REPORT ON THE MIGRATION OF BULGARIAN JEWS TO PALESTINE, 1948

Sanitized Copy Approved for Release 2011/10/17: CIA-RDP82-00457R001600160006-5
CENTRAL INTELLIGENCE AGENCY REPORT

INFORMATION REPORT

COUNTRY   Bulgaria/Palestine
DATE DISTRIBUTED   11 June 1948
SUBJECT   Migration of Bulgarian Jews to Palestine
NO. OF PAGES   2
PLACE ACQUIRED   (......................)
DATE ACQUIRED   (......................)

1. (..........) there are approximately 46,000 Jews in Bulgaria, of whom 44,000 are Sephardic (Spanish) Jews and 2,000 are Ashkenazic (German, Austrian, Polish) Jews. (.....) all of these Jews desire to emigrate to Palestine, for one of the following reasons: (a) religious motives; (2) desire to join relatives now in Palestine (.......) there are approximately 10,000 Jewish families in Bulgaria having sons or close relatives in Palestine, primarily as the result of the first migration which took place in 1925); and (c) opposition to communism.

2. The first migration of Bulgarian Jews since the war took place late in December 1947 when several hundred Jews between the ages of 17 and 35 departed from Burgas aboard the PAN CRESCENT and PAN YORK. The local Zionist organization allegedly selected emigrants on the basis of loyalty to the Zionist cause, number of relatives residing in Palestine and potential contribution to the economy of Palestine. The Bulgarian government refused to permit the removal of any property from the country and each emigrant departed with not more than a knapsack or suitcase. A collective passport was issued for the group.

3. A second group left Bulgaria around the middle of February, via Proag Prague, Paris and Marseilles. Each person carried a Bulgarian passport and a Palestinian certificate issued by the British. These emigrants were in the same age group, and, as in the first migration, 60 percent of the migrants were men.

4. A third group departed early in March, also bearing Bulgarian passports and Palestinian certificates; while a fourth group is waiting to leave for Palestine. There are said to be about 40 communist agents in the latter group.

5. Not more than two percent of the Bulgarian Zionists, which comprise the largest group of Jews desiring to go to Palestine, are communists. It is stated that about half of this number are idealists who were communists before 9 September 1944, when the communists gained control in Bulgaria, and that the remainder are opportunists who "still want to do business".

6. (..................................) the Bulgarian government considered the Jews anti-communist and non-assimilable, and that their opposition to communism cancelled any economic value they might have had. (........................) the Bulgarian government would probably change its policy in the near future, however, in line with action taken by Rumania, Czechoslovakia and other satellite countries which have made it increasingly difficult for Jews to leave.

7. (............................) none of the Jewish emigrants has had any military training. (............) prior to 9 September 1944, no Jews were permitted in the Bulgarian Army. Instead, they served in the labor corps. Since 9 September only a few Jews have been called on for military service, and no Jews are being remobilized in the current mobilization because none had served in the Bulgarian Army prior to 9 September.

CONFIDENTIAL

BIBLIOGRAPHY OF BOOKS AND OTHER SOURCES

(Andric, 1977) Andric, Ivo. *The Bridge on the Drina* (Translated by Lovette F. Edwards), University of Chicago Press (Phoenix Fiction Series), Chicago, 1977

(Alhalel) Alhalel, Mayer Rafael. *Mayer Rafael Alhalel with fellow camp workers in a Jewish labor camp, 1943* http://www.centropa.org/photo/mayer-rafael-alhalel-fellow-camp-workers-jewish-labor-camp

(Anzhel, 2006) Anzhel, Leon. *Labor camp in the village of Rudnik*, Year of Interview - 2006, http://www.centropa.org/photo/labor-camp-village-rudnik

(Arendt, 2006) Arendt, Hannah. *Eichmann in Jerusalem: A Report on the Banality of Evil*, New York, Penguin Books, 2006

(Auschwitz Bombing Controversy, August, 1944) *Auschwitz Bombing Controversy: War Department Rejects World Jewish Congress Request to Bomb Auschwitz (August 9-14, 1944)*, Jewish Virtual Library, at: https://www.jewishvirtuallibrary.org/war-department-rejects-world-jewish-congress-request-to-bomb-auschwitz-august-1944

(Balabanov to Arditti Letter, 1960) *Reports written by the Bulgarian Ambassador N. Balabanov in Ankara on the Jewish problem in Bulgaria (in Bulgarian)*, Yad Vashem Archive, item ID 4314902, file 268

(Bar-Zohar, 2013) Bar-Zohar, Michael. *Beyond Hitler's Grasp: The Heroic Rescue of Bulgaria's Jews*, 2013 (electronic edition)

(Barkai, 1990) Barkai, Avraham. *German Interests in the Haavara-Transfer Agreement 1933-1939*, The Leo Baeck Institute Yearbook, vol. 35, issue 1, 1990

(Barkley, 1876) Barkley, Henry C. *Between the Danube and Black Sea or Five Years in Bulgaria*, John Murray, London, 1876

(Ben-Naeh, 2006) Ben-Naeh, Yaron. *Blond, Tall, with Honey-*

Colored Eyes: Jewish Ownership of Slaves in the Ottoman Empire, Jewish History, 2006, volume 20, issue 3-4, p. 315-332

(Beorn, 2018) Beorn, Waitman Wade. *The Holocaust in Eastern Europe: At the Epicenter of the Final Solution*, London, Bloomsbury, 2018

(Boyadjieff, 1989) Boyadjieff, Christo. *Saving the Bulgarian Jews in World War II*, Free Bulgarian Center, Ottawa, 1989

(Brown, 1673) Brown, Edward. *A Brief Account of Some Travels in Hungaria, Servia, Bulgaria, Macedonia, Thessaly, Austria, Styria, Carniola, and Friuli*, printed for T.R. for Benj. Tooke, London, 1673

(Brustein, 2004) Brustein, William I. and King Ryan D. *Balkan Anti-Semitism: The Cases of Bulgaria and Romania before the Holocaust*, East European Politics and Societies, 2004, volume 18, issue 3, p. 430-454

(Brustein, Ronnkvist, 2002) Brustein, William and Ronnkvist, Amy. *The roots of anti-Semitism: Romania before the Holocaust*, Journal of Genocide Research, 2002, volume 4, issue 2, p. 211-235

(Burds, 2013) Burds, J. *Holocaust in Rovno: The Massacre at Sosenki Forest, November 1941*, Palgrave Macmillan, New York, 2013

(Circular of Ratnik, 1943) *Circular of the Ratnik organization, 03 April 1943 (in Bulgarian).* – in: Documentation on antisemitism in Bulgaria, 1918-1943, Yad Vashem, item 4060292, file 148

(Chary, 1972) Chary, Frederick B. *The Bulgarian Jews and the Final Solution, 1940-1944*, The University of Pittsburgh Press, Pittsburgh, PA, 1972

(Churchill & Roosevelt, Vol.2) *Churchill & Roosevelt: The Complete Correspondence, Volume II. Alliance Forged: November 1942 – February 1944*, London, Collins, 1988

(CIA Report, Bulgaria 1948) *Central Intelligence Agency Report on Migration of Bulgarian Jews to Palestine*, June 11, 1948

(Cohen, 2014) Cohen, Julia Phillips. *Becoming Ottomans: Sephardi Jews and the Imperial Citizenship in the Modern Era*, Oxford University Press, 2014

(Crimes in Yugoslavia) *The Crimes of the Fascist Occupants and Their Collaborators Against Jews in Yugoslavia (in Serbian)*, Belgrade, Federation of Jewish Communities of the FPR of Yugoslavia, 1957

(Crampton, 2007) Crampton, R.J. *Bulgaria*, Oxford University Press, 2007

(Deletant, 2012) Deletant, Dennis. *Ion Antonescu and the Holocaust in Romania*, East Central Europe, 2012, issue 39

(Desires for Solution of the Jewish Question, 1941) *Memorandum Entitled "Desires and Ideas of the Foreign Office in Connection with the Intended Total Solution of the Jewish Question in Europe," Prepared by Referat D III of the Department Germany, and Submitted to Luther on 8 December 1941 in Preparation for the Wannsee Conference.* – in: Trials of War Criminals before the Nuernberg Military Tribunals, vol. 13, Washington D.C., 1982

(Deutscher Schulatlas, 1943) *Deutscher Schulatlas, herausgegeben von der Reichsstelle fuer das Schul- und Unterrichtsschrifttum*, 1943, Gemeinschaftsverlag deutscher Schulatlas-Verleger

(Diaries of Theodor Herzl, Vol.1) *[Theodor Herzl Visits Bulgaria]* – in: *The Complete Diaries of Theodor Herzl, Volume 1 (Book 3, April 1896)*, Herzl Press and Thomas Yoseloff, New York-London, 1960, pp. 366-369

(Diaries of Theodor Herzl, Vol.2) *[Theodor Herzl Meets Prince Ferdinand of Bulgaria]* – in: *The Complete Diaries of Theodor Herzl, Volume 2 (Book 4, July 1896)*, Herzl Press and Thomas Yoseloff, New York-London, 1960, pp. 436-439

(Dimitroff, 1985) Dimitroff, Pashanko. *King Boris III of Bulgaria: Toiler, Citizen, King 1894-1943*, Lewes, The Book Guild, 1986

(Dolapchiev, 1953) Dolapchiev, Nikola. *Law and Human Rights in Bulgaria*, International Affairs, Vol. 29, No. 1, Jan. 1953, pp. 59-68

(Donchev, 1968) Anton Donchev. *Time of Parting: A Novel* (Translated from the Bulgarian by Marguerite Alexieva), William Morrow & Company, New York, 1968

(Dostoevsky, Karamazov, 2000) Dostoevsky, F. *The Brothers Karamazov* (transl. by Constance Garnett), Pennsylvania State University, 2000 (Electronic Edition)

(Edelheit, 1994) Edelheit, Abraham J. *Jewish Responses to the Nazi Threat, 1933-1939: An Evaluation*. – in: Jewish Political Studies Review, vol. 6, no. 1-2 (Spring 1994), p. 135-152

(East and West, 1868) *The East and the West by an Oriental and a Former Rayah*, Athens, National Printing Office, 1868

(Encyclopaedia Judaica, 2007, 9) *Encyclopaedia Judaica (Second Edition), Volume 9*, Thomson Gale, Detroit-New York, 2007

(Finkel, 2017) Finkel, Evgeny. *Ordinary Jews: Choice and Survival during the Holocaust*, Princeton, Princeton University Press, 2017

(Fischel, 2010) Fischel, Jack R. *Historical Dictionary of the Holocaust (Second Edition)*, The Scarecrow Press, Latham-Toronto, 2010

(Foreign Relations US, Vol. 1, 1943) *Foreign Relations of the United States: Diplomatic Papers, 1943, General, Volume 1*, Washington, D.C., US State Department

(Foreign Relations US, Vol. 1, 1944) *Foreign Relations of the United States: Diplomatic Papers, 1944, General, Volume 1*, Washington, D.C., US State Department

(Foreign Relations US, Vol. 4, 1943) *Foreign Relations of the United States: Diplomatic Papers, 1943, The Near East and Africa, Volume 4*, Washington, D.C., US Department of State, 1964

(Fraser, 1906) Fraser, John Foster. *Pictures from the Balkans*, Cassell and Company, London-Paris-New York-Melbourne, 1906

(Freeman, 1877) Freeman, Edward A. *The Ottoman Power in Europe: Its Nature, Its Growth and Its Decline*, Macmillan & Co.,

London, 1877

(Friedman, 1957) Friedman, Philip. *Their brothers' keepers*, Crown Publishers, New York, 1957

(Gallagher, 2001) Gallagher, Tom. *Outcast Europe: The Balkans, 1789-1989, from the Ottomans to Milosevic*, Routledge, London-New York, 2001

(Georgeoff, 1985) Georgeoff, Peter John. *National Minorities in Bulgaria, 1919-1980* – in: *Eastern European National Minorities, 1919-1980, a Handbook*, published by Libraries Unlimited, Littleton, CO, 1985, pp. 274-308

(Gerlach, 2016) Gerlach, Christian. *The Extermination of the European Jews*, Cambridge University Press, Cambridge, 2016

(Gerlach, 1998) Gerlach, Christian. *The Wannsee Conference, the Fate of German Jews, and Hitler's Decision in Principle to Exterminate All European Jews*, The Journal of Modern History, 1998, volume 70, issue 4

(Gladstone, 1877) Gladstone, Right Hon. W.E. *Lessons in Massacre or, The Conduct of the Turkish Government in and about of Bulgaria Since May 1876*, John Murray, London, 1877

(Gladstone, 1876) Gladstone, Right Hon. W.E. *Bulgarian Horrors and the Question of the East*, Lovell, Adam, Wesson & Company, London, 1876

(Goebbels, 1948) *The Goebbels Diaries 1942-1943*, edited, translated and with an introduction by Louis P. Lochner, Doubleday & Co., Garden City, NY, 1948

(Graf, 2017) Graf, Tobias P. *The Sultan's Renegades: Christian-European Converts to Islam and the Making of the Ottoman Elite, 1575–1610*, Oxford University Press, New York, 2017

(Groth, 2011) Groth, Alexander J. *Accomplices: Churchill, Roosevelt, and the Holocaust*, New York, Peter Lang Publishing, 2011

(Groth, 2014) Groth, Alexander J. *Absolving the Allies? Another Look at the Anglo–American Response to the Holocaust*, Israel Journal of Foreign Affairs, 2014, Vol.8, Issue 1

(Guttman, 2013) Guttman, Nathan. *Controversy Erupts over Effort to Honor Bulgarian Who Saved Jews from Nazis*, Forward, June 11, 2013 at: http://archive.is/XxACQ

(Herzl, 1960, Vol.1) *[Theodor Herzl Visits Bulgaria]* – in: *The Complete Diaries of Theodor Herzl*, Volume 1 (Book 3, April 1896), Herzl Press and Thomas Yoseloff, New York-London, 1960, pp. 366-369

(Herzl, 1960, Vol.2) *[Theodor Herzl Meets Prince Ferdinand of Bulgaria]* – in: *The Complete Diaries of Theodor Herzl*, Volume 2 (Book 4, July 1896), Herzl Press and Thomas Yoseloff, New York-London, 1960, pp. 436-439

(Heydrich, 1939) Heydrich, Reinhard. *Express letter to the chiefs of all Einstatzgruppen of the Security Police*, September 21, 1939. – in: Trials of War Criminals before the Nuernberg Military Tribunals, vol. 13, Washington D.C., 1982

(Hitler, Reden 1932-1945) *Domarus, Max. Hitler: Reden und Proklamationen 1932-1945*, Leonberg, Pamminger & Partner, 1988

(Hitler, Speeches 1932-1945, Vol. IV) *Domarus, Max. Hitler. Speeches and Proclamations 1932-1945. Volume IV: The years 1941 to 1945*, Wauconda, IL, Bolchazy-Carducci Publishers Inc., 2004

(Hitler's Order about Secrets, 1941) *Basic Order of Hitler, 25 September 1941, Concerning the Handling and Safeguarding of Secrets.* – in: Trials of War Criminals before the Nuernberg Military Tribunals under Control Council Law No. 10, vol. XIII, Washington D.C., US Government Printing Office, 1982

(Hitler's Table Talk, 2000) *Hitler's Table Talk 1941-1944: His Private Conversations* (Introduced and with a Preface by H.R. Trevor-Roper), Enigma Books, New York, 2000

(Hitler's Ten-Year War, 1943) *Hitler's Ten-Year War on the Jews*, Institute of Jewish Affairs of the American Jewish Congress, New York, 1943

(Hollander, 2013) Hollander, Ethan J. *The Banality of Goodness Collaboration and Compromise in the Rescue of Denmark's Jews*, Journal of Jewish Identities, Issue 6, Number 2, July 2013

(Imber, 2002) Imber, Colin. *The Ottoman Empire, 1300-1650: The Structure of Power*, Palgrave Macmillan, Houndmills-New York, 2002

(Intelligence Study of Bulgaria, 1943) *Joint Army-Navy Intelligence Study of Bulgaria, Janis No.38, Volume 2, October 1943*, USA, Joint Intelligence Study Board, October 1943

(Ioanid, 1990) Ioanid, Radu. *The Sword of the Archangel: Fascist Ideology in Romania (East European Monographs, no. CCXCII)*, Columbia University Press, New York, 1990

(Ioanid, January 1992) Ioanid, Radu. *The Pogrom of Bucharest, 21-23 January 1941*, Holocaust and Genocide Studies, 1992, volume 6, issue 4, pp. 373-382

(Ioanid, 1993) Ioanid, Radu. *The Holocaust in Romania: The Iasi Pogrom of June 1941*, Contemporary European History, 1993, volume 2, issue 2, pp. 119-148

(Joint Study Bulgaria, 1943) *Joint Army-Navy Intelligence Study of Bulgaria*, Janis No.38, USA, Volume 2, October 1943

(Karpat, 1985) Karpat, Kemal H. *Ottoman Population, 1830-1914: Demographic and Social Characteristics*, The University of Wisconsin Press, 1985

(Kershaw, 2008) Kershaw, Ian. *Hitler, the Germans, and the Final Solution*, International Institute for Holocaust Research Yad Vashem, Jerusalem, 2008

(Keshales) *Booklet regarding the history of the Jews of Bulgaria written by Haim Keshales, Volume I, (Typewritten manuscript in Bulgarian)*, Yad Vashem Archives, item ID 5083411, file 1

(Kohler, 1916) Kohler, Max and Wolf, Simon. *Jewish Disabilities in the Balkan States: American Contributions Toward Their Removal, with Particular Reference to the Congress of Berlin*, published by the

American Jewish Committee, New York, 1916

(Labor Battalions 1941-1943) *Documentation regarding the labor battalions in Bulgaria, 1941-1943 (in Bulgarian)*, Yad Vashem Archives, item 4061375, file 165

(Letter to Ribbentrop on Einsatzgruppen, 1941) *Letter from the Chief of the Security Police and SD to von Ribbentrop, 30 October 1941, Transmitting the First Five Reports of the Einsatzgruppen. –* in: Trials of War Criminals before the Nuernberg Military Tribunals, vol. 13, Washington D.C., 1982.

(Lower, 2005) Lower, Wendy. *Nazi Empire-Building and the Holocaust in Ukraine*, The University of North Carolina Press, 2005

(Macdonald, 1913) Macdonald, John. *Czar Ferdinand and His People*, T.C. & E.C. Jack, London, 1913

(Marinov, 2017) Marinov, Miroslav. *Saved: Japan and the Jews in World War II*, MPM Publishing, Toronto, 2017

(Marx, 1959) Marx, Karl. *A World without Jews*, New York, Philosophical Library, 1959

(Macgahan, 1876) Macgahan J.A. *The Turkish Atrocities in Bulgaria: Letters of the Special Commissioner of the "Daily News" J.A. Macgahan, Esq., with an Introduction and Mr. Schuyler's Preliminary Report*, Bradbury, Agnew & Co., London, 1876

(Mason, 1988) Mason, Henry L. *Implementing the Final Solution: The Ordinary Regulating of the Extraordinary*, World Politics: A Quarterly Journal of International Relations, 1988, volume 40, issue 4

(Medoff, 1987) Medoff, Rafael. *The Deafening Silence*, New York, Shapolsky Publishers, 1987

(Memoirs of Heskia Finzi) *Memoirs of Heskia Finzi on David Iosifov and his activities, 1943-1944 (Handwritten manuscript in Bulgarian)*, Yad Vashem Archives, item ID 4272821, file 259

(Memoirs of Mihalev) *Memoirs of Petar Georgiev Mihalev on the events in Kyustendil, March 1943 (typewritten manuscript in Bulgarian, dated September 12, 1973)*, Yad Vashem Archives, item ID 4064714, file 202

(Memoirs of Momchilov) *Memoirs of Ivan Momchilov on the events in Kyustendil and Sofia, 08-09 March 1943 (typewritten manuscript in Bulgarian, dated December 15, 1966)*, Yad Vashem Archives, item ID 4298229, file 264

(Memoirs of the son of Yohanan Avraam Benbassat) *Memoirs of the son of Yohanan Avraam Benbassat who was convicted of blood libel in Vratsa; Comments of the trial against Bokhor Yeshuyu Shishedji, 1898, manuscripts in Bulgarian* (Documentation on the phenomenon of antisemitism in Vratsa and Yambol, late 19th century, in: "Archive of Benjamin Arditti: Documentation Regarding the History of Bulgarian Jewry", 1850-1964, Yad Vashem Archives, item 78520, file 118)

(Memorandum Eden-Roosevelt, 1943) *Memorandum Concerning Conference Between Eden and Roosevelt (March 27, 1943)*, archived at: http://archive.is/8In77

(Memorandum on Expulsion of Jews to Madagascar, 1940) *Memorandum by Rademacher, 3 July 1940, Entitled "The Jewish Question in the Peace Treaty," Noting That the Desirable Solution Is to "Get All the Jews Out of Europe," Proposing That Madagascar Become a German Mandate to Which European Jews Be Sent.* – in: Trials of War Criminals before the Nuernberg Military Tribunals, vol. 13, Washington D.C., 1982

(Miller, 1975) Miller, Marshall Lee. *Bulgaria during the Second World War*, Stanford University Press, Stanford, 1975

(Monastir During the Holocaust) *Monastir During the Holocaust: Liquidation of the Jewish Community in Monastir*, Yad Vashem http://archive.is/Motma

(Monroe, 1914) Monroe, Will S. *Bulgaria and Her People with an Account of the Balkan Wars, Macedonia, and the Macedonian Bulgars*, The Page Company, Boston, 1914

(Morcan, 2016) Morcan, James & Lance. *Debunking Holocaust Denial Theories: Two Non-Jews Affirm the Historicity of the Nazi Genocide*, Bay of Plenty, NZ, 2016

(Nazi-Soviet Relations, 1948) *Nazi-Soviet Relations 1939-1941: Documents from the Archives of the German Foreign Office*, Washington, D.C., Department of State, 1948

(New York Times, 1913) *Bulgarian Jews Protest*, New York Times, February 27, 1913

(Ofer, 1990) Ofer, Dalia. *Escaping the Holocaust: Illegal Immigration to the Land of Israel, 1939-1944*, New York-Oxford, Oxford University Press, 1990

(Oren, 1971) Oren, Nissan. *Bulgarian Communism: The Road to Power, 1934-1944*, Columbia University Press, New York-London, 1971

(Overy, 2013) Overy, Richard. *The Bombing War: Europe 1939–1945*, London, Penguin Books, 2013

(Patchoff, 1919) Patchoff, Dragomir and Katzeff, Danail (ed.). *The Roumanian Atrocities over the Bulgarian Population in Dobroudja Abducted into Moldova*, published by the Dobroudja Organization in Bulgaria, 1919

(Paulsson, 1995) Paulsson, Gunnar S. *The 'Bridge over the oresund': The Historiography on the Expulsion of the Jews from Nazi-Occupied Denmark*, Journal of Contemporary History, Vol. 30, No. 3, July 1995.

(People's Court Session No.9, 1945) *Proceedings of People's Court Session No. 9 in Sofia, 16 March 1945 (in Bulgarian)*, Item ID 4440080, file 1

(People's Court Session No.10, 1945) *Proceedings of People's Court Session No. 10 in Sofia, 17 March 1945 (in Bulgarian)*, Yad Vashem Archives, item ID 4741749, file 2

(People's Court Session No.11, 1945) *Proceedings of People's Court Session No.11 in Sofia (in Bulgarian), 19 March 1945*, Yad Vashem Archives, Item ID 4741841, file 3

(People's Court Session No.14, 1945) *Proceedings of People's Court Session No.14 in Sofia, 22 March 1945 (in Bulgarian)*, Yad Vashem Archives, record group TR.6 - People's Court, Sofia, item ID 4832504, file 6

(People's Court Session No.15, 1945) *Proceedings of People's Court Session No.15 in Sofia, 23 March 1945 (in Bulgarian)*, Yad Vashem Archives, item ID 4832589, file 7

(People's Court Session No.16, 1945) *Proceedings of People's Court Session No.16 in Sofia, 24 March 1945(in Bulgarian)*, Yad Vashem Archives, item ID 4897640, file 8

(People's Court Session No.18, 1945) *Proceedings of People's Court Session No.18 in Sofia, 29 March 1945*, Yad Vashem Archives, item ID 4973586, file 10

(People's Court Session No.20, 1945) *Proceedings of People's Court Session No.20 in Sofia (in Bulgarian), 31 March 1945*, Yad Vashem Archives, Item ID 4973827, file 12

(Polikar, 2006) Polikar, Samy. *Bulgaria and linguistic matters of Bulgarian Jews*, International Journal of the Sociology of the Language, 2006, issue 179, pp. 101-113

(Report on Balkan Wars, 1914) *Report of the International Commission to Inquire into the Causes and Conduct of the Balkan Wars* (Carnegie Endowment for International Peace, Division of Intercourse and Education, Publication No.4), published by the Endowment, Washington, D.C., 1914

(Reports by US diplomatic representations, 1944) *Reports by US diplomatic representations in Europe to the War Refugee Board (WRB) in Washington regarding relief and rescue operations for the Jews of Yugoslavia, Romania and Bulgaria, May-October 1944*, Yad Vashem Archives, item ID 3736781, file 89

(Rescue of Russe in 1877) *Memoirs regarding the rescue of Russe from burning, robbery and murder of its residents, 1877*, Yad Vashem Archives, item ID 4019833, file 131

(Righteous Among the Nations, 2016) *Names and Numbers of Righteous Among the Nations - per Country & Ethnic Origin, as of January 1, 2016*, at: http://archive.is/fQHMB

(Rubenov) *Memoirs of Robert Rubenov on the Kailaka concentration camp and his partisan sister Mati Rubenova* (Typewritten Manuscript in Bulgarian), Yad Vashem Archives, item ID 4314836, file 266

(Sakowicz, 2005) Sakowicz, Kazimierz. *Ponary Diary 1941-1943: A Bystander's Account of a Mass Murder*, New Haven, Yale University Press, 2005

(Schaffer, 1985) Schaffer, Ronald. *Wings of Judgment: American Bombing in World War II*, NY, Oxford University Press, 1985

(State Security, 2012) *State Security and the Jewish Community in Bulgaria, Documentary Volume (in Bulgarian)/ Държавна сигурност и еврейската общност в България 1944 г. – 1989 г.,*

Документален сборник, София, КРДОПБГДСРСБНА, 2012

(Stefanov, 2002) Stefanov, Pavel. *Bulgarians and Jews throughout History*, Occasional Papers on Religion in Eastern Europe, 2002, volume 22, issue 6

(Tamir, 1979) Tamir, Vicki. *Bulgaria and Her Jews: The History of a Dubious Symbiosis*, New York, Sepher-Hermon Press, 1979

(Telegram Boris III) *Telegram from King Boris III to Bulgarian Zionists* - in: Documentation on the relations between the court of the Bulgarian King and Bulgarian Jewry, 1915-1975, Yad Vashem Archives, item ID 4061322, file 163

(Thompson, 1886) Thompson, Geo. Carslake. *Public Opinion and Lord Beaconsfield 1875-1880, Volume 1*, Macmillan & Co., London, 1886

(Trevor-Roper, 1966) Trevor-Roper, H.R. (ed.) *Hitler's War Directives 1939-1945*, Pan Books, London, 1966

(Trial of Adolf Eichmann, Session 47, part 3) *The Trial of Adolf Eichmann, Session 47, part 3 of 8 (King Boris III and the Bulgarian Jews)*, The Nizkor Project, at: http://archive.is/GCOVc

(Trubakov, 2013) Trubakov, Ziama. *The Riddle of Babi Yar: The True Story Told by a Survivor of the Mass Murders in Kiev, 1941-1943*, CreateSpace Publishing, USA, 2013

(Two essays by Isaak Naimovich and Matey Yulzari) *Two essays written by Isaak Naimovich and Matey Yulzari regarding the rescue of Bulgarian Jewry (in Bulgarian)*, Yad Vashem Archives, item ID 5120483, Record Group 0.13-Bulgaria Collection, file 60

(Varsano) *"Evlag" - Memoirs written by Albert Varsano regarding the Somovit detention camp for Jews* (Typewritten Manuscript in Bulgarian), Yad Vashem Archives, item ID 5091768, record group O.13 - Bulgaria Collection, file 58

(Vasileva, 1959) Vasileva, Nadejda Slavi. *On the Catastrophe of the Thracian Jews: Recollection,* Yad Washem (Vashem) Studies on the European Jewish Catastrophe and Resistance, Volume III, Jerusalem, Publishing Department of the Jewish Agency, 1959

(Vilhjalmsson, Bludnikow, 2006) Vilhjalmur Orn Vilhjalmsson and Bent Bludnikow. *Rescue, Expulsion, and Collaboration: Denmark's Difficulties with Its World War II Past*, Jewish Political Studies Review, Vol. 18, No. 3-4, Fall 2006.

(Volovici, 1991) Volovici, Leon. *Nationalist Ideology and Antisemitism: The Case of Romanian Intellectuals in 1930s*, Pergamon Press, Oxford, 1991

(Wannsee Protocol, 1942) The Wannsee Protocol (January 20, 1942) at http://archive.is/Zi7cu

(Windth, 1907) Windt, Harry De. *Through Savage Europe, Being the Narrative of a Journey (Undertaken as a Special Correspondent of the "Westminster Gazette"), Throughout the Balkan States and European Russia*, T. Fisher Unwin, London, 1907

(72 години от бомбардировките над София) *10 януари 1944 г. : 72 години от една от най-страшните и кръвопролитни англо-*

американски бомбардировки над София, http://archive.is/xx99l

(Адроки) *"Из живота на лагера Сомовит". Спомени на Алберт Адроки за пребиваването му в еврейския лагер в Сомовит през лятото на 1943 г.* (Typewritten Manuscript in Bulgarian), Централен Държавен Архив, фонд 1568К, опис 1, а.е. 191, л. 1-16

(Ардити, 2014) *Племенникът на Елиас Канети: Хазартът е мъжка слабост на Симеон (Самуел Ардити), 2 ноември 2014,* http://archive.is/2aNZc

(Ардити, 1952) Ардити Б. *Ролята на Цар Борис III при изселването на евреите от България,* Тел-Авив, 1952

(Ардити, спомени) *Спомени от годините на Холокоста – 1940-1943, Кратка автобиография на Самуил Ардити,* at: http://archive.is/bAh9

(Ардити, Човекът който изигра Хитлер) Ардити, Самуил. *Човекът, който изигра Хитлер или Цар Борис III гонител или приятел на евреите,* at: http://archive.is/WwuqU

(Бар-Зоар, Йоанид) *Проф. Михаел Бар-Зоар: Една малка държава каза „Не" на Хитлер. Раду Йоанид: Трябва да изнесете цялата истина.* at: http://archive.is/b7sNx

(Барух, 1991) Барух, Нир. *Откупът – Цар Борис и съдбата на българските евреи,* София, Университетско издателство «Св. Климент Охридски», 1991

(Барух, Спомени 1941-1943) Барух, Яко. *Спомени за периода 1941-1943.* - in: Documentation from the 1950's on persecution against the Jews in Bulgaria during World War II including the events of the 9-10 March 1943, Yad Vashem Archives, item ID 4272702, file 258

(Барух, Спомени 9 март 1943) Барух, Яко. *Спомени за 9 март 1943.* - in: Documentation from the 1950's on persecution against the Jews in Bulgaria during World War II including the events of the 9-10 March 1943, Yad Vashem Archives, item ID 4272702, file 258

(Бележка от Княгиня Евдокия) *Бележка от княгиня Евдокия върху лекарската експертиза за смъртта на цар Борис III, Кобург, 22 март 1949 г.,* at http://archive.is/QS6op

(Благодарствено писмо, 1937) *Благодарствено писмо от министъра на народното просвещение до Анжело Куюмджийски за учредения паричен фонд за подпомагане на бедни студенти. София, 20 авг. 1937.* Централен Държавен Архив, фонд 177К, опис 2, а.е. 944, л. 16

(Благодарствено писмо, 1943) *Благодарствено писмо от „една майка" до цар Борис III за освобождаването на пловдивските евреи,* София, 11 март 1943, Централен държавен архив, фонд 3К, опис 12, а.е. 963, л. 1

(Василева, 1992) Василева, Бойка. *Евреите в България 1944-1952,* София, Университетско издателство "Св. Климент Охридски", 1992

(Вълчева, 2006) Вълчева Р. *Антисемитски отношения 19 - 20 в.,* публикувана на 5 септември 2006, at: https://archive.is/AIAAF

(Гаврилова, 2016) Гаврилова, Милица. *Лиляна Паница – забравената спасителка на българските евреи*, Bulgarian History, 11 юли 2016, at: http://archive.is/O8XLR

(Генов, Дизраели) Генов, Румен. *Дизраели, еврейството и антисемитизмът в България*, Instute Centre of Excellence 'Dialogue Europe' http://dialogueeurope.org/uploads/JewsCol/Panel101.pdf

(Гринберг, 1945) Гринберг, Натан. *Документи*, публикувана от Централната консистория на евреите в България, 1945

(Груев, 1991) Груев, Стефан. *Корона от тръни: Царуването на Цар Борис Трети 1918-1943*, Български писател, София, 1991

(Данни за Сомовит) *Данни за въдворените евреи в лагера Сомовит, разпределени като: близки на политически провинени; заподозрени като неблагонадеждни; с провинение по Закона за защита на нацията; отлъчили се трудовомобилизирани; по неизвестна причина*, 1944, Централен държавен архив, фонд 1568К, опис 1, а.е. 86, л. 13

(Джераси) *Яков Джераси: Да бъдеш български евреин беше голям плюс по време на Втората световна война*, at: http://archive.is/EcEfc

(Джераси, Работните лагери) Джераси, Яков. *Работните лагери спасиха българските евреи от лагерите на смъртта*, at: http://archive.is/2Pdku

(Довеждането на Рафаел Камхи) *Преписка на Министерство на външните работи и изповеданията за довеждането на Рафаел Моис Камхи от Солун и уреждането на престоя му в София*, София, 23 март 1943 – 29 юни 1944, Централен държавен архив, фонд 176К, опис 21, а.е. 2897, л. 1-8

(Доклад ЕЦО, 1946) *Доклад на Централния комитет на Единната Ционистическа организация в България пред 23-та редовна конференция, състояла се в София на 5, 6, 7 и 8 януари 1946 година - Documentation of the 23rd Zionist Organization conference in Bulgaria*, 1946, Yad Vashem Archives, item ID 4032747, file 85

(Докъде стигнаха) *Докъде стигнаха американските евреи: В САЩ заспориха за спасяването на българските евреи*, at: http://archive.is/9grmI

(Донесение за Жак Нисимов Шоев) *Донесение от В. Борачев, делегат по еврейските въпроси, до комисаря по еврейските въпроси за изпращането на Жак Нисимов Шоев в лагера Сомовит*, Нова Загора, 10 август 1943, Централен държавен архив, фонд 1568К, опис 1, а.е. 86, л. 12

(Донесение за инж. Давидов) *Донесение от Ст. Иванов, околийски управител в Горна Джумая, до комисаря по еврейските въпроси за изпращането на инж. Давидов в лагера Соомовит*, Горна Джумая, 7 септември 1943, Централен държавен архив, фонд 1568К, опис 1, а.е. 86, л. 8

(Донесение за Митрополит Кирил, 1944) *Донесение от*

началник щаба на II дивизионна област до Министерство на войната за съдействието на Пловдивския митрополит Кирил за освобождаването на арестувани евреи. Пловдив, 28 май 1944, Централен Държавен Архив, фонд 1318К, опис 1, а.е. 2202, л. 1

(Донесение за Хана Нисим Мордехай) Донесение от Христо Талев, делегат по еврейските въпроси, до комисаря по еврейските въпроси за изпращането на Хана Нисим Мордехай в лагера Соомовит, Дупница, 23 ноември 1943, Централен държавен архив, фонд 1568К, опис 1, а.е. 86, л. 9

(Досие за пререгистриране, 1930) Досие за пререгистриране на Културно-просветния институт "Еврейски народен университет", съгласно чл.10 от Закона за държавен надзор върху дружествата и сдруженията. София, 21 ноем. 1930 – 21 дек. 1939. Централен Държавен Архив, фонд 264К, опис 5, а.е. 1630, л. 1-6

(Досие за пререгистриране, 1938) Досие за пререгистриране на Ешкеназкото женско благотворително дружество "Подкрепа", съгласно чл.10 от Закона за държавен надзор върху дружествата и сдруженията. София, 25 авг. 1938 – 13 окт. 1947. Централен Държавен Архив, фонд 264К, опис 5, а.е. 1622, л. 1-59

(Досие на книга против антисемитизма, 1937) "Българската общественост за расизма и антисемитизма". Досие на книгата в бюро "Преса и печат" на Дирекция на полицията. София, 10 юли 1937. Централен Държавен Архив, фонд 370К, опис 2, а.е. 2967, л. 1-5

(Евреи загинали във войните, 1940) Списък на загиналите през войните български евреи, изпратен до XXV ОНС като приложение №1 към изложение на Централната консистория на евреите в България. София, 1940, Централен Държавен Архив, фонд 173К, опис 6, а.е. 1087, л. 27-28

(Еврейски работни групи, 2008) Еврейски работни групи в Трудова повинност 1941-1945 г., София, Държавна агенция „Архиви", 2008

(Живков) Живков, Тодор. Избрани съчинения, том 23: Януари-септември 1975, Партиздат, София

(Закон за защита на нацията, 1941) Закон за защита на нацията (Приложения: Правилник по прилагане на закона за защита на нацията; Наредба I № 2556 по Правилника по прилагане на закона за защита на нацията; Наредба по приложението на чл. 25 от закона за защита на нацията; Минстерски постановления по приложението на закона за защита на нацията), Държавно книгоиздателство, София, 1941

(Законопроект за данък върху еврейски имущества, 1941) Законопроект за еднократен данък върху имуществата на лица от еврейски произход с приложен доклад от министъра на финансите Добри Божилов. София, 10–11 юли 1941, Централен

Държавен Архив, фонд 173К, опис 6, а.е. 1787, л. 1-16

(Златева) Златева А. *Осъдените карикатури: Художниците пред VI състав на Народния съд (1945)*, "Дриновски сборник", том 4, 2011, Издателство на БАН "Проф. Марин Дринов", стр.277-293

(Изложение на Централната консистория по ЗЗН, 1940) *Изложение от Централната консистория на евреите в България по законопроекта за защита на нацията. София, 22 окт. 1940*, Централен Държавен Архив, фонд 1335К, опис 1, а.е. 118, л. 1-10

(Изложение от БЛС против ЗЗН, 1940) *Изложение от Управителния съвет на Българския лекарски съюз до председателя на XXV ОНС срещу законопроекта за защита на нацията. София, 5 ноем. 1940.* Централен Държавен Архив, фонд 173К, опис 6, а.е. 1087, л. 56-58

(Изложение от СБА против ЗЗН, 1940) *Изложение от Съюза на българските адвокати до министър-председателя Богдан Филов срещу расовия характер на подготвения законопроект за защита на нацията. София, 30 окт. 1940*, Централен Държавен Архив, фонд 833К, опис 2, а.е. 18, л. 341-344

(Илков, 1908) Илков, Димитър. Принос към историята на град Стара Загора, издава Старо-Загорското Градско Общинско Управление, Пловдив, 1908

(Инджов, 2012) *Инджов, Иво. „Еврейският въпрос" в огледалото на българската преса: 1940-1944 г.* In: „Еврейската тема" в българския печат (1940-1944 г.) и в киното, published by Институт за модерна политика – Център за еврейски изследвания при СУ „Св. Климент Охридски", София, 2012

(Истината за македонските евреи) *Истината за македонските и тракийски евреи бе представена пред европейски дипломати*, at: http://archive.is/mXwjm

(Казасов, писмо до Филов, 1940) *Писмо от Димо Казасов до министър-председателя Богдан Филов и народните представители от XXV ОНС срещу законопроекта за защита на нацията. София, 18 ноем. 1940*, Централен Държавен Архив, фонд 409К, опис 1, а.е. 64, л. 1-5

(Коен, 2004) Ст.н.с.д-р Давид Коен. *Еврейските трудови лагери в България*, 2004 http://archive.is/mNXqs

(Коен, Ти вярваш, 2012) Коен, Леа. *Ти вярваш: Осем погледа върху Холкоста на Балканите*, годишник „Либерален преглед" – 2012, том 3 (септември – октомври)

(Коминтерн, 1998) *Коминтерн и идея мировой революции. Документы*, Москва, Наука, 1998

(Конституция) *Конституция на Българското Княжество* (Приета на 16.04.1879 г.), http://www.parliament.bg/bg/17

(Кореспонденция по прилагане на ЗЗН в училищата, а.е. 1836, 1941-1943) *Кореспонденция на Министерство на народното просвещение по прилагането на Закона за защита на нацията в българските училища (писма против изключване на *еврейски ученички през 1943)*. София, 1941–1943, Централен Държавен Архив, фонд 177К, опис 2, а.е. 1836, л. 82-104

(Криспин, 1970) Криспин, Донна. *Протестната демонстрация на софийските евреи на 24 май 1943 година*, Годишник на Обществена културно-просветна организация на евреите в НРБ, София, година 5, 1970

(Круглов, 1997) Круглов, Александр Иосифович. *Уничтожение еврейского населения Украины в 1941 -1944 гг. Хроника событий*, published by the author, 1997

(Леверсон, 1993) *Последните дни на Цар Борис – Срещата с Адолф Хитлер*, София, МКИ, 1993

(Лулчев, 1992) Лулчев, Любомир. *Тайните на дворцовия живот, дневник (1938—1944)*, СК „Веселие", София, 1992

(Майер, 1969) Майер, Израел. *Придобивките на българските евреи при народната власт*, Годишник на Обществена културно-просветна организация на евреите в НР България, том 4, 1969, с. 57-77

(Маринова-Христиди) Маринова-Христиди, доц. д-р Румяна. *Евреите в социалистическа България*, at: https://www.uni-sofia.bg/index.php/bul/content/download/152099/1095507/version/1/file/Doc.+Rumiana+Marinova-+Hristidi.pdf

(Месечен доклад, август 1943) *Месечен доклад от служба "Държавна сигурност" при Пловдивска полицейска област до Дирекция на полицията, 4 август 1943*, Централен Държавен Архив, фонд 370К, опис 6, а.е. 1902, л. 28-32

(Методиева, 2016) Методиева, Юлиана. *Да се изучава цялата технология на българския Холокост, изселванията, стигмата, лагерите*, годишник „Либерален преглед", 2016, том 2

(Митев) Митев. *Българи и евреи – съседи и съграждани*, at: http://www.thebulgarianjews.org.il/_Uploads/dbsAttachedFiles/BulgariEvreiMitev.pdf

(Надежда Василева, писмо, 1947) *Писмо от Надежда Василева до Еврейския научен институт с посочени уточнения по спомените й за престоя на беломорските евреи в Лом през 1943 г. Лом, 30 авг.1947*, ЦДА, фонд 1568К, опис 1, а.е. 190, л. 36

(Наредба за прилагане на ЗЗН, 1941) *Наредба I по Правилника за прилагане на Закона за защита на нацията. София, 18 февр. 1941*, Централен Държавен Архив, фонд 371К, опис 5, а.е. 1016, л. 2

(Народен съд, свидетел Матилда Жак Враджали, 1945) *Протокол от 22-ро заседание на Втори състав на Народния съд в София с разпит на свидетеля Матилда Жак Враджали за подсъдимия Георги Липовански, София, 17 януари 1945 г.*, Централен Държавен Архив, фонд 1449, опис 1, а.е. 54, л. 2040-2041

(Народен съд, разпит на Георги Липовански, 1944) *Протокол от 4-то заседание на Втори състав на Народния съд в София с разпит на подсъдимия д-р Георги Липовански, София, 23*

декември 1944 г., Втори състав, Централен Държавен Архив, фонд 1449, опис 1, а.е. 44, л. 248-282

(Нойков, 1995) Нойков, Стилиян. *Цар Борис Трети в тайните документи на Третия райх 1939-1943,* София, Университетско издателство „Св. Климент Охридски", 1995

(Нотариален акт, 1937) *Нотариален акт за учредяване на Фондация за подпомагане на бедни студенти с посочени цели и задачи, подписан от учредителя Анжело Нисим Куюмджийски. София, 30 юли 1937,* Централен Държавен Архив, фонд 177К, опис 2, а.е. 944, л. 18, 19

(Окръжно на Софийската Митрополия, 1940) *Окръжно №4870 на Софийската митрополия за приемането на евреи в лоното на Българската православна църква, София, 23 ноем.1940,* Централен Държавен Архив, фонд 166К, опис 6, а.е. 11, л. 16

(Петрински, 2015) Петрински, Иван. *71 години от бомбардировките: на англо-американската жестокост бе дадена пълна власт,* 15 януари 2015, вестник „Сега" at: https://archive.is/TKoi2

(Писмо от Анжело Куюмджийски, 1937) *Писмо от Анжело Куюмджийски до министъра на народното просвещение за откриване на банкова сметка с номинална стойност от 7 милиона лв. за подпомагане на бедни студенти. София, 10 авг. 1937.* Централен Държавен Архив, фонд 177К, опис 2, а.е. 944, л. 17

(Писмо от евреи до царица Йоанна, 1943) *Писмо от представители на "верноподанно еврейство" до царица Йоанна за изселването на софийските евреи. София, 24 май 1943,* ЦДА, фонд 250Б, опис 1, а.е. 47, л. 15

(Писмо от Калицин, 1943) *Писмо от Ярослав Калицин, началник административно отделение в Комисарството по еврейските въпроси, до делегата на Комисарството при еврейската община в Разград за пристигането на 400 лица от еврейски произход от Южна България в Разград, София, 2 юли 1943,* Централен държавен архив, фонд 1568К, опис 1, а.е. 94, л. 8

(Писмо от митрополит Неофит, декември 1940) *Писмо от Неофит, митрополит Видински и наместник-председател на Светия синод на Българската православна църква, до министъра на вътрешните работи и народното здраве за признатите в Царство България вероизповедания, сред които е иизраилтянското, и включване на секти и религиозни движения, уронващи престижа на господстващата в България религия като допълнение в законопроекта за защита на нацията. София, 18 дек. 1940,* Централен Държавен Архив, фонд 371К, опис 5, а.е. 1573, л. 18

(Писмо от митрополит Неофит, ноември 1940) *Писмо от Неофит, митрополит Видински и наместник-председател на Светия синод на Българската православна църква, до министър-председателя и председателя на XXV ОНС, с предложение за:*

смекчаване предвидените в законопроекта за защита на нацията мерки срещу евреите, приели християнството; да не се предвиждат разпоредби против евреите като народностно малцинство; предвиждане на мерки срещу всички религиозни пропаганди, които разпокъсват духовното единство на българския народ. София, 15 ноем. 1940, Централен Държавен Архив, фонд 371К, опис 5, а.е. 1573, л. 19-20

(Пити, 1937) Пити, Буко. *Българската общественост за расизма и антисемитизма: Анкета между видни представители на българската общественост, наука, литература, изкуство,* София, 1937

(Постановление на МС №116, 1943) *Постановление на Министерския съвет №116, протокол 32, за лишаване от българско поданство на всички лица от еврейски произход, изселени извън пределите на страната.* София, 2 март 1943, Централен Държавен Архив, фонд 250Б, опис 1, а.е. 47, л. 10

(Постановление на МС №126, 1943) *Постановление на Министерския съвет №126, протокол 32, за реда и начина на отчуждаване на недвижимите имоти на лица от еврейски произход.* София, 2 март 1943, Централен Държавен Архив, фонд 250Б, опис 1, а.е. 47, л. 9

(Предложение за недоверие на Пешев) *Предложение за изказване на недоверие на подпредседателя на Народното събрание Димитър Пешев.* София, 25 март 1943, Централен Държавен Архив, фонд 173К, опис 6, а.е. 2608, л. 1

(Преписка за евреи напускащи България, 1944) *Преписка на Дирекция на полицията с Щаба на войската, Комисарството по еврейските въпроси и Министерство на външните работи и изповеданията за евреи, напускащи България през Свиленград.* София, Кюстендил, Свиленград, 10 февр. – 27 май 1944, Централен Държавен Архив, фонд 370К, опис 6, а.е. 1457, л. 12-28

(Престъпност сред евреите, 1940) *Сведение за участието на евреите в общата престъпност в България – приложение № 4 към изложение на Централната консистория на евреите в България до XXV ОНС срещу законопроекта за защита на нацията.* София, 1940, Централен Държавен Архив, фонд 173К, опис 6, а.е. 1087, л. 31-32

(Протест на Пешев и 42 парламентаристи, 1943) *Протестно изложение от Димитър Пешев, подпредседател на XXV ОНС, и от 42-ма народни представители до министър председателя Богдан Филов против изселването на евреите извън границите на България.* София, 17 март 1943, Централен Държавен Архив, фонд 1335К, опис 1, а.е. 126, л. 1-3

(Професии на евреите в София, 1940) *Таблица за професионалното разпределение на евреите в София – приложение № 3 към изложение на Централната консистория на евреите в България до XXV ОНС срещу законопроекта за защита* на нацията. *София, 1940*, Централен Държавен Архив, фонд 173К, опис 6, а.е. 1087, л. 30

(Ред за напускане на България от евреи, 22 юни-25 август 1944) *Преписка на Дирекция на полицията с областните директори, Министерство на външните работи и изповеданията, Русенската еврейска община и българската легация в Букурещ за разрешаване транзитното преминаване през България на 1000 евреи, румънски поданици. София, Русе, Букурещ, 22 юни – 25 август 1944*, Централен Държавен Архив, фонд 370К, опис 6, а.е. 1457, л. 1-8

(Романо, Леви, 1961) Романо, Алберт А.; Леви, Д-р Нисим (Буко). *По кой път бяха спасени евреите в България? (комунисти и ционисти) (По повод книгата на Натан Гринберг "Хитлеристкият натиск за унищожаване на евреите от България")*, Израел, 1961

(САЩ искали) *САЩ искали да спасят българските евреи чрез изпращането им в Турция*, http://www.duma.bg/node/161423

(Сведение за евреи изселени от София, юни 1943) *Сведение на Комисарството по еврейските въпроси за изселените от София лица от еврейски произход. София, 8 юни 1943*, Централен Държавен Архив, фонд 1568К, опис 1, а.е. 71, л. 15-16

(Свети синод, Протокол №4, 1943) *Протокол №4 от извънредна сесия на пълния състав на Българската православна църква срещу опитите на правителството да изсели евреите от различни градове в страната. София, 2 апр.1943*, Централен Държавен Архив, фонд 791К., опис 1, а.е. 70, л. 23-33

(Свети синод, Протокол №6, 1943) *Протокол №6 на пълния състав на Светия синод на Българската православна църква за проведена на 15 март 1943 г. в двореца Враня среща на намаления състав на Синода с цар Борис III и министър-председателя Богдан Филов за смекчаване прилагането на Закона за защита на нацията. София, 22 юни 1943*, Централен Държавен Архив, фонд 791К, опис 1, а.е. 70, л. 41-52

(Свети синод, Протокол №9, 1943) *Протокол №9 на пълния състав на Светия синод на Българската православна църква за покръстването на евреи и разпространяваните анонимни позиви срещу Софийския митрополит Стефан. София, 29 юни 1943*, Централен Държавен Архив, фонд 791К, опис 1, а.е. 70, л. 58-64

(Свети синод, Протокол №12, 1940) *Протокол №12 на пълния състав на Светия синод на Българската православна църква за разглеждане на законопроекта за защита на нацията и определяне състава на комисия за изготвяне на изложение до Народното събрание. София, 14 ноем. 1940*, Централен Държавен Архив, фонд 791К, опис 1, а.е. 65, л. 35-40

(Свети синод, Протокол №13, 1940) *Протокол №13 на пълния състав на Светия синод на Българската православна църква за приемане текста на изложението до председателя на*

Народното събрание по Закона за защита на нацията. София, 15 ноем. 1940, Централен Държавен Архив, фонд 791К, опис 1, а.е. 65, л. 40-44

(Свети синод, Протокол №8, 1943) *Протокол №8 на пълния състав на Светия синод на Българската православна църква за положението на евреите след разселването им в страната. София, 25 юни 1943*, Централен Държавен Архив, фонд 791К, опис 1, а.е. 70, л. 55-58

(Свети синод, Протокол №19, 1943) *Протокол №19 на намаления състав на Светия синод на Българската православна църква за събитията на 24 май 1943 г. и срещата на митрополит Стефан със софийските евреи. София, 27 май 1943*, Централен Държавен Архив, фонд 791К, опис 1, а.е. 69, л. 188-200

(Секретна записка от Мартин Лутер до Рибентроп, 1942) *Секретна докладна записка на заместник държавния секретар на Германското министерство на външните работи Мартин Лутер до имперския външен министър Йоахим фон Рибентроп за политиката на цар Борис III и правителството на проф. Богдан Филов спрямо българските евреи. Берлин, 11 септ. 1942*, Централен Държавен Архив, фонд 1568К, опис 1, а.е. 172, л. 9, 10

(София и войната) Асланян, Крикор. *София и войната (през очите на дете очевидец)* at: http://stara-sofia.blogspot.ca/2010_07_01_archive.html

(Спомени на Надежда Василева) *Спомени на Надежда Слави Василева за изселването на евреи от Беломорието и за престоя им в Лом през март 1943 г., София, 19 юли 1947*, ЦДА, фонд 1568К, опис 1, а.е. 190, л. 2-20, 23-33

(Справка за броя на евреите, 1943) *Справка на Комисарството по еврейските въпроси за броя на еврейското население по градове и за броя на лицата от еврейски произход, изселени от София в различни градове. София, 10 юни 1943*, Централен Държавен Архив, фонд 1568К, опис 1, а.е. 71, л. 12

(Справка за броя на еврейските изселници, 1944) *Справка на Министерство на външните работи и изповеданията за броя на еврейските изселници от България в Палестина за периода 1 ян. – 9 септ. 1944 г. София, 27 дек. 1944*, Централен Държавен Архив, фонд 198, опис 1, а.е. 114, л. 1-5

(Тайны дипломатии Третьего рейха) *Тайны дипломатии Третьего рейха: Германские дипломаты, руководители зарубежных военных миссий, военные и полицейские атташе в советском плену. Документы из следственных дел. 1944—1955*, Москва, Международный фонд "Демократия", 2011

(Ташев) Ташев, Спас. *Холокостът във вардарска Македония и Беломорието през 1943 г. и неговото съвременно измерение*, at: https://www.scribd.com/document/81027797/Broshura-Holokostat-v-Makedoniya

(Телеграми от аптекари, 1941-1942) *Протестни телеграми*

от аптекари в цялата страна срещу законопроекта за ликвидиране на еврейските аптеки. София, 1941–1942, Централен Държавен Архив, фонд 173К, опис 6, а.е. 1753, л. 6-49, 55-70

(Телеграми от занаятчии против ЗЗН, 1940) *Телеграми от столари, сладкари, шивачи, обущари и други занаятчии до XXV ОНС срещу законопроекта за защита на нацията, ноември-декември 1940.* Централен Държавен Архив, фонд 173К, опис 6, а.е. 1087, л. 74, 76, 80-87, 149, 153.

(Тенчев, 2008) Тенчев, Желязко. *Български орли в безсмъртен полет*, вестник „Дума", 2008, at http://old.duma.bg/2008/1108/131108/obshtestvo/ob-8.html

(Транзитни визи, архив) *Работни бележки, извадки от регистри на легации и спомени на Любен Златаров, за дейността на Н. Вачев, Х. Левинсон, Л. Златаров и Н. Пецев, свързани с транзитното преминаване на евреи по време на Втората световна война през България.* Б.м, б.д, Централен държавен архив, фонд 1870К, опис 1, а.е. 17, л. 17-115

(Удостоверение на Рафаел Камхи, 1943) *Удостоверение, издадено от командващия областта Солун – Егея, заверено и подписано от Българския царски офицер за свръзка, за сваляне на еврейска звезда №41 367 на Рафаел Моис Камхи и отвеждането му от Солун в България. Солун, 2 апр.1943*, ЦДА, фонд 1568К, опис 1, а.е. 195, л. 455

(Факти, евреи защитили България, 1940) *Факти и прояви на българското еврейство в защита на България – приложение към изложение на Централната консистория на евреите в България до XXV ОНС срещу законопроекта за защита на нацията. София, 1940*, Централен Държавен Архив, фонд 173К, опис 6, а.е. 1087, л. 33-37

(Хаджийски, 2002) Хаджийски, Иван. *Психология на Априлското въстание*, в: Оптимистична теория за нашия народ, Избрани съчинения в 3 тома, том 3, Изток-Запад, София, 2002, стр. 211-265

(Шимон Перес) *Шимон Перес: Спасяването на българските евреи е уникален пример*, Вести, 6 март 2013, https://archive.is/XPJuY

1. Bulgaria in 1878 after the San Stefano treaty and the Berlin Congress.

2. King Ferdinand declares the independence of Bulgaria (1908).

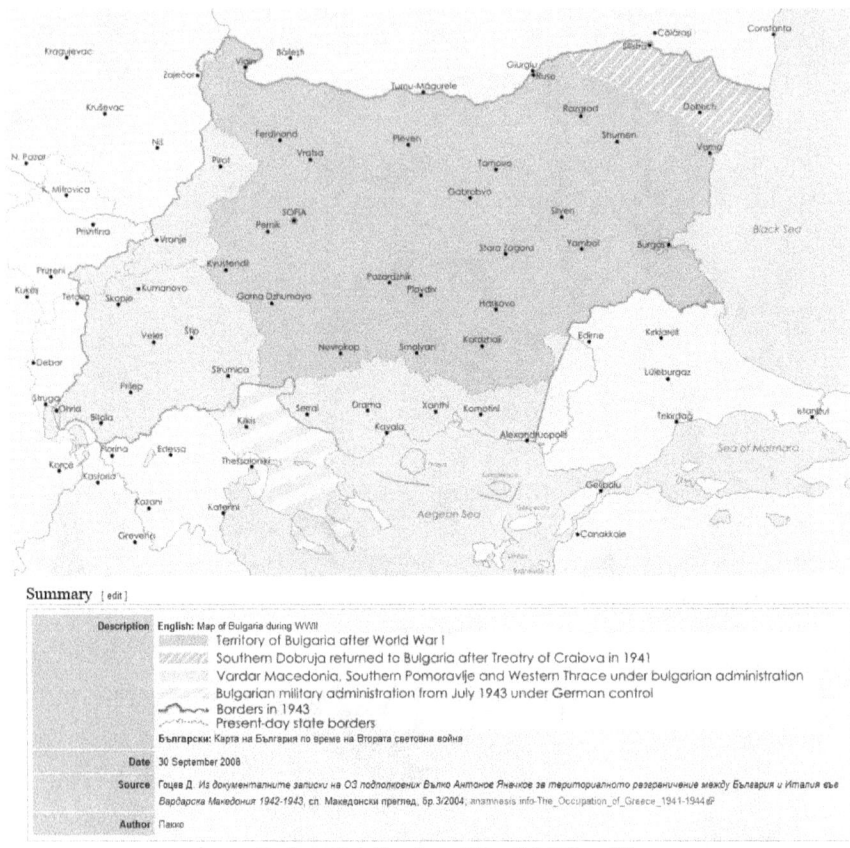

3. Bulgaria during World War II.

4. Map of Europe from Deutsche Schulatlas (1942). Bulgaria's old borders are shown clearly.

5. Detail of the previous map showing the old borders of Bulgaria.

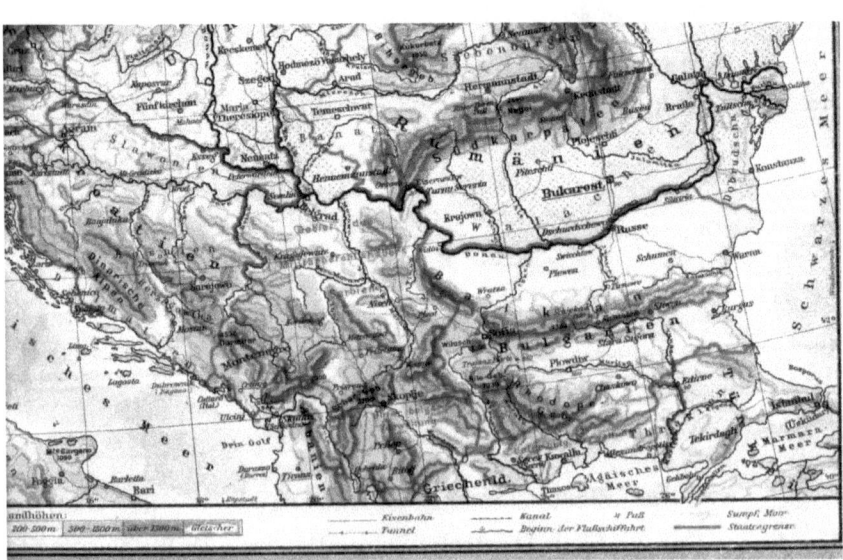

6. German map showing Thrace and Macedonia as territories under Bulgarian administration.

7. Church St. Nedelya before 1925.

8. Church St. Nedelya after the terrorist act in April 1925.

9. Children's Day, Sofia, 1928, with Metropolitan-Stefan.

10. King Boris III with Prime Minister Kimon Georgiev (right, holding a hat), ca. 1935.

11. King Boris III of Bulgaria, official portrait, ca. late 1930s.

12. The Bulgarian Royal Family: King Boris III, Queen Ioanna, Princess Maria Louisa, and Prince Simeon.

13. The Central Synagogue in Sofia, opened in 1909.

14. The old Synagogue Francos in Sofia, ca. late 19th century.

15. The liberation of southern Dobruja, 1940.

16. Rose harvest in Bulgaria, ca. 1930s.

17. Jewish students march on an official holiday, Vidin, Bulgaria, 1932.

18. The Bulgarian Jewish athletes parading in the stadium at the 2nd Maccabi Games opening ceremony, 1935.

19. Plastic yellow star worn by the Jews in Bulgaria from 1941 to 1944.

20. Jewish labor group, Bulgaria, 1940s.

21. People's Assembly, Sofia, after Allied bombing in 1944.

22. School "St. Sedmochislenitsi" in Sofia, hit by Allied bombs, 1944.

23. Holocaust memorial to Bulgarian Jews in Israel.

24. Dimitur Peshev Memorial Square in Jaffa

PHOTO CREDITS

Cover photo: Jewish star used in Bulgaria, Wikimedia Commons, commercial use right, author "The devious diesel".

Back photo: The Synagogue in Sofia, Bulgaria, Wikimedia Commons, commercial use right, author "Pudelek (Marcin Szala)".

1: Wikimedia Commons, TodorBozhinov.
2: Wikimedia Commons, public domain.
3: Wikimedia Commons, public domain.
4: Web Archive, public domain.
5: Web Archive, public domain.
6: Wikimedia Commons, public domain.
7: Wikimedia Commons, public domain.
8: Wikimedia Commons, public domain.
9: Wikimedia Commons, Bulgarian Archives State Agency, BASA-389K-1-361-5.
10: Wikimedia Commons, Bulgarian Archives State Agency, BASA-3K-15-263-2.
11: Wikimedia Commons, Bulgarian Archives State Agency, BASA-3K-7-342-28.
12: Web Archive, public domain.
13: Wikimedia Commons, commercial use right, "kuchin ster".
14: Wikimedia Commons, public domain.
15: Wikimedia Commons, Bulgarian Archives State Agency, BASA-3K-7-436-63.
16: Wikimedia Commons, Bulgarian Archives State Agency, BASA-1323K-1-46-73.
17: Wikimedia Commons, public domain.
18: Wikimedia Commons, public domain.
19: Wikimedia Commons, commercial use right, "The devious diesel".
20: Wikimedia Commons, commercial use right, "Yossi Nevo".
21: Wikimedia Commons, Bulgarian Archives State Agency, BASA-45K-1-18-19.
22: Wikimedia Commons, Bulgarian Archives State Agency, BASA-45K-1-18-1.
23: Wikimedia Commons, public domain, author avishai teicher.
24: Wikimedia Commons, commercial use right, author avishai teacher.

ABOUT THE AUTHOR

Miroslav Marinov is a Toronto-based writer, blogger and translator. His major fields of interest are philosophy, religion and history, specifically Eastern Orthodox Christian theology and the political philosophy of the early Confucianism. He holds a Ph.D. degree in Philosophy.

He is author of the books *Confucian Treatises* (in Bulgarian), *Lynched: The Media War against Rob Ford* and *Saved: Japan and the Jews in World War II*.

You can contact him with questions, opinions or hate mail at:

marinov@mpmpublishing.com

www.ingramcontent.com/pod-product-compliance
Lightning Source LLC
Chambersburg PA
CBHW050100170426
43198CB00014B/2402